The Good Retirement Guide

25TH EDITION

The Good Non Retirement Guide

Everything you need to know about health, property, investment, leisure, work, pensions and tax

FRANCES KAY

KoganPage

LONDON PHILADELPHIA NEW DELHI

Publisher's note

Every possible effort has been made to ensure that the information contained in this book is accurate at the time of going to press, and the publishers and author cannot accept responsibility for any errors or omissions, however caused. No responsibility for loss or damage occasioned to any person acting, or refraining from action, as a result of the material in this publication can be accepted by the editor, the publisher or the author.

This 25th edition published in Great Britain in 2011 by Kogan Page Limited

Apart from any fair dealing for the purposes of research or private study, or criticism or review, as permitted under the Copyright, Designs and Patents Act 1988, this publication may only be reproduced, stored or transmitted, in any form or by any means, with the prior permission in writing of the publishers, or in the case of reprographic reproduction in accordance with the terms and licences issued by the CLA. Enquiries concerning reproduction outside these terms should be sent to the publishers at the undermentioned address:

Kogan Page Limited
120 Pentonville Road
London N1 9JN
United Kingdom

www.koganpage.com

© Kogan Page, 2011

The right of Kogan Page to be identified as the author of this work has been asserted by them in accordance with the Copyright, Designs and Patents Act 1988.

British Library Cataloguing in Publication Data
A CIP record for this book is available from the British Library.

ISBN 978 0 7494 6244 4
E-ISBN 978 0 7494 6245 1

Typeset by Saxon Graphics Ltd, Derby
Production managed by Jellyfish
Printed and bound in Great Britain by CPI Antony Rowe

Stop press

Spending Review announcements

On 20th October 2010 the Chancellor of the Exchequer announced the Spending Review. This outlined the Government's spending plans to 2014/15 and represented £81 billion of cuts in public spending over four years. The following items are of most relevance to readers of *The Good Non Retirement Guide*.

State pension age to be raised

Millions of workers will have to delay their retirement after the state pension age was raised to 66. Retirement age for men will start rising from 65 in 2018, reaching 66 by 2020. For women who can collect their pension at 60, the pension age will start rising in 2016, also reaching 66 by 2020 – this represents an increase of six years in a decade. These measures, which are being taken four years earlier than expected, will save £5bn a year by the end of the next parliament. But this move leaves those approaching retirement very little time to plan properly for a delayed retirement.

Current increasing longevity has meant maintaining the retirement age of 60 for women and 65 for men is unsustainable. The time-scale for raising the pension age to 67 and 68 is also likely to be accelerated. The Chancellor justified the move by saying that many other countries are now increasing the pension age. As a result of these changes, about 5.1 million people who had expected to retire at 65 will have to continue working for an extra year, saving the country about £30 billion in pensions and benefits between 2015 to 2025. A further £13 billion will be raised from additional income tax and national insurance contributions paid by workers who would have retired. The planned changes are intended to ensure that pensions remain sustainable for everyone. The trade off for a later retirement has to be a better state pension.

For younger people, however, the situation may get worse: the Government is considering increasing the pension age to 70 or even higher in future decades. If this does happen, at least it gives people plenty of time to plan ahead to ensure they can pay for their retirement.

The Government are to go ahead with plans to link the state pension to wage increases or inflation – whichever is higher – from 2011. Most importantly, these moves taken by the Government to cut the cost of supporting Britain's ageing population underlines the need for individuals to take action to ensure they can still achieve the retirement they want.

Some good news for pensioners

Pensioners were largely protected when the Chancellor preserved a host of free measures which could have been axed. Universal benefits such as free eye tests, free prescription charges, free bus passes at 60, and free TV licences for the over 75s are untouched. There are no plans to means-test them. They will all be available to every person over a certain age.

Winter fuel payments are protected, although most people over 60 will receive £200 from 2011, compared to £250 in 2010. The additional temporary cold weather payments, of £25, paid to millions of people on low incomes and disabled people, which apply when the local daily temperature has been at or below freezing for seven consecutive days, have been made permanent.

Reform of public sector pensions

Public sector workers will have to pay a new levy on their salaries to fund their pensions. The average state employee will pay an extra three per cent of their salary towards their retirement schemes. The increased contributions are expected to cost public sector workers £1.76 billion a year by 2014, with some set to pay higher occupational pension contributions if they are members of big public service pension schemes. Payouts will no longer be based on final salaries, but on average earnings, from 2012. This decision was made in the wake of Lord Hutton's independent commission (due to report in full in spring 2011) which has described the gulf between public and private sector schemes as "fundamentally unfair". The chancellor announced that any increases in pension contributions would be "staggered and progressive", with the lowest paid and members of the armed forces being protected. But those who gained the highest pensions from final-salary schemes are expected to pay the most.

NHS budget is being increased

Health is one of the few departments not to have been cut. The health budget in England will rise by £10bn by 2014 to £114bn. However that amounts to only 0.1 per cent annual rise once inflation is taken into account. This rise is likely to be more than swallowed up by increasing demands from factors such as obesity, the ageing population and the cost of new drugs.

Pension credit savings award frozen

Pensioners who have modest savings or a small private pension (up to £80 per week) are entitled to a payment of up to £20.52 a week on top of the basic state pension. This upper rate will not rise in line with prices or earnings for the next four years – which represents a loss of up to £100 per year for the average claimant. This freeze reinforces the need for savers not to rely on government payouts to help them out in old age.

Council tax benefit cut

The Chancellor announced a 10 per cent cut in the council tax benefit budget from April 2013. Local councils will be expected to cut the amount of council tax benefit they pay by this amount. Those in receipt of this benefit are either too poor to pay council tax or the unemployed.

Working tax credit working hours threshold raised

There is to be an increase in the working hours threshold for working tax credits for couples with children from 2013. It is proposed that couples with children should work at least 24 hours a week between them in order to be eligible for working tax credit. Also, the percentage of childcare claimable under the family element of working tax credit will be trimmed from 80 per cent to 70 per cent.

Child benefit cuts

Cuts to child benefit for higher rate tax payers is estimated to generate £2.5bn. From 2013 child benefit will be withdrawn from families in which one or both parents are higher-rate tax payers (ie earning more than £44,000 a year). If both parents earn less than £44,000, they will continue to receive child benefit. But families with one main earner on, for example, £45,000, will see their benefit stopped. This is expected to save £2.5bn for the Government and affect 300,000 more people.

There will be a £2bn investment in new universal credit. In the longer term the government plan to introduce a 'universal benefit' which would replace the current system of Jobseekers' Allowance, Income Support and Employment and Support Allowance with a single benefit. This is an attempt to try to simplify the system. It is estimated that the setting up of this will initially cost about £2bn.

Time limit on ESA (Employment and Support Allowance)

It was announced that there is a new 12 month time limit for the one million people on Employment and Support Allowance to find work or face benefit cuts. This payment is for people whose ability to work is limited by disability or illness. It will be a big saving for the government once this time limit is implemented. Payment is to be limited to one year for those who are able to do some work and whose payment is based on their National Insurance contributions. The ESA has replaced the former Incapacity Benefit.

Compensation claim

Pensioners who were the victims of the Equitable Life scandal are to share £1.5 billion in compensation. The payments to about 1.5 million policyholders will begin in 2011, bringing to a close a decade-long fight for compensation. Campaigners, innocent victims of a gross failure of regulation, had fought for compensation of £5 billion. Those hardest hit will benefit most.

Contents

Chapter One
Are you looking forward to retirement?

I have enjoyed greatly the second blooming ... suddenly you find – at the age of 50, say – that a whole new life has opened before you. AGATHA CHRISTIE

This is the 25th edition of *The Good Non Retirement Guide*, which contains a wealth of information on retirement issues for 2011 and beyond. With so much recent press coverage about how difficult and expensive life has become for the older generation, and with the government planning to scrap the default retirement age in the UK from October 2011, it is not surprising that many people when thinking about their retirement do so with some apprehension. While this volume does not promise to be packed from cover to cover with good news, irresistible bargains and unbeatable offers, it does attempt to be positive and cautiously optimistic about the choices and opportunities available to the recently retired. Since negative thoughts tend to be depressing, we hope that readers of *The Good Non Retirement Guide 2011* will find within its pages plenty of sound, sensible advice and suggestions. These are intended to remove some of the fear of the unknown and help make life after 60 as enjoyable and rewarding as possible.

Retirement is after all a significant life-changing event. Maybe you have been contemplating for a long time what to do once you stop working. Some people find that the years simply slip by and they are facing their retirement without having done much planning. One important thing to remember is that with better health and increased longevity, many people are now 'retired' for 25 years or more. Indeed the older generation could be divided into three separate groups. Those between the age range of 55 to 64 years are sometimes referred to as being at pre-retirement age. The next age group starts at 65 (currently the official retirement age but not for much longer) and goes to 75 years. This includes a large percentage of the population, fit, healthy and active. The third group are those aged over 75, and have been retired for about a decade, sometimes referred to as the long-term retired.

Regardless of age or grouping, and there are obviously wide extremes in each category, some retired people have limited means on which to live while others have substantial personal savings. Since an increasing number of people now expect to work long past the traditional retirement age, regardless of what the government decides to do, the solution for some is to retire on a part-time basis, continuing to do a number of hours paid work each week whilst enjoying some leisure time as well.

Anyone over the age of 50 wishing to minimize levels of stress and worry about retirement needs to make some effort with their advance planning. Important events always require good preparation to get best results. The benefit of reading *The Good Non Retirement Guide* is that it gives you all the help you'll need. It is packed with information, suggestions and advice on every aspect of retirement and beyond. It will inspire you to do things you've never thought of, and help you to sort out the practicalities should you not already have explored the options available. It is an invaluable resource book, and its purpose is to help you enjoy your retirement to the full.

Key concerns amongst all three age groups of the over-55s are finances, health and leisure. Other issues may well include where you live and how retirement affects relationships and friendships. Chapter 7 contains a very practical Budget Planner. Unless you have already worked out in detail how much you'll have to live on in retirement, completing this is time well spent. You may be pleasantly surprised to find that the difference between income pre- and post-retirement is not as great as you'd feared.

As with all questions affecting retirement, preparation makes good sense. Assessing your likely savings, including lump sums from your pension or any insurance policies you may have, can give you a clearer idea of the future. From this you can draw up a plan as to how to maximize their value. You will have to consider carefully how to invest your money, whether it would make sense to buy an annuity, and what tax planning should be considered. Best advice is to consult a good accountant, stockbroker or other professional adviser. Should you not have one already, there is advice in the book on how to find a reputable person to assist you and explain the options available to you.

Your retirement income may well depend on whether you start a new career, especially if – as happens to thousands of people – you were made redundant with no immediate job prospects on offer. While starting afresh is not easy and may not be appropriate for everyone, increasing numbers of people over retirement age find continuing to work rewarding. While some individuals turn their talents to something entirely new, others go freelance or become consultants in their existing area of expertise. There is some sound advice in Chapter 11, Looking for Paid Work, which gives many useful leads and suggestions.

People who start their own business in retirement are now referred to as 'mature entrepreneurs'. Being your own boss at any age is exciting and should this be one of your, so far, unfulfilled ambitions it can be tremendously rewarding. There are many who, having taken the plunge, derive enormous satisfaction from building up a profitable family enterprise. If you are seriously considering the idea, Chapter 10, Starting Your Own Business, provides some basic information that could help you decide whether this course of action is right for you.

A worthwhile alternative to becoming a business tycoon is to devote your energies to voluntary work. There are literally scores of opportunities for retired people to make a valuable contribution within their own community covering many different types of work, or nationally with larger not-for-profit organizations. Whether you can spare only the occasional day or can help on a regular basis, Chapter 12, Voluntary Work, has a wealth of suggestions you might like to consider.

Good health is essential to a happy and fulfilling retirement. Without it, energy is lacking and many activities are restricted. No amount of money can compensate for poor health. While anyone can be unfortunate enough to be struck down by an unexpected illness, your future good health is largely in your own hands. Obesity and associated health issues have a considerable impact on how long someone lives. In terms of life expectancy there is a big gap between those who look after their health and those who make little or no attempt to follow healthy lifestyle choices. As well as all the obvious advice about not smoking, becoming overweight or drinking to excess, there is the important question of exercise. This book has suggestions for a number of interesting ways of keeping fit.

There are opportunities throughout the country for almost every kind of sport, many with 50-plus beginners especially welcome. Additionally, dancing, yoga, keep-fit-to-music and relaxation classes are readily available through most local authorities. They are also offered by the many specialist bodies listed in the Leisure Activities and Health chapters (Chapters 9 and 13). The choice of leisure pursuits is enormous and the main problem may be fitting everything in. Many recently retired people often wonder how they ever found the time to work. If you want to improve your IT skills, take a degree, join a choir, become proficient in a craft, play competitive Scrabble, start a coin collection or become a bee-keeper, you will find an organization that caters for your enthusiasm.

The type of activities you enjoy may affect your decision as to where you will live. Lots of people are conditioned to think of retirement as being the time for selling up and moving to a new home. It is something that should be considered carefully, as many people relocate without giving enough thought to such essentials as proximity to family and friends and whether there is the same scope for pursuing their interests. An all-too-common mistake is for people to retire to a place where many years previously they once spent an idyllic holiday. Resorts that are glorious in midsummer can be bleak and damp in winter, as well as pretty dull when the tourist season is over. Equally, many people sell their house and move somewhere smaller without sufficient thought. It may be that when spending more time at home they actually want more space rather than less.

While moving may be the right solution, especially if you want to realize some capital to boost your retirement income, there are plenty of ways of adapting a house to make it more convenient and labour-saving. Likewise, you may be able to cut the running costs, for example with better insulation. These and other possibilities, including taking in a paying guest or creating a granny flat, are explored in Chapter 8, Your Home. On the subject of granny flats, if you are caring for elderly parents there may come a time when a little bit of outside help could make all the difference. The range of organizations that can provide you with back-up is far more extensive than you might realize. For single people especially, who may feel that they have no choice but to give up a career, knowing what facilities are available could prove a veritable godsend.

Many people find adjusting to retirement quite difficult. It can take time because of the inevitable changes in living patterns. Moving from full-time employment into retirement has different social, emotional and mental impacts on people. Maintaining interaction with others and keeping mentally stimulated are reasons some people cite for worrying about how best to organize their time in retirement. No problem is insurmountable but it is wise to resist making huge changes in a hurry and to wait until you have got used to the reduction of pressure on your time. Relatives may try to impose new pressures once you are no longer at work. Likewise, close friendships sometimes alter when one friend retires and not the other. Additionally, people who live on their own admit that they had not realized how much they relied on their job for companionship and sometimes even for part of their social life. Taken a step at a time, retirement is full of opportunity and choice – but it is important to consider each decision carefully.

Pre-retirement courses

If you are wondering what to do when you retire, talk to other people who have recently stopped working. Friends who have already tackled the challenges and opportunities of retirement will be happy to offer suggestions. Good advice is useful and a large number of companies recognize this need by offering pre-retirement courses for their employees who are coming up to retirement age. If you are in a firm where this is not offered, or if you are self-employed, there are a number of organizations that can give you advice and help.

Before deciding on a particular course, it is worth thinking about the most appropriate time for you to attend one and the subjects that it should cover. The traditional view is that the ideal time is somewhere between one and two years before you are due to retire. While this is probably true for most people, it is also important to remember that preparing for retirement is best taken in stages. Some financial decisions, such as those affecting company or personal pension planning, need to be taken as early as possible. Others, such as whether to move house, can probably only be made much later.

The basic subjects that the best courses address are: finance, health, activity, leisure, housing and the adjustments that will need to be made by both you and your family when you retire. The crucial test, however, is not so much the amount of factual information the course contains but the extent to which it helps to focus and stimulate your own thoughts on the various issues and to lead to discussion with your partner and others in the same situation.

The following is a list of some organizations offering pre-retirement courses and advice:

Laterlife Learning runs retirement workshops for the modern generation who wish to maximize their enjoyment in later life. Retirement is now a 25–30 year project and one of the most significant lifestyle changes. Laterlife is the leading provider of planning retirement workshops, running over 100 open workshops annually in more than

30 locations all around the UK, as well as programmes for leading organizations in both public and private sector. Website: www. laterlife.com and www.retirement-courses.co.uk

Life Academy is a charity that enables people to learn about managing the changes in their lives through life and retirement planning and financial education. In both finance and health, the importance of adequate preparation for the future is all the greater given our increasing longevity. Contact: 01483 301170; website: www.life-academy.co.uk.

Retirement Education Services is one of the biggest specialist training consultancies in the field of planning for retirement. It runs around 100 courses/seminars a year. Its headquarters are in Oxfordshire, but it has associates in Newcastle and Edinburgh. Contact: 01491 833 696; website: www.retirementeducationsers.co.uk.

Scottish Pre-Retirement Council provides pre-retirement courses in and around Glasgow to facilitate the change from working life to retirement. Courses are normally two one-day sessions held over consecutive weeks. Contact: 0141 332 9427; website: www.sprc.org.uk.

PRIME (Prince's Initiative for Mature Enterprise) is a UK charity founded by HRH The Prince of Wales that provides free information, events and training to help older people get back into work by starting their own businesses. The charity's activities are needed because the over-50s face huge problems of unemployment and age discrimination in the conventional job market. For further information see www.primeinitiative.co.uk.

Should you wish to see which useful government bodies and support organizations there are for the over-50s, look at www.direct.gov.uk and search under 'Pensions and Retirement Planning'. There are many relevant sections, including 'Planning for Retirement' and 'Over 50s Health and Wellbeing'.

Also, a number of universities run retirement planning courses. These are typically held once or twice a year and are normally arranged by the department of extra-mural studies.

Commercial organizations

The following organizations offer an attractive mix of courses with something to suit almost everyone. There are residential and day courses. Several are specifically for senior executives:

Millstream International helps senior people make the most of new opportunities when they leave their main employment, whether from an enforced or considered career break or on retirement. Contact: 01730 825 711; website: www.mill-stream.co.uk.

Retirement Counselling Service is an independent organization offering a range of in-house and external retirement seminars and services throughout the UK. Contact: 01494 433553; website: www.the-retirement-site.co.uk.

Adult education

If you wish to consider further education in retirement, you could consult **Workers' Educational Association**, which is the UK's largest voluntary provider of adult education. Founded in 1903 to support the educational needs of working men and women, today's WEA runs over 10,000 courses each year, providing learning for more than 110,000 adults of all ages and drawn from all walks of life. The WEA is one of the UK's biggest charities and operates at local, regional and national levels. There are nine regions in England, a Scottish association and over 450 local branches. Contact: 020 7426 3450; website: www.wea.org.uk.

New focus for the retired

There are now a growing number of organizations to represent the interests of retired people. The over-50s represent a large proportion of the population, and it is essential that they have a means of putting forward their views on issues that affect their lives at both national and local levels. Two of the best known, which in addition to their campaigning role arrange a variety of social and other events, are:

Age UK, which is dedicated to improving later life for everyone. Contact: 0800 169 6565; website; www.ageuk.org.uk.

National Pensioners Convention, which is Britain's biggest pensioner organization, representing over 1,000 local, regional and national pensioner groups with a total of over 1.5 million members. The NPC's main objective is to promote the welfare and interests of all pensioners, as a way of securing dignity, respect and financial security in retirement. Contact: 020 7383 0388; website: www.npcuk.org.

And don't forget the hugely successful **Retirement Shows.** This unique forum for all who are retired, semi-retired or who aspire to retire (sponsored by Prudential) is held every year in three locations – Manchester, London and Glasgow. Great value and a fun-packed day out. Included is a wide variety of activities and features as well as free informative seminars and expert-panel sessions. Contact: 01372 743 837; website: www.the-retirement-show.com.

Chapter Two
Money in general

> Money is better than poverty, if only for financial reasons.
> **WOODY ALLEN.**

According to research conducted by LV= in 2010, almost 70 per cent of people aged over 50 are concerned about their income during retirement. Increasing numbers of people are delaying retiring because of the impact of the global economy. The government is planning to scrap the default retirement age in the UK from October 2011 so fixed retirement age may be a thing of the past. The hope is that this change will encourage people to work for longer, against a background of an ageing population. Longer working is widely seen as necessary to keep income tax receipts up and reduce the burden on pension funds as Britain's population ages.

However, a government-backed study estimated that educated middle-class households suffered the biggest financial losses from the economic downturn (falling house prices, tumbling stock markets and cuts in pension rights being the three main factors), forcing many people to delay retirement as a result. Contrastingly, households with little wealth had less to worry about since they could rely on state benefits and other assistance in retirement.

In a recent survey conducted by Barclays Wealth (www.bbc.co.uk/news/business-11416323) retirement is shunned by 60 per cent of UK wealthy individuals, which means almost two thirds of wealthy people in the United Kingdom want to keep working and never retire. The number of these so-called 'nevertirees' may well increase in future since more and more people are likely to shun the traditional concept of retiring. Since the UK government wants people to work longer to fund their retirement, having already scrapped the default retirement age of 65 from October 2011, there may be many who relish the challenges of continuing to work.

The wealthy were still likely to have sufficient assets to fund their retirement, while for those middle-earners nearing the end of working life, losses are more important because of the effect on resources available in retirement. Those with large shareholdings or who took out annuities in the middle of the crisis were worst hit. So one of the many questions facing the pre-retirement age group is, can you afford to retire? Is it better to wait until asset prices recover? Whether you are one or 10 years away from retirement, the most important thing to do is to review your retirement plans and see what options there are for maximizing your future income. The worst thing to do is ignore the situation and hope that things will miraculously improve on their own. Whatever the state of the global economy, wise handling of your personal economy is most likely to have a beneficial effect on your financial well-being during retirement.

In a lot of instances anticipation is far worse than reality. Retirement can be, and often is, better than many people imagine. The key to managing your retirement well is to know how to make whatever money you have go as far as possible. So what steps should you take to secure a better retirement? Getting a financial health check is important and, depending on the standard of living you want, see whether a review of your retirement date is necessary or whether other options should be considered to augment your income. As long as people are realistic, hopefully drastic economies will not have to be made. For many men and women who have only a rough idea as to their likely income and expenditure, the best advice is to do your sums.

Doing the sums

The best way to get an objective view of your financial affairs is to draw up a budget showing your income and outgoings. Getting to know the facts, do some figures – these are the essential first steps in your pre-retirement planning. To make a proper assessment, you need to draw up several lists:

- expected sources of income on retirement;
- essential outgoings;
- normal additional spending (such as holidays and other luxuries).

The following options should also be considered:

- possible ways to boost your retirement income;
- spending now for saving later;
- your wish list, if affordable.

The third list is composed of variables and unknowns and is therefore the most difficult to work out. Who would have predicted the economic turbulence of the last three years? The two most important items to consider in retirement planning are tax and inflation. Other things like stocks and shares, property prices and energy costs can go up or down and affect retirement financial planning. Emergency situations can and do arise, such as health issues for example, so if possible special provisions should be made. The other imponderable is predicting how long you, your partner or any dependants are likely to live, so it pays to consider such matters when budgeting in retirement.

Planning for the future is never a waste of time, neither can it be done too early. If you base your calculations on current commitments and expenditure this could be way off the mark, since your lifestyle and spending habits may change considerably. To get the figures into perspective, imagine yourself already retired. While some items will probably take a heftier slice of your budget, others will certainly be cheaper or no longer cost you anything at all. So it's not all bad news.

The possible areas where savings can be made and extra outgoings need to be considered are discussed below. The most practical way of using the list is to tick off the items that will definitely apply to you and, where possible, write down the expenditure involved (see Budget Planner, Chapter 7). While this will be no more than a draft – since there will obviously be gaps – the closer you are to retirement, the more sensible it is to do this exercise.

Possible savings

If you consider that going out to work costs money, when you leave your job you could save quite a lot: there will be a number of items you no longer have to pay for. These include travelling costs to work, bought lunches and special clothes, out-of-pocket incidentals such as drinks with colleagues, collections for presents or the Christmas party. National Insurance Contributions cease and, unless you choose to invest in a private plan, your pension payments will also stop. Additionally, when you retire, you may be in a lower tax bracket.

At the same time, you may have reached the stage when your children are now independent, your mortgage is substantially paid off and you have stopped subscribing to a life assurance policy. On reaching state retirement age – state pension age is still 65 for men and 60 for women but is expected to increase to 66 for all by 2016 – you become eligible for a variety of benefits. Currently these include concessionary travel and free NHS prescriptions, as well as cheaper theatre and cinema tickets (usually matinees), reduced entrance charges for exhibitions and a wide choice of special holiday offers. Some benefits apply to both men and women from age 60.

Many insurance companies give discounts to mature drivers, some of which apply from age 50. Other companies restrict eligibility to those aged 55 or even 60. This scheme could be terminated when the policy holder reaches 75 but a number of companies extend the cover to a spouse or other named person with a good driving record. The discount for people over 50 ranges from 10 to 15 per cent. There are considerable extra savings for drivers with a five-year claim-free record. The best advice is to approach your existing insurance company first and ask what terms they will give you. If these do not seem good, it could pay to shop around. A growing number of insurers give discounts to those buying a policy online so don't forget to check the internet.

Extra outgoings

There is no escaping the fact that when you retire some of your expenses will be heavier than at present. First, you will probably be spending more time at home, so expect utility bills to go up due to increased consumption.

With lots of leisure time you may spend more on outings, hobbies and short breaks and holidays. To avoid having to make serious cutbacks, these need to be budgeted for well in advance. Even voluntary activities have hidden expenses, for example more use of the telephone, petrol costs and supporting fund-raising occasions.

Looking ahead, home comforts become increasingly important. There may come a time when you will be paying other people to do some of the jobs that you previously managed yourself. Anticipating such areas of additional expenditure is not being pessimistic. On the contrary, it is the surest way of avoiding future money worries. You may find, once you have sat down and worked out your retirement income and expenditure in detail, that you'll manage very well.

Expected sources of income on retirement

Your list will include at least some of the following. Once you have added up the figures in the Budget Planner (Chapter 7) you will have to deduct Income Tax to arrive at the net spending amount available to you:

- State basic pension;
- State graduated pension;

- SERPS;
- State second pension;
- occupational pension;
- personal pension;
- stakeholder pension;
- State benefits.

Additionally, you may receive income or a capital sum from some of the following:

- company share option scheme;
- sale of business or personal assets;
- investments (stocks and shares, unit trusts, etc);
- other existing income (from a trust, property, family business);
- bank/building society savings;
- National Savings & Investments bond or certificate;
- endowment policy.

You might also be in receipt of income from an annuity. However, since at this stage you will be unlikely to have purchased one, this really belongs in the category of investment decisions.

Unavoidable outgoings

One person's priority is another person's luxury – and vice versa. For this reason, the divide between 'unavoidable outgoings' and 'normal additional expenditure' (see section following) is likely to vary with each individual. For example, pet owners would consider pet food and veterinary bills as an essential item of expenditure, whereas those who do not have a pet are able to disregard such costs. Almost everyone will want to juggle some of the items between the two lists or add their own particular requisites or special enthusiasms.

Whatever your own essentials, some of the following items will certainly feature on your list of unavoidable expenses:

- food;
- rent or mortgage repayments;
- Council Tax;
- repair and maintenance costs;

- heating;
- lighting and other energy;
- telephone/mobile and internet connection;
- postage (including Christmas cards);
- TV licence/Sky/digital subscriptions;
- household insurance;
- clothes;
- domestic cleaning products;
- laundry, cleaners' bills, shoe repairs;
- miscellaneous services, ie property maintenance, such as plumber, window cleaner;
- car, including road tax, fuel, insurance, road rescue such as RAC or AA, servicing;
- other transport;
- regular savings and life assurance;
- HP/other loan repayments;
- outgoings on health.

Normal additional expenditure

This may well include:

- gifts;
- holidays;
- newspapers/books/CDs/DVDs;
- computer expenses (including broadband);
- drink;
- cigarettes/tobacco;
- hairdressing;
- toiletries/cosmetics;
- entertainment (hobbies, outings, DVD purchase/rental, home entertaining, etc);
- miscellaneous subscriptions/membership fees;
- charitable donations;

- expenditure on pets;
- garden purchases.

Work out the figures against these lists. Then, to compare your expenditure against likely income, jot them down on the Budget Planner (see page 151).

Possible ways of boosting your retirement income

Other than luck – winning the lottery or coming into a legacy – there are three main possibilities for providing you with extra money: your home, work and investment skill.

Your home

Your home offers several different options: moving somewhere smaller, taking in lodgers or raising money on your home.

Moving somewhere smaller

You could sell your present home, move into smaller accommodation and collect a capital sum at the same time as reducing your running costs. It is essential to look at the sums as the cash difference on the exchange – in other words, your profit – could be less than you expect. Moving home is always an expensive business, with lawyers' fees and removal costs. Make allowances for some decorating expenses and a possible period of overlap when sorting out payments for telephone rental, extra electricity bills and so on.

If you are planning to buy, you will need to add Stamp Duty. First-time buyers only are exempt from Stamp Duty on properties up to £250,000. Otherwise Stamp Duty Land Tax of between 1 and 4 per cent is payable on the whole purchase price. Moving may well be an excellent decision, but if money is the main criterion you need to be thoroughly realistic when calculating the gains.

Transferring an existing mortgage to your new property or getting a new one might be another option. Mortgages are available to people over retirement age. However, there may be good reasons why a mortgage would not be sensible for you. If in doubt, consult an accountant or solicitor who will help you work out the details.

Taking in lodgers

You may have more space than you need in your current home. If you do not wish to move you could consider taking in lodgers, either as paying guests or, if your property lends itself to the creation of a separate flatlet, in a tenancy capacity. When assessing the financial rewards, it is wise to assume that there will be times when the accommodation is empty – so you will not be receiving any rent. The good news is that you may be able to keep more of any earnings you make.

You can, under the government's Rent a Room scheme, let out a furnished room in your home and claim tax relief of up to £4,250 a year (£2,125 if letting jointly). Any excess rental over £4,250 will be assessed for tax in the normal way. The scheme does not apply if you let unfurnished accommodation in your home. You don't even have to be a home-owner to take advantage of the Rent a Room scheme, but if you are renting you should check whether your lease allows you to take in a lodger.

If you're paying a mortgage, it is best to check the mortgage lender's and insurer's terms too. The relief applies only to accommodation that is 'part of your main home', so if you are thinking of creating a separate flatlet you will need to take care that this qualifies and that it is not at risk of being assessed as a commercial let. It is best to check the technical requirements with your architect or other professional adviser.

Raising money on your home

A third option is to part-sell your home for either a capital sum or regular payments, under an equity-release scheme, and continue to live in it for as long as you wish. Sounds wonderful? There are both attractions and drawbacks that need to be considered carefully, and you would be strongly advised to discuss the matter with your solicitor.

All these possibilities are explored in greater detail in Chapter 8, Your Home. If you think any of the ideas sound interesting, see the following sections in Chapter 8: 'Moving to a new home', 'Raising money on your home' and 'Letting rooms in your home'.

Work

You might wish to continue working. If this is the case, one of the simplest solutions is for you to talk to your employer to see what options are available for you to remain with your present organization. The age discrimination legislation should be a point in your favour, as it strengthens the rights of individuals who want to postpone their retirement. If you stay, you could either defer your pension or, if you prefer and the scheme rules allow it, you could start drawing your pension benefits – perhaps as a way to boost your income if you ease down to part-time work.

Alternatively, you may look on retirement as the opportunity for a job switch or the chance you have always wanted of setting up on your own. When assessing your budget plans, it is as well to err on the side of caution with regard to any additional income you will be likely to earn. Becoming self-employed or setting up a business may seem attractive but you have to meet the start-up costs and few new enterprises make much profit during the first two or three years. If you are self-employed or own a business, there may be certain tax advantages as well as possible scope for improving your pension. There is more information on work opportunities in Chapters 10, 11 and 12.

Investment

Despite recent gloomy economic conditions, with markets still depressed, now could be an excellent time to consider investing. Don't assume that it requires a huge amount of money. If it is something you haven't done before, it can be fascinating and rewarding. As you will see from Chapter 5, investment can take many different forms, and among the list of different options there should be something to suit almost everyone. Although you may consider this to be specialist reading, it is worth taking a look. Maximizing your income in retirement could make all the difference between being able to enjoy life and a few luxuries or worrying about money.

One significant change for pensioners is that they will no longer be forced to use most of their pension to buy a guaranteed income for life. Rules requiring most people to spend three-quarters of their pension savings on annuities have been scrapped. From April 2011 pensioners are allowed to delay the purchase for longer, or not to buy one at all. This would mean they are able to pass their pension savings on to their heirs subject to a 55 per cent tax, instead of the 82 per cent tax at present. The rule change is positive news and intended to encourage people to put more into their pension pots.

Spending now for saving later

You may normally take the view that there is never a best time for spending money. But, remember, retirement planning is different in that sooner or later you will need, or want, to make certain purchases. These could include paying off outstanding commitments, such as a mortgage. Most people's basic list – at least to think about – includes one or more of the following:

- expenditure on their home;
- the purchase of a car;
- the termination of HP or other credit arrangements.

Additionally, there may be a number of general domestic or luxury items that you have been promising yourself you would buy for some time. The question is simply one of timing: that is, determining the right moment to buy. To help you decide whether a policy of 'spending now' is sensible, or possibly self-indulgent, there are two very simple questions you should ask: Can I afford it more easily now – or in the future? By paying now rather than waiting, will I be saving money in the long run? True, the issue may be complicated by tax and other considerations, but for most choices this very basic analysis helps greatly to clarify the financial arguments on both sides.

Home improvements

If you plan to remain in the same property, the likelihood is that at some point you will want to make some changes or improvements: install double glazing, insulate the loft, modernize the kitchen or perhaps convert part of the house to a granny flat for an elderly parent who is becoming too frail to live alone. It is normally accepted that any significant expenditure on your home is best undertaken several years prior to retirement. The question largely depends on individual circumstances. Some people find it easier, and more reassuring, to pay major household bills while they are still earning. Others specifically plan to use part of the lump sum from their pension to create a dream home. To arrive at the answer that makes best financial sense, present commitments have to be weighed against likely future expenditure (together with what money you will have available).

Another very important consideration is to make sure you know how long you intend to stay in your present home. Investing a fortune in a property and then moving a couple of years later is not wise. Despite what people may think, it is rare to recoup all your expenditure on a property you've modified to your own taste. Though it involves a few minutes' paperwork, a worthwhile exercise is to jot down your own personal list of pros and cons under the headings 'spending now' and 'spending later'. If still in doubt, waiting is normally the more prudent course.

Purchasing a car

There could be two good reasons for buying a new car ahead of your retirement. One is that you have a company car that you are about to lose; the other is that your existing vehicle is getting old and is beginning (or will probably soon start) to give you trouble. If either of these applies, then it probably makes sense to buy a replacement sooner rather than later.

Company car owners should first check whether they might be entitled to purchase their present car on favourable terms. A number of employers are quite happy to allow this. Also, in terms of reducing carbon footprints, two-car families should think seriously come retirement whether both vehicles are necessary.

Paying off HP, loans and similar

In general, this is a good idea, since delay is unlikely to save you any money – and may actually cost you more. The only precaution is to check the small print of your agreement, to ensure that there is no penalty for early repayment. A further exception to the rule could be your mortgage. An accountant could advise you; or, if you are thinking of moving (and the issue is really whether to transfer an existing mortgage or possibly acquire a new one), include this among the points to raise with your solicitor.

Cherished plans, if affordable

The Budget Planner (Chapter 7) is designed to help you work out whether your various luxuries and plans are destined to remain dreams or are achievable. Perhaps as this is such a very personal decision area, only you can really make the assessments. However, if you plan your finances with a specific objective in view, you may find that against expectations an idea that first seemed impossible is actually affordable. Or, when you really think about the choices, some of your earlier priorities may seem less important.

Money – if you become redundant

Much of the information in the earlier part of this chapter is equally valid whether you become redundant or retire in the normal way. However, there are several key points with regard to money that it could be to your advantage to check:

- *You may be entitled to statutory redundancy pay.* Your employer is obliged to pay the legal minimum, which is calculated on your age, length of service and weekly pay. To qualify, you will need to have worked for the organization for at least two years. Redundancy pay is 1.5 weeks' pay for each year worked if you are over 41 years, up to a maximum of £380 a week. See the **Redundancy Help** website: www.redundancyhelp.co.uk.

- *Ex gratia payments.* Many employers are prepared to be more generous. As long as it's not more than £30,000, statutory redundancy pay is not taxable. Any payment over this limit is subject to tax and National Insurance.

- *Benefits that are not part of your pay.* Redundancy may mean the loss of several valuable benefits, such as a company car, life assurance and health insurance. Some insurance companies allow preferential rates to individuals who were previously insured with them under a company scheme.

- *Holiday entitlement.* You could be owed holiday entitlement for which you should be paid.

- *Your mortgage.* Your mortgage lender should be notified as soon as possible and might agree to a more flexible repayment system. Check whether your mortgage package includes insurance against redundancy. There is help available from the State if you are claiming benefits, such as income support or income-based jobseeker's allowance. Those claiming these benefits could have their interest payments covered for two years if their mortgage is below £200,000. However, no help is available to pay off the capital of your mortgage.

- *Other creditors/debts.* Any creditors that you may have difficulty in paying (electricity, gas, a bank overdraft) should be informed as early as possible in the hope of agreeing easier payment terms. There could be an argument for paying off credit card bills immediately, even if this means using some of your redundancy pay.

- *Company pension.* Company pension scheme members normally have several choices. See the 'Early leavers' section in Chapter 3, Pensions.

- *Jobseeker's allowance (JSA).* Even if you are hoping to get another job very soon, you should sign on without delay. Your National Insurance Contributions will normally be credited to you. This is important to protect your State pension. To qualify for JSA you need to be under State pension age and must either have paid sufficient

Class 1 National Insurance Contributions or have a low income. You must also be both available for and actively seeking work. For further information about JSA and other possible benefits, look on the **Directgov** website: www.direct.gov.uk.

- *Redundancy helpline.* The helpline can answer queries on all aspects of redundancy. Contact: 0845 145 0004; website: www.redundancyhelp.co.uk.

Money left unclaimed

With over £850 million lying unclaimed in dormant bank, building society and NS&I (National Savings and Investments) accounts, it might be worth checking to see if any of these funds are yours. More than one in 10 people think they may have forgotten assets but many people do not know how to try to find their money. If you think this could apply to you, there is a free lost account tracing website: www.mylostaccount.org.uk, which helps people track down their missing funds. It is easy to use and is a one-stop site covering UK banks and building societies as well as all NS&I accounts. Any savers who think they have mislaid details of a long-unused account should use 'mylostaccount.org' to help trace it.

Extra income

There are a number of State benefits and allowances available to give help to many pensioners. Although public spending cuts have impacted greatly on millions of people, support is available for those most in need. Definitions of 'need' cover a very wide range and apply, among others, to problems connected with health, housing and care of an elderly or disabled relative, as well as widowhood. Pensioners are failing to claim up to £5.4 billion in benefits every year, even though many of them are struggling to make ends meet. This is according to a recent study by Age UK, which suggests that 1.97 million older people who are eligible for Council Tax benefit are not claiming it. The two main reasons cited for older people not claiming what they are entitled to are the claims process being too complicated and feeling too proud to claim.

While many of these benefits are 'means-tested', some, such as Disability Living Allowance, are not dependent on how poor or how wealthy, you are. Moreover, even when means-testing is a factor, for some of the benefits income levels are nothing like as low as many people imagine. Because this information is not widely enough known, many individuals – including over a million pensioners – are not claiming help to which they are entitled and for which in many cases they have actually paid through their National Insurance Contributions.

A number of voluntary organizations also provide assistance to individuals, sometimes in cash or sometimes in the form of facilities, such as special equipment for disabled people. Details are given in the relevant chapters. For further advice and information contact the following organizations:

Jobcentre Plus Office: 0800 055 6688; website: www.dwp.gov.uk.

Citizens Advice Bureau: free confidential advice at over 3,000 locations throughout the UK; website: www.citizensadvice.org.uk.

Age UK: 0800 169 6565; website: www.ageuk.org.uk.

Making your money go further

The **Consumer Financial Education Body (CFEB)** is an independent organization, established in April 2010 by the Financial Services Authority (FSA) and has the responsibility for helping consumers understand financial matters and manage their finances better. It provides free, impartial information and education, Moneymadeclear guides and a money guidance service. Contact: 0300 500 5000; website: www.moneymadeclear.org.uk or www.cfebuk.org.uk.

Savvy Woman is a finance website for women who want more from their money. It is packed with articles and information on everything from pensions and retirement planning to protecting your money and investing in property. You can also get your money questions answered by a panel of experts and receive money tips and information by signing up for an e-mail newsletter. Website: www.savvywoman.co.uk

Utility Warehouse is a company that offers telephone, broadband, mobile, gas and electricity at very competitive rates. There is also the opportunity to use a 'cashback' card for your shopping that will lessen the cost of your other bills. Contact: 0800 131 3000; website: www.utilitywarehouse.co.uk.

You can also access all age-specific discounts and promotions in the **Seniors Discounts** Directory if you register as a member of Seniors

Discounts. All new discounts are automatically added to the home page under 'Latest Discounts' so it pays to check regularly. To enrol, go to www.seniorsdiscounts.co.uk and follow the instructions.

Useful reading

The Pensioners' Guide is an easy-to-read booklet that provides information on the range of government benefits and services for pensioners, obtainable from Jobcentre Plus or social security offices, Citizens Advice Bureau and Post Offices. It is also available in pdf downloadable format from the website: www.thepensionservice.gov.uk or www.direct.gov.uk/pensions

Another excellent book for those wanting detailed information about planning their finances is *Talking about Retirement* by Lyn Ashurst, published by Kogan Page. The author is an authority in her field and gives a comprehensive and detailed study of a careful and planned approach to the retirement process, based on about 50 case studies. For more information and other recommended titles on retirement and associated issues published by Kogan Page, see www.koganpage.com.

Chapter Three
Pensions

> *The future, according to some scientists, will be exactly like the past, only more expensive.* JOHN SLADEK

In life there are many significant choices that have to be made. Few, however, are as important as deciding how to fund the level of income you wish to receive for the rest of your life. Many people have worked for years, saving money into a pension pot, assuming this will guarantee them a more comfortable old age. However, pension prospects for thousands of people who are facing retirement are not good at present. Indeed recent statistics point to the huge number of people born in the post-war years who are fearful about their financial future. The main reasons for this are volatile stock markets, which have made it difficult to build up a decent pension fund; many employers having withdrawn generous company-based schemes; and property, which had been a rock solid investment for so long has been less certain in recent years.

A government-backed research study showed that the wealthiest households had not suffered significantly since they still had sufficient assets to fund their retirement. Households with the lowest incomes had less to worry about since they could rely on State benefits and other assistance in retirement. In most cases those in the middle earnings bracket were worst hit because of the triple whammy of falling house prices, tumbling stock markets and cuts in pension rights. But despite this, next to your home your pension is still almost certainly your most valuable asset. It is therefore important to check where you stand – and take advice on what you can best do if damage limitation is required – to ensure that when you retire you receive the maximum benefit.

In June 2010 the government announced the de-linking of RPI (Retail Price Index) and switching to CPI (Consumer Price Index) for calculating rises in benefits, tax credits and public service pensions. This change will mean that many people are likely to receive smaller increases in government payouts, as CPI tends to be lower than RPI. The CPI includes different things: spending by pensioners who get most of their income from State benefits is in, while Council Tax and mortgage payments are out. This has usually pushed CPI inflation below RPI inflation, although it can have the opposite effect when interest rates and house prices are falling. Additionally, the CPI makes price increases look smaller because it takes account of how we switch to alternative products to avoid them. The Index switch announced in June 2010 came as a surprise to many because it unpicks the pensions people were expecting to receive. Whatever the rights and wrongs of the decision, it means lower pension increases in the short term and for the government a welcome contribution to cutting the current budget deficit.

State pensions

State pension age is the earliest age you can claim a State pension. It is not the same as retirement age. Retirement age is when you choose to retire. You can still work when you reach State pension age. Currently, if you are a man born before 6 April 1959 your State pension age is 65. A woman born on or before 5 April 1950 has a State pension age of 60. Women born on or after 6 April 1950 will find their state pension age increasing to 65 between 2010 and 2020 to equalize the pension age for men and women at 65. The government wishes to speed up the rise in state pension age for men to 66 by 2016 – eight years earlier than planned. The pension age for women will also rise to 66 by 2020. These changes are needed, according to the government, to help reduce the UK's national debt.

In July 2010, the government announced plans to scrap the default retirement age in the UK from October 2011. Under this proposal, employers would not be allowed to dismiss staff because they had reached the age of 65. This has been welcomed by campaigners against ageism. Under the plans no forced retirement notices could be issued by an employer after 6 April 2011 (six months before the October 2011 change).

Your right to a State pension

Your right to a State pension depends on your (or your spouse's) National Insurance Contributions (NIC). Most people have to pay into the NIC scheme while they are working. If you are an employee, your employer will have automatically deducted Class 1 NIC from your salary, provided your earnings were above a certain limit (2010/11: £110 a week – the 'earnings threshold'). If you are self-employed, you will have been paying a flat-rate Class 2 NIC of £2.40 every week and possibly the earnings-related Class 4 NIC as well. You may also have paid Class 3 voluntary contributions at some point in your life in order to maintain your contributions record. If you are over pension age you do not pay NIC. There may have been times during your working life when you have not – either knowingly or unwittingly – paid NIC. If you have not paid sufficient contributions to qualify for a full-rate basic pension you may be entitled to a reduced rate of pension. However, your NIC record will have been maintained in the following circumstances.

If you have lived or worked outside Great Britain

If you have lived in Northern Ireland or the Isle of Man, any contributions paid there will count towards your pension. The same should also apply in most cases if you have lived or worked in an EU country or any country whose social security is linked to Britain's by a reciprocal arrangement. However, there have sometimes been problems with certain countries so, if you have any doubts, you should enquire what your position is at your pension centre.

If you have received Home Responsibilities Protection (HRP)

If you have not worked regularly at some time since 1978, because you have had to stay at home to care for either a child or a sick or elderly person, you may have protected your right to a pension by claiming HRP. This benefit allows you to deduct the years when you were required to give up work from the normal qualifying period for a basic pension and so, in effect, shorten the number of years when you would otherwise have been required to make contributions.

There are two important points to note. First, if you are a woman and were claiming Child Benefit, HRP should have been credited to you automatically, whereas a man staying at home to care for a child would have needed to arrange the transfer of Child Benefit to himself. Second, HRP is available only for complete tax years in which earnings were less than 52 times the lower earnings limit.

Although HRP can be claimed by both sexes, it predictably applies more frequently to women. For more information, see 'Pensions for women' at the end of this chapter, or check the website: www.direct.gov.uk/pensions.

If you have been in any of the following situations

You will have been credited with contributions (instead of having to pay them) if:

- you were sick or unemployed (provided you sent in sick notes to your social security office, signed on at the unemployment benefit office or were in receipt of Jobseeker's Allowance);
- you were a man aged 60–64 and not working;
- you were entitled to maternity allowance, invalid care allowance or unemployability supplement;
- you were taking an approved course of training;
- you had left education but had not yet started working;
- since April 2000, your earnings had fallen between what are known as the lower earnings limit and the primary threshold, ie between £97 and £110 a week (2010/11).

Married women and widows

Married women and widows who do not qualify for a basic pension in their own right may be entitled to a basic pension on their husband's contributions at about 60 per cent of the level to which he is entitled (see 'Pensions for women' at the end of this chapter).

Since the introduction of independent taxation, husband and wife are assessed separately for tax. As a result, a married woman is now entitled to have her section of the joint pension offset against her own personal allowance, instead of being counted as part of her husband's taxable income. For many pensioner couples, this should mean a reduction in their tax liability.

Reduced-rate contributions note: many women retiring today may have paid a reduced-rate contribution under a scheme that was abolished in 1978. Women who were already paying a reduced-rate contribution were, however, allowed to continue doing so. These reduced-rate contributions *do not count* towards your pension and you will not have had any contributions credited to you. If you are still some years away from retirement, it could be to your advantage to cancel the reduced-rate option, as by doing so you may be able to build up a wider range of benefits without paying anything extra. This applies if you are currently (2010/11) earning between £97 and £110 a week, ie between the lower earnings limit and the primary threshold. If you are earning above the primary threshold (£110), to get the same extra benefits you would have to start paying extra contributions. For advice, contact your local tax office or see the website: www.hmrc.gov.uk.

How your pension is worked out

Anyone trying to decide whether they can afford to retire should get their State pension forecast from **The Pension Service.** It is worth getting an early estimate of what your pension will be, as it may be possible to improve your NI Contribution record by making additional Class 3 voluntary contributions. Contact: 0845 300 0168; website: www.direct.gov.uk/pensions

Basic State pension

The full basic pension for a man or woman (April 2010/11) is £97.65 a week, and £156.15 for a married couple. These are the maximums available. If you do not have the maximum qualifying years to qualify for the full basic state pension, you will be entitled to a lower amount based on the number of qualifying years on your record. State pensions are increased in April each year. In the June 2010 Budget it was announced that from April 2011 pensions would be uprated by the highest of the price index, earnings or 2.5 per cent. All pensions are taxable other than one or two special categories, such as war widows and the victims of Nazism.

The amount of basic State pension you receive at State pension age is based on your National Insurance Contribution record over your working life. The rules for the State pension have changed and the number of qualifying years you need for a full basic State pension now depends on when you reach State pension age. Those reaching State pension age on or after 6 April 2010 require 30 qualifying years to get a full basic State pension. Each qualifying year of paid or credited contributions will be worth 1/30th of the full basic State pension.

Due to improvements in service arrangements, you only need to claim a State pension two months before your State pension birthday date. The **Department for Work and Pensions** (DWP) has launched an online service where you can now claim benefits from home or abroad. Contact: 0800 731 7898; website: www.dwp.gov.uk/pensions

If you do not qualify for a full basic State pension you may be able to pay Class 3 National Insurance Contributions if you have gaps in your National Insurance record. Paying them would mean that years that would not normally be qualifying years would count towards your basic State pension. Your forecast letter will tell you whether or not you can do this. There are time limits for paying Class 3 National Insurance Contributions and you must normally pay them within six years of the end of the tax year for which you are paying.

Additional State pension

If you are (or have been) in employment you may have been building up an additional State pension – the State Second Pension. (This was formerly known as SERPS – the State Earnings Related Pensions Scheme.) The amount of State Second Pension (S2P) you get depends on your earnings and your NICs record. There are other means of entitlement to some S2P: for example if you earn below a certain amount set by the government; or if you cannot work through long-term illness or disability; or you are a carer.

The S2P is not available to the self-employed, for whom the alternative pension choices are either a personal pension or a stakeholder pension. If you are an employee, you are automatically included in S2P unless you decide to contract out, or you are a member of an employer's occupational pension scheme that is contracted out. If you decide to contract out, you stop building up your S2P entitlement and build up a replacement for it in your own pension. You will continue to be contracted out of S2P unless you decide to contract back in.

For more information about contracting out, or if you have any queries regarding the S2P scheme, ask The Pension Service: 0845 606 0265; website: www.direct.gov.uk/pensions.

Deferring your pension

Your pension will be increased if you delay claiming it past State retirement age. You can do so whether you are still in work or not. For every year you defer taking your pension, there will be an increase in its value. You can continue deferring your pension for as long as you like. The extra money will be paid to you when you eventually decide to claim your pension. You can choose whether to take it as a taxable lump sum or in higher weekly pension payments. If you choose to receive higher weekly payments, you will need to defer your pension for at least five weeks. If you go for the lump sum, deferral must be for at least one year. You will receive a one-off lump sum payment and your State pension paid at the normal rate.

If you plan to defer your pension, you should also defer any graduated pension to which you may be entitled – or you risk losing the increases you would otherwise obtain. The Pension Service can advise you. Contact: 0845 606 0265; website: www.direct.gov.uk/pensions.

Increases for dependants

Since 6 April 2010 it has not been possible to claim an increase in your State pension for another adult. If you were already entitled to this increase on 5 April 2010 you will be able to keep it until you no longer meet the conditions for the increase, or until 5 April 2020, whichever is first.

Age addition

Your pension will be automatically increased once you reach 80. The current rate is 25p a week.

Income Support

If you have an inadequate income, you may qualify for Income Support. There are special premiums (ie additions) for lone parents, disabled people, carers and pensioners. A condition of entitlement is that you should not have capital, including savings, of more than £16,000. A big advantage is that people entitled to Income Support receive full help with their rent and should also not have any Council Tax to pay. See 'Housing benefit' and 'Council Tax benefit', in Chapter 8.

Pension Credit

There are two different types of Pension Credit. Guarantee Credit is for those who have reached the minimum qualifying age; Savings Credit is for those aged 65 and over. The basic rate for the standard minimum guarantee for 2010/11 is £132.60 a week for single people and £202.40 for couples. These amounts could be increased if you are disabled, caring for someone, or for certain housing costs, such as mortgage interest payments. If you are not already receiving Pension Credit but think you would be entitled to do so, the enquiry line is: 0800 99 1234 or website: www.direct.gov.uk/pensioncredit For general enquiries about pensions, contact The Pensions Service: 0845 60 60 265.

Other sources of help

Social Fund. If you are faced with an exceptional expense you find difficult to pay, you may be able to obtain a budgeting or crisis loan, community care grant or funeral payment from the Social Fund.

These are dealt with through Jobcentre Plus. See website: www.direct.gov.uk.

There are two other online sources of help relating to information on benefits. These are **Turn2Us** (www.turn2us.org.uk), a charity set up specifically to identify potential sources of funding for those facing financial difficulty; and **EntitledTo** (www.entitledto.co.uk), which will help you work out which benefits you may be entitled to.

According to Age UK, around 1.97 million pensioners are failing to claim Council Tax benefit to which they are entitled. Every year £5.4 billion is left unclaimed by pensioners despite many of them struggling to make ends meet. The main reasons for their failure to claim are the complicated claims process and those who are too independent and proud to claim benefits.

Early retirement and your pension

Because many people retire early, some people assume it is possible to get an early pension. While the information is correct as regards many employers' occupational pension schemes, as well as for stakeholder and personal pensions, it does not apply to the basic State pension. If you take early retirement before the age of 60, it may be necessary for you to pay voluntary Class 3 NIC to protect your contributions record for State pension purposes. Your local tax office can advise you about NICs.

How you get a State pension

You should claim your pension a few months before you reach State pension age. The Department for Work and Pensions (DWP) should send you a claim form (BR1) at the proper time, but if this doesn't arrive it is your responsibility to contact the DWP. If you have moved recently, make sure it has your current address. After you claim, you are told in writing exactly how much pension you will get. You will also be told what to do if you disagree with the decision. Contact: 0800 731 7898; website: www.direct.gov.uk/pensions

How your State pension can be paid

Pensions are usually paid direct into a bank account. This can be a bank or building society account or, if you prefer, a Post Office Card Account. Individuals who prefer to receive their money every week have the option of receiving a weekly cheque, which can be cashed at the Post Office or paid direct into a Post Office Card Account.

Other situations

Pensions can be paid to an overseas address, if you are going abroad for six months or more. See website: www.direct.gov.uk/pensions, the section on Britons Living Abroad.

If you are in hospital, your pension can still be paid to you and you will receive your pension in full for the duration of your stay, regardless of how long you have to remain in hospital. For advice contact either The Pensions Service or the Citizens Advice Bureau.

Christmas bonus

Pensioners usually get a small tax-free bonus shortly before Christmas each year. The amount and due date are announced in advance. For many years the sum has been £10. The bonus is combined with your normal pension payment for the first week in December.

Advice

The Pension Service provides information to current and future pensioners so that making informed decisions about pension arrangements is straightforward. The Pensions Service plans for everyone to have more independence in later life by tackling pensioner poverty and reforming the pension process. If you need help with your retirement plans it can assist you. It will explain what the State will provide when you retire and let you know what pension-related benefits you may be entitled to.

If you have any queries or think you may not be obtaining your full pension entitlement, you should contact the Pension Service as soon as possible. If you think a mistake has been made, you have the right to appeal and can insist on your claim being heard by an independent tribunal. Before doing so, you would be strongly advised to consult a solicitor at the Citizens Advice Bureau or the Welfare Advice Unit of your social security office. Some areas have special Tribunal Representation Units to assist people to make claims at tribunals. If you are contacting the Pension Service with a query, you should quote either your National Insurance number (or your spouse's) or your pension number if you have already started receiving your pension. Contact: 0845 606 0265; website: www.directgov.uk/pensions.

For further information about pensions, there is a booklet full of advice entitled *Pensioners' Guide* (latest edition April 2010) obtainable from The Pensions Service, part of the Department for Work and Pensions. Contact: 08457 31 32 33 or website: www.direct.gov.uk pensions.

Private pensions

Pension savings are still one of the most tax-effective investments available because you receive Income Tax relief on contributions at your highest tax rate and the growth in your pension fund is totally exempt from Income Tax and Capital Gains Tax. Another advantage is that part of the pension can be taken as a tax-free cash sum when you retire. Private pension schemes fall into two broad categories: those arranged by employers (occupational pensions), and those you can arrange for yourself. If your employer does not offer a pension scheme, or you are self-employed, the best alternative is a stakeholder pension.

On the subject of occupational pensions, recent changes introduced by the Coalition Government are likely to reduce the value of all occupational pensions. Pension funds will now only be required to increase pensions by the rate of inflation measured by the Consumer Price Index (CPI) rather than the Retail Price Index (RPI), which is currently used to increase pension payments. The CPI has consistently been lower than the RPI and the government's decision to change the rules on indexation will affect schemes in both the public and private sectors.

Company pension schemes

Company pension schemes vary from company to company but the two most general types are 'salary related' and 'money purchase' schemes. In a salary related scheme, the amount of money you receive is based either on your final salary or career average earnings. The benefits provided at retirement are based on the member's service and earnings.

The other types are defined contribution schemes. These can be money purchase, group personal pension plans or group stakeholder pension schemes. The benefits provided at retirement are based on how much is paid in and how the chosen investment performs. On retirement your fund is used to provide your pension, usually by buying an annuity (a regular income for life).

About 10 million people are now participating in company schemes. While the schemes can vary considerably, the following basic features apply to all of them.

Pension fund

Pension contributions go into a pension fund that is quite separate from your employer's company. It is set up under trust and run by trustees, appointed from management and from pension scheme members. It is the job of the trustees to manage the fund and its investments and to ensure that the benefit promises are kept.

Payments into the fund

Your scheme may or may not ask for a contribution from you. For this reason, schemes are known as 'contributory' or 'non-contributory'. If (as is normally the case) you are required to make a contribution, this will be deducted from your pay before you receive it. Your employer's contributions to the scheme represent the money your employer is setting aside for your pension and other benefits. In some schemes the amount is calculated as a fixed percentage of your earnings; in others the scheme actuary will estimate the amount that your employer needs to pay to ensure your (and other members') benefits in the future.

Benefits from the scheme

All pension scheme members should be given a booklet describing how the scheme works, what benefits it provides and other information, including the address of the Pensions Ombudsman. If you do not receive one, you should ask the person in the company responsible for the pension scheme – this is often the personnel manager – to supply you with a booklet. You can also ask to see a copy of the trust deed as well as the latest annual report and audited accounts. The key benefits applicable to most pension schemes include:

- A pension due at whatever age is specified by the scheme, usually somewhere between 60 and 65 (although many companies offer early retirement provision).
- Death benefit (sometimes known as 'lump sum life assurance'), paid out if you die before retirement age.
- A widow's or widower's pension paid for life no matter when you die. Same-sex couples who enter a civil partnership are now treated as married couples, which entitles them to receive an equivalent survivor's pension on the death of their partner.

Contribution and benefit limits

The government sets limits (for tax relief) on the contributions that individuals can invest in their pension plan and on the pension benefits they can receive. All company and personal pension schemes are now under a single tax regime.

Among other important changes, the earnings cap is no longer a factor. Instead, individuals can now invest up to 100 per cent of annual earnings into their plan (or plans) with the benefit of tax relief, up to a maximum figure – known as the annual allowance. For the tax year 2010/11 this amount is £255,000. Yearly pension savings above this amount are taxed at 40 per cent. The lifetime limit for 2010/11 is £1.8 million for total pension funds. Funds in excess of the lifetime limit are subject to the lifetime allowance charge. This applies in addition to the usual Income Tax due on pension payments. If you take benefits above your lifetime allowance as a pension, the lifetime allowance charge on the excess amount will be 25 per cent if taken as income, or 55 per cent if taken as a lump sum. The ceiling on tax relief given to people with pension funds up to £1.8 million will be maintained until 2015/16.

Tax-free lump sum

Provided your scheme rules allow it, you can take up to a maximum of 25 per cent of the value of your fund – including Additional Voluntary Contributions (AVCs) and contracted-out benefits from the State Second Pension scheme – from age 55 without having to retire. Unless you are in a final salary scheme, you are no longer obliged to take any pension income when accessing your lump sum but can leave the money in the fund to continue to grow. A major new benefit for those nearing retirement is that they can ease into part-time work, take their lump sum and, if they wish to do so, start drawing some pension income.

Scheme rules

The fact that HMRC has changed the rules is unfortunately no guarantee that individuals will be able to take full advantage of all the new options that have become available. Their employer's pension scheme rules will also need to have been altered accordingly, which may not always be the case. Before making any definite plans, it is advisable first to check with whoever is responsible for the company scheme.

Types of scheme

With so many over-55s realizing they may not have saved enough to comfortably fund their retirement, people are faced with having to do far more themselves to obtain adequate pension provision.

Final salary scheme

Now increasingly rare, this is where your pension is calculated as a proportion of your final pay, which could mean literally the last year you work, or possibly for controlling directors the average of three consecutive years during the last 10. The amount you receive depends on two factors: the number of years you have worked for the organization and the fraction of final pay on which the scheme is based, typically 1/60th or 1/80th. So, if you have worked 30 years for a company that has a 1/60th pension scheme, you will receive 30/60ths of your final pay – in other words, half. Final pay schemes can be contracted into or out of the additional State pension scheme. If a scheme is contracted out, it must provide a pension that is broadly equal to, or better than, its State equivalent.

Money purchase scheme

Unlike final salary schemes, the amount of pension you receive is not based on a fixed formula but (within HMRC limits) is dependent on the investment performance of the fund into which your own and your employer's contributions on your behalf have been paid. Although there is an element of risk with money purchase schemes, in that no one can forecast with certainty how well or badly a pension fund might do, in practice most trustees act very conservatively.

Different schemes have different ways of determining how members' pension entitlements are calculated. You should enquire what the rules are and additionally (if you have not already received one) you should request a statutory money purchase illustration (SMPI), which should give you an idea of what size pension you might realistically expect once inflation has been taken into account. You should receive a fresh SMPI statement every year, based on the actuarial assumptions that have been used to calculate its growth and the (inflation-adjusted) income it should yield on purchase of an annuity. One of the more important changes of the new rules is that it is no longer compulsory to purchase an annuity. Individuals who prefer to keep their fund invested can opt, at 75, for an alternatively secured pension.

Group personal pension scheme

Employers sometimes arrange group schemes for employees wishing to build up a personal pension. They are usually more advantageous than individual personal pensions because employers normally make contributions of 3 per cent (or more) into all participants' pension funds. Also, because of the group savings, the charges tend to be lower than for individually administered schemes. All personal pensions, whether group or individual, are a form of money purchase scheme.

Contracted-out mixed benefit scheme (COMBS)

This is an occupational pension scheme contracting out of the state second pension on both a salary-related and money purchase basis. A COMB scheme has two sections, one of which can hold both guaranteed minimum pensions and section 9(2B) rights, the other protected rights arising both before and after 6 April 1997.

Average earnings scheme

As its name implies, this is based on your average earnings over the total period of time that you are participating in the scheme. Every year, an amount goes into the scheme on your behalf, calculated in accordance with your level of earnings. As your salary increases, so too do your potential benefits. Each year your 'profits' from the scheme are worked out from a formal table and the total of all these annual sums constitutes your pension.

Flat-rate pension scheme

Your level of pay is not a factor. Instead, the same flat rate applies to everyone, multiplied by the number of years in which they have been participants of the scheme. So, for example, if the flat rate is £500 a year of pension and you have been a member of the scheme for 20 years, your pension will be £10,000 a year.

Section 32s

Section 32s (S32) are policies available from insurance companies for the purpose of taking a transfer from an occupational pension scheme. The transfer can be effected by the scheme member or by the trustees. A S32 can also be used by someone who is awarded a share of their ex-spouse's occupational pension as part of a divorce settlement. After the transfer has been paid into the S32, usually no further contributions can be paid.

Advice

There is an organization that is committed to helping anyone who has an occupational pension in the UK. It has over 200 branches around the country which offer fellowship and support locally. **NFOP (National Federation of**

Occupational Pensioners) is the oldest and the largest occupational pensioner organization in UK. Contact: 01582 721 652; website: www.nfop.org.uk.

Executive pension plans

These are individual pension plans arranged by an employer for the benefit of some or all executives above a certain grade. Designed primarily for directors, senior executives and key employees, an Executive Pension Plan is a money purchase scheme. Features usually include a large range of possible funds and flexibility – payments may be changed at any time and they represent a tax-efficient saving. Normally, one of the following four types of investment policy is used: with profits, unit linked, deposit administration and non-profit.

Possible changes to your scheme

Money purchase schemes are not as good as final salary ones, but with so many employers discontinuing final salary schemes, do not be deterred. You will be better off remaining in your employer's scheme than leaving it in favour of, say, a personal pension. Your employer will still be making contributions into the scheme on your behalf, which very few employers do in the case of personal pensions, and additionally you will not have any management charges to pay. If you had a personal pension these would come out of your own fund. Also, if you fear that your pension will be insufficient, you have several possible ways of helping to improve it. You can make additional voluntary contributions (AVCs) or you can invest in a stakeholder scheme or personal pension. If you like, you can do all three.

High earners

The maximum tax-free lump sum is now limited to 25 per cent of their fund value or 25 per cent of their lifetime limit, whichever is lower. For many high earners, this is likely to be a positive gain. But not all pension schemes have changed their rules accordingly, so when it comes to the lump sum this might well be a point to check. Equally, a couple of other former rules may well still apply. In particular, until recently, high earners who joined a new pension scheme were required to base their final salary assessment on their average earnings over any three consecutive years during their last 10. Similarly, controlling directors were not permitted to resign just before retirement to boost their salary but, instead, had to use the three-year average method of calculation. Also, gains from share options in the final year of employment were not allowed in the calculation of final salary.

Accelerated accrual rates

Some schemes allow individuals to enjoy an enhanced accrual scale to qualify for full pension benefits after an agreed minimum number of years' service.

Top-up schemes

Employers can still set up 'top-up' pension schemes to provide additional benefits above the HMRC limits, but such schemes are now taxable and their former advantages have largely gone as a result of new pension rules introduced in 2006. There is some transitional relief for individuals with existing schemes. If you have a FURBS (funded, unapproved retirement benefit scheme), SUURBS (secured, unfunded, unapproved retirement benefit scheme) or similar, expert advice is strongly recommended to explore your best course of action.

Compulsory purchase annuities

Pensioners are no longer required to buy annuities. Rules that made most people spend three-quarters of their pension savings on annuities have been scrapped. Until April 2006, virtually everyone with a personal pension, S32 policy, retirement annuity, contracted-out company money purchase scheme (COMPS) or AVC arrangement was required by law to purchase an annuity. Although today individuals have greater choice in the matter – see 'Alternatively secured pension', below – for most people the purchase of an annuity will still be the most sensible arrangement. Generally annuities offer greater security than most other ways of providing you with an income in retirement. Even if you are not planning to buy an annuity at the present time, it is still worth understanding how annuities work and the amount of choice you have to determine which of the various possibilities suits you best.

The basics

An annuity is a regular income paid in exchange for a lump sum, usually accrued through years of investing in an approved, tax-free pension scheme.

There are different types of annuity; the vast majority are conventional and pay a risk-free income that is guaranteed for life. The amount you will receive depends on your age, whether you are male or female, the size of your pension fund and, in some circumstances, the state of your health. You have the choice of using the whole of your accumulated pension fund or you can take all, or part, of your tax-free lump sum. If you take your lump sum, this will reduce the size of your annuity and the amount of annual income you receive.

Other important factors that can affect your annuity 'earnings' include: what add-on options you may choose, the timing of when you buy your annuity, and the choice of provider. A further consideration could be your life expectancy. Some providers offer annuities that pay enhanced rates to people suffering from ill health or who have been regular smokers for some years.

Add-on options

The most typical options that you will be offered include: a spouse's pension; annual increases, which may either be fixed at, say, 3 or 5 per cent or may be linked to retail price inflation; and a return of some of the capital (either in the form of a lump sum or in annual payments over five or 10 years) should you die unexpectedly early. Wise as such options usually are to protect you and your dependants' long-term security, there will almost invariably be some additional cost that, if you were to go for all the possible extras, could reduce the annual income by around 50 per cent.

Timing

The requirement to purchase an annuity was put back to age 77 from 22 June 2010 by the Chancellor of the Exchequer. Today everyone with a money purchase scheme, including those with a free-standing AVC (FSAVC), can choose when they wish to purchase an annuity between the ages of 55 and 77, or whether on reaching 77, instead of purchasing an annuity, they would prefer to extend a drawdown scheme (see below) and opt for an alternatively secured pension.

The two key factors when it comes to a question of timing are what age you are when you purchase an annuity and what the level of interest rates are at the time. As a general rule, the older you are and the higher the level of interest rates, the bigger the annual income you will receive. The earliest age you can take a pension is now 55.

If you choose to wait, you have what is known as the *income withdrawal option,* or drawdown as it is sometimes called. This allows you to take your tax-free lump sum any time from age 55 to 77, and to withdraw a limited income from the fund (the maximum permitted is broadly equal to the annuity your fund could have provided) during the deferral period. The rest of the money has to remain in the fund, where it can continue to be invested and grow tax-free. In case of death, the fund may pass to the surviving spouse, who can either continue with the income withdrawal option or purchase an annuity. Alternatively, the fund can be paid out to the surviving spouse (or to the estate of the deceased) as a lump sum, minus a 35 per cent tax charge.

Attractive as this sounds, income withdrawal is not a decision to be entered into lightly. While the big gain of the withdrawal option is that it allows individuals both to delay purchase of an annuity until interest rates are favourable and to obtain their lump sum and – if wanted – an income in the meantime, there are also very considerable risks. In particular: the stock market could fall, reducing the capital value of your pension fund; interest rates could be even less favourable when you eventually need to purchase an annuity; commission rates are usually high compared with those for conventional annuities and there could also be substantial administration charges to pay; and some plans are more tax-efficient than others.

Not only is independent financial advice very strongly recommended if you are considering deferring the purchase of an annuity, but many experts advise that the income withdrawal option is not suitable for anyone with less than £250,000 in their pension fund. The issue is not that clear cut, however, and those with smaller funds may be advised to use income withdrawal to give themselves greater flexibility together with some additional income if, for example, they move to part-time work. Sensible as this may be in certain circumstances, you would need to ensure that you do not run down your fund too far and so risk ending up with an inadequate pension.

An alternative to drawdown, for those who have no need to take their tax-free lump sum up front, is *phased retirement.* It is, however, not available to people in an employer's scheme but only to those with personal pensions. The scheme works broadly as follows. In effect, your pension fund is divided into slices – say 1,000 – and each year you can withdraw a number of these to purchase an annuity or income drawdown scheme, while at the same time taking up to 25 per cent of the money as tax-free income. The remainder of your money stays in the fund and can continue to be invested.

As well as allowing you greater control over your annuity purchase (since, as opposed to just one, you would be buying a series of smaller annuities), one of the major advantages of phased retirement is that all money left in your pension fund on death can (unless the present rules are changed) be passed on to your spouse, or other beneficiaries, free of tax.

However, as with drawdown, there are risks as well as advantages, and expert advice is strongly recommended. For further information about withdrawal schemes, the FSA has published *The FSA Guide to Pension Annuities and Pension Fund Withdrawal*. To obtain a copy call 0845 606 9966; or order via website: www.fsa.gov.uk.

Choice of provider

Whether you intend to buy a normal retirement annuity, a drawdown pension plan as described above or one of the newer with-profits or unit-linked annuities, this is one area above all where expert independent advice is essential. Annuity rates offered by life companies can vary by as much as 20 per cent, and the difference between the best and worst choice could greatly affect your income. There is no obligation to buy your annuity from the company that has been managing your pension plan. Indeed, the best people for pension plans are not usually the most competitive for annuities and, while there may be attractions in remaining with the same company (some offer loyalty bonuses), your decision will need to be based on the best all-round terms you can get at the time of purchase. Once you have made a choice, it is extremely difficult to switch.

Alternatively secured pension

ASPs have been available since 6 April 2006. The requirement to purchase an annuity was put back by the Chancellor of the Exchequer to age 77 from 22 June 2010. The alternatively secured pension (ASP), which is a variation on the drawdown scheme, is available to individuals over age 77. With this scheme individuals can continue to invest their pension savings and draw an income from their fund within laid down limits. The minimum that must be drawn as an income from the fund is 55 per cent of an amount calculated by applying the funds available to a table produced by the Government Actuaries Department (GAD). The maximum is 90 per cent. The GAD table is based on the level of single-life lifetime annuity rates for a person of the same sex and aged 77. No allowance is made in the annuity rate used for any level of annual pension increases. These rates were introduced with effect from 6 April 2007 following a review of ASPs by the government.

You should take advice from an independent financial adviser, a pensions consultant or from one of the several companies that specialize in tracking annuity rates. **The Annuity Bureau,** for example, monitors the rates on a daily basis and will track the optimum rate that best suits your particular circumstances. Depending on the amount of personalized advice you require, there may be a fee for using this service. Contact: 0800 071 8111; website: www.annuity-bureau.co.uk. Another annuity specialist that offers similar services is **Annuity Direct,** Tel: 0500 506 575; website: www.annuitydirect.co.uk.

Pension pot of less than £15,000

People with a pension pot of under £15,000 are not required to buy an annuity. Instead, once they reach 60, they can take all the money as a lump sum – with a quarter of their lump sum being tax-free and the remainder subject to Income Tax. If annuity rates remain at their current low, some individuals might be better off paying the tax. Your pension provider, or an independent financial adviser (IFA), should be able to advise you at the time. An important point if you have more than one pension plan is that the 'exempt' amount of £15,000 does not apply to each of them but is the total aggregate value of all your plans. If you wish to take a lump sum from all of them, this will need to have been arranged within a 12-month period, at any time between age 60 and 75.

Additional voluntary contributions (AVCs)

If, as you approach retirement, you become aware that you are not going to have a big enough pension to live as comfortably as you would like, you might seriously consider the possibility of making AVCs. Although no longer as valuable as they once were, because the 2006 rule changes allow individuals similar ways of boosting their pension, nevertheless for some people AVCs might still offer the best solution. Their particular attractions are that AVCs – as well as the growth of the plan – enjoy full tax relief, so for basic-rate taxpayers HMRC is in effect paying £20 of every £100 invested. A further advantage is that some AVCs allow you to purchase 'added years', to make up any shortfall in your entitlement to benefit under a company scheme.

However, an option known as 'free-standing AVCs' (FSAVCs) is also on offer. As the name implies, these are not linked to a company scheme but can be purchased independently from insurance companies, building societies, banks, unit trusts, friendly societies and Independent Financial Advisers (IFAs). Individuals can, if they wish, contribute both to company AVCs and to a free-standing plan or plans. To enjoy the tax relief, the total of all your AVCs plus other contributions to the pension plan is not allowed to exceed your annual earnings, or your annual allowance if this is lower.

Rule changes

Over the years, there have been several rule changes of which you should be aware:

- Previously, individuals had to make a commitment to pay regular contributions for a period of at least five years. This requirement has been abolished and (provided the actual scheme rules permit) both the amount and the timing of payments can be varied to suit members according to their personal circumstances.

- AVCs purchased between April 1987 and 5 April 2006 can now go towards your pension or towards your lump sum, as you prefer.

- AVC benefits, provided your scheme rules allow, can now be taken at any time between ages 55 and 75 (or earlier if an individual is forced to leave employment owing to incapacity). If you choose to draw your AVC benefits before you retire, they would normally have to be taken as part of your tax-free lump sum or in the form of income drawdown.

Choosing an AVC plan

The best schemes can yield excellent value and for many individuals can be one of the most effective ways of increasing their security in retirement. All scheme providers (ie both company AVC and FSAVC schemes) must give prospective investors 'key features' information including, in particular, details of the charges. Also, anyone advising you about the purchase of FSAVCs must at the very least explain the basic differences between the FSAVCs being recommended and the AVCs offered by your employer's scheme.

IFAs must go further and give you an analysis of the specific differences to help you decide which type of scheme – or possible alternative type of investment – would be in your best financial interest. When discussing the options, a particular question you might ask is whether it would be more sensible for you to invest in an ISA. In general, the charges are likely to be lower with a collective AVC scheme offered by an employer than for free-standing contracts. Also, some employers match members' contributions to a company AVC scheme with extra contributions to the occupational scheme. Against this, if the performance is pedestrian or if there are early retirement penalties, you might still be better off with FSAVCs or a SIPP (Self-Invested Personal Pension) or other personal pension.

As with any other important investment decision, you would be well advised to take your time and do some basic research into the track record of any policies you might be considering (specialist publications such as *Money Management* provide a good starting point). On no account sign any document without first being absolutely certain that you fully understand all the terms and conditions. Finally, if you are already subscribing to company AVCs, before investing in a new plan check on your present level of contributions and the benefits that these are expected to yield. You should be aware that current taxation, legislation and HMRC practice are all liable to change without notice, and the impact of taxation (and any tax reliefs) depends on individual circumstances. Please check details with your company pension adviser or IFA, who should be only too happy to answer any questions.

Early leavers

In the past, early leavers tended to do very badly, but the government has introduced new rules that help considerably. For example, employers can now pay a full pension, without actuarial reduction, at any age between 55 and 70. Companies are under no obligation to do so but, for those people lucky enough to work for an organization that has amended its pension scheme rules accordingly, this provision could make an immense difference to the financial position of early retirees. It has to be said, however, that most employers still apply actuarial reductions (although these are sometimes waived in special cases such as redundancy), so if you are thinking of taking early retirement it is advisable to work out very carefully how this might affect your pension.

Another important change concerns what are known as your *preserved rights* – in other words, your financial rights with regard to your pension. To qualify, you should have been with the pension scheme for two years. If you leave earlier but have at least three months' qualifying service in the scheme, you have three choices available: leave your pension with the scheme, take your pension to a new scheme, or take your pension to an insurance company.

1. Leaving the pension with the scheme

You remain a member of the scheme and receive a pension at the scheme's normal retirement age. If the scheme is a final salary one, the value would probably be calculated on 1/60th (or 1/80th) of your earnings at the time of your leaving and the number of years you have worked for the company. Whereas previously most pensions were frozen, today company schemes are obliged to increase the accrued pension rights by 2.5 per cent a year or the rate of inflation, whichever is lower. Another advantage of remaining in the scheme is that you keep any benefits – such as a widow's pension and possibly others – that are already included. Also, once you start receiving your pension, you would be entitled to any extra increases that may be given. In the case of money purchase schemes, your accumulated assets would normally remain invested in the fund, hopefully growing every year to buy you a bigger pension on retirement. You would also be entitled to any benefit that the scheme provided under the rules.

2. Taking your pension to a new scheme

You do not have to make an immediate decision. You can transfer your pension scheme at any time, provided you do so over a year before you retire. If you wish to switch to a new scheme, this could be to another company scheme, a personal pension or a stakeholder pension. Personal and stakeholder pensions are described later in this chapter, so if you are interested in taking advantage of either of these you should read the sections carefully. Here, we explain the various possibilities if you wish to join a scheme run by your new employer.

Early leavers now have the right to move their pension – or, more precisely, its transfer value – to a new employer's scheme willing to accept it. The transfer value is the cash value of your current pension rights. Calculating this can be problematic, and early leavers are often at a disadvantage compared with those who remain in the scheme. Joining a new employer's scheme does not necessarily oblige you to transfer your previous benefits. In some circumstances, there may be very good arguments for leaving your existing benefits with your former scheme and joining your new employer's scheme from scratch for the remaining years that you are working. Since you could be at risk of giving up more than you stand to gain by transferring your benefits to a new scheme, expert advice is strongly recommended.

3. Taking your pension to an insurance company

If neither of the two previous options appeal, or your new company will not accept your old pension value into its own scheme, you can go independent and have the transfer value of your pension invested by a life company into a personal scheme. After deducting its charges, the life company would invest the balance of the money in the fund, or funds, of your choice.

Advice

Deciding on your best option is not easy, so before taking action you should at least consult your company pension scheme manager to give you an assessment of the likely value of your pension if you leave it in the scheme. An important point to bear in mind is that your present company scheme may include valuable extras, such as a spouse's pension, life cover and attractive early retirement terms in the event of ill health.

If you are planning to switch, you will need to decide between a Section 32 buy-out, a personal pension and a stakeholder pension. Although for the majority of employees a personal or stakeholder pension is usually likely to offer a higher return, there are certain limitations. For example, the older the employee and the larger the transfer value, the more attractive a Section 32 buy-out becomes. Because this is a complex area – and making the wrong decision could prove expensive – independent expert advice is very strongly recommended. It could pay you to get the advice of a pension consultant, particularly if a large sum of money is involved. For a list of those operating in your area, contact the **Society of Pension Consultants,** Tel: 020 7353 1688; website: www.spc.uk.com.

Becoming self-employed

If, as opposed to switching jobs, you leave paid employment to start your own enterprise, you are allowed to transfer your accumulated pension rights into a new fund. There are three main options. The most obvious solution is to invest your money with an insurance company, as mentioned above, or to take either a personal or a stakeholder pension. Alternatively, if you expect to be in a high earning bracket, you might consider setting up a limited company, even if you are the only salaried employee, rather than launching the same business as a self-employed individual. The company could set up a self-administered pension scheme with loan-back facilities plus other advantages. However, there are various pros and cons that will need to be weighed up carefully, depending on the transfer value of your earlier pension and the anticipated annual amount available for investing in your new scheme. Since this is rather a complex area, before taking any action you are strongly advised to consult your financial adviser. A third possibility, which might be more attractive if you are fairly close to normal retirement age, is to leave your pension in your former employer's scheme.

Useful reading

Transferring a Pension to another Scheme and *Ill-Health Early Retirement*, obtainable from the **Pensions Advisory Service:** 0845 601 2923; website: www.pensionsadvisoryservice.org.uk.

Leaflet PM4, *Personal Pensions – Your Guide*, obtainable from the **Pensions Info** order line: 0845 731 3233; website: www. thepensionservice.gov.uk.

Stakeholder Pensions and Decision Trees, obtainable from the **Financial Services Authority:** 0300 500 5000; website: www.fsa.gov.uk.

Minimum retirement age

The minimum age at which you are allowed to take early retirement and draw your pension has been 55 since 6 April 2010.

Questions on your pension scheme

Most people find it very difficult to understand how their pension scheme works. However, your pension is a valuable asset, especially as you approach retirement, and it is important that you should know the main essentials, including any options that may still be available to you.

If you have a query or if you are concerned in some way about your pension, you should approach whoever is responsible for the scheme in your organization. If the company is large, there may be a special person to look after the scheme on a day-to-day basis: this could be the pensions manager or, quite often, it is someone in the personnel department. In a smaller company, the pension scheme may be looked after by the company secretary or managing director. The sort of questions you might ask will vary according to circumstance, such as before you join the scheme, if you are thinking of changing jobs, if you are hoping to retire early and so on. You will probably think of plenty of additional points of your own. The questions listed here are simply an indication of some of the key information you may require to plan sensibly ahead.

If you want to leave the organization to change jobs

- Could you have a refund of contributions if you were to leave shortly after joining?
- How much will your deferred pension be worth?
- Should you want to move the transfer value to another scheme, how long would you have to wait from the date of your request? (This should normally be within three to six months.)

If you leave for other reasons

- What happens if you become ill – or die – before pension age?
- What are the arrangements if you want to retire early? Most schemes allow you to do this if you are within about 10 years of normal retirement age, but your pension may be reduced accordingly. Many schemes, in fact, operate a sliding scale of benefits, with more generous terms offered to those who retire later rather than earlier.

If you stay until normal retirement age

- What will your pension be on your present salary? And what would it be assuming your salary increases by, say, 5 or 10 per cent before you eventually retire?
- What spouse's pension will be paid? Can a pension be paid to other dependants?
- Similarly, can a pension be paid to a partner, male or female?
- What happens if you continue working with the organization after retirement age? Normally, any contributions you are making to the scheme will cease to be required and your pension (which will not

usually be paid until you retire) will be increased to compensate for its deferment. NB: since April 2006, provided their scheme rules allow it, members of occupational pension schemes can draw their pension benefits, if they wish, without having to wait until after they leave.

- What are the arrangements if you retire from the organization as a salaried employee but become a retained consultant or contractor?

If you just want information

- Are any changes envisaged to the scheme? For example, if it is a final salary one, is there any chance that it might be wound up and a money purchase one offered instead?
- If there were a new money purchase scheme, would the company be making the same contributions as before or would these be lower in future?
- Is there any risk that benefits – either members' own or those for dependants – could be reduced?
- Is there a possibility that members might be required to pay higher contributions than at present?

What to do before retirement

In addition to understanding your current pension scheme, you may also need to chase up any previous schemes of which you were a member. This is well worth pursuing, as you could be owed money from one or more schemes, which will all add to your pension on retirement day.

You may be able to get the information from your previous employer(s). If you have difficulty in locating them – perhaps because the company has been taken over – contact the **Pension Tracing Service,** which assists individuals who need help in tracing their pension rights. This is a free service, run by the Pension Service, part of the Department for Work and Pensions (DWP). Its database contains the details of over 200,000 occupational and personal pension scheme administrators. Applicants can either write to the Pension Tracing Service, giving as much detail about the employer and pension scheme as possible, or alternatively request a trace application form (PTI) to complete. Contact: 0845 600 2537; website: www.direct.gov.uk/pensions. Choose the link to the Pension Tracing Service.

Other help and advice

If you have any queries or problems to do with your pension, in addition to the Pension Tracing Service there are three main sources of help available to you. These are the trustees or managers of your pension scheme, the Pensions Advisory Service and the Pensions Ombudsman.

Trustees or managers

These are the first people to contact if you do not properly understand your benefit entitlements or if you are unhappy about some point to do with your pension. Pensions managers (or other people responsible for pensions) should give you their names and tell you how they can be reached.

The Pensions Advisory Service

The Pensions Advisory Service provides members of the public with general information and guidance on pension matters and assists individuals with disputes with personal, company and stakeholder pensions. The PAS has been providing free services since 1983. Sustained by a nationwide network of highly experienced pension professional volunteer advisers who are supported by London-based pension technical and administrative staff, the service is provided via a helpline, written advice, mediation and employee meetings. They are funded by the DWP. The service is available to any member of the public who either has a specific query or just needs general information. Contact the **Pensions Advisory Service:** 0845 601 2923; website: www.pensionsadvisoryservice.org.uk.

Pensions Ombudsman

You would normally approach the Ombudsman *only* if neither the pension scheme manager (or trustees) nor the Pensions Advisory Service is able to solve your problem. The Ombudsman can investigate: 1) complaints of maladministration by the trustees, managers or administrators of a pension scheme or by an employer; 2) disputes of fact or law with the trustees, managers or an employer. The Ombudsman does not, however, investigate complaints about mis-selling of pension schemes, a complaint that is already subject to court proceedings, one that is about a State social security benefit, or a dispute that is more appropriate for investigation by another regulatory body. There is also a time limit for lodging complaints, which is normally within three years of the act, or failure to act, about which you are complaining.

Provided the problem comes within the Ombudsman's orbit, he will look into all the facts for you and will inform you of his decision, together with his reasons. There is no charge for the Ombudsman's service. The Pensions Ombudsman has now also taken on the role of Pension Protection Fund Ombudsman and will be dealing with complaints about, and appeals from, the Pension Protection Fund. He will also be dealing with appeals from the Financial Assistance Scheme. Contact the **Pensions Ombudsman:** 020 7630 2200; website: www.pensions-ombudsman.org.uk.

If you have a personal pension, contact the **Financial Ombudsman Service (FOS):** 0800 0234 567; website: www.financial-ombudsman.org.uk. It is possible you may be referred to the Pensions Ombudsman, but if so you will be informed very quickly.

Protection for pension scheme members

New rules have been introduced to protect pension scheme members in the event of a company takeover or proposed bulk transfer arrangement. A welcome reform is that, in the event of a scheme in deficit being wound up, the deficiency becomes a debt on the employer that the trustees can pursue. As an additional safeguard, self-investment by occupational pension funds is now restricted to 5 per cent. Equally important, solvent companies choosing to wind up their scheme on or since 11 June 2003 will need to protect members' accrued pension rights in full.

The regulatory system has also become much more stringent since April 2005, with the creation of the **Pensions Regulator,** a body with wide powers and a proactive approach to regulation, whose top priority is to identify and tackle risks to members' benefits. There is now also a **Pension Protection Fund (PPF)** to help final salary pension scheme members who are at risk of losing their pension benefits owing to their employer's insolvency. Members over the normal pension age will receive 100 per cent of their current benefits plus annual increases (the lower of RPI and 2.5 per cent) on pensions accrued from 6 April 1997. Members below the scheme's normal retirement age will receive 90 per cent of the Pension Protection Fund level of compensation plus annual increases, subject to a cap and the standard Fund rules. Contact: 0845 600 2541; website: www.pensionprotectionfund.org.uk.

There is more help too for members who lost pension savings in a company scheme before the introduction of the Pension Protection Fund. The **Financial Assistance Scheme (FAS)** offers help to some people who have lost out on their pension. The scheme is managed by the DWP and is administered by the FAS Operational Unit (FAS OU). It makes payments to top-up scheme benefits to eligible members of schemes that are winding up or have wound up. Assistance is also payable to the survivor of a pension scheme member. It is payable from normal retirement age (subject to a lower age limit of 60 and an upper age limit of 65). Contact: 0845 604 4585; website:www.pensionprotectionfund.org.uk.

Personal pensions for employees

A main aim behind personal pensions is to give people working for an employer the same freedom as the self-employed to make their own independent pension arrangements, should they wish to do so. Before making any decision, a basic point to understand is that nearly everyone who pays NI Contributions as an employee is already contributing towards an additional pension: either to the State Second Pension or to a contracted-out company pension scheme. You have the right to take a personal pension (PP) in place of the State Second Pension or, alternatively, in place of your employer's scheme (whether this is contracted in or out). If you like you can also invest in a personal pension in addition to your employer's scheme, provided the total of your contributions does not exceed your annual allowance.

To judge whether a personal pension is a good idea, you need to understand the advantages and possible limitations of your present arrangements compared with the attractions – but also risks – of a PP. If you are a member of a good contracted-out final salary scheme – or have the opportunity of joining one – it is very unlikely that a PP would be in your best interest. If, however, your employer does not have a pension scheme, if you are ineligible to join, if the scheme is contracted into the State scheme, if you think you could do better for yourself than your current scheme, or if you think that it could be to your advantage to have an extra pension, then a PP might be worth considering.

A main advantage of a personal pension is that if you change jobs you can take it with you without penalty. You will have real choice as to how your pension payments are invested. If you have built up a big enough fund, you can retire at any age between 55 and 75. Also, if you change your mind after having taken a personal pension, you can switch back into the State scheme or, if the scheme rules allow it, you can transfer your payments into a company contracted-out scheme.

The biggest drawback of a personal pension, particularly for an older person, is that it may not offer you such attractive benefits as your present scheme. For a start, most employers do not make extra contributions to a personal pension so, other than your rebate from the State Second Pension (see 'Minimum contributions', below), all the investment towards your pension will need to come out of your earnings. You may also lose out on valuable extra benefits that are often included in an employer's scheme, including a pension before normal age were you to become ill, protection for your dependants should you die, attractive early retirement terms if you were made redundant, and any increases in pension payments that the scheme may give to help offset inflation.

Before taking a decision, a first essential is to understand how personal pensions work. The main points are discussed below.

Starting date

You can decide to start a personal pension at any time you want and then, in order to receive all the minimum contributions that will be paid into your pension plan, backdate it to the start of the tax year on 6 April. The formalities involved are very easy.

Contributions into your pension plan

There are three possible ways (previously four, see 'Special incentive payments', below) of building up savings in your pension plan.

1. Minimum contributions

These will be paid into your new scheme automatically. They are worked out according to the level of NIC that both you and your employer are required to pay by law. Instead of going into either the State Second Pension or a contracted-out company pension scheme, they will be paid directly into your personal pension plan at the end of the tax year to which they relate. The older you are, the bigger the contribution rebate. Whereas previously there was a fixed percentage for all personal pension members (with those over 30 receiving an extra 1 per cent), since April 1997 contribution rebates are calculated on an age and earnings-related basis.

2. Extra contributions made by you

You can make extra contributions into your pension plan. If you do so, you will not only build up more savings for your retirement but you also enjoy full tax relief on these contributions.

3. Voluntary contributions by your employer

Your employer might decide that it wants to help you improve your pension by making contributions over and above the statutory NI Contributions into your pension plan. If you are considering leaving a company pension scheme, this could be one of the questions you should ask as a means of comparing the value of a personal pension against your existing scheme. The total of contributions from you and your employer is not allowed to exceed your annual earnings.

4. Special incentive payments

An extra 2 per cent payment was given by the government as part of the launch of personal pensions. These payments have now ceased. Anyone who previously received them can look forward to enjoying the benefit when they retire.

Your pension receipts

As with all money purchase schemes, the amount of pension you eventually receive will depend on two main factors: the size of the fund you have been able to build up and the fund's investment performance. Generally speaking, the longer you have been saving towards a personal pension and the bigger the total contributions paid, the larger your pension will stand to be. Many pension advisers suggest that a useful formula is to halve your age at the time of first starting to save for your pension and use this figure as a percentage of your gross salary that you should invest annually in your pension for the remainder of your working life. Thanks to the new rules, you can average this out over the years, making lower contributions when money is tight and higher ones when you can more easily afford to do so. You have a great deal of choice in the matter, but there are also certain rules designed to protect you.

A basic rule concerns what are known as your *protected rights*. These are the minimum contributions (including the value of the extra 2 per cent introductory payment) and tax relief you may have received – together with their accumulated investment growth. Your protected rights can only be invested in a single contract, in contrast to your and your employer's extra or voluntary contributions, which can be invested in as many different personal plans as you please. You can choose whether to use your protected rights towards your annuity or towards your tax-free lump sum, as you prefer.

Choosing a pension plan

Personal pensions are offered by insurance companies, building societies, unit trusts, friendly societies and IFAs. Before you make up your mind, you should aim to look at a variety of plans. Furthermore, you should not hesitate to ask as many questions as you want about any points that are unclear or any technical term that you do not fully understand – including in particular any questions you may have about the level of charges.

Understanding the figures has become very much easier over the past few years. Today, not only are all life and pension policy providers required to state their charges in writing but they must also disclose any salesperson's commission – stated in cash terms – in advance of any contract being signed. These, together with other essential 'consumer' information about the policy, should be included in what are called the 'key facts' documents. Advisers must now also state in writing their reasons for any recommendations to you.

Because choosing both the right type of investment and the particular institution with which you are likely to feel happiest is such an important decision, even after you have chosen a scheme you will have a *14-day cooling-off period* that gives you a chance to change your mind.

Is a personal pension a wise decision?

This is a question that only you, or an adviser who knows your personal circumstances, can answer. As a general rule, if you are in a good company pension scheme the advice is to stay there. Those for whom opting out is likely to be least advised are older people in a good company or public sector pension scheme.

The key issue is how your existing pension arrangements compare with the alternatives. You will therefore need to know what the value of your pension would be if you stay in the additional State pension scheme or in your company scheme, whichever is applicable.

For information about the value of your state scheme rights, complete form BR19, *State Pension Forecast*, from The Pensions Service, part of the

Department for Work and Pensions. Contact: 08457 313 233; website: www.direct.gov.uk/pensions

In the case of an employer's scheme, ask the pensions department or the person responsible for pensions (this could be the personnel manager or company secretary) to provide you with full information about your pension and future benefits, including details of death and disability cover.

Other points you will need to consider include: what type of investment policy would suit you; what size contributions (within HMRC-allowed limits) you could realistically afford; and what, after deduction of administrative and other charges, your plan might be worth when you come to retire. This is not to say that taking a personal pension is either a right or a wrong decision, simply that you need to be aware of all the various factors before opting out of your present arrangements. Since the sums are often very complex, if you are thinking of making a change you would be strongly advised to consult an independent pensions specialist.

Useful reading

Leaflets QG1, *A Quick Guide to Pensions*; PM3, *Occupational Pensions – Your Guide*; PM4, *Personal Pensions – Your Guide*; and PM5, *Pensions for the Self-Employed – Your Guide*. Contact: 08457 313 233; website: www.direct.gov.uk/pensions.

Stakeholder Pensions and Decision Trees and *FSA Guide to Pensions*, obtainable free from the Financial Services Authority (FSA). Contact: 0845 606 1234; website: www.fsa.gov.uk.

Stakeholder pensions

Stakeholder pensions were launched in April 2001 with the aim of encouraging more people to begin saving towards a pension. While essentially targeted at more modest earners, anyone else should they wish to do so can start, or switch to, a stakeholder pension. (The rule excluding individuals in occupational schemes with earnings over £30,000 was abolished in April 2006.)

Stakeholders are very similar to personal pensions but with the advantage that they are required to meet specified government standards, including limiting maximum annual charges (excluding financial advice) to 1.5 per cent for the first 10 years of the policy. This was increased from 1 per cent in April 2005, but if you were investing in a stakeholder prior to this date the maximum charge you would have to pay for the next few years is held at 1 per cent.

Whereas until fairly recently pension contributions were always linked to earnings, anyone with a stakeholder policy can invest up to 100 per cent of their earnings or £3,600 a year, whichever is the greater. A husband or wife could make contributions for a non-earning partner. Those wishing to contribute more than £3,600 a year to their own scheme can do so, provided they have earnings of over £3,600 a year. Also, savers can stop, start or alter payments without penalty.

All contributions paid are net of basic-rate tax, with the pension provider reclaiming the tax from HM Revenue & Customs. Higher-rate taxpayers will need to reclaim the excess tax through the self-assessment system. From April 2008, when basic-rate tax reduced to 20 per cent, the cost for basic-rate taxpayers increased to £2,880. Most higher-rate taxpayers should be unaffected. However, as now, they will only be able to claim the excess relief if the stakeholder scheme is in their own name, rather than that of a partner or other person.

Early retirees who are already drawing an occupational pension can, if they wish, start contributing to a stakeholder pension. A good reason for doing so might be to take advantage of an immediate self-vesting pension or series of immediate self-vesting pensions. As with personal pensions, stakeholder pensions can be taken at any age between 55 and 75.

How to obtain

Stakeholder pensions are available from banks, Post Offices, insurance companies and other financial institutions. Although the basic charges may not be very different between one provider and another, you are nevertheless strongly advised to investigate at least two or three plans and ask for much the same sort of information as you would if you were considering a personal pension. This is even more important if you are actually thinking of switching from a PP to a stakeholder pension or, as is possible, having a stakeholder as well as a PP.

Advantages and drawbacks

Some experts are of the view that, if you are happy with your present arrangements, you might be best staying as you are. Though stakeholder policies are usually cheaper, you could face penalties if you terminate your existing scheme early. Equally, if you are thinking of switching from an employer's money purchase scheme, you will lose the extra contributions that your employer is making on your behalf. Against this, the flexibility you would get with a stakeholder to alter or stop payments without penalty is attractive. Since weighing up the pros and cons of making a change is not easy, you are strongly recommended to get expert advice or, if you have a particular query, contact the **Pensions Advisory Service** Helpline: 0845 601 2923; website: www.pensionsadvisoryservice.org.uk.

Useful reading

PM8, *Stakeholder Pensions – Your Guide*, obtainable from The Pensions Service. Contact: 08457 313 233; website: www.direct.gov.uk/pensions.

Types of investment policy

There are four different types of investment policy: with-profits, unit-linked, deposit administration and non-profit policies. Brief descriptions of each follow.

1. With-profits policies

These are one of the safest types of pension investments. They guarantee you a known minimum cash fund and/or pension on your retirement and, although the guaranteed amount is not usually very high, bonuses are added at regular intervals, according to how the investments in the fund perform. Additionally, a terminal (or final) bonus is given when the pension policy matures. Over the past few years most terminal bonuses have been lower than projected, reflecting low interest rates and patchy performance by equities. However, an important feature is that once bonuses are given, they cannot later be withdrawn or put at risk due to some speculative investment.

2. Unit-linked policies

These are less safe than with-profits policies but they offer the attraction of potentially higher investment returns. However, the risks are greater and the size of your pension will obviously be affected. For this reason, many advisers recommend that their clients swap their unit-linked policies to the with-profits type about five years before they retire, provided market conditions are favourable at the time. The decision as to what is best will very much depend on timing. Clearly if the stock market is depressed, then cashing in equity-based contracts before you need to could lose you money, unless of course your adviser takes the view that the stock market is likely to plunge even further. Another factor that should be taken into account is the prevailing level of interest rates, since these affect annuity rates.

3. Deposit administration policies

These lie somewhere between with-profits and unit-linked policies in terms of their risk/reward ratio. They operate rather like bank deposit accounts, where the interest rate is credited at regular intervals.

4. Non-profit policies

Although these provide a guaranteed pension payment, the return on investment is usually very low. As a rule, they tend only to be recommended for people starting a plan within five years of their retirement.

Choosing the right policy

Great care is needed when choosing the organization with which to invest your pension savings. Once you have committed yourself to a policy, you will not usually be able to move your money without considerable financial penalty. As a general rule, it is sensible to select a large, well-known company that has been in the market for a long time. Before deciding, you should compare several companies' investment track records. What you should look for is evidence of good, consistent results over a period of 10 to 20 years.

You should aim at the very least to talk to two or three financial institutions or independent financial advisers (IFAs) and make it clear to all of them that you are doing so. If you need further advice – and particularly if a large sum of money is involved – there could be a strong argument for consulting an independent pension consultant or IFA who charges fees rather than earns commission.

Self-Invested Personal Pension

Another possibility is to set up your own Self-Invested Personal Pension (SIPP). These are do-it-yourself schemes that among other assets can include directly held shares and commercial property. Residential property cannot be held in a SIPP nor can luxury items such as antiques, wine, classic cars and yachts. The big advantage of SIPPs is that they offer greater flexibility than ordinary pensions. On the other hand, administration costs are usually higher. Pension experts advise that such schemes are only suitable for fairly sophisticated investors with at least £100,000 in their pension fund. This is not to say that you should necessarily rule out SIPPS, simply that before you go ahead you should ensure that you understand the drawbacks as well as the advantages.

Complaints

If you have a complaint about advice you have received in relation to your SIPP or other personal pension, obtain advice from the **Financial Ombudsman Service (FOS)**: 0800 0234 567; website: www.financial-ombudsman.org.uk. It is possible you may be referred to the Pensions Ombudsman, but if so you will be informed very quickly.

Opting back into the State scheme

You may have been told by a financial adviser that, rather than continue with your personal pension, you might be better off switching into the State Second Pension (S2P). One reason you may have been given is that the rebates paid to those who have contracted out of the State scheme are insufficient in the light of increased longevity and the expected return on equity investments.

The advice is most likely to be pertinent if you are already over 43 and have average, or modest, earnings. However, if you can afford to do so, there is nothing to stop you from contracting back into the State scheme and also having a personal pension. Before you decide, check that your adviser has taken account of all the factors. Particular points you might want to discuss include:

- the likely value of your pension if:
  - you stay as you are,
  - you contract back into the State scheme,
  - you contribute to both S2P and a personal pension;
- what contributions you would need (or be advised) to make in each of the above situations;
- whether there would be a penalty if you stopped paying into your personal pension;
- how easy it would be to restart the plan should a PP be more advantageous when the S2P changes from being earnings-related to flat-rate, as the government has planned should happen in the next few years.

Another point to take into account could be your financial adviser's charges, as these may come out of the fund that you are building towards your pension. As guidance, many PP managers have recently reduced their fees to around 1.5 per cent – in line with the norm (excluding financial advice) for stakeholder pensions.

A lump sum?

All pension scheme members, whether in an employer's scheme or having a private pension plan, are entitled to take a tax-free lump sum from their fund. The maximum amount allowed is 25 per cent of their fund or 25 per cent of their lifetime limit, whichever is lower. The minimum age at which you can retire or take your lump sum now is 55.

Taking a lump sum reduces the pension you receive, but on the other hand, if you invest the money wisely, you could end up with a higher income. The first priority, however, is to ensure that you will have enough income for your own needs.

If you take a lump sum, the amount by which your pension will be reduced is mainly determined by your age. The younger you are, the smaller the reduction. Another consideration is your tax status. Since the lump sum is tax-free, as a general rule the higher your top rate of tax after retirement, the greater the advantage in opting for a lump sum. Your life expectancy can also be an important factor. The shorter this is, the more sense it makes to take the lump sum.

Before consulting an expert, it would be helpful to both of you if you could work out – at least in very general terms – what your financial priorities are. The sort of questions your adviser will ask are: whether you are investing for income now or capital growth in the future; whether you need to go for absolute security with every penny you have or whether you can afford slightly more risky investments in the hope of making more money in the long run; and what other sources of income you have or might expect to receive.

Pension rights if you continue to work after retirement age

When you reach normal retirement age, you will usually stop making contributions into your company pension scheme, even if you decide to carry on working. Your employer, of course, would have to agree to your continuing to work but, thanks to the age discrimination legislation, this should not normally be a problem if you are under 65 and are physically and mentally capable of doing your job. Even if you are over 65, you may find that your employer will be only too happy for you to stay – and, even then, if your employer wants you to leave, it will have to give you at least six months' notice in writing. If you are facing such a decision, here are some points to bear in mind:

- You can continue working, draw your company pension and put some (or possibly all) of your earnings into a separate scheme.

- You can leave your pension in the fund, where it will continue to earn interest until you retire. In most private schemes, you could expect to receive in the region of an extra 8 per cent for every year that you delay retirement. If you continue working, say, for an additional five years, your pension would then be 40 per cent higher than if you had started taking it at the normal age. You will also have been earning a salary meanwhile, so you are likely to be considerably better off as a result.

- You can leave your pension in the fund, as described above, and additionally contribute to a personal or stakeholder pension, provided your contributions do not exceed the (2010/11) £255,000 annual allowance.

- Since April 2006, provided your scheme rules allow, you can continue working for your existing employer and draw your pension benefits, as opposed to – as previously – having to defer them until you left the organization.

Equal pension age

Employers are required to treat men and women equally with regard to retirement and pension issues. This means that by law they must have a common retirement age that applies equally to both sexes. Similarly, they must also have a common pension age, and pension schemes must offer the same benefits to their male and female members.

Divorce

Pension-sharing became legally available in respect of divorce or annulment proceedings commenced on or after 1 December 2000. While an advantage of pension-sharing is that it allows a clean break on divorce, many experts believe that it may well have the effect of so diminishing the pension scheme member's retirement fund that he or she may not have sufficient left to rebuild an adequate pension. The situation could apply to men or women. Although women usually benefit most from pension-sharing, the legislation equally allows an ex-husband to have a share in his former wife's pension rights.

The question of pension-sharing could be a subject to raise with your solicitor if you are in the process of divorce proceedings. But however much in favour your legal adviser may be, in the final analysis it is up to the court to decide on what it sees as the fairest arrangement – and pension-sharing is only one of several options available.

Divorced wives

If you have a full basic pension in your own right, this will not be affected by divorce. However, if, as applies to many women, despite having worked for a good number of years you have made insufficient contributions to qualify for a full pension, you should contact your pension centre, quoting your pension number and NI number. It is possible that you may be able to obtain the full single person's pension, based on your ex-husband's contributions.

Your right to use your ex-husband's contributions to improve or provide you with a pension depends on your age and/or whether you remarry before the age of 60. As a general rule, you can use your ex-husband's contributions towards your pension for the years you were married (ie until the date of the decree absolute). After that, you are expected to pay your own contributions until you are 60, unless you remarry.

If you are over 60 when you divorce, then whether you remarry or not you can rely on your ex-husband's contributions. If you remarry before the age of 60, then you cease absolutely being dependent on your former husband and instead your pension will be based on your new husband's contribution record. The same rules apply in reverse. Although it happens less frequently, a divorced man can rely on his former wife's contribution record during the years they were married to improve his basic pension. A divorced wife might have some claim to her former husband's occupational pension benefits.

Pension-sharing

As previously mentioned, provisions to enable the court to share occupational or personal pension rights at the time of divorce or annulment came into law on 1 December 2000. The legislation now equally applies to the additional State pension. Sharing, however, is only one option for dealing with pension rights and would not necessarily apply in all cases.

Separated wives

Even if you have not lived together for several years, from an NI point of view you are still considered to be married. The normal pension rules apply including, of course, the fact that, if you have to depend on your husband's contributions, you will not be able to get a pension until he is both 65 and in receipt of his own pension.

If you are not entitled to a state pension in your own right, you will receive the dependant's rate of benefit, which is about 60 per cent of the full rate (or less if your husband is not entitled to a full pension). In such a case, you can apply for Income Support to top up your income. Once you are 60, you can personally draw the wife's pension of £58.50 a week, without reference to your husband.

If your husband dies, you may be entitled to bereavement benefits in the same way as other widows. If there is a possibility that he may have died but that you have not been informed, you can check by contacting the **General Register Office:** 0845 603 7788; website: www.gro.gov.uk. The indexes to all birth, marriage and death entries in England and Wales are available at the **National Archives:** 020 8876 3444; website: www. nationalarchives.gov.uk.

Widows

There are three important benefits to which widows may be entitled: Bereavement Benefit, Bereavement Allowance and Widowed Parent's Allowance. All are largely modelled on the former widows' benefits (Widow's Payment, Widow's Pension and Widowed Mother's Allowance), with the important difference that all are now also applicable to widowed men. To claim the benefits, fill in form BB1, obtainable from any social security or Jobcentre Plus office. You will also be given a questionnaire (BD8) by the registrar. It is important that you complete this, as it acts as a trigger to help speed up payment of your benefits.

Widows who were already in receipt of the Widow's Pension before it was replaced by Bereavement Allowance in April 2001 are not affected by the change and will continue to receive their pension as normal.

Bereavement Benefit

This has replaced what used to be known as 'Widow's Payment'. It is a tax-free lump sum of £2,000, paid as soon as a woman is widowed, provided that: 1) her husband had paid sufficient NI contributions; 2) she is under state retirement age; or 3) if she is over 60, her husband had not been entitled to a retirement pension. Her claim will not be affected if she is already receiving a State pension, provided this is based on her own contributions. Bereavement Benefit applies equally to widowers. In such cases, the male State retirement age (65) applies and receipt is dependent on the wife's NI contributions.

Bereavement Allowance

This has replaced the Widow's Pension. As stated earlier, women already in receipt of Widow's Pension before 6 April 2001 are not affected and will continue to receive their pension as normal. Bereavement Allowance is for those aged between 45 and State pension age who do not receive Widowed Parent's Allowance. It is payable for 52 weeks and, as with Widow's Pension before, there are various levels of payment: the full-rate and age-related Bereavement Allowance. Receipt in all cases is dependent on sufficient NI contributions having been paid. See the website for more information: www.direct.gov.uk.

Full-rate Bereavement Allowance is paid to widows and widowers between the ages of 55 and 59 inclusive. The weekly amount is £97.65, which is the same as the current pension for a single person. Age-related Bereavement Allowance is for younger widows and widowers who do not qualify for the full rate. It is payable to widowed persons who are aged between 45 and 54 inclusive when their partner dies. Bereavement Allowance is normally paid automatically once you have sent off your completed form BB1, so if for any reason you do not receive it you should enquire at your social security or Jobcentre Plus office. In the event of your being ineligible, owing to insufficient NI contributions having been paid, you may still be entitled to receive Income Support, housing benefit or a grant or loan from the social fund. Your social security or Jobcentre Plus office will advise you. As applies to Widow's Pension, widows who remarry or live with a man as his wife cease to receive Bereavement Allowance. See website: www.direct.gov.uk.

Widowed Parent's Allowance

This is paid to widowed parents with at least one child for whom they receive Child Benefit. The current value (2010/11) is £97.65 a week. The allowance is usually paid automatically. If for some reason, although eligible, you do not receive the money, you should inform your social security or Jobcentre Plus office. See website: www.direct.gov.uk.

Retirement pension

Once a widow reaches 60, she will normally receive a State pension based on her own and/or her late husband's contributions. If at the time of death the couple were already receiving the State retirement pension, the widow will continue to receive her share. An important point to remember is that a widow may be able to use her late husband's NI contributions to boost the amount she receives.

Other important points

Separate from the basic pension, a widow may also receive money from her late husband's occupational pension, whether contracted in or out of the State scheme. She may also get half of any of his graduated pension.

War widows and widowers

Until recently war widows who remarried or cohabited lost their War Widow's Pension, unless either the cohabitation ceased or they became single again as a result of the death of the new husband, divorce or legal separation, in which circumstances it was restored. After years of campaigning by many groups, at last the rules have been changed and war widows can now keep their pension for life. The new rules also include men, and war widowers equally can keep a late spouse's pension for life.

Part-timers

Thanks in large part to the sex discrimination legislation being extended to include access to pension schemes, many part-timers who were previously excluded can now join their employer's occupational pension scheme as of right – or may even be able to claim retrospective membership for the years they were 'unlawfully excluded'. Their claim can be backdated only to 1976 or, if later, to the start date of their employment and must be made (at the absolute latest) within six months of their leaving the job.

Part-timers who wish to claim must apply to an employment tribunal and, as a condition of receiving any backdated benefits due, must pay contributions in respect of those years. Although it is perhaps stating the obvious, successful appeals are not automatic, as the issue will be judged solely on grounds of sex discrimination (and not on exclusion for other reasons).

Pensions for women

Women who have worked all their adult lives and paid full Class 1 contributions should get a full basic State pension in their own right at the age of 60. The current amount is £97.65 a week. This rises every April and is linked to earnings from April 2011.

Women who have worked for only part of their adult lives may not have enough contributions to get a full basic State pension on their own record. Instead, they may receive a reduced pension or one based on their husband's contributions, or one topping up the other. A wife entitled to a reduced pension on her own contributions can claim it at 60, regardless of whether or not her husband is receiving his pension.

Married women who have never worked are also entitled to a pension based on their husband's contributions. In money terms, the value is about 60 per cent of the level of basic pension to which the husband is entitled. There are several important conditions, however. First, a woman can receive a pension based on her husband's contributions only if he himself is in receipt of a basic pension. He will have to have reached 65 and must have retired. Additionally, the wife herself must be over 60 to qualify.

If a wife has had her 60th birthday but her husband has not yet reached 65 (or has decided to defer his retirement), she must wait until her husband retires to receive her share of the married couple's pension. An important point to note is that, since the introduction of independent taxation, a married woman is entitled to have her section of the joint pension offset against her own personal allowance instead of it being counted as part of her husband's taxable income. For many pensioner couples, this should have the happy result of reducing their tax liability.

If a wife who formerly worked is over 60 and retired but cannot yet get a basic pension on either her own or her husband's contributions, she may be able to qualify for an additional pension or graduated pension based on her own contributions. These are described a little further on; but first a word about two other important matters: reduced-rate contributions and Home Responsibilities Protection.

Reduced-rate contribution

Many women retiring today have paid a reduced rate of NIC, also known as 'the small stamp'. This option was given to working wives in 1948 and withdrawn in 1978, but women who had already chosen to pay the reduced rate were allowed to continue, provided they did not take more than a two-year break from employment after 1978. If you have never paid anything but reduced-rate contributions, you are not entitled to a basic pension in your own right but instead must rely on your husband's contributions for the married couple's pension.

Home Responsibilities Protection (HRP)

Men and women, whether single or married, who have been unable to work regularly because they have had to stay at home to care for children and/or a disabled or elderly person may be able to safeguard their pension by claiming Home Responsibilities Protection. This is a very important benefit, especially for the many single women in their 50s who are sacrificing their career to look after an elderly parent. This measure was introduced in 1978, and protection therefore applies only from this date. The person you are caring for must belong to one of the following categories:

- a child under 16 for whom you are getting Child Benefit;
- someone whom you are looking after regularly for at least 35 hours a week, who is in receipt of attendance allowance, constant attendance allowance or disability living allowance;
- someone – for example, an elderly person – for whom you have been caring at home and in consequence have been getting Income Support (or Supplementary Benefit in the past);
- a combination of the above situations.

A married woman or widow cannot get HRP for any tax year in which she was liable to pay only reduced-rate NIC. HRP can be given only for complete tax years (6 April to 5 April), so if you simply gave up work for a few weeks to help out you would be unlikely to qualify. Additionally, HRP cannot be used to reduce your total working life to below 20 years. To obtain a claim form, you should ask your pension centre for leaflet CF411.

Since 1978, anyone in receipt of Child Benefit, Supplementary Benefit or Income Support who is caring for someone in one of the eligible categories listed above is automatically credited with HRP. All other claimants should obtain leaflet CF411 from their pension centre.

There are concerns that up to 500,000 women over the age of 60 may be losing out on more than £1 billion in State pension entitlement through not receiving HRP. Because the HRP system reduces the number of qualifying years to receive a full State pension for women who have taken time off work to bring up children, this benefit should have been given automatically to women who were not working and who were receiving Child Benefit at any time after April 1978, when the system was introduced. Thousands of women are unaware of this and are not receiving full pensions because the government's system has failed to adjust their qualifying pension years automatically.

To get clarification, any woman over 60 or within two months of retirement should contact the Pension Service to find out whether her state pension is calculated with the benefit of HRP. Contact: 0800 731 7898; website: www.direct.gov.uk/pensions.

Additional pension

The State Second Pension (S2P) applies to women with contracted-out pension schemes. They are entitled either to a pension that is broadly equal to or better than its State equivalent, or to what are known as 'protected rights' (ie their and their employer's compulsory contributions together with their accumulated investment growth).

Useful information

A useful website if you want general information in a clear format, sometimes described as 'a rough guide to pensions', is www.pensionsorter.co.uk.

Pensions for Women – Your Guide (PM6) and *State Pensions for Parents and Carers – Your Guide* (PM9), obtainable from the Pensions Information order line: 0845 731 3233; website: www.direct.gov.uk/pensions.

Managing in Retirement and *Just the Facts about Pensions*, free booklets available from the FSA Money Made Clear information line: 0300 500 5000; website: www.fsa.gov.uk/consumer.

Chapter Four
Tax

Death, taxes and childbirth; there's never a convenient time for any of them. MARGARET MITCHELL, AUTHOR OF *GONE WITH THE WIND*

Since recent budget changes have been particularly hard hitting, a chapter that provides information on taxes is necessary because most of us are affected by a number of different taxes. While you were employed you may have been contributing many thousands of pounds to HM Revenue & Customs (or HMRC, for short), but in practice you may have had very little direct contact with the tax system. The accounts department will have automatically deducted – and accounted for – the PAYE on your earnings as a salaried employee. If you were self-employed or had other money unconnected with your job, you may have had more dealings with your tax office. On reaching retirement you should be able to calculate how much money (after deduction of tax) you will have available to spend: the equivalent, if you like, of your take-home pay. Understanding the broad principles could help you save money by not paying more in taxation than you need.

The purpose of this chapter is not to give tax planning advice; tax planning is a job for a specialist. Your tax adviser should be fully conversant with your financial affairs so that he or she can advise in the light of your own particular circumstances. The aim here is simply to remind you of the basics and to draw your attention to some of the latest provisions that could have a bearing on your immediate or longer-term plans. The following information is based on our understanding, as at November 2010, of current taxation, legislation and HMRC practice, all of which are liable to change without notice. The impact of taxation (and any tax relief) depends on individual circumstances.

Income Tax

This is calculated on all (or nearly all) your income, after deduction of your personal allowance and, in the case of older married people, of the Married Couple's Allowance. The reason for saying 'nearly all' is that some income you may receive is tax-free: types of income on which you do not have to pay tax are listed a little further on.

Most income counts, however. You will be assessed for Income Tax on: your pension, interest you receive from most types of savings, dividends from investments, any earnings (even if these are only from casual work), plus rent from any lodgers if the amount you receive exceeds £4,250 a year. Many social security benefits are also taxable. The tax year runs from 6 April to the following 5 April, so the amount of tax you pay in any one year is calculated on the income you receive (or are deemed to have received) between these two dates. The four different rates of Income Tax for 2010/11 are:

1 the 10 per cent starting rate for savings, which applies to the first £2,440 of any savings income;

2 the 20 per cent basic-rate tax for income up to £37,400;

3 the 40 per cent higher-rate tax, which is levied on all taxable income over £37,400 up to £150,000; and

4 the top rate of 50 per cent on incomes in excess of £150,000.

Another change that affects many earners' take-home pay is the increase in National Insurance Contributions; the upper earnings limit for employees' Class 1 NIC and the Class 4 National Insurance upper profits limit, applicable to the self-employed, increased. Since 2009 these limits have been aligned to the upper limit for basic-rate Income Tax, making some people worse off.

Tax allowances

Personal allowance

You don't pay tax on every single penny of your money. You are allowed to retain a certain amount before Income Tax becomes applicable. This is known as your personal allowance. When calculating how much tax you will have to pay in any one year, first deduct from your total income the amount represented by your personal allowance. You should add any other tax allowance to which you may be entitled – see further on. You will not have to pay any Income Tax if your income does not exceed your personal allowance (or total of your allowances), and you may be able to claim a refund for any tax you have paid, or that has been deducted from payments made to you, during the year.

Calculating your personal allowance since the introduction of independent taxation has become easier. Everyone receives the same basic personal allowance regardless of whether they are male, female, married or single. It does not matter where the income comes from, whether from earnings, an investment, a pension or another source.

The basic personal allowance (2010/11) is £6,475. The personal allowance for those aged under 65 will be increased by £1,000 to £7,475 in April 2011. (This will benefit 23 million taxpayers and remove hundreds of thousands more from Income Tax altogether.) People aged 65 to 74 are entitled to a higher personal allowance than the basic, by virtue of their age. For the year 2010/11 this is unchanged at £9,490. For those over 75 this is also unchanged at £9,640. From 2010/11 the Personal Allowance reduces where the income is above £100,000 – by £1 for every £2 of income above the £100,000 limit. This reduction applies irrespective of age.

NB: the extra allowance linked to age is normally given automatically. If you are not receiving it but believe you should be doing so, contact your local tax office. If you have been missing out, you may be able to claim back anything you have lost for up to six years and should receive a tax rebate. The amounts have been altered several times in recent years, so any rebate would only apply to allowances that would have been due to you at the time. Contact the **HMRC** general information line: 0845 900 0444; website: www.hmrc.gov.uk.

Married Couple's Allowance

Married Couple's Allowance (for those born before 6 April 1935 but aged under 75) is no longer applicable. Age-related Married Couple's Allowance (aged 75 and over) is £6,965. The minimum amount of Married Couple's Allowance is £2,670.

Some important points you should know:

- Married Couple's Allowance is restricted to 10 per cent tax relief.
- A widowed partner, where the couple at the time of death were entitled to Married Couple's Allowance, can claim any unused portion of the allowance in the year he or she became widowed.

- *Registered blind people* can claim an allowance of £1,890 a year. If both husband and wife are registered as blind, they can each claim the allowance. It is called the Blind Person's Allowance. If you think you would be eligible, you should write to your local tax office with full relevant details of your situation. If you were entitled to receive the allowance earlier but for some reason missed out on doing so, you may be able to obtain a tax rebate.

Useful reading

For more detailed information about tax allowances, see the following HMRC leaflets obtainable free from any tax office: IR 121, *Income Tax and Pensioners* and *Rates and Allowances 2010/11*. Contact: 0845 900 0444; website: www.hmrc.gov.uk.

Same-sex partners

Same-sex couples are treated the same as married couples for tax purposes. As a result, they gain all the same tax advantages but also the same disadvantages. The most important is that only one property can qualify as their principal home for exemption from Capital Gains Tax. Against this, there is no CGT to pay on transfer of assets between the couple, and similarly any assets left in a will to each other are free of Inheritance Tax. Other major areas that stand to be affected are pension rights (other than the State scheme) and, though not specifically a tax issue, settlements between the couple in the event of a divorce.

Tax relief

Separate from any personal allowances, you can obtain tax relief on the following:

- a covenant for the benefit of a charity, or a donation under the Gift Aid scheme;
- contributions to occupational pensions, self-employed pension plans and other personal pensions;
- some maintenance payments, if you are divorced or separated and were aged 65 or older at 5 April 2000.

Mortgage interest relief

Mortgage interest relief was abolished on 6 April 2000. The only purpose for which relief is still available is in respect of loans secured on an older person's home to purchase a life annuity. However, to qualify the loan must have been taken out (or at least processed and confirmed in writing) by 9 March 1999. Borrowers in this situation can continue to benefit from the relief for the duration of their loan. As before, the relief remains at 10 per cent on the first £30,000 of the loan.

Maintenance payments

Tax relief for maintenance payments was also withdrawn on 6 April 2000. Individuals in receipt of maintenance payments are not affected and will continue to receive their money free of Income Tax. Those who had to pay tax under the pre-March 1988 rules now also receive their payments free of tax. Most individuals paying maintenance, however, face higher tax bills. This applies especially to those who set up arrangements before the March 1988 Budget. While previously they got tax relief at their highest rate, from 6 April 2000 when maintenance relief was withdrawn they no longer get any relief at all. An exception has been made in cases where one (or both) of the divorced or separated spouses was aged 65 or over at 5 April 2000. Those paying maintenance are still able to claim tax relief – but only at the 1999/2000 standard rate of 10 per cent.

Pension contributions

HMRC sets limits on the contributions that individuals can invest in their pension plan and on the pension benefits they can receive. All company and personal pensions are now set under a single tax regime.

Among other important changes, the earnings cap is no longer a factor. Instead, individuals can now invest up to 100 per cent of annual earnings into their plan (or plans) with the benefit of tax relief up to a maximum figure – known as the annual allowance – of £255,000. Higher contributions are allowed but without any tax relief on the excess. If you have a stakeholder or personal pension, you can make contributions of up to £3,600 a year irrespective of your earnings (or even if you earn nothing at all). You pay the contributions net of basic-rate tax, and your pension provider will then reclaim the tax from HMRC.

The annual allowance is not the only capped amount. There is also a lifetime limit of £1.8 million for total pension funds, including any fund growth. Funds in excess of the lifetime limit are subject to a 25 per cent recovery charge (ie tax) if taken as income, or 55 per cent if taken as a lump sum. The lifetime limit of £1.8 million will remain in place until 2015/16.

Fund protection

Individuals whose pension fund was already over the lifetime limit before 6 April 2006 – or anticipated to become so before they draw their pension – were able to protect their fund from the recovery charge, provided the fund was formally registered with HMRC within three years of 6 April 2006 (A-day), ie 5 April 2009.

Tax-free lump sum

A further major change concerns the tax-free lump sum. Everyone (provided the scheme rules permit) is entitled to take up to 25 per cent of the value of their fund or 25 per cent of their lifetime limit, whichever is lower. Additional Voluntary Contributions (AVCs) and the opted-out benefits from the State Second Pension can count towards the lump sum instead of, as before, having to remain in the fund to provide pension income.

There is no longer any requirement for members of company schemes to wait until they retire before accessing their lump sum. Should they wish to do so, they can now take the money at any time from the age of 55. Members of final salary schemes cannot take their lump sum in isolation. There is now also greater flexibility for employees nearing retirement, who as well as taking their tax-free lump sum can also (provided their scheme rules allow) start drawing some pension income while still remaining at work part time.

Scheme rules

The fact that HMRC has changed the rules is unfortunately no guarantee that individuals will be able to take full advantage of all the new options that have become available. Their employer's pension scheme rules will need to have been altered accordingly, which may not always be the case. Before making any definite plans, it is advisable to check first with whoever is responsible for the company pension scheme.

Pension Credit

Pension Credit is a means-tested State benefit for those over 60, giving certain pensioners extra money each week. It's made up of two elements – the 'Guarantee Credit' element and the 'Savings Credit' element. Pension

Credit guarantees everyone aged 60 and over an income of at least £132.60 a week if you are single and £202.40 a week if you have a partner. Also, if you or your partner are 65 or over you may be rewarded for saving for your retirement, up to £20.52 a week if you are single; or £27.09 a week if you have a partner. You may get more Pension Credit if you have caring responsibilities, are severely disabled or have certain housing costs.

If you apply over the phone for Pension Credit and, at the same time, for housing and Council Tax benefits, the Pension Service will automatically send its claim information to the appropriate local authority. This does away with the need for another claim form to be completed and signed. Also claimants are now able to spend up to 13 weeks abroad (increased from four weeks) and still retain entitlement to Pension Credit. This brings the benefit into line with housing and Council Tax benefits. The backdating of pension credit claims is now limited to three months, to bring it into line with other benefits.

For further information, see Chapter 3, Pensions, or the **Pension Credit Helpline:** 0800 99 1234; website: www.direct.gov.uk/pensions.

Tax-free income

Some income you may receive is entirely free of tax. It is not taxed at source. You do not have to deduct it from your income, as in the case of personal allowances. Nor do you have to go through the formality of claiming relief on it. If you receive any of the following, you can forget about the tax aspect altogether – at least as regards these particular items:

- Disability Living Allowance;
- industrial injuries disablement pension;
- Income Support (in some circumstances, such as when the recipient is also getting Jobseeker's Allowance, Income Support benefit will be taxable);
- housing benefit;
- Council Tax benefit;
- all pensions paid to war widows (plus any additions for children);
- pensions paid to victims of Nazism;
- certain disablement pensions from the armed forces, police, fire brigade and merchant navy;
- annuities paid to the holders of certain gallantry awards;

- the £10 Christmas bonus (paid to pensioners);
- National Savings Premium Bond prizes;
- SAYE bonuses;
- winnings on the football pools and on other forms of betting;
- rental income of up to £4,250 a year from letting out rooms in your home;
- the winter fuel payment (paid to pensioners);
- the extra £400 winter fuel payment paid to households with a resident aged 80 and over;
- income received from certain insurance policies (mortgage payment protection, permanent health insurance, creditor insurance for loans and utility bills, various approved long-term care policies) if the recipient is sick, disabled or unemployed at the time the benefits become payable;
- all income received from savings in an Individual Savings Account (ISA);
- all dividend income from investments in venture capital trusts (VCTs).

Other tax-free money

The following are not income, in the sense that they are more likely to be one-off rather than regular payments. However, as with the above list they are tax-free:

- virtually all gifts (in certain circumstances you could have to pay tax if the gift is above £3,000 or if, as may occasionally be the case, the money from the donor has not been previously taxed);
- a redundancy payment, or a golden handshake in lieu of notice, up to the value of £30,000;
- a lump sum commuted from a pension;
- a matured endowment policy;
- accumulated interest from a Tax Exempt Special Savings Account (TESSA) held for five years;
- dividends on investments held in a Personal Equity Plan (PEP);
- compensation money paid to people who were mis-sold personal pensions;

- compensation paid to those who were mis-sold free-standing AVCs (FSAVCs). To qualify for exemption from tax, the money must be paid as a lump sum as opposed to annual payments.

Income Tax on savings

For the year 2010/11 the 10 per cent starting rate applies to savings income up to £2,440.

Income Tax on other investments

For most investments on which you are likely to receive dividends, basic-rate tax will have been deducted before the money is paid to you. If you are a basic-rate taxpayer, the money you receive will be yours in its entirety. If you pay tax at the higher rate, you will have to pay some additional tax and should allow for this in your budgeting.

Exceptionally, there are one or two types of investment where the money is paid to you gross – without the basic-rate tax deducted. These include NS&I income bonds, capital bonds, the NS&I Investment Account and all gilt interest. (People who prefer to receive gilt interest net can opt to do so.) As with higher-rate taxpayers, you will need to save sufficient money to pay the tax on the due date.

Avoiding paying excess tax on savings income

Banks and building societies automatically deduct the normal 20 per cent rate of tax from interest before it is paid to savers. As a result, most working people, except higher-rate taxpayers, can keep all their savings without having to worry about paying additional tax. While convenient for the majority, a problem is that some 4 million people on low incomes – including in particular many women and pensioners – are unwittingly paying more tax than they need. Those most affected are non-taxpayers (anyone whose taxable income is less than their allowances) who, although not liable for tax, are having it taken from their income before they receive the money.

Non-taxpayers can stop this happening quite simply by requesting their bank and/or building society to pay any interest owing to them gross, without deduction of tax at source. If applicable, all you need do is request form R85 from the institution in question or HMRC Enquiry Centre, which you will then need to complete. If you have more than one bank or building society account, you will need a separate form for each account. People who have filled in an R85 should automatically receive their interest gross. If your form was not completed in time for this to happen, you can reclaim the tax from your tax office after the end of the tax year in April.

Reclaiming tax overpaid

If you are a non-taxpayer and have not yet completed an R85 form (or forms), you are very likely to be eligible to claim a tax rebate. To obtain a claim form and, if relevant, copies of form R85 for you to complete and give to your bank or building society contact the special **Taxback Helpline** on 0845 077 6543.

Mistakes by HMRC

HMRC does sometimes make mistakes. Normally, if it has charged you insufficient tax and later discovers the error, it will send you a supplementary demand requesting the balance owing. However, under a provision known as the 'Official Error Concession', if the mistake was due to HMRC's failure 'to make proper and timely use' of information it received, it is possible that you may be excused the arrears. For this to be likely, you will need to convince HMRC that you could reasonably have believed that your tax affairs were in order. Additionally, HMRC itself will need to have been tardy in notifying you of the arrears: this will normally mean more than 12 months after the end of the tax year in which HMRC received the information indicating that more tax was due.

Undercharging is not the only type of error. It is equally possible that you may have been overcharged and either do not owe as much as has been stated or, not having spotted the mistake, have paid more than you needed to previously. In time HMRC may notice the error and send you a refund, but equally it may not. So if you have reason to think your tax bill looks wrong, check it carefully. Then, if you think there has been a mistake, write to your tax office explaining why you think the amount is too high. If a large sum is involved it could well be worth asking an accountant to help you.

As part of the Citizen's Charter, HMRC has appointed an independent Adjudicator to examine taxpayers' complaints about their dealings with

HMRC and, if considered valid, to determine what action would be fair. Complaints appropriate to the Adjudicator are mainly limited to the way HMRC has handled someone's tax affairs, for example excessive delay, errors, discourtesy or how discretion has been exercised. In deciding fair treatment, the Adjudicator has power to recommend the waiving of a payment or even the award of compensation if, as a result of error by HMRC, the complainant had incurred professional fees or other expenses. Before approaching the Adjudicator, taxpayers are expected to have tried to resolve the matter, either with their local tax office or, should that fail, with the regional office.

Genuine mistakes are excused by HMRC but individuals may need to convince officials that they had not been careless in completing their returns, otherwise they could be at risk of incurring a penalty. More immediately, the deadline for filing paper self-assessment forms for the 2010/11 tax year is 31 October 2011. Those filing online will have until 31 January 2012.

For further information, see HMRC booklet Code of Practice 1, *Putting Things Right: How to Complain*, available from tax offices. Contact the Adjudicator's Office for information about referring a complaint. The Adjudicator acts as a fair and unbiased referee looking into complaints about HMRC, including the Tax Credit Office, the Valuation Office and the Office of the Public Guardian and the Insolvency Service. Contact the **Adjudicator's Office:** 0300 057 1111; website: www.adjudicatorsoffice.gov.uk.

Other useful organizations

The TaxPayers' Alliance has a campaign team of energetic volunteers committed to achieving a low-tax society. It has over 18,000 supporters and is regularly mentioned in the media. Contact the **TaxPayers' Alliance:** 0845 330 9554; website: www.taxpayersalliance.com.

TaxHelp for Older People (TOP) is an independent, free tax advice service for over-60s whose household income is less than £17,000 a year. This organization offers the service originally provided through the Low Incomes Tax Reform Group (associated with the Chartered Institute of Taxation) but is now provided by Tax Volunteers, an independent organization. Contact TOP: 0845 601 3321; website: www.taxvol.org.uk. Tax forms that can help you:

R40 – If you want to claim back tax paid on savings and investments you need to complete this form. Remember that you need one for each year you are claiming for.

R85 – Getting your interest paid without tax being taken off. Not a taxpayer? This form will save you having to claim tax back each year. You can use this if your total taxable income (before tax is taken) is below your personal allowance. Ask for one at your bank or building society, sign it and hand it back.

P161 – Are you going to be 65 (60 for a woman) in this tax year? Or is your income changing, for example, State pension and private pensions are due to start? If yes, this is a very important form. It will help you inform HMRC of your age and income, allowing it to give you your age allowance and your new tax codes.

R27 – This form helps you to settle the tax affairs of someone who has died. If you have recently been bereaved and have informed HMRC, it should send you one. It is worth completing because it often creates a repayment and helps to sort out any final transfer of married couples' allowance. Your solicitor, if you have one, will usually deal with it for you.

P53 – If you have recently taken a lump sum rather than buying an annuity (pension), you will have noticed that an enormous amount of tax was deducted before you received it. If you want to claim this back immediately rather than waiting until the end of the tax year, you should complete a P53.

P45 – You should receive one of these when you finish work with an employer. If you start a new job in the same tax year it is important that you give it to your new employer. It will ensure you are given the correct tax code and the right tax is deducted.

P46 – As important as the P45. If you start a new job and you do not have a P45 you must complete a P46. Your employer should prompt you to do this. If not, ask for one. This form also sorts out your tax codes.

Forms 575 and 18 – If you are thinking of transferring some of your married couples' allowance, Form 575 allows you to transfer the excess at the end of the tax year. Form 18 allows you to transfer the minimum amount.

Most forms can be obtained by calling the **HMRC Taxback Helpline**: 0845 077 6543; website: www.hmrc.gov.uk.

Tax Credits

There are two tax credits that could be of possible interest: the Working Tax Credit (WTC) and the Child Tax Credit (CTC). The amount of tax credits you get depends on how many children you have living with you, whether you work and how many hours you work, if you pay for childcare, if you or any child living with you has a disability, or if you are coming off benefits. A recent budget change is that from April 2012 the 50-plus element will no longer be available for those claiming Working Tax Credit.

Working Tax Credit

This is an earnings top-up given to low-income workers, including the self-employed. Eligibility is normally restricted to couples and single parents with a low income. In certain circumstances, including in particular households with three or more dependent children or where a member of the family has a disability, those with slightly higher incomes could still be eligible to apply. HMRC advises that the easiest way to check is to complete the form, listed under 'Tax credits', on its website www.hmrc.gov.uk. Contact the **Tax Credit Helpline:** 0845 300 3900; website: www.direct.gov.uk/MoneyTaxandBenefits.

To qualify, claimants must usually work for at least 30 hours a week. However, for those with a disability and/or dependent children, the minimum requirement is 16 hours a week. Working parents can receive up to 80 per cent of eligible childcare costs. All recipients receive the payment direct from HMRC into their bank, building society, Post Office or National Savings account either weekly or four-weekly.

Child Tax Credit

This is a cash payment given to all families with a low household income that have at least one child under 16, or under 20 if in full-time education. The money, which is on top of Child Benefit, is paid direct to the main carer. The amount of credit varies according to parental income but, from 6 April 2011, families with an income of more than £40,000 will see their eligibility for child tax credits reduced. The baby element of Child Tax Credits is also abolished from 6 April 2011.

Need to claim

Payment is not automatic. In both cases – Working Tax Credit and Child Tax Credit – you need to complete an application form, obtainable from any Tax Enquiry Centre or the Tax Credit Helpline: 0845 300 3900 (for Northern Ireland, Tel: 0845 603 2000); website: www.direct.gov.uk/MoneyTaxandBenefits.

NB: Child Tax Credit is one area where independent taxation could be said not to apply, as eligibility is based on the combined income of the parents.

Tax rebates

When you retire, you may be due for a tax rebate. If you are, this would normally be paid automatically, especially if you are getting a pension from your last employer. The matter could conceivably be overlooked, either if you are due to get a pension from an earlier employer (instead of from your last employer) or if you will be receiving only a State pension and not a company pension in addition.

In either case, you should ask your employer for a P45 form. Then either send it – care of your earlier employer – to the pension fund trustees or, in the event of your receiving only a State pension, to the tax office together with details of your age and the date you retired. Ask your employer for the address of the tax office to which you should write. If the repayment is made to you more than a year after the end of the year for which the repayment is due – and is more than £25 – HMRC will automatically pay you (tax-free) interest. HMRC calls this a 'repayment supplement'.

Post-war credits

Post-war credits are extra tax that people had to pay in addition to their Income Tax between April 1941 and April 1946. The extra tax was treated as a credit to be repaid after the war. People who paid credits were given certificates showing the amount actually paid. Repayment started in 1946, initially only to men aged 65 or over and to women aged 60 or over, but the conditions for claiming varied over the years until 1972, when it was announced that there would be a 'general release' and that all credits were to be repaid without any further restrictions. In 1972 people who could produce at least one of their post-war credit certificates were invited to claim. In cases where the original credit holder has died without claiming repayment and the post-war credit certificate is still available, repayment can be made to the next of kin or personal representative of the estate. Interest is payable on all claims at a composite rate of 38 per cent. The interest is exempt from Income Tax. All claims should be sent to the **Special Post-War Credit Claim Centre** at HM Revenue & Customs, HM Inspector of Taxes – PWC Centre V, Ty Glas, Llanishen, Cardiff CF4 5TX, Tel: 0845 300 3949.

Capital Gains Tax (CGT)

You may have to pay Capital Gains Tax if you make a profit (or, to use the proper term, 'gain') on the sale of a capital asset, for example stocks and shares, jewellery, any property that is not your main home, and other items of value. CGT applies only to the actual gain you make, so if you buy shares to the value of £100,000 and sell them later for £125,000 the tax officer will be interested only in the £25,000 profit you have made.

Not all your gains are taxable. There is *an exemption limit of £10,100* (2010/11) a year so, if during the year your total gains amount to £14,500, tax will be levied only on £4,400. A very important point for married couples to know is that as a result of independent taxation each partner now enjoys his or her own annual exemption of £10,100 instead of, as before, their gains being aggregated (ie added together) for tax purposes. This means in effect that, provided both partners are taking advantage of their full exemption limit, a couple can make gains of £20,200 a year free of CGT. However, it is not possible to use the losses of one spouse to cover the gains of the other. Transfers between husband and wife remain tax-free, although any income arising from such a gift will of course be taxed. Income will normally be treated as the recipient's for tax purposes.

Gains made before April 2008 are taxed at the same rate as your income: 10 per cent where the gains fall below the starting-rate limit for Income Tax of £2,440; 20 per cent where they fall between the starting-rate and basic-rate limits for Income Tax, ie between £2,441 and £37,400; or at 40 per cent where they fall above the basic-rate limit for Income Tax, ie £37,401 and above. However, since 22 June 2010 any gains you make are taxed at 28 per cent for higher-rate and additional-rate tax payers.

Taper relief was abolished in April 2008 and the new single tax rate of 28 per cent applies across the board since 22 June 2010. The 10 per cent rate for entrepreneurial business activities will be extended from the first £2 million to the first £5 million of qualifying gains made over a lifetime.

Free of Capital Gains Tax

The following assets are not subject to CGT and do not count towards the gains you are allowed to make:

- your main home (but see the note below);
- your car;
- personal belongings up to the value of £6,000 each;
- proceeds of a life assurance policy (in most circumstances);
- profits on UK government stocks;
- National Savings certificates;
- SAYE contracts;
- building society mortgage cashbacks;
- futures and options in gilts and qualifying corporate bonds;
- Personal Equity Plan (PEP) schemes (now automatically ISAs);
- gains from assets held in an Individual Savings Account (ISA);
- Premium Bond winnings;
- betting and lottery winnings and life insurance policies if you are the original owner;
- gifts to registered charities;
- small part-disposals of land (limited to 5 per cent of the total holding, with a maximum value of £20,000);
- gains on the disposal of qualifying shares in a Venture Capital Trust (VCT) or within the Enterprise Investment Scheme (EIS), provided these have been held for the necessary holding period (see below).

Enterprise Investment Scheme (EIS)

The EIS allows individuals investing in qualifying unquoted companies 20 per cent Income Tax relief on investments up to £500,000 and exemption from Capital Gains Tax on disposal of the shares, provided these have been held for at least three years. Losses qualify for Income Tax or CGT relief. A further advantage is that, whereas deferral relief has been withdrawn in respect of VCTs since 6 April 2004, those investing in an EIS can still defer any CGT liability, provided gains are invested in qualifying unquoted companies within three years. Also, an investor can become a paid director, provided he or she was not previously connected with the company at the time of the first investment. See **HMRC** website: www.hmrc.gov.uk.

Your home

Your main home is usually exempt from CGT. However, there are certain 'ifs and buts' that could be important. If you convert part of your home into an office or into self-contained accommodation on which you charge rent, the part of your home that is deemed to be a 'business' may be separately assessed – and CGT may be payable when you come to sell it. (CGT would not apply if you simply take in a lodger who is treated as family, in the sense of sharing your kitchen or bathroom.)

If you leave your home to someone else who later decides to sell it, then he or she may be liable for CGT when the property is sold (although only on the gain since the date of death). There may also be Inheritance Tax implications, so if you are thinking of leaving or giving your home to someone you are strongly advised to consult a solicitor or accountant. If you own two homes, only one of them is exempt from CGT, namely the one you designate as your 'main residence'.

Selling a family business

With taper relief having been abolished in April 2008, the CGT now payable if you are selling a family business is 28 per cent. One possible option is the CGT deferral relief allowable to investors in an EIS.

Investors – including entrepreneur owners or directors with gains arising from the sale of shares in their own companies – can defer paying CGT and in many cases can also obtain Income Tax relief at 20 per cent on investments of up to £500,000 a year, provided gains are reinvested in qualifying unquoted companies (including AIM and Ofex companies) within three years. In recent years, some of the rules have been altered to create a more unified system of venture capital reliefs. The key changes that potential investors should note are:

- the amount that can be invested is now £500,000 (previously £400,000);
- the amount an individual may invest in shares issued in the first half of the tax year and qualifying for Income Tax relief for the previous year is now £50,000 (previously £25,000);

- qualifying companies are limited to £7 million of gross assets before an investment (£8 million after an investment); and

- companies with property-backed assets, such as farming and nursing homes, no longer qualify as eligible trading companies.

This is a very complex field, so before either retiring or selling shares you are strongly recommended to seek professional advice.

Useful reading

For further information about Capital Gains Tax, see booklet CGT1, *Capital Gains Tax: An Introduction*, available from any tax office. Consult the HMRC website: www.hmrc.gov.uk.

Inheritance Tax (IHT)

Inheritance Tax (IHT) is the tax that is paid on your 'estate'. Broadly speaking this is everything you own at the time of your death, less any debts you have. It's sometimes payable on assets you may have given away during your lifetime. Assets include property, possessions, money and investments.

In the 22 June 2010 Emergency Budget, the Chancellor froze the Inheritance Tax Threshold (the level at which you'll need to pay tax) at £325,000 until 2014. The threshold amount for married couples and civil partners is £650,000. The value of estates over and above the allowance is taxed at 40 per cent.

Before any tax is calculated, there are a number of exemptions and other concessions that may be relevant. There is no immediate tax on lifetime gifts between individuals. The gifts become wholly exempt if the donor survives for seven years. When the donor dies, any gifts made within the previous seven years become chargeable and their value is added to that of the estate. The total is then taxed on the excess over £325,000. Chargeable gifts benefit first towards the £325,000 exemption, starting with the earliest gifts and continuing in the order in which they were given. Any unused balance of the £325,000 threshold goes towards the remaining estate.

Under the new rules, the £325,000 threshold allows married couples or civil partners to transfer the unused element of their IHT-free allowance to their spouse or civil partner when they die. For many couples this effectively doubles the tax-free amount they can bequeath to their children. IHT will, however, still be levied at 40 per cent above £325,000 on the estate of anyone who is single or divorced when they die.

Gifts or money up to the value of £3,000 can also be given annually free of tax, regardless of the particular date they were given. Additionally, it is possible to make small gifts to any number of individuals free of tax, provided the amount to each does not exceed £250.

A previous loophole, whereby it was possible for an owner to dispose of assets such as houses, paintings or boats but continue to enjoy the benefit of them, no longer exists. Under the current rules, designed to tighten up on avoidance of IHT, people who continue to have some usage of the property they formerly owned but do not pay the market rent will be charged yearly Income Tax on the retained benefit.

As an alternative to the Income Tax charge, taxpayers can elect for IHT treatment on the relevant property in due course. The time limit for electing is the same as the self-assessment deadline for making a return for the tax year in which an individual is first liable for the pre-owned asset (POA) charge. Contact the **Probate and Inheritance Tax Helpline: 0845 302 0900.**

While most ex-owners or their heirs will end up paying one way or another, the Chancellor has built in certain exclusions and exemptions, including preserving the important principle that transfers of property between spouses remain exempt from any tax. Tax will equally not be charged if the asset is sold for full market value or if, owing to a change in circumstance, an owner who had previously given away a property needs to reoccupy his or her former home.

Quite apart from IHT, Capital Gains Tax may have to be paid on any asset you left to a beneficiary, or as part of your estate, that is subsequently sold. HMRC treats such assets as having been acquired at the date of death and at their prevailing market value at the time. By the same token, CGT will have to be paid on any gain that has built up on an asset you gave away during your lifetime and that is subsequently sold.

Another important consideration that should not be overlooked is the need to make a will. The rules of intestacy are very rigid, and neglecting to make a proper will can have serious consequences for those whom you might wish to benefit. (For further information, see 'Wills', in Chapter 16.) Likewise, if you have already written a will, it is strongly recommended that you have this checked by a professional adviser to ensure that you do not give money unnecessarily to HMRC. In view of the recent changes to IHT, check with your professional adviser or HMRC.

Tax treatment of trusts

Under the new rules for aligning the Inheritance Tax treatment for trusts, those who have set up or have an interest in 'accumulation & maintenance' trusts (A&Ms) and/or 'interest in possession' trusts (IIPs) that do not meet new IHT rules about their terms and the circumstances in which they were created are most affected. The new rules came into effect on 22 March 2006 for new trusts, additions of new assets to existing trusts, and other IHT-relevant events in relation to existing trusts. Transitional rules provided for a period of adjustment for certain existing trusts to 6 April 2008.

Discretionary trusts are assessed for IHT on their tenth anniversary and every 10 years thereafter. Distributions from the trust may also trigger an IHT charge. These rules apply to trusts created during the settler's lifetime and those created within the settler's will. Since 2008, the same treatment applies to funds gifted on or after 22 March 2006 into most IIP and A&M trusts.

This is a particularly complex area, and professional advice is recommended. Further information is available from the **Probate/Inheritance Tax Helpline:** 0845 302 0900; website: www.hmcourts-service.gov.uk.

Independent taxation

Both husband and wife are taxed independently on their own income. Each has his or her own personal allowance and rate band, and both independently pay their own tax and receive their own tax rebates. Moreover, independent taxation applies equally to the age-related additions, and both husband and wife are now eligible for their own higher tax allowance from the age of 75.

A further important point for many couples is that independent taxation does not apply simply to Income Tax but equally to both Capital Gains Tax and Inheritance Tax. As a result, both husband and wife enjoy their own Capital Gains Tax exemption (£10,100 in the 2010/11 tax year) and their own exemption from IHT (£325,000 – this limit frozen until 2014). Property left to a surviving spouse remains, as before, free of Inheritance Tax.

Self-assessment

If you are one of the 9 million people who need to complete a tax return, you will probably be all too familiar with self-assessment. The tax return forms are sent out in April, and the details you need to enter on the form you receive in April 2011 are those relating to the 2010/11 tax year.

Even if a taxpayer has never had a tax return, and so is unlikely to be directly affected by self-assessment unless his or her circumstances change, all taxpayers now have a legal obligation to keep records of all their different sources of income and capital gains. These include:

- details of earnings plus any bonus, expenses and benefits in kind received;
- bank and building society interest;
- dividend vouchers and/or other documentation showing gains from investments;
- pension payments, eg both State and occupational or private pensions;
- miscellaneous income, such as freelance earnings, maintenance payments and taxable social security benefits;
- payments against which tax relief can be claimed (eg charitable donations or contributions to a personal pension).

HMRC advises that taxpayers are obliged to keep these records for 22 months after the end of the tax year to which they relate.

If you are self-employed or a partner in a business, as well as the above list you also need to keep records of all your business earnings and expenses, together with sales invoices and receipts. All records (both personal and business) need to be kept for five years after the fixed filing date.

Those most likely to be affected by the self-assessment system include anyone who normally receives a tax return, higher-rate taxpayers, company directors, the self-employed and partners in a business. If your only income is from your salary, from which tax is deducted at source, you will not have to worry about self-assessment. If, however, you have other income that is not fully taxed under PAYE (eg possibly benefits in kind or expenses payments) or that is not fully taxed at source, you need to notify HMRC within six months of the end of the tax year, and you may need to fill in a tax return.

The same may be true when you retire. Even though you may not think of yourself as wealthy, if your financial affairs change, as they sometimes do on retirement (eg if you become self-employed or receive income that has not already been fully taxed), it is your responsibility to inform HMRC and, depending on the amount of money involved, you may need to complete a tax return. The government has recently revised the guidelines, and higher-rate taxpayers will no longer automatically receive a self-assessment form if their affairs can be handled through the PAYE system.

A very important point to know for anyone who might be feeling worried is that *self-calculation is optional.* If you think the calculations are too complicated or that you might be at risk of making a mistake, HMRC will continue as before to do the sums for you. Until recently, taxpayers who wanted HMRC to calculate their tax liability for them had to file their return by an earlier date. Today, this is no longer an issue. Instead, what matters is whether you file online or submit a paper return. Paper returns must be filed by 31 October each year; the deadline for online filing is 31 January the following year.

Further information

See booklets SA/BK4, *Self-Assessment – A General Guide to Keeping Records*; SA/BK6, *Self-Assessment – Penalties for Late Tax Returns*; SA/BK7, *Self-Assessment – Surcharges for Late Payment of Tax* and SA/BK8, *Self-Assessment – Your Guide*, all obtainable free from any tax office. Contact the Self-Assessment Helpline: 0845 900 0444; website: www.direct.gov.uk or HMRC website: www.hmrc.gov.uk.

Retiring abroad

There are many examples of people who retired abroad in the expectation of being able to afford a higher standard of living and who returned home a few years later, thoroughly disillusioned. As with other important decisions, this is where it is essential to research your options thoroughly. It is crucial to investigate property prices, as well as the cost of health care. As anyone who has ever needed a doctor or dentist abroad knows, the term 'free health service' does not always mean what it says. While these and similar points are perhaps obvious, a vital question that is often overlooked is the taxation effects of living overseas. If you are thinking of retiring abroad, do look into the effect this will have on your finances before you go.

Taxation abroad

Tax rates vary from one country to another: a prime example is VAT, which varies considerably in Europe. Additionally, many countries levy taxes that don't apply in the UK. Wealth tax exists in quite a few parts of the world. Estate duty on property left by one spouse to another is also fairly widespread. There are all sorts of property taxes, different from those in the UK, which – however described – are variously assessable as income or capital. Sometimes a special tax is imposed on foreign residents. Some countries charge income tax on an individual's worldwide income, without the exemptions that apply in the UK.

Apart from the essential of getting first-class legal advice when buying property overseas, if you are thinking of retiring abroad the golden rule must be to investigate the situation thoroughly before you take an irrevocable step, such as selling your home in the UK. An even more common mistake is for people to misunderstand their UK tax liabilities after their departure.

Your UK tax position if you retire overseas

Many intending emigrants cheerfully imagine that, once they have settled themselves in a dream villa overseas, they are safely out of the clutches of the UK tax office. This is not so. You first have to acquire non-resident status. If you have severed all your ties, including selling your home, to take up a permanent job overseas, this is normally granted fairly quickly. But for most retirees, acquiring unconditional non-resident status can take up to three years. The purpose is to check that you are not just having a prolonged holiday but are actually living as a resident abroad. During the check period, HMRC may allow you conditional non-resident status and, if it is satisfied, full status will be granted retrospectively.

Rules

The rules for non-residency are pretty stringent. You are not allowed to spend more than 182 days in the UK in any one tax year, or to spend more than an average of 90 days per year in the UK over a maximum of four tax years. Even if you are not resident in the UK, some of your income may still be liable for UK taxation.

UK Income Tax

All overseas income (provided it is not remitted to the UK) is exempt from UK tax liability.

Income deriving from a UK source is, however, normally liable for UK tax. This includes any director's or consultant's fees you may still be receiving, as well as more obvious income such as rent from a property you still own.

An exception may be made if the country in which you have taken up residency has a double tax agreement with the United Kingdom (see below). If this is the case, you may be taxed on the income in your new residence – and not in the UK.

Additionally, interest paid on certain British government securities is not subject to tax. Non-residents may be able to arrange for their interest on a British bank deposit or building society account to be paid gross.

Some former colonial pensions are also exempt.

Double tax agreement

A person who is a resident of a country with which the UK has a double taxation agreement may be entitled to exemption or partial relief from UK Income Tax on certain kinds of income from UK sources and may also be exempt from UK tax on the disposal of assets. The conditions of exemption or relief vary from agreement to agreement. It may be a condition of the relief that the income is subject to tax in the other country.

NB: if, as sometimes happens, the foreign tax authority later makes an adjustment and the income ceases to be taxed in that country, you have an obligation under the self-assessment rules to notify HMRC.

Capital Gains Tax (CGT)

This is only charged if you are resident or ordinarily resident in the UK; so if you are in the position of being able to realize a gain, it is advisable to wait until you acquire non-resident status. However, to escape CGT, you must wait to dispose of any assets until after the tax year of your departure and must remain non-resident (and not ordinarily resident) in the UK for five full tax years after your departure. Different rules apply to gains made from the disposal of assets in a UK company; these are subject to normal CGT.

Inheritance Tax (IHT)

You escape tax only if:

- you were domiciled overseas for all of the immediate three years prior to death;
- you were resident overseas for more than three tax years in your final 20 years of life; and
- all your assets were overseas.

Even if you have been resident overseas for many years, if you do not have an overseas domicile you will have to pay IHT at the same rates as if you lived in the UK.

Domicile

Broadly speaking you are domiciled in the country in which you have your permanent home. Domicile is distinct from nationality or residence. A person may be resident in more than one country, but at any given time he or she can be domiciled in only one. If you are resident in a country and intend to spend the rest of your days there, it could be sensible to decide to change your domicile. If, however, you are resident but there is a chance that you might move, the country where you are living would not qualify as your domicile. This is a complicated area, where professional advice is recommended if you are contemplating a change.

UK pensions paid abroad

Any queries about your pension should be addressed to the International Payments Office, **International Pensions Centre: 0191 218 7777**; website: www.direct.gov.uk/pensions.

Technically your State pension could be subject to Income Tax, as it derives from the UK. In practice, if this is your only source of UK income, tax is unlikely to be charged. If you have an occupational pension, UK tax will normally be charged on the total of the two amounts.

Both State and occupational pensions may be paid to you in any country. If you are planning to retire to Australia, Canada, New Zealand or South Africa, it would be advisable to check on the up-to-date position regarding any annual increases you would expect to receive to your pension. Some people have found the level of their pension frozen at the date they left the UK, while others have been liable for unexpected tax overseas.

If the country where you are living has a double tax agreement with the UK, as previously explained, your income may be taxed there – and not in the UK. The UK now has a double tax agreement with most countries. For further information, check the position with your local tax office.

If your pension is taxed in the UK, you will be able to claim your personal allowance as an offset.

Health care overseas

People retiring to another EU country before state retirement age can apply for a form E106, which will entitle them to state health care in that country on the same basis as for local people. An E106 is valid only for a maximum of two and a half years, after which it is usually necessary to take out private insurance cover until State retirement age is reached. More information and a form are available from **DWP Overseas Contributions:** 0845 915 4811; website: www.dwp.gov.uk/international/further-help-and-advice.

Thereafter, UK pensioners can request the International Pensions Centre at Newcastle (see under 'UK pensions paid abroad' above) for a form E121, entitling them and their dependants to state health care as provided by the country in which they are living.

Useful reading

Residents and Non Residents – Liability to Tax in the UK, (IR20) available from any tax office.

Leaflet SA29, *Your Social Security Insurance, Benefits and Health Care Rights in the European Community*, contains essential information about what to do if you retire to another EU country. It is available from any social security or Jobcentre Plus office or website: www. jobcentreplus.gov.uk.

Chapter Five
Investment

Small opportunities are often the beginning of great enterprises. DEMOSTHENES (384 BC – 322 BC)

Investing is something everyone should consider, whatever age they are. Most people have some form of savings because such funds tend to be for short-term goals such as a holiday, a new car, special family occasions or an emergency. Investing however is for the longer term. As a general rule, you are in a position to start investing if you have a cash cushion already set aside in an instant access savings account (or similar) equal to at least six month's expenditure, or £10,000, whichever is the higher.

If you feel you are in a position to tie up a sum of money you don't need and take some risk to get a better return, there are a number of ways to do this. In essence investments involve balancing the risk of a short-term loss against the chance of a long-term gain. Just as no one is exactly the same, each person has a different attitude to risk. If you have a qualified financial adviser, he can help you determine your risk profile. As there are so many different types of investment, and each offers a different route to growth, it is important to define exactly what you're investing for.

Potential gains over the long term can be much higher than you might at first think. The most important thing is to get the balance right. You will read many articles on the subject of financial planning for retirement that concentrate on ways of boosting your immediate income. Although this would compensate for your loss of earnings, this could be misleading and short-sighted advice. A more critical consideration must be to safeguard your long-term security. Statistics show that an ever growing number of people live for 20 years or more after they retire. Your investment strategy must be aimed not just for your 60s and 70s but also for your 80s or even your 90s.

Inflation is another essential factor that must be taken into account. People on fixed incomes are the hardest hit when inflation rises. So many people have suffered as a result of their savings being slashed in value. Even when inflation rates are low it takes its toll to an alarming extent. The good news is that there's plenty that can be done to make what money you have work hard for you, so it is worth spending some time reviewing all your options.

Sources of investable funds

Possible sources of quite significant capital include:

- Commuted lump sum from your pension. There is now one set of rules for all types of pension scheme, with members allowed a maximum of 25 per cent of their pension fund or 25 per cent of their lifetime limit, whichever is lower. There is no tax to pay when you receive the money.

- Insurance policies designed to mature around your retirement. These are normally tax-free.

- Profits on your home, if you sell it and move to smaller, less expensive accommodation. Provided this is your main home, there is no capital gains tax to pay.

- Redundancy money, golden handshake or other farewell gift from your employer. You are allowed £30,000 redundancy money free of tax. The same is usually true of other severance pay up to £30,000, but there can be tax if, however worded, your employment contract indicates that these are deferred earnings.

- Sale of SAYE and other share option schemes. The tax rules vary according to the type of scheme, the date the options were acquired and how long the shares were held before disposal. Since the rules are liable to change with each Budget statement, for further information see HMRC website: www.hmrc.gov.uk.

General investment strategy

Investments differ in their aims, their tax treatment and the amount of risk involved. One or two categories are best suited to the wealthy who can afford to take significant risks. Others, such as certain types of National Savings, would be more appropriate for the less affluent. The aim for most people is to acquire a balanced portfolio: in other words, a mix of investments variously designed to provide some income to supplement your pension and also some capital appreciation to maintain your standard of living in the long term.

Except for annuities, National Savings & Investments and property, which have sections to themselves, the different types of investment are listed by groups, as follows:

- variable interest accounts;
- fixed interest securities;
- equities;
- long-term lock-ups.

As a general strategy and particularly in the current economic climate, it is a good idea to mix and match, so your investments are spread across several groups.

Annuities

Definition

In essence an annuity is a contract with an insurance company to pay you an income for the rest of your life in return for you handing over your pension savings. The money is paid to you by the annuity provider (insurer) and can be monthly, quarterly or annually. These will remain exactly the same year in, year out. Once you've chosen your annuity provider, you cannot change your mind. That is why it is so important to think carefully before deciding which product to choose. Payments are calculated according to life expectancy tables, and for this reason annuities are not such an attractive investment for those under 70. Other than your age, the key factor affecting the amount you will receive in payments is the level of interest rates at the time you buy: the higher these are, the more you will receive.

Savers are no longer forced to use most of their pension to buy a guaranteed income for life. Rules requiring most people to spend three-quarters of their pension savings on annuities have been scrapped. From April 2011 pensioners can delay the purchase for as long as they wish or not buy one at all. This means they could pass their pension savings on to their heirs.

However, should you wish to purchase an annuity it would probably give you more immediate income than any other form of investment. But whether you actually get good value depends on how long you live. When you die, your capital will be gone and there will be no more payments. So if you die a short while after signing the contract, it will represent very bad value indeed. On the other hand, if you live a very long time, you may more than recoup your original capital. As a precaution against early death, it is possible to take out a capital-protected annuity, an annuity that includes a guaranteed payment period, or an annuity that transfers to your partner for the duration of his or her life. Any of these options will reduce the annuity income you receive but could be worth considering if your primary concern is to give your partner (or other beneficiaries) added security.

Most annuities fall into one of two main categories: conventional and investment-linked.

Conventional/level annuities

You will receive a fixed income for life – either at one level or varying (linked to inflation). This is the simplest and most straightforward annuity available. Approximately 85 per cent of people choose this type because they have the benefit of certainty. You know what your income will be for the rest of your life. But you will no longer gain from the investment of your pension fund. They are not flexible, so if you die (even if this is after one payment) the fund is lost. Also, if the annuity rates are low at the time you lock into the scheme, your retirement income will be smaller than it possibly could be.

Investment-linked annuities

The amount you get for your annuity is dependent on the performance of one or more stock market type investments. These annuities expose your pension funds to the ups and downs of the stock market. There is the possibility of rising retirement income. You are taking the risk that you may get less for the hope you will get more. Income levels will fluctuate and reduce in poor investment conditions. There is however a minimum limit below which your annuity income cannot fall. This type of annuity should be considered only after taking independent financial advice, and by those who have other assets on which they can live should the income level drop.

Remember: it is your choice whether you go down the conventional annuity route or choose the investment-linked product. Whichever route you choose, there's no going back on your decision, so take your time.

There are a few variations on each type: some additions can be made to whichever option you choose.

Guaranteed annuity

These pay out for a set number of years, even if you die. Such guarantees reduce the income, but not dramatically if you're younger. If you die within the guarantee period, your nominee will receive the balance of the guarantee as gradual income.

Joint-life annuities

These annuities continue to pay out after one partner dies. They are particularly suitable if you are married or in a civil partnership, and more especially if one partner has no pension. But they come at a cost: you will receive a lower income level. Joint-life annuities pay out as long as one of a couple is living and you have a choice of percentages for the survivor's pension.

Escalating annuities

There is a conventional annuity which allows income to grow with inflation. This type is linked to a measure of inflation (like RPI) or set to rise by a certain percentage each year. These are known as inflation-linked annuities. Annuities can also be linked to the stock market through an investment annuity.

Enhanced/impaired annuities

These annuities offer extra cash if your life is likely to be shorter than average. Poor health can mean a richer annuity because the insurance company calculates the length of time you are likely to live. You might like to opt for this type even if you feel fit and don't smoke. Some 40 per cent of people should consider buying an enhanced annuity as it could make a huge difference to your income.

NB: don't forget that you can combine annuities. You do not have to use your pension pot for just one product. There are a number of imponderables however – factors about which you cannot ever be certain. These include how long you will live, whether inflation will increase or decrease, and whether your personal situation will change.

Variable annuities

These products are also known as 'third-way' products and guaranteed drawdown plans. They are sort of half-way between standard and investment annuities. They provide a guaranteed lifetime income which is payable regardless of investment returns. Also included are regular investment lock-ins, so if the fund increases so does the level of income. However, if the fund value falls, the income remains at the level of the last lock-in. Funds can be paid to beneficiaries on death. The guarantee depends on the financial strength and solvency of the insurance company. So the question is: how strong are the guarantees likely to be if the firm got into difficulties?

There are some caveats with these products, such as commission being paid to financial advisers who sell them, they are expensive and in many cases people would be better off with an annuity or an unsecured pension. Be careful and take specialist advice before considering this option.

Tax

Income tax on optional annuities is relatively low, as part of the income is allowed as a return on capital that is not taxable. Pension-linked annuities are fully taxable.

How to obtain

The annuity market is expanding rapidly and there is a vast choice of products. Specialists in annuity advice are:

Annuity Direct	0500 50 65 75; www.annuitydirect.co.uk
Annuity Advisor	0800 1444 144; www.annuity-advisor.co.uk
Annuity Bureau	0800 071 8111; www.annuity-bureau.co.uk
Annuities Online	0800 019 6629; www.annuities-online.com
Hargreaves Lansdown	0117 980 9940; www.h-l.co.uk/pensions
Origen Annuities	0845 603 0836; www.origenfsannuities.co.uk
William Burrows	020 7484 5366; www.williamburrows.com

You can buy an annuity either direct from an insurance company or via an intermediary, such as an independent financial adviser (IFA). But shop around, since as mentioned above the payments vary considerably. If you already have an IFA, he or she will talk you through the various options. Otherwise, **to find an IFA,** consult the professional advice website: www.unbiased.co.uk. Choose the search service you need, tick your requirements and receive details of appropriate, qualified advisers close to your home or office.

National Savings & Investments (NS&I)

NS&I is one of the biggest savings institutions in the country, guaranteed by the government, and all investments are backed by HM Treasury. It is extremely easy to invest in NS&I products, as all you need do is go to the Post Office for information or telephone **NS&I Customer Enquiries:** 0500 007 007 or visit the website: www.nsandi.com. Most types of investment offered by NS&I are broadly similar to those provided by banks and other financial bodies.

NS&I Savings Certificates, of which there are two types (fixed interest and index-linked), are free of tax. Although in most cases they do not pay a particularly high rate of interest, any investment that is tax-free is worth considering. For non-taxpayers who invest in NS&I products there is no need to complete an HM Revenue & Customs (HMRC) form to receive their money in full, as this is automatic.

The main investments offered by National Savings & Investments are:

Easy Access Savings Account. This is an easy way to build up your savings, with instant access to your money and the option to save regularly by standing order. You can open one with £100 and invest up to £2 million. The account offers variable, tiered rates of interest and allows instant access through the Post Office or cash machines.

Income Bonds. These are worth considering if you are interested in earning monthly income and having easy access to your money. They pay fairly attractive, variable, tiered rates of interest, increasing with larger investments. Interest is taxable, but paid in full without deduction of tax at source. You can invest between £500 and £1 million. There is no set term for the investment.

Fixed Interest Savings Certificates. These will earn you guaranteed and tax-free returns. They offer a moderate rate of interest. You can invest from £100 to £15,000 per issue. There are two terms: two years and five years. For maximum benefit, you must hold the certificates for five years.

Inflation-beating Savings Certificates. These are worth considering if you want to make sure your investment grows ahead of inflation, tax-free. You can invest from £100 to £15,000 per issue and they are not tied in to the tax year, unlike ISAs. There is a fixed rate of interest, index-linked to the Retail Prices Index. No index-linking or interest will be earned on certificates cashed in within one year of purchase. Certificates must be retained for either three or five years. Interest is tax-free.

Children's Bonus Bonds. These are for those who want to give a child a long-term tax-free investment. Bonds are sold in multiples of £25, and the maximum purchase per child is £3,000 for each issue. The investment term is five years at a time until the 21st birthday. Interest rates are fixed for five years at a time plus a guaranteed bonus. These are tax-free for parents and children and need not be declared to HMRC.

Complaints

If you have a complaint about any NS&I product, you should raise this with the Director of Savings. Should the matter not be resolved to your satisfaction you can contact the **Financial Ombudsman Service:** 0845 080 1800; website: www.financial-ombudsman.org.uk.

The safety of your investment

Investors are protected by the legislative framework in which societies operate and, in common with bank customers, their money (up to a maximum of £50,000) is protected under the **Financial Services Compensation Scheme (FSCS).** For further details, contact: 020 7892 7300; website: www.fscs.org.uk.

Variable interest accounts

Most banks and building societies offer interest-bearing current accounts. Because there are around 54 million current accounts in the UK, there is a lot of competition amongst banks to get business and persuade people to switch their accounts. The difference between in-credit and overdraft rates vary considerably so check very carefully what charges apply before you move. Another point to investigate is whether there is a fixed monthly or other charge. This can sometimes change at fairly short notice. You should check your monthly statement carefully and consider moving your account if you are dissatisfied. Banks and building societies frequently introduce new accounts with introductory bonuses, which are then slashed in value after a few months. Although this could equally apply to internet accounts, they could still be worth investigating as, generally speaking, they tend to offer more competitive rates.

Although keeping track may be fairly time-consuming, at least comparing the rates offered by different savings institutions has become very much easier, as all advertisements for savings products must now quote the annual equivalent rate (AER). Unlike the former variety of ways of expressing interest rates, the AER provides a true comparison taking into account the frequency of interest payments and whether or not interest is compounded.

Definition

Other than the interest-bearing current accounts described above, these are all savings accounts of one form or another, arranged with banks, building societies, the National Savings & Investments Bank, and some financial institutions that operate such accounts jointly with banks. The accounts include, among others, instant access accounts, high interest accounts and fixed-term savings accounts.

Your money collects interest while it is in the account, which may be automatically credited to your account or for which you may receive a regular cheque. Some institutions pay interest annually; others – on some or all of their accounts – will pay it monthly. If you have a preference, this is a point to check.

Although you may get a poor return on your money when interest rates drop, your savings will nearly always be safe, as you are not taking any kind of investment risk. Moreover, provided you deal with an authorized bank, up to £50,000 of your money will be 100 per cent protected under the **Financial Services Compensation Scheme**. Contact: 020 7892 7300; website: www.fscs.org.uk

Access

Access to your money depends on the type of account you choose: you may have an ATM card and/or chequebook and withdraw your money when you want; you may have to give a week's notice or slightly longer; or, if you enter into a term account, you will have to leave your money deposited for the agreed specified period. In general, accounts where a slightly longer period of notice is required earn a better rate of interest.

Sum deposited

You can open a savings account with as little as £1. For certain types of account, the minimum investment could be anything from £500 to about £5,000. The terms tend to vary according to how keen the institutions are, at a given time, to attract small investors.

Tax

With the exception of cash ISAs which are tax-free, and of the National Savings & Investments Bank, where interest is paid gross, tax is deducted at source – so you can spend the money without worrying about the tax implications. However, you must enter the interest on your tax return and, if you are a higher-rate taxpayer, you will have additional liability.

Basic-rate taxpayers pay 20 per cent on their bank and building society interest. Higher-rate taxpayers pay 40 per cent. Non-taxpayers can arrange to have their interest paid in full by completing a certificate (R85, available from HMRC or the bank) that enables the financial institution to pay the interest gross. If you largely rely on your savings income and believe you are or have been paying excess tax, you can reclaim this from HMRC. For further information, see 'Income Tax on savings' in Chapter 4.

NB: savers with cash ISAs should soon find it quicker to transfer their money between providers since the OFT ruled on a 'super complaint' issued by the consumer body Consumer Focus. The main complaint was the lengthy delays many ISA holders experienced in transferring their money during the 'ISA season' each Spring. Transfer times should improve from around 23 to 15 days since this ruling. However, reductions in transfer time were not effective before December 2010. If you are transferring your savings from one account to another, keep an eye on this 15-day transfer guideline.

Choosing a savings account

There are two main areas of choice: the type of savings account and where to invest your money. The relative attractions of the different types of account and of the institutions themselves can vary according to the terms being offered at the time. Generally speaking, however, the basic points are as follows.

Instant access savings account

This attracts a relatively low rate of interest, but it is both easy to set up and very flexible, as you can add small or large savings when you like and can usually withdraw your money without any notice. It is an excellent temporary home for your cash if you are saving short-term for, say, a holiday. However, it is not recommended as a long-term savings plan.

High interest savings account

Your money earns a higher rate of interest than it would in an ordinary savings account. However, to open a high interest account you will need to deposit a minimum sum, which could be £500 to £1,000. Although you can always add to this amount, if your balance drops below the required minimum your money will immediately stop earning the higher interest rate. Terms vary between providers. There may be a minimum and/or maximum monthly sum you can pay into the account. Also, some accounts have a fixed term, at the end of which your money will no longer earn the more favourable rate of interest.

Fixed-term savings account

You deposit your money for an agreed period of time, which can vary from a few months to over a year. In return for this commitment, you will normally be paid a superior rate of interest. As with high interest accounts, there is a minimum investment: roughly £1,500 to £10,000. If you need to withdraw your money before the end of the agreed term, there are usually hefty penalties. Before entering into a term account, you need to be sure that you can afford to leave the money in the account. Additionally, you will need to take a view about interest rates: if they are generally low, your money may be better invested elsewhere.

Equity-linked savings account

This offers a potentially better rate of return, as the interest is calculated in line with the growth in the stock market. Should the market fall, you may lose the interest, but your capital should normally remain protected. The minimum investment varies from about £500 to £5,000 and, depending on the institution, the money may need to remain deposited for perhaps as much as five years. Do ensure you fully understand all the terms and conditions as rules vary.

ISA savings

See later in this chapter, page 120.

Information

For banks, enquire direct at your nearest high street branch. There will be leaflets available, describing the different accounts in detail, or if you have any questions you can ask to see your bank manager. You can also investigate the other banks to see whether they offer better terms. For building societies, enquire at any building society branch. There is such a wide range of these that it is advisable to look at a number of them, as the terms and conditions may vary quite widely.

The **Building Societies Association** offers a free range of helpful leaflets and information sheets, including: *Lost Savings? Taxation of Building Society Interest*; *Individual Savings Accounts and Building Societies*; and *The Child Trust Fund*. A list of members, giving head office addresses and telephone numbers, is also available. All leaflets can be ordered by calling the Consumer Helpline: 020 7520 5900; website: www.bsa.org.uk.

The safety of your investment

Investors are protected by the legislative framework in which societies operate and, in common with bank customers, their money (up to a maximum of £50,000) is protected under the **Financial Services Compensation Scheme (FSCS)**. Contact: 020 7892 7300; website: www.fscs.org.uk.

Complaints

If you have a complaint against a bank or building society, you can appeal to the **Financial Ombudsman Service (FOS)** to investigate the matter, provided the complaint has already been taken through the particular institution's own internal disputes procedure – or after eight weeks if the problem has not been resolved – and provided the matter is within the scope of the Ombudsman Scheme. Generally speaking, the FOS can investigate complaints about the way a bank or building society has handled some matter relating to its services to customers. Contact: 0845 080 1800; website: www.financial-ombudsman.org.uk.

Fixed interest securities

In contrast to variable interest accounts, fixed interest securities pay interest at a rate that does not change with any external variable. The coupon payments are known in advance. Coupons are almost always all for the same amount and paid at regular intervals, regardless of what happens to interest rates generally. There are two risks with fixed income securities: credit risk and interest rate risk.

Credit risk is one of the main determinants of the price of a bond. The price of a debt security can be explained as the present value of the payments (of interest and repayment of principal) that will be made. Credit risk is an issue for lenders such as banks. In this context, the key is the risk of losses to the bank so correlation with the bank's other lending is what matters, not correlation with debt available in the market.

Interest rate risk is simply the risk to which a portfolio or institution is exposed because future interest rates are uncertain. Bond prices are interest rate sensitive so if rates rise, then the present value of a bond will fall sharply. This can also be thought of in terms of market rates: if interest rates rise, then the price of a bond will have to fall for the yield to match the new market rates. The longer the duration of a bond, the more sensitive it will be to movements in interest rates. Banks can have significant interest rate risk: they may have depositors locked into fixed rates and borrowers on floating rates or vice versa. Interest rate risk can be hedged using swaps and interest rate-based derivatives.

If you buy when the fixed rate is high and interest rates fall, you will nevertheless continue to be paid interest at the high rate specified in the contract note. However, if interest rates rise above the level when you bought, you will not benefit from the increase. Generally these securities give high income but only modest, if any, capital appreciation. The list includes high interest gilts, permanent interest-bearing shares, local authority bonds and stock exchange loans, debentures and preference shares.

Gilt-edged securities

Definition

Gilts, or gilt edged securities, are bonds issued by the UK government that offer the investor a fixed interest rate for a predetermined, set time. Investment in gilts is best suited to people who desire a fixed, predictable income with a return of capital guaranteed. While their value, like shares, are prone to fluctuation, gilts are well-known for their security and are viewed as the safest of investments, hence their original name, 'gilt edged securities'. While stock has a redemption date, typically between five and 25 years, it can be sold at any time for the present market price. Investors are not tied down and there are no penalties for selling the stock. By the time the redemption date is reached, the government will pay the investor the face value of the stock, which could be more or less than the original price, providing a capital gain or loss.

You can buy and sell gilts on the stock market or by using the Bank of England's postal dealing service. Gilt value is influenced by many factors, including inflation, other competing forms of investment and the time left till maturity. Buying gilts is best done when interest rates are high and look likely to fall. When general interest rates fall, the value of the stock will rise and can be sold profitably.

There are many types of UK gilts on offer. For example, a stock may be quoted as 10 per cent Treasury Stock 2015, 99½–100¼. In plain English, this means the following:

- 10 per cent represents the interest you will be paid. The rate is fixed and will not vary, whatever happens to interest rates generally. You will receive the interest payment twice-yearly, 5 per cent each time.
- You are buying Treasury Stock.
- The maturity date is 2015.
- To buy the stock, you will have to pay £100.25p (ie 100¼).
- If you want to sell the stock, the market price you will get is £99.50 (ie 99½).

In addition, when buying or selling, consideration must be given to the accrued interest that will have to be added to or subtracted from the price quoted. Gilts are complicated by the fact that you can either retain them until their maturity date, in which case the government will return the capital in full, or sell them on the London Stock Exchange at market value.

Index-linked gilts

The first index-linked gilt issue was in 1981. These inflation-indexed bonds were originally for institutional investors. Index-linked gilts differ from conventional gilts in that both the semi-annual coupon payments and the principal payment are adjusted in line with movements in the RPI as their value is geared to the cost of living. They are most valuable when inflation is high but are even more sensitive than other gilts to optimum timing when buying or selling.

Recently UK index-linked gilts have slumped because of fears that existing issuance will become linked to the consumer price index rather than the retail price index. This is as a result of the government having announced that private sector final salary pension schemes are to be linked to the CPI rather than the RPI to bring them in line with public sector arrangements, following the Emergency Budget changes announced in June 2010. RPI has been 0.55 per cent higher than CPI over the last 20 years, so although the change helps pension funds cut their deficits by an estimated £100 billion, investors are taking a hit as a result.

Tax

Gilt interest from whatever source is paid gross. Gross payment does not mean that you avoid paying tax, simply that you must allow for a future tax bill before spending the money. Recipients who prefer to receive the money net of tax can request for this to be arranged. A particular attraction of gilts is that no capital gains tax is charged on any profit you may have made, but equally no relief is allowed for any loss.

How to buy

You can buy gilts through banks, building societies, a stockbroker or a financial intermediary, or you can purchase them through **Computershare Investor Services**: 0870 703 0143; website: www.uk.computershare.com In all cases, you will be charged commission. Prices of gilts are published every day in all the quality newspapers under the heading 'British Funds'. You may also find it helpful to refer to the section headed 'Bonds' on page 126.

Assessment

Gilts normally pay reasonably good interest and offer excellent security, in that they are backed by the government. You can sell at very short notice, and the stock is normally accepted by banks as security for loans, if you want to run an overdraft. However, gilts are not a game for amateurs as, if you buy or sell at the wrong time, you could lose money; and, if you hold your stock to redemption, inflation could take its toll on your original investment. Index-linked gilts, which overcome the inflation problem, are generally speaking a better investment for higher-rate taxpayers – not least because the interest paid is very low.

Gilt plans

This is a technique for linking the purchase of gilt-edged securities and with-profit life insurance policies to provide security of capital and income over a 10- to 20-year period. It is a popular investment for the commuted lump sum taken on retirement. These plans are normally obtainable from financial intermediaries, who should be authorized by the Financial Services Authority (FSA).

Permanent interest-bearing shares (PIBS)

These are a form of investment offered by some building societies to financial institutions and private investors as a means of raising share capital. They have several features in common with gilts, as follows. They pay a fixed rate of interest that is set at the date of issue; this is likely to be on the high side when interest rates generally are low and on the low side when interest rates are high. The interest is usually paid twice-yearly and – again, similarly to gilts – there is no Stamp Duty to pay or Capital Gains Tax on profits. Despite the fact that PIBS are issued by building societies, they are very different from normal building society investments and have generally been rated as being in the medium to high risk category. Anyone thinking of investing their money should seek professional advice. To buy the shares, you will need to go to a stockbroker or financial adviser.

Equities

These are all stocks and shares, purchased in different ways and involving varying degrees of risk. They are designed to achieve capital appreciation as well as give you some regular income. Most allow you to get your money out within a week. Today, the number of shareholders is estimated at well over 15 million people. Equity securities usually provide steady income as dividends but there is always some risk. They may fluctuate significantly in their market value with the ups and downs in the economic cycle and the fortunes of the issuing firm. Investing has become very much easier, largely as a result of the increase in the number of internet and telephone share-dealing facilities.

For those who believe in caution, the gamble can be substantially reduced by avoiding obviously speculative investments and by choosing a spread of investments, rather than putting all your eggs in one basket. Equities include ordinary shares, unit trusts, OEICs (see below), investment trusts and REITs.

Unit trusts and OEICs

Definition

Unit trusts and OEICs (open-ended investment companies, a modern equivalent of unit trusts) are forms of shared investments, or funds, that allow you to pool your money with thousands of other people and invest in world stock markets. Your money is pooled in a fund run by professional managers, who invest the capital in a wide range of assets including equities, bonds and cash. The advantages are that it is usually less risky than buying individual shares, it is simple to understand, you get professional management and there are no day-to-day decisions to make. Additionally, every fund is required by law to have a trustee (called a 'depository' in the case of OEICs) to protect investors' interests.

Unit trusts have proved incredibly popular because your money is invested in a broad spread of shares and your risk is reduced. But they are rapidly being replaced by the OEIC (pronounced 'oik'). The FSA's rules governing which types of fund can convert to OEICS were relaxed in 2001 and since then the majority of fund management groups have converted their unit trusts to OEICs or launched such funds.

The minimum investment in some of the more popular funds can be as little as £25 a month or a £500 lump sum; both are relatively painless and a good way to get on the first rung of investing in the stock market. You could, however, invest a much higher amount. Investors' contributions to the fund are divided into units (shares in OEICs) in proportion to the amount they have invested. Unit trusts and OEICs are both open-ended investments. As with ordinary shares, you can sell all or some of your investment by telling the fund manager that you wish to do so. The value of the shares you own in an OEIC, or units in a unit trust, always reflects the value of the fund's assets.

The key differences between the two are:

- *Pricing:* when investing in unit trusts, you buy units at the offer price and sell at the lower bid price. The difference in the two prices is known as the spread. To make a return the bid price must rise above the offer before you sell the units. An OEIC fund contrastingly has a single price, directly linked to the value of the fund's underlying investments. All shares are bought and sold at this single price. An OEIC is sometimes described as a 'what you see is what you get' product.

- *Flexibility:* an OEIC fund offers different types of share or sub fund to suit different types of investor. The expertise of different fund management teams can be combined to benefit both large and small investors. There is less paperwork as each OEIC will produce one report and accounts for all sub funds.

- *Complexity:* unit trusts are, legally, much more complex, which is one of the reasons for their rapid conversion to OEICs. Unit trusts allow an investor to participate in the assets of the trust without actually owning any. Investors in an OEIC buy shares in that investment company.

- *Management:* with unit trusts, the fund's assets are protected by an independent trustee and managed by a fund manager. OEICs are protected by an independent depository and managed by an authorized corporate director.

- *Charges:* unit trusts and OEICs usually have an up-front buying charge, typically 3–5 per cent and an annual management fee of between 0.5 and 1.5 per cent. It is possible to reduce these charges by investing through a discount broker or fund supermarket, but bear in mind that this means acting without financial advice. Charges on OEICs are relatively transparent, shown as a separate item on your transaction statement.

How to obtain

Units and shares can be purchased from banks, building societies, insurance companies, stockbrokers, specialist investment fund providers and independent financial advisers, directly from the management group and via the internet. Some firms advertise in the national press and financial magazines and also, increasingly, on the internet. Some have their own sales forces. Many of the larger firms may use all these methods. You may be asked to complete a form – stating how much you want to invest in which particular fund – and then return it to the company with your cheque. Alternatively, you may be able to deal over the telephone or internet.

For a list of unit trusts and OEICs you can look in the *Financial Times,* or to obtain information and various fact sheets on such topics as ISAs, ethical investment, unit trusts and tax contact **Investment Management Association:** 020 7831 0898; website: www.investmentuk.org. More information is available on the following websites:

www.thisismoney.co.uk/investing

www.moneyweek.com

www.investment-advice.org.uk

www.investorschronicle.co.uk

www.investmentfunds.org.uk

Tables comparing the performance of the various funds are published in specialist magazines or on websites such as *Money Management, Money*

Observer and *What Investment*. With over 2,000 funds from which to choose, it is important to get independent professional advice. For further information on where to obtain this, see Chapter 6, Financial Advisers.

However, should the DIY approach appeal to you, and developing skills to trade stock markets yourself is something you would consider, maybe the organization **Knowledge to Action Ltd** is for you. This company offers courses teaching the skills required to trade on the stock market. The courses are held at various locations around the country. You can find out what it means to be a trader and how it could boost your income by contacting: 020 7751 8924; website: www.knowledgetoaction.co.uk.

Tax

Units and shares invested through an ISA have special advantages (see 'Individual Savings Account (ISA)', below). Otherwise, the tax treatment is identical to that of ordinary shares.

Assessment

Unit trusts and OEICs are an ideal method for smaller investors to buy stocks and shares: both less risky and easier. This applies especially to tracker funds, which have the added advantage that charges are normally very low. Some of the more specialist funds are also suitable for those with a significant investment portfolio.

Complaints

Complaints about unit trusts and OEICs are handled by the **Financial Ombudsman Service (FOS)**. It has the power to order awards of up to £100,000. Before approaching the FOS, you must first try to resolve the problem with the management company direct via its internal complaints procedure. If you remain dissatisfied, the company should advise you of your right to refer the matter to the FOS. Contact: 0845 080 1800; website: www.financial-ombudsman.org.uk.

The safety of your investment

Investors are protected by the legislative framework in which societies operate and, in common with bank customers, their money (up to a maximum of £50,000) is protected under the **Financial Services Compensation Scheme (FSCS)**. Contact: 020 7892 7300; website: www. fscs.org.uk.

Ordinary shares listed on the London Stock Exchange

Definition

Public companies issue shares as a way of raising money. When you buy shares and become a shareholder in a company, you own a small part of the business and are entitled to participate in its profits through a dividend, which is normally paid six-monthly. Dividends go up and down according to how well the company is doing, and it is possible that in a bad year no dividends at all will be paid. However, in good years, dividends can increase very substantially.

The money you invest is unsecured. This means that, quite apart from any dividends, your capital could be reduced in value – or if the company goes bankrupt you could lose the lot. Against this, if the company performs well you could substantially increase your wealth. The value of a company's shares is decided by the stock market. Thousands of large and small investors are taking a view on each company's prospects, and this creates the market price. The price of a share can fluctuate daily, and this will affect both how much you have to pay if you want to buy and how much you will make (or lose) if you want to sell. You could visit the **London Stock Exchange** website, www.londonstockexchange.com, to find a list of brokers in your area who would be willing to deal for you. Alternatively, you can go to the securities department of your bank or to one of the authorized share shops, which will place the order for you.

Whether you use a stockbroker, a share shop, a telephone share-dealing service or the internet, you will be charged both commission and Stamp Duty, which is currently 0.5 per cent. Unless you use a nominee account (see below), you will be issued with a share certificate that you or your financial adviser must keep, as you will have to produce it when you wish to sell all or part of your holding. It is likely, when approaching a stockbroker or other share-dealing service, that you will be asked to deposit money for your investment up front or advised that you should use a nominee account. This is because of the introduction of several new systems, designed to speed up and streamline the share-dealing process.

There are three types of share, all quoted on the London Stock Exchange, that are potentially suitable for small investors. These are investment companies, REITs and convertible loan stocks. Other possibilities, but only for those who can afford more risky investments, are zero coupon loan stocks and warrants:

> *Investment companies* are companies that invest in the shares of other companies. They pool investors' money and so enable those with

quite small amounts to spread the risk by gaining exposure to a wide portfolio of shares, run by a professional fund manager. There are over 300 different companies from which to choose. For a range of fact sheets on investment companies, contact the **Association of Investment Companies**: 020 7282 5555; website: www.theaic.co.uk.

Real estate investment trusts (REITs). This type of fund, quoted on the London Stock Exchange, operates similarly to investment trusts. It pools investors' money and invests it for them collectively in commercial and residential property. They offer individuals a cheap, simple and potentially less risky way of buying shares in a spread of properties, with the added attraction that the funds themselves are more tax-efficient, as both rental income and profits from sales are tax-free within the fund. Also, if wanted, REITs can be held within an ISA or Self-Invested Personal Pension (SIPP). There are numerous UK companies that have converted to REIT status. Stockbrokers and independent financial advisers are able to provide information and it is recommended that professional advice is taken before investing.

Convertible loan stocks give you a fixed guaranteed income for a certain length of time and offer you the opportunity to convert them into ordinary shares. While capital appreciation prospects are lower, the advantage of convertible loans is that they usually provide significantly higher income than ordinary dividends. They are also allowable for ISAs.

Zero coupon loan stocks provide no income during their life but pay an enhanced capital sum on maturity. They would normally only be recommended for higher-rate taxpayers, and professional advice is strongly recommended.

Warrants are issued by companies or investment trusts to existing shareholders either at launch or by way of an additional bonus. Each warrant carries the right of the shareholder to purchase additional shares at a predetermined price on specific dates in the future. Warrants command their own price on the stock market. They are a high-risk investment, and professional advice is essential.

Tax

All UK shares pay dividends net of 10 per cent Corporation Tax. Basic-rate and non-taxpayers have no further liability to income tax. Higher-rate taxpayers must pay further Income Tax at 22 per cent. Quite apart from Income Tax, if during the year you make profits by selling shares that in total exceed £10,100 (the annual exempt amount for an individual in 2010/11) you will be liable for Capital Gains Tax, which is now calculated at a flat rate of 28 per cent.

Assessment

Although dividend payments generally start low, in good companies they are likely to increase over the years and so provide a first-class hedge against inflation. The best equities are an excellent investment. In others, you can lose all your money. Good advice is critical, as this is a high-risk, high-reward market.

A green option? Ethical and sustainable investments

Protecting the planet and investing money for profit are not always compatible. However, consider the option offered by **Living Investments UK**. This company works with private and institutional investors, building portfolios of commercially sustainable teak plantations that benefit the planet and provide the potential to earn excellent returns for investors over the medium to long term. Investors lease plots of forest for the time it takes the trees to mature. When the trees are thinned/felled (after eight years of ownership) revenue is generated. For further information see website: www. livinginvestmentsuk.com

Individual Savings Account (ISA)

Definition

ISAs are savings accounts launched in April 1999 as a replacement for PEPs and TESSAs. They contain many of the same advantages in that all income and gains generated in the account are tax free. They are simply a tax-free savings account. There is a subscription limit. There are two types of ISA: cash ISAs and stocks and shares ISAs. Since 6 April 2010 it has been possible for anyone, whatever age, to invest £5,100 in a cash ISA and up to £10,200 in a stocks and shares ISA.

From 6 April 2011 the ISA limits increase in line with the RPI on an annual basis. In the event that the RPI is negative, the ISA limits will remain unchanged. The cash ISA limit remains half the value of the stocks and shares ISA limit.

Tax

ISAs are completely free of all Income Tax and Capital Gains Tax. You should be aware that a 20 per cent charge is levied on all interest accruing from non-invested money held in an ISA that is not specifically a cash ISA.

Assessment

ISAs offer a simple, flexible way of starting, or improving, a savings plan, although sadly they are no longer as attractive as they once were, and some readers may now find better homes for investing their money. While cash ISAs remain useful, as all interest is tax-free, stocks and shares ISAs – while still potentially worthwhile for higher-rate taxpayers – offer fewer advantages to basic-rate taxpayers as a result of the charges and the removal of the dividend tax credit.

Child Trust Funds

Children born after December 2010 are not eligible for a Child Trust Fund. However, accounts set up for eligible children will continue to benefit from tax free investment growth. Withdrawals will not be possible until the child reaches 18. The child, friends and family will be able to contribute £1,200 per year and it will still be possible to change the type of account and move it to another provider. See website: www.childtrustfund.gov.uk.

Long-term lock-ups

Certain types of investment, mostly offered by insurance companies, provide fairly high guaranteed growth in exchange for your undertaking to leave a lump sum with them or to pay regular premiums for a fixed period, usually five years or longer. The list includes life assurance policies, investment bonds and some types of National Savings Certificates.

Life assurance policies

Definition

Life assurance can provide you with one of two main benefits: it can either provide your successors with money when you die or it can be used as a savings plan to provide you with a lump sum (or income) on a fixed date. In the past, it was very much an 'either or' situation: you chose whichever type of policy suited you and the insurance company paid out accordingly. In recent years, however, both types of scheme have become more flexible, and many policies allow you to incorporate features of the other. This can have great advantages from the point of view of enabling you to 'have your cake and eat it', but the result is that some of the definitions appear a bit contradictory. There are three basic types of life assurance: whole life policies, term policies and endowment policies:

1 *Whole life policies* are designed to pay out on your death. In its most straightforward form, the scheme works as follows: you pay a premium every year and, when you die, your beneficiaries receive the money. As with an ordinary household policy, the insurance holds good only if you continue the payments. If one year you did not pay and were to die, the policy could be void and your successors would receive nothing.

2 *Term policies* involve a definite commitment. As opposed to paying premiums every year, you elect to make regular payments for an agreed period, for example until such time as your children have completed their education, say eight years. If you die during this period, your family will be paid the agreed sum in full. If you die after the end of the term (when you have stopped making payments), your family will normally receive nothing.

3 *Endowment policies* are essentially savings plans. You sign a contract to pay regular premiums over a number of years and in exchange receive a lump sum on a specific date. Most endowment policies are written for periods varying from 10 to 25 years. Once you have committed yourself, you have to go on paying every year (as with term assurance). There are heavy penalties if, having paid for a number of years, you decide that you no longer wish to continue.

An important feature of endowment policies is that they are linked in with death cover. If you die before the policy matures, the remaining payments are excused and your successors will be paid a lump sum on your death. Endowment policies have long been a popular way of making extra financial provision for retirement. They combine the advantages of guaranteeing you a lump sum with a built-in life assurance provision. The amount of money you stand to receive, however, can vary hugely, depending on the charges and how generous a bonus the insurance company feels it can afford on the policy's maturity. Over the past few years, pay-outs have been considerably lower than their earlier projections might have suggested. Aim to compare at least three policies before choosing.

Options

Both whole life policies and endowment policies offer two basic options: with profits or without profits. Very briefly the difference is as follows:

- *Without profits.* This is sometimes known as 'guaranteed sum assured'. What it means is that the insurance company guarantees you a specific fixed sum (provided of course you meet the various terms and conditions). You know the amount in advance and this is the sum you – or your successors – will be paid.

- *With profits.* You are paid a guaranteed fixed sum plus an addition, based on the profits that the insurance company has made by investing your annual or monthly payments. The basic premiums are higher and, by definition, the profits element is not known in advance. If the insurance company has invested your money wisely, a 'with profits' policy provides a useful hedge against inflation. If its investment policy is mediocre, you could have paid higher premiums for very little extra return.

- *Unit linked.* This is a refinement of the 'with profits' policy, in that the investment element of the policy is linked in with a unit trust.

Other basics

Premiums can normally be paid monthly or annually, as you prefer. The size of premium varies enormously, depending on the type of policy you choose and the amount of cover you want. Also, of course, some insurance companies are more competitive than others. As a generalization, higher premiums tend to give better value, as relatively less of your contribution is swallowed up in administrative costs.

As a condition of insuring you, some policies require that you have a medical check. This is more likely to apply if very large sums are involved. More usually, all that is required is that you fill in and sign a declaration of health. It is very important that this should be completed honestly: if you make a claim on your policy and it is subsequently discovered that you gave misleading information, your policy could be declared void and the insurance company could refuse to pay.

Many insurance companies offer a better deal if you are a non-smoker. Some also offer more generous terms if you are teetotal. Women generally pay less than men of the same age because of their longer life expectancy.

How to obtain

Policies are usually available through banks, insurance companies, independent financial advisers (IFAs) and building societies. The biggest problem for most people is the sheer volume of choice. Another difficulty can be understanding the small print: terms and conditions that sound very similar may obscure important differences that could affect your benefit. An accountant could advise you, in general terms, whether you are being offered a good deal or otherwise. However, if it is a question of choosing a specific policy best suited to your requirements, it is usually advisable to consult an IFA. **For help in finding an IFA in your area**, see website www.unbiased.co. uk. See also Chapter 6, Financial Advisers.

Disclosure rules

Advisers selling financial products have to abide by a set of disclosure rules, requiring them to give clients certain essential information before a contract is signed. Although for a number of years the requirements have included the provision of both a 'key features' document (explaining the product, the risk factors, charges, benefits, surrender value if the policy is terminated early, tax treatment and salesperson's commission or remuneration) and a 'suitability letter' (explaining why a particular product or policy was recommended), the FSA recently decided to revamp the rules to provide consumers with clearer and more comprehensive information.

As a result, advisers must now give potential clients two 'key facts' documents: one entitled 'About our services', describing the range of services and the type of advice on offer; and a second entitled 'About the cost of our services', including among other information details of the advisers' own commission charges and – for comparison purposes – the average market rate. Importantly too, IFAs must offer clients the choice of paying fees or paying by commission.

The **Association of British Insurers (ABI)** has a number of useful information sheets on life insurance; contact: 020 7600 3333; website: www.abi.org.uk.

Tax

Under current legislation, the proceeds of a qualifying policy – whether taken as a lump sum or in regular income payments (as in the case of family income benefit) – are free of all tax. If, as applies to many people, you have a life insurance policy written into a trust, there is a possibility that it could be hit by the new Inheritance Tax rules affecting trusts if the sum it is expected to pay out is above the (2010/11) £325,000 IHT threshold. The best advice is to check with a solicitor.

Assessment

Life assurance is normally a sensible investment, whether the aim is to provide death cover or the benefits of a lump sum to boost your retirement income. It has the merit of being very attractive from a tax angle, and additionally certain policies provide good capital appreciation – although a point to be aware of is that recent bonuses have tended to be considerably lower than their projected amount. However, you are locked into a long-term commitment. So, even more than in most areas, choosing the right policy is very important. Shop around, take advice and, above all, do not sign anything unless you are absolutely certain that you understand every last dot and comma.

Complaints

Complaints about life assurance products, including alleged mis-selling, are handled by the **Financial Ombudsman Service** (FOS). Before approaching the FOS, you first need to try to resolve a dispute with the company direct. Contact: 0845 080 1800; website: www.financial-ombudsman.org.uk.

For your protection

The **Financial Services Compensation Scheme** (FSCS) is the compensation fund of last resort for customers of authorized financial services firms. If a firm becomes insolvent or ceases trading the FSCS may be able to pay compensation to its customers. Contact: 020 7892 7300; website: www.fscs.org.uk.

Alternatives to surrendering a policy

There are heavy penalties if you surrender an endowment policy before its maturity. Some people, however, may wish to terminate the agreement, regardless of any losses they may make or investment gains they may sacrifice. Instead of simply surrendering the policy to the insurance company, people in this situation may be able to sell the policy for a sum that is higher than its surrender value. Contact the **Association of Policy Market Makers: 0845 011 9406;** website: www.apmm.org

For those looking for investment possibilities, second-hand policies could be worth investigating. Known as traded endowment policies (TEPs), they offer the combination of a low-risk investment with a good potential return. Owing to increased supply, there is currently a wide range of individual policies and a number of specialist funds managed by financial institutions. A full list of appropriate financial institutions and authorized dealers that buy and sell mid-term policies is obtainable from the Association of Policy Market Makers. It can also arrange for suitable policies to be valued by member firms, free of charge.

Bonds

Bonds generally offer less opportunity for capital growth, they tend to be lower risk as they are less exposed to stock market volatility, and also have the advantage of producing a regular guaranteed income. There are many different types of bonds, with varying degrees of risk. The three main types are government bonds (called gilt-edged securities or 'gilts'), corporate bonds and investment bonds:

1 *Gilts,* which are explained earlier in this chapter, are the least risky. They are secured by the government, which guarantees both the interest payable and the return of your capital in full if you hold the stocks until their maturity.

2 *Corporate bonds* are fairly similar except that, as opposed to lending your money to the government, you are lending it to a large company or taking out a debenture. The risk is higher because, although you would normally only be recommended to buy a corporate bond from a highly rated company, there is always the possibility that the company could fail and might not be able to make the payments promised. In general, the higher the guaranteed interest payments, the less totally secure the company in question. Gilts and corporate bonds are normally recommended for cautious investors.

3 *Investment bonds* are different in that they offer potentially much higher rewards but also carry a much higher degree of risk. Because

even gilts can be influenced by timing and other factors, if you are thinking of buying bonds, expert advice is very strongly recommended. They are discussed in more detail below.

Investment bonds

Definition

This is the method of investing a lump sum with an insurance company, in the hope of receiving a much larger sum back at a specific date – normally a few years later. All bonds offer life assurance cover as part of the deal. A particular feature of some bonds is that the managers have wide discretion to invest your money in almost any type of security. The risk/reward ratio is, therefore, very high. They can produce long-term capital growth but can also be used to generate income.

While bonds can achieve significant capital appreciation, you can also lose a high percentage of your investment. An exception is guaranteed equity bonds, which, while linked to the performance of the FTSE 100 or other stock market index, will protect your capital if shares fall. However, while your capital should be returned in full at the end of the fixed term (usually five years), a point not always appreciated is that, should markets fall, far from making any return on your investment you will have lost money in real terms: first, because your capital will have fallen in value, once inflation is taken into account; second, because you will have lost out on any interest that your money could have earned had it been on deposit.

All bond proceeds are free of basic-rate tax, but higher-rate tax is payable. However, higher-rate taxpayers can withdraw up to 5 per cent of their initial investment each year and defer the higher-rate tax liability for 20 years or until the bond is cashed in full, whichever is earlier. Although there is no Capital Gains Tax on redemption of a bond (or on switching between funds), some Corporation Tax may be payable by the fund itself, which could affect its investment performance. Companies normally charge a front-end fee of around 5 per cent plus a small annual management fee, usually not related to performance.

Tax

Tax treatment is very complicated, as it is influenced by your marginal Income Tax rate in the year of encashment. For this reason, it is generally best to buy a bond when you are working and plan to cash it after retirement.

Offshore bonds

As tax reliefs vanish, some investors are looking for alternatives and it has been suggested that offshore bonds are the new pensions. There has been a recent surge of interest in offshore bonds from high earners looking for an alternative to pensions for their retirement savings. From April 2011 those earning in excess of £130,000 gradually lose their higher-rate tax relief under changes confirmed in the Emergency Budget in June 2010. Offshore bonds provide significant tax savings for investors because up to 5 per cent of capital can be withdrawn while deferring higher-rate tax for up to 20 years with no immediate tax to pay.

Offshore bonds are an insurance 'wrapper' round a portfolio of investments, which receive tax advantages by allowing you to defer the tax on the growth of the investments. Capital growth in an onshore bond is taxed at 20 per cent, whereas offshore bond capital grows tax free. While basic-rate taxpayers have no more tax to pay when they cash in an onshore investment bond, higher-rate taxpayers must pay a further 20 per cent and top-rate taxpayers must pay 30 per cent. With offshore bonds there is no tax to pay until you encash the bond, when higher-rate taxpayers will pay the entire 40 per cent and the top-rate payers will be liable for 50 per cent.

Charges for offshore bonds are high: typically 0.3 to 1 per cent upfront plus £400 to 0.25 per cent a year, depending on how much is invested. Adviser commission on top means the bonds are generally best for investments greater than £100,000 and held for more than five years. In comparison with pensions, these schemes are being increasingly recommended for retirement savings for higher-rate taxpayers who use their ISA and capital gains allowance, and no longer benefit from high-rate tax relief.

Investor protection

There are now stringent rules on businesses offering investment services and a powerful regulatory body, the Financial Services Authority (FSA). This is charged by Parliament with responsibility for ensuring that firms are 'fit and proper' to operate in the investment field and for monitoring their activities on an ongoing basis. The main effects of these safeguards are as follows.

Investment businesses (including accountants or solicitors giving investment advice) are not at liberty to operate without authorization or exemption from the FSA. Operating without such authorization or exemption is a criminal offence.

Previously, under what was known as 'polarization', businesses providing advice on investment products either could operate as 'tied agents', limited to selling their own in-house products (or those of a single provider), or had to be independent financial advisers, advising on products across the whole market. The FSA recently took the view that this was too restrictive and, with the aim of providing consumers with greater choice, has now authorized a new category of adviser known as a 'multi-tied agent', able to offer the products from a chosen panel of providers.

Whether tied, multi-tied or independent, advisers must give customers certain information before a contract is signed. Under the disclosure rules, this includes two 'key facts' documents – 'About our services' and 'About the cost of our services' – plus a 'suitability letter' explaining the rationale on which recommendations are based.

Among other important details, the information must provide a breakdown of the charges (expressed in cash terms), describe the payment options (commission and/or fee) and, in the case of commission, must quote both the adviser's own commission and the average market rate.

Investment businesses must adhere to a proper complaints procedure, with provision for customers to receive fair redress, where appropriate.

Unsolicited visits and telephone calls to sell investments are for the most part banned. Where these are allowed for packaged products (such as unit trusts and life assurance), should a sale result the customer will have a 14-day cooling-off period (or a seven-day 'right to withdraw' period if the packaged product is held within an ISA and the sale follows advice from the firm). The cooling-off period is to give the customer time to explore other options before deciding whether to cancel the contract or not.

A single regulatory authority

Finding out whether investment businesses are authorized or not and checking up on what information they are required to disclose is now much easier. All former self-regulating organizations (including the PIA, IMRO and SFA) have now been merged under the Financial Services Authority, with the purpose of improving investor protection and of providing a single contact point for enquiries. Contact **FSA Money Made Clear**: 0300 500 5000; website: www.moneymadeclear.org.uk.

A single Ombudsman scheme

The single statutory Financial Ombudsman Service (FOS) was set up in December 2001. It replaced the various former schemes that used to deal with complaints about financial services. It provides a 'one-stop shop' for dissatisfied consumers. The schemes concerned are: Banking Ombudsman, Building Societies Ombudsman, Insurance Ombudsman, Personal Insurance Arbitration Service, PIA Ombudsman, Investment Ombudsman, SFA Complaints Bureau (and Arbitration Schemes) and FSA Complaints Unit.

A welcome result of there being a single Ombudsman scheme is that the FOS covers complaints across almost the entire range of financial services and products – from banking services, endowment mortgages and personal pensions to household insurance and stocks and shares. The list equally includes unit trusts and OEICs, life assurance, FSAVCs and equity release schemes. A further advantage is that the FOS applies a single set of rules to all complaints. Since April 2007 the Financial Ombudsman Service has also covered – for the first time – the consumer-credit activities of businesses with a consumer-credit licence issued by the Office of Fair Trading. Consumer-credit activities now covered by the Ombudsman range from debt consolidation and consumer hire to debt collecting and pawnbrokers.

Complaints

If you have a complaint against an authorized firm, in the first instance you should take it up with the firm concerned. You may be able to resolve the matter at this level, since all authorized firms are obliged to have a proper complaints-handling procedure.

The Financial Ombudsman Service advises that the best approach is to start by contacting the person you originally dealt with and, if you phone, to keep a written note of all telephone calls. If complaining by letter, it helps to set out the facts in logical order, to stick to what is relevant and to include important details such as customer policy or account numbers. You should also keep a copy of all letters, both for your own record purposes and as useful evidence should you need to take the matter further.

If you have gone through the firm's complaints procedure, or if after eight weeks you are still dissatisfied, you can approach the FOS, which will investigate the matter on your behalf and, if it finds your complaint is justified, may require the firm to pay compensation; depending on your losses, this could be up to £100,000. If you disagree with the Ombudsman's decision, this does not affect your right to go to court should you wish to do so. Contact the **Financial Ombudsman Service** (**FOS**): 0845 080 1800; website: www.financial-ombudsman.org.uk.

For your protection

The **Financial Services Compensation Scheme** (**FSCS**) is the compensation fund of last resort for customers of authorized financial services firms. If a firm becomes insolvent or ceases trading the FSCS may be able to pay compensation to its customers. Contact: 020 7892 7300; website: www.fscs.org.uk.

Warning

The existence of the FSA enables you to check on the credentials of anyone purporting to be a financial adviser or trying to persuade you to invest your money in an insurance policy, bond, unit or investment trust, equity, futures contract or similar. However, if either they or the organization they represent is not authorized by the FSA, you are very strongly recommended to leave well alone. You can check whether a firm is authorized by contacting **FSA Money Made Clear** on 0300 500 5000; website: www.moneymadeclear.org.uk

Useful reading

There are a number of Money Made Clear guides published by the FSA. For a list of these booklets contact FSA Money Made Clear: 0300 500 5000; website: www.moneymadeclear.org.uk.

Chapter Six
Financial advisers

Many receive advice, few profit by it. **PUBLILIUS SYRUS, WRITER OF MAXIMS (c.100 BC)**

If there is one golden rule when it comes to money matters, it must be: if in doubt, ask. Financial advisers are professionals who offer financial planning services to individuals and companies. This can include investment advice, pension planning, life assurance and other insurances. Although most professional advisers are extremely sound, not everyone who proffers advice is qualified to do so. Before parting with your money, it is essential to ensure that you are dealing with a registered member of a recognized institution. Checking credentials has become much easier under the Financial Services Act.

Before making contact with a financial adviser it is generally a good idea to try to sort out your priorities. What are you looking for? Is it capital growth, or is your main objective to increase your income? If you have special plans, such as helping your grandchildren, or if you need several thousand pounds to improve your home, these should be thought through in advance. They could have a bearing on the advice you receive. A further reason for doing some pre-planning is that certain types of advisers – for example, insurance brokers – do not specifically charge you for their time. Other professional advisers, such as accountants and solicitors, charge their fees by the hour. Check on the fee structure before accepting an expensive leisurely lunch while discussing retirement plans because you may be footing the bill.

Choosing an adviser

When choosing an adviser, there are usually four main considerations: respectability, suitability, price and convenience. Where your money is concerned, you cannot afford to take unnecessary risks. Establishing that an individual is a member of a recognized institution is a basic safeguard. But it is insufficient recommendation if you want to be assured of dealing with someone who will personally suit you. The principle applies as much with friends as with complete strangers. If you are thinking of using a particular adviser, do you already know him or her in a professional capacity? If not, you should certainly check on the adviser's reputation, ideally talking to some of his or her existing clients. No one who is any good will object to your asking for references. Most reputable professionals will be delighted to assist, as it means that the relationship will be founded on a basis of greater trust and confidence.

Accountants

Accountants are specialists in matters concerning taxation. If there is scope to do so, they can advise on ways of reducing your tax liability and can assess the various tax effects of the different types of investment you may be considering. They can also help you with the preparation of tax returns. Should you be considering becoming self-employed or starting your own business, they can assist you with some of the practicalities. These could range from registering for VAT to establishing a system of business accounts. Many accountants can also help with raising finance and offer support with the preparation of business plans. Additionally, they may be able to advise in a general way about pensions and your proposed investment strategy. Most accountants, however, do not claim to be experts in these fields. They may refer their clients to stockbrokers or other financial advisers for such specialized services. If you need help in locating a suitable accountant, any of the following should be able to advise:

> **Association of Chartered Certified Accountants (ACCA):** 020 7059 5000; website: www.accaglobal.com.

> **Institute of Chartered Accountants in England and Wales (ICAEW).** If your enquiry is regarding membership or a specific member of the ICAEW, or to check if a firm is registered with the ICAEW, call the ICAEW Membership Enquiry Line: 0207 920 8100; website: www.icaew.com.

> **Institute of Chartered Accountants of Scotland (ICAS).** For enquiries regarding members' registration: 01383 882 645; website: www.icaew.com.

Complaints

Anyone with a complaint against an accountancy firm should contact the company's relevant professional body for advice and assistance – see ACCA, ICAEW or ICAS, above.

Banks

Most people need no introduction to the clearing banks since, if they have a bank account, they are probably regularly bombarded with information on the latest products and services. But there are now fewer banks to choose from than there were. Lloyds Banking Group owns more than 30 per cent of the current account market and 30 per cent of the mortgage market. A number of the building societies that were visible on the high streets have been taken over by the Spanish Santander Group.

Banks provide comprehensive services, in addition to the normal account facilities. These include investment, insurance and tax-planning services, as well as how to draw up a will. Brief information follows on the main ones. Other more specialized banks such as Hoare's, Coutts and overseas banks are all part of the UK clearing system and can offer a very good service. The contact details given are those of the head office:

Barclays Bank plc offers customers a range of accounts to suit a variety of personal savings requirements. Additionally, a number of financial planning services are available through Barclays Bank subsidiary companies. These include personal investment advice, investment management, stockbroking, unit trusts, personal taxation, wills and trusts. You can apply through your local branch of Barclays Bank, or contact: 08457 555 555; website: www.barclays.co.uk.

Co-operative Bank has a comprehensive range of products including current accounts, savings accounts, mortgages, credit cards, loans, insurance and investment services. For assistance with financial planning, apply at your local branch or contact: 08457 212 212; website: www.co-operativebank.co.uk.

HSBC offers a comprehensive choice of financial products ranging from OEICs and ISAs to life assurance, which are selected according to a customer's requirements by a financial planning manager. HSBC Premier IFA offers investment management and estate planning services to clients who prefer to have a local specialist to look after their affairs on a regular basis. Clients typically have an income over £75,000 or liquid assets of over

£100,000. Any HSBC branch can arrange a meeting if you would like to discuss these services, or contact: 08457 404 404; website: www.hsbc.co.uk.

Lloyds TSB offers a wide range of financial services, including current and savings accounts, home insurance, investment management, and life assurance through Scottish Widows. As well as the classic account, which offers all the normal current account facilities, and the Gold Service, which among other facilities includes free travel insurance, there is Private Banking, which is a comprehensive wealth-management service tailored to individual requirements for customers with £250,000 or more of liquid assets. Details of all these services, as well as life assurance and investment products, are available at all Lloyds TSB branches, contact: 0845 3000 000; website: www.lloydstsb.com.

NatWest (part of the RBS Group) financial planning managers can advise on a wide range of banking and financial planning services for retirement, including investment funds and ISAs. To make an appointment, contact your local NatWest branch or contact: 0800 200 400; website: www.natwest.com.

RBS (Royal Bank of Scotland) offers a comprehensive range of current accounts and savings products. The bank's Private Trust and Taxation Department offers free advice on making a will, although the usual legal fees are applicable if you proceed. Royal Scottish Assurance, the Royal Bank of Scotland's life assurance, pensions and investment company, offers a full financial planning service free of charge. Financial planning consultants can also recommend ISAs and unit trusts provided by the Royal Bank of Scotland unit trust managers. Further information is available from any branch of the bank, or contact: 0808 100 0808; website: www.rbs.co.uk.

Santander Group (formerly Abbey and now including Alliance & Leicester) offers a range of savings, mortgage, pension, current account, and medical and other insurance products plus loans for such items as home improvements, a car or money to finance a holiday. A broad range of savings accounts is available that includes branch-based, postal and internet instant access accounts, and fixed- and variable-rate savings bonds, including a retirement income bond for the over-55s. There is also a range of ISAs. Full details of all services can be obtained from any high street branch or contact: 0800 555 100; website: www.santander.co.uk.

Complaints

If you have a complaint about a banking matter, you must first try to resolve the issue with the bank or building society concerned. If you remain dissatisfied, you can contact the **Financial Ombudsman Service:** 0845 080 1800; website: www.financial-ombudsman.org.uk.

For your protection

The **Financial Services Compensation Scheme** (FSCS) is the compensation fund of last resort for customers of authorized financial services firms. If a firm becomes insolvent or ceases trading the FSCS may be able to pay compensation to its customers. Contact: 020 7892 7300; website: www.fscs.org.uk.

Independent financial advisers (IFAs)

IFAs can advise you across the whole spectrum of investment policies and products: endowment policies, personal pensions, life assurance, permanent health insurance, critical illness cover, unit trusts, ISAs and other forms of personal investment such as, for example, mortgages. Their job is to help you work out whether the type of policy you have in mind would be most suitable and where, depending on your circumstances and objectives, you could obtain best value for money. In other words, they act as your personal adviser and handle all the arrangements for you.

To be able to offer 'best advice', an IFA needs to try to ensure that you would not be at risk of over-committing yourself or taking some other risk that might jeopardize your security. He or she will, therefore, need an understanding of your existing financial circumstances (and future expectations) including, for example, your earnings, employment prospects and any other types of investment you might already have. In turn, you should also ask your adviser a number of questions including – as a first essential – by whom they are regulated. This should normally be the FSA but could be one of a small number of designated professional bodies, which themselves are answerable to the FSA. If you have any doubts, you can check via the **FSA's Central Register Money Made Clear helpline:** 0300 500 5000; website: www.fsa.gov.uk.

Your adviser should provide you with two 'key facts' documents entitled 'About our Services' and 'About the Cost of our Services', plus a 'suitability letter' explaining all these points, but if for some reason you do not receive these or if there is anything you do not understand you should not hesitate to ask. Under rules brought in by the FSA, advisers who want to call themselves 'independent' have to offer clients the option of paying by fee.

This means of course that clients incur an upfront charge. The following organizations provide information on locating local IFAs:

The Institute of Financial Planning will help you in your search for a certified financial planner by region, speciality or name. Contact: 0117 945 2470; website: www.financialplanning.org.uk.

The Personal Finance Society (PFS) will also help you identify an adviser by postcode or specific financial need. Its website has a useful extra function in that it allows you to look for only chartered financial advisers. Once you have found an adviser, you can make sure that the adviser is approved by checking his or her credentials with the FSA, which is responsible for regulating the industry. Contact: 020 8530 0852; website: www.thepfs.org.

The professional advice website, **unbiased.co.uk** will help you find local professional advice for an IFA, mortgage adviser, solicitor or accountant. Website: www.unbiased.co.uk.

Insurance brokers

The insurance business covers a very wide range, from straightforward policies – such as motor or household insurance – to rather more complex areas, including life assurance and pensions.

Although many people think of brokers and IFAs as doing much the same job, IFAs specialize in advising on products and policies with some investment content, whereas brokers primarily deal with the more straightforward type of insurance, such as motor, medical, household and holiday insurance. Some brokers are also authorized to give investment advice.

A broker should be able to help you choose the policies that are best suited to you, help you determine how much cover you require and explain any technical terms contained in the documents. He or she can also assist with any claims, remind you when renewals are necessary and advise you on keeping your cover up to date. An essential point to check before proceeding is that the firm the broker represents is regulated by the FSA.

A condition of registration is that a broker must deal with a multiplicity of insurers and therefore be in a position to offer a comprehensive choice of policies. The FSA disclosure rules require brokers to provide potential customers with a 'key facts' document. This should include the cost of the policy (but not commission), as well as a 'suitability' statement explaining the reasons for the recommendation. The information must also draw attention to any significant or unusual exemptions. Generally speaking, you are safer using a larger brokerage with an established reputation. Also, before you take out a policy, it is advisable to consult several brokers in order to get a better feel for the market.

The **British Insurance Brokers' Association** represents nearly 2,200 insurance broking businesses. It can put you in touch with a member broker in your area. Contact: 0870 950 1790; website: www.biba.org.uk.

Complaints

The **Association of British Insurers (ABI)** represents some 400 companies (as opposed to Lloyd's syndicates or brokers), providing all types of insurance from life assurance and pensions to household, motor and other forms of general insurance. About 90 per cent of the worldwide business done by British insurance companies is handled by members of the ABI. It publishes a wide range of information sheets, obtainable from the ABI, on: 020 7600 3333; website: www.abi.org.uk.

Other pension advisers

If you have a query to do with your pension, there are some organizations that may be able to assist, discussed below.

Individuals in paid employment

If you are (or have been) in salaried employment and are a member of an occupational pension scheme, the normal person to ask is your company's personnel manager or pensions adviser or, via him or her, the pension fund trustees. Alternatively, if you have a problem with your pension you could approach your trade union, since this is an area where most unions are particularly active and well informed.

If you are in need of specific help, a source to try could be the **Pensions Advisory Service.** It is an independent non-profit organization that provides free information, advice and guidance on the whole spectrum of pensions, including State, company, personal and stakeholder schemes. With a network of 500 professional advisers the PAS can give free help and advice on all matters to do with any type of pension scheme. Contact: 0845 601 2923; website: www.pensionsadvisoryservice.org.uk.

As with most other financial sectors, there is also a **Pensions Ombudsman.** You would normally approach the Ombudsman if neither the pension scheme trustees nor the Pensions Advisory Service are able to solve your problem. Also, as with all Ombudsmen, the Pensions Ombudsman can only investigate matters that come within his orbit. These are: 1) complaints of maladministration by the trustees, managers or administrators of a pension scheme or by an employer; and 2) disputes of fact or law with the trustees, managers or an employer. You can contact the Pensions Ombudsman: 020 7630 2200; website: www. pensions-ombudsman.org.uk. Unlike many of the other Ombudsman services, the Pensions Ombudsman has not become part of the single statutory Financial Ombudsman Service and will continue to remain as a separate scheme.

Another source of help is the **Pension Tracing Service,** which can provide individuals with contact details for a pension scheme with which they have lost touch. It is run by the Pension Service, part of the Department for Work and Pensions. As with the Ombudsman, there is no charge for the service. For further information, contact the Pension Tracing Service, 0845 600 2537. You can also fill in a tracing request form online by visiting the website: www.thepensionservice.gov.uk and following the links to the Pension Tracing Service.

Two other organizations that, although they do not advise on individual cases, are interested in matters of principle and broader issues affecting pensions, are:

National Association of Pension Funds: 020 7601 1700; website: www. napf.co.uk.

The Pensions Regulator, which is the UK regulator of work-based pension schemes. Contact: 0870 606 3636; website: www. thepensionsregulator.gov.uk.

Solicitors

Solicitors are professional advisers on subjects to do with the law or on matters that could have legal implications. They can assist with the purchase or rental of property, with drawing up a will, or if you are charged with a criminal offence or are sued in a civil matter. Additionally, their advice can be invaluable in vetting any important document before you sign it. If you do not have a solicitor (or if your solicitor does not have the knowledge to advise on, say, a business matter), often the best way of finding a suitable lawyer is through the recommendation of a friend or other professional adviser, such as an accountant. If you need a solicitor specifically for a business or professional matter, organizations such as Chambers of Commerce, small business associations, your professional institute or your trade union may be able to put you in touch with someone in your area who has relevant experience. Another solution is to contact the **Law Society:** 020 7242 1222; website: www.lawsociety.org.uk.

A further resource of possible interest is **Solicitors for Independent Financial Advice (SIFA).** This is a network of law firms offering financial as well as legal services, with the aim of providing clients with a 'one-stop shop' when making important financial decisions. It maintains a nationwide register and will help source the best firm according to what advice is needed – such as investments, pension planning, wills or choosing a long-term care policy. Contact: 01372 721 172; website: www.sifa.co.uk.

Community Legal Service (Legal Aid) funding

If you need a Community Legal Service (CLS) solicitor, or want to find out if you are eligible for Community Legal Service funding, the place to go is a solicitor's office or an advice centre. Ask for the leaflet *A Practical Guide to Community Legal Service Funding* by the Legal Services Commission. You can ask an adviser to go through this with you to help you work out whether you are eligible. If you have a low income or are in receipt of benefits and would welcome independent advice about tax credits, debt, employment or housing problems, you might usefully contact the Community Legal Advice helpline. The Community Legal Service works in partnership with solicitors and not-for-profit organizations to provide information, advice and representation to people in need. The Service lists solicitors and advice agencies that do CLS work. **The Community Legal Service helpline:** 0845 345 4345; website: www.legalservices.gov.uk.

Complaints

All solicitors are required by the Law Society to have their own in-house complaints procedure. If you are unhappy about the service you have received, you should first try to resolve the matter with the firm through its complaints-handling partner. If you still feel aggrieved you can approach the Law Society's Legal Complaints Service (LCS), which is an independent arm of the Law Society responsible for handling complaints against solicitors.

If you believe you have a complaint of negligence, the LCS will help you either by putting you in touch with a solicitor specializing in negligence claims or by referring you to the solicitor's insurers. If it arranges an appointment for you with a negligence panellist, the panel solicitor will see you free of charge for up to an hour and advise you as to your best course of action. If you believe that you have been overcharged, you should ask to be sent the booklet *Can We Help?* This explains the procedure for getting your bill checked, the various time limits involved and the circumstances in which you might be successful in getting the fee reduced.

For practical assistance if you are having problems with your solicitor, you can ring the **Legal Complaints Service helpline: 0845 608 6565**; website: www.legalcomplaints.org.uk. If this has failed to resolve the problem, you can approach the Legal Services Ombudsman. You must try to do so within three months of the LCS's, or other professional body's final decision or your complaint will risk being out of time and the Ombudsman will not be able to help you. Contact the **Legal Services Ombudsman, 0845 601 0794**; website: www.olso.org.

General queries

For queries of a more general nature, you should approach the **Law Society: 020 7242 1222**; website: www.lawsociety.org.uk. If you live in Scotland or Northern Ireland, the LCS will not be able to help you; instead you should contact the Law Society at the relevant address:

> **The Law Society of Scotland: 0131 226 7411**; website: www.lawscot. org.uk.

> **The Law Society of Northern Ireland: 028 9023 1614**; website: www. lawsoc-ni.org.

Stockbrokers

Stockbrokers buy and sell shares quoted on the main market of the London Stock Exchange and on AIM (alternative investment market), which trades mainly in the shares of young and growing companies that cannot afford the full listing on the London Stock Exchange (LSE). Investments can be made in British and international equities, bonds, investment trusts and gilts (government stocks). As well as trading for clients, stockbrokers can advise on the prospects of different companies, help individuals choose the best type of investment according to their financial situation, and also provide a wide range of other financial services including tax planning.

It is difficult to be specific about the cost of using a stockbroker. While some now charge fees in the same way as, say, a solicitor, generally stockbrokers make their living by charging commission on every transaction. You will need to enquire what the terms and conditions are before committing yourself, as these can vary quite considerably between one firm and another. A growing number of provincial stockbrokers are happy to deal for private investors with sums from about £5,000. Additionally, nearly all major stockbrokers now run unit trusts. Because through these they are investing collectively for their clients, they welcome quite modest investors with around £2,000.

There are several ways of finding a stockbroker: you can approach an individual through recommendation or you can check the 'Locate a Broker' service on the **London Stock Exchange** website: www.londonstockexchange. com Alternatively there is the **Association of Private Client Investment Managers and Stockbrokers (APCIMS),** which provides a free directory of stockbrokers and investment managers, together with details of their services. APCIMS also has an online directory, which is searchable by region and type of service. Contact: 020 7448 7100; website: www.apcims.co.uk.

Complaints

If you have a complaint about a stockbroker or other member of the former Securities and Futures Authority (SFA), you should put this in writing to the compliance officer of the stockbroking firm involved. If the matter is not satisfactorily resolved, you can then contact the Financial Ombudsman Service (FOS), which will investigate your complaint and, if the Ombudsman considers this justified, can award compensation. Contact **Financial Ombudsman Service:** 0845 080 1800; website: www.financial-ombudsman.org.uk.

A note of warning

Despite the safeguards of the Financial Services Act, when it comes to investment – or to financial advisers – there are no cast-iron guarantees. Under the investor protection legislation, all practitioners and/or the businesses they represent offering investment or similar services must be authorized by the FSA or, in certain cases, by a small number of Designated Professional Bodies that themselves are answerable to the FSA. A basic question, therefore, to ask anyone offering investment advice or products is: are you registered and by whom? The information is easy to check by telephoning **FSA's Consumer Helpline:** 0845 606 1234; website: www.fsa.gov.uk. For further information, see 'Investor protection' at the end of Chapter 5.

For your protection

The Financial Services Compensation Scheme (FSCS) is the compensation fund of last resort for customers of authorized financial services firms. If a firm becomes insolvent or ceases trading the FSCS may be able to pay compensation to its customers. Contact: 020 7892 7300; website: www.fscs.org.uk.

Financial Ombudsman Service (FOS)

There is now a single contact point for dissatisfied customers, as the FOS covers complaints across almost the entire range of financial services, including consumer-credit activities (such as store cards, credit cards and hire purchase transactions). The service is free, and the FOS is empowered to award compensation of up to £100,000. However, before contacting the FOS you must first try to resolve your complaint with the organization concerned. Also, the Ombudsman is powerless to act if legal proceedings have been started. Contact the **Financial Ombudsman Service:** 0845 080 1800; website: www.financial-ombudsman.org.uk.

Useful reading

Further reading and information on choosing a financial adviser is available from Money Made Clear (part of the Consumer Financial Education Body, established by the Financial Services Authority). Contact: 0300 500 5000; website: www.moneymadeclear.org.uk.

Chapter Seven
Budget planner

If you can count your money, you don't have a billion dollars. JOHN PAUL GETTY, 1892–1976

It doesn't matter whether you are about to retire tomorrow or not for several years, some people are constantly worrying about not having enough money. The best way of making your money work for you in retirement is to complete a Budget Planner. The more accurate you can be, the more helpful it will be.

If retirement is imminent, then doing the arithmetic in as much detail as possible will not only reassure you but also help you plan your future life with greater confidence. You'll feel better knowing how you stand financially. Don't forget that even at this stage there are probably a number of options open to you. Examining the figures written down will highlight the areas of greatest flexibility. One tip, offered by one of the retirement magazines, is to start living on your retirement income some six months before you retire. Not only will you see if your budget estimates are broadly correct, but since most people err on the cautious side when they first retire you will have the bonus of all the extra money you will have saved.

If retirement is still some years ahead, there will be more unknowns and more opportunities. When assessing the figures, you should take account of your future earnings. Perhaps you should also consider what steps you might be able to take under the pension rules to maximize your pension fund. You could also consider whether you should be putting money aside now in a savings plan and/or making other investments. Imprecise as they will be, the Budget Planner estimates you have made in the various income and expenditure columns should indicate whether, unless you take action now, you could be at risk of having to make serious adjustments in your standard of living later on. To be on the safe side, assume an increase in inflation. Everyone should, if they possibly can, budget for a nest egg. This is to help cover the cost of any emergencies or special events – perhaps a family wedding – that may come along.

1. Possible savings when you retire

Items	Estimated monthly savings
National Insurance contributions	....
Pension payments	....
Travel expenses to work	....
Bought lunches	....
Incidentals at work, eg drinks with colleagues, collections for presents	....
Special work clothes	....
Concessionary travel	....
Free NHS prescriptions	....
Free eye tests	....
Mature drivers' insurance policy	....
Retired householders' insurance policy	....
Life assurance payments and/or possible endowment policy premiums	....
Other	....
TOTAL	....

NB: you should also take into account reduced running costs if you move to a smaller home; any expenses for dependent children that may cease; other costs, such as mortgage payments, that may end around the time you retire; and the fact that you may be in a lower tax bracket.

2. Possible extra outgoings when you retire

Items	Estimated monthly cost
Extra heating and lighting bills	....
Extra spending on hobbies and other entertainment	....
Replacement of company car	....
Private health care insurance	....
Longer, or more frequent, holidays	....
Life and permanent health insurance	....
Cost of substituting other perks, eg expense account lunches	....
Out-of-pocket expenses for voluntary work activity	....
Other	....
TOTAL	....

NB: looking ahead, you will need to make provision for any extra home comforts you might want and also, at some point, for having to pay other people to do some of the jobs that you normally manage yourself. If you intend to make regular donations to a charity or perhaps help with your grandchildren's education, these too should be included in the list. The same applies to any new private pension or savings plan that you might want to invest in to boost your long-term retirement income.

3. Expected sources of income on retirement

Many people have difficulty understanding the tax system, and you should certainly take professional advice if you are in any doubt at all. However, if you fill in your expected sources of income and likely tax implications carefully below, it should give you a pretty good idea of your net income after retirement and enable you to make at least provisional plans. Remember too that you may have one or two capital sums to invest, such as:

- the commuted lump sum from your pension;
- money from an endowment policy;
- gains from the sale of company shares (SAVE or other share option scheme);
- profits from the sale of your home or other asset;
- money from an inheritance.

A. Income received *before* tax

Basic State pension	....
State graduated pension	....
SERPS/State Second Pension	....
Occupational pension(s)	....
Stakeholder or personal pension	....
State benefits	....
Investments and savings plans paid gross, eg gilts, National Savings	....
Possible rental income	....
Casual or other pre-tax earnings	....
TOTAL	....
Less: Personal tax allowance and possibly also married couple's allowance	....
Basic-rate tax	....
TOTAL A	....

3. continued

B. Income received *after* tax

Dividends (unit trusts, shares, etc)	....
Bank deposit account	....
Building society interest	....
Annuity income	....
Other (including earnings subject to PAYE)	....
TOTAL B	....
Total A + Total B	....
Less: higher-rate tax (if any)	....
Plus: Other tax-free receipts, eg some State benefits income from an ISA	....
Investment bond withdrawals, etc	....
Other	....
TOTAL NET INCOME	....

4. Unavoidable outgoings

Items	Estimated monthly cost
Food	....
Rent or mortgage repayments	....
Council Tax	....
Repair and maintenance costs	....
Heating	....
Lighting and other energy	....
Telephone/mobile/internet	....
Postage (including Christmas cards)	....
TV licence/Sky/digital subscription	....
Household insurance	....
Clothes	....
Laundry, cleaner's bills, shoe repair	....
Domestic cleaning products	....
Miscellaneous services, eg plumber and window cleaner	....
Car (including licence, petrol, etc)	....
Other transport	....
Regular savings and life assurance	....
HP and other loan repayments	....
Outgoings on health	....
Other	....
TOTAL	....

NB: before adding up the total, you should look at the 'Normal additional expenditure' list below, as you may well want to juggle some of the items between the two.

5. Normal additional expenditure

Items	Estimated monthly cost
Gifts	....
Holidays	....
Newspapers/books/CDs/DVDs	....
Computer (including broadband)	....
Drink	....
Cigarettes/tobacco	....
Hairdressing	....
Toiletries/cosmetics	....
Entertainment (hobbies, outings, home entertaining, etc)	....
Miscellaneous subscriptions/ membership fees	....
Charitable donations	....
Expenditure on pets	....
Garden purchases	....
Other	....
TOTAL	....

NB: for some items, such as holidays and gifts, you may tend to think in annual expenditure terms. However, for the purpose of comparing monthly income versus outgoings, it is probably easier if you itemize all the expenditure in the same fashion. Also, if you need to save for a special event such as your holiday, it helps if you get into the habit of putting so much aside every month (or even weekly).

Chapter Eight
Your home

A man travels the world over in search of what he needs and returns home to find it. GEORGE MOORE

Home sweet home is what matters to most people, especially as they grow older. For many people of retirement age, their home is their major financial asset. The Council of Mortgage Lenders estimates that the over-65s own £100 billion of unmortgaged equity in property. That figure equates to half the housing wealth in this country. One of the most important decisions to be taken as you approach retirement is whether you should move house or stay put and consider making changes to where you live.

To many people, one of the biggest attractions once they've finished work is the pleasure of being able to move home. No longer are they tied to an area within easy commuting distance; at last they can indulge their long-held plans of living in a new area (possibly a new country). Although this could turn out to be everything they desire, without any real assessment of the pros and cons, some do regret having made a hasty decision. It is sensible at least to examine the various options. An obvious possibility is to stay where you are and perhaps adapt your present home to make it more suitable for your requirements. You might decide to move nearer to family or friends. Looking further ahead, you could consider buying or renting some form of purpose-built retirement accommodation.

Lots of people are conditioned to think of retirement as being a time for selling up and relocating. An all-too-common mistake is for people to retire to a place where they once spent an idyllic holiday, perhaps 15 or 20 years previously, without further investigation. Resorts that are glorious in midsummer can be bleak and damp in winter. They can also be pretty dull when the tourist season is over. Equally, many people sell their house and move somewhere smaller without sufficient thought. It may be that spending more time at home they will want more space, rather than less.

Although moving may be the right solution for some, especially if you want to realize some capital to boost your retirement income, there are plenty of ways of adapting a house to make it more convenient and labour-saving. Likewise, you may be able to cut the running costs, for example, with better insulation. Before you come to any definite decision, first ask yourself a few down-to-earth questions. What are your main priorities? Do you want to be closer to your family? Would a smaller, more manageable home be easier for you to run – and less expensive? What about realizing some capital to provide you with extra money for your retirement? How about living in a specific town or village, which you know you like and where you have plenty of friends? Or does the security of being in accommodation that offers some of the facilities you may want as you become older sound attractive? Would, say, a resident caretaker and the option of having some of your meals catered for, appeal to you? Whatever choice you make is bound to have advantages and drawbacks; life is full of compromises. But it is important that you weigh up the pros and cons carefully so that you don't end up making a decision that – while attractive in the short term – you regret later on.

New rules on garden-grabbing

One point to mention is that the new government has announced rules to curb building on garden land. This may be a mixed blessing for home-owners. 'Garden-grabbing' (the practice where developers build in the back gardens of existing homes) is to be discouraged. In the past many new homes have been built on the site of large gardens belonging to older properties. Nothing has been banned but two small bureaucratic changes have been made that will give councils less incentive to give planning permission for new homes in the gardens of existing properties.

In essence, the definition of brownfield land has been changed so that it will no longer include gardens. (This is important because councils are set targets for the proportion of new homes that must be built on previously developed land.) The second change introduced is the abolition of targets for minimum housing density. Together these changes will make it easier for councils to resist applications from developers to build in back gardens and some councils have already begun to fight garden-grabbing. The results may please some people if homes are not being built in back gardens, but others may be offended if, instead, those homes are built on greenfield sites.

In 2008, 68 per cent of new homes were built in back gardens so it is unlikely that garden-grabbing will come to a complete stop. On one hand it will remain popular among the home-owners who could stand to make a fortune from gaining planning permission on their gardens. On the other there are many who will be frustrated by this rule change as it can only increase the shortage of homes and increase inflationary pressures since there has been no simultaneous loosening of planning rules on greenfield land to compensate for the move against garden-grabbing.

Staying put

With property prices still uncertain, it makes a lot of sense for some householders to opt to improve rather than move. If you're a home-owner who needs more space, it makes sound common sense to extend rather than sell up in the current climate. House prices are not going to rise significantly in the foreseeable future, so many people's instinct is to sit tight. Instead of looking in estate agents' windows, it might be more sensible to seek the services of an architect, reputable builder, plumber and electrician.

There may be plenty of arguments for moving, and there are probably just as many for staying where you are. Moving house can be a traumatic experience at the best of times, and even more so as you become older. Emotional ties are harder to break and precious possessions more painful to part with, as is usually necessary, especially if moving somewhere smaller.

Although ideally you may want to remain where you are, you may feel that your home is really too large or inconvenient for you to manage in the future. However, before you heave your last sigh of regret and put it on the market, it is worth considering whether there are ways of adapting it to provide what you want. If your house is too big, you might think about reusing the space in a better way. Would it be possible, for example, to turn a bedroom into an upstairs study? Or perhaps you could convert a spare room into a separate workroom for hobbies and get rid of the clutter from the main living area? Have you thought about letting one or two rooms? As well as solving the problem of wasted space, it would also bring in some extra income.

Ways of increasing the size of your property

Before embarking on any improvements, it is sensible to work out which ones will add the most value to your property. The loft conversion is popular as it can add an extra bedroom and possibly even a bathroom. Building an extra room as an extension is the next favourite, followed by adding a conservatory, a new kitchen, central heating, bathrooms and new windows. But there are some exciting options available to those ready for a challenge.

If you are considering building an extension, what sort will it be? The most ambitious of course would be to become your own neighbour, by purchasing the next-door property and knocking through. This solution to requiring more space (whatever the reason might be – such as moving relatives close to you while retaining some independence) works for some people. Knocking through allows more space than an extension without incurring moving costs or leaving the neighbourhood. This option is neither cheap nor simple but it is possible to knock through almost any age or style of property so long as they are adjoining. Professional advice from an architect is essential so that the required planning permissions can be sought. Also it is sensible to take an holistic approach so that the finished conjoined house looks right. This makes selling the property much easier in the future and it is vital to bear this firmly in mind however you plan to extend your property. Alternatively, if you live in an apartment you might be able to buy the adjoining unit or the one above or below then knock through or install a staircase to achieve double living space. Any construction work being undertaken must, of course, adhere strictly to planning and building regulations and you must ensure the project is completed properly. Although it may be tempting to cut corners, it is never advisable as things can come back to haunt you at a later date should you want to sell.

The next possibility could be to build an extension. Depending on the style of property you own you may be able to extend by building on the back, side or front of your home. A two-storey extension would give additional ground floor living space as well as two rooms upstairs and an extra bathroom. Any scheme is subject to local planning approval but once the permissions have been granted, the project can proceed relatively quickly. Provided you can remain living in the property while the building work is being carried out, the disruption is less dramatic. Owners living on-site often make for a smoother and swifter conclusion to the project.

Another popular way to increase space in your home is to build above a garage. Converting this type of space increases the size of your home easily and quickly. Remember to do your sums before you start to compare building costs with how much value the extra rooms are likely to add to your home. Any scheme would be subject to appropriate planning permission being granted. This is needed because of the extra height and alteration to the roof line. Whether your garage is single size or double, attached or detached, this type of extension is one of the quickest 'wins' because you are working with what you've got and you are spared the necessity of digging new foundations. However, existing foundations will need to be checked to prove they can sustain the extra load. Also there are few implications for disruption to the rest of the house, particularly if the garage is detached. You could of course extend into the garage itself as well as building above, as long as it's not needed to house the car. Rooms above a detached garage make an ideal guest suite, office, study, granny or nanny flat (or somewhere to carry on a noisy hobby). Should this idea appeal, there are some specialist companies dealing solely with garage conversions.

Some possible changes

A few judicious home improvements carried out now could make the world of difference in terms of comfort and practicality. Many of us carry on for years with inefficient heating systems that could be improved relatively easily and cheaply. Stairs need not necessarily be a problem, even when you are very much older, thanks to the many types of stair lifts now available. Even so, a few basic facilities installed on the ground floor could save your legs in years to come. Similarly, gardens can be redesigned to suit changing requirements. Areas that now take hours to weed could be turned into extra lawn or a patio.

For some people, the problem is not so much the size or convenience of their home as the fact that they are unable to buy the freehold or extend the lease. They fear for their long-term security. But since the Leasehold Reform, Housing and Urban Development Act 1993 extended the right of enfranchisement to thousands of flat leaseholders, they now have the collective right to buy the freehold of their building and the individual right to extend their leases at a market price.

Among other requirements to enfranchise, your flat must be held under a lease that was originally granted for more than 21 years, and the eligible tenants of at least half of the flats in the block must also wish to buy the freehold. Before proceeding, you would be advised to obtain a professional valuation as a first step to establishing a fair price to which the landlord will be entitled. 'Fair price' is made up of the open market value of the building, half of any mortgage value that may be payable, plus possible compensation to the landlord for any severance or other losses. If you have a dwindling lease but do not wish to enfranchise, the more straightforward purchase of a 90-year lease extension might be a better option. For further information see leaflets *Collective Enfranchisement – Getting Started; Collective Enfranchisement – Valuation; Lease Extension – Getting Started* and *Lease Extension – Valuation*, obtainable free from LEASE at the address below.

If, as applies to many people, you want protection from a landlord but do not want to buy the freehold or extend your lease, you will be glad to know that leaseholders' rights have been strengthened recently. Among other rights, where leaseholders believe that their service charges are unreasonable they can ask a leasehold valuation tribunal, rather than a court, to determine what charge is reasonable. This includes work that has been proposed but not yet started. Also, where there are serious problems with the management of a building, tenants can ask the tribunal to appoint a new manager. Importantly, leasehold valuation tribunals are less formal than a court and avoid the risk of potentially unknown costs being awarded, which can be the case with court proceedings. (Tribunals can award costs of up to £500 where they believe a person has acted abusively or otherwise unreasonably in connection with the proceedings.) For further information, obtain the booklet *Residential Long Leaseholders – Your Rights and Responsibilities* (ISBN 978 1409 809 593), available from Citizens Advice Bureau or from the Department for Communities and Local Government Publications Centre, Tel: 0300 123 1124; website: www.communities.gov.uk.

Additionally, the Common-hold and Leasehold Reform Act 2002 introduced a new right to take over the management of flats without having to prove fault on the part of the landlord. It made buying the freehold or an extended lease of a flat easier, strengthened leaseholders' rights against unreasonable service charges, prevented landlords from taking any action for unpaid ground rent unless this has first been demanded in writing, made lease variations easier to obtain and provided further protection for the holding of leaseholders' monies. Furthermore, landlords are not able to commence forfeiture proceedings to obtain possession of the property unless they have first proved an alleged breach of the lease before a leasehold valuation tribunal. Where the breach relates to arrears, they must also have proved that the sum demanded is reasonable.

Landmark Leasehold Advisory Services specializes in providing legal services to residential leaseholders of England and Wales. It represents leaseholders and leaseholders alone and is a one-stop competent legal product base that provides the leaseholder with every right and protection afforded to them by law. Contact: 0845 475 2002; website: www.landmarklease.com.

For publications issued by LEASE such as *The Right to Manage* and *Service Charges and Other Issues,* and for general advice on leasehold, including leaseholders' rights and responsibilities, contact the **Leasehold Advisory Service (LEASE)**, Tel: 020 7374 5380; website: www.lease-advice. org. For advice on leasehold legislation and policy, consult the **Department for Communities and Local Government** website: www.communities.gov. uk; Tel: 020 7944 4400.

Moving to a new home

If you do decide to move, the sooner you start looking for your new home the better. There is no point in delaying the search until you retire and then rushing round expecting to find your dream house in a matter of weeks. With time to spare, you will have a far greater choice of properties and are less likely to indulge in any panic buying. While a smaller house will almost certainly be easier and cheaper to run, make sure that it is not so small that you are going to feel cramped. Remember that, when you and your partner are both at home, you may need more room to avoid getting on top of each other. Also, if your family lives in another part of the country, you may wish to have them and your grandchildren to stay. Conversely, beware of taking on commitments such as a huge garden. While this might be a great source of enjoyment when you are in your 60s, it could prove a burden as you become older.

If you are thinking of moving out of the neighbourhood, there are other factors to be taken into account such as access to shops and social activities, proximity to friends and relatives, availability of public transport and even health and social support services. While these may not seem particularly important now, they could become so in the future. Couples who retire to a seemingly 'idyllic' spot often return quite quickly. New friends are not always easy to make.

Something to bear in mind when considering re-locating is that some rural areas have hidden levels of deprivation. A new report (compiled by Gloucestershire Rural Community Council – GRCC) states that around a third of that county's population – about 200,000 – lives in rural areas and some 16,000 are classified as income deprived. This comes as a shock to many people who believe that everyone who lives in the countryside has an idyllic existence. If you are elderly or infirm, living in the country can create massive challenges, particularly if you have a long-term illness. Lack of public transport is one of the main causes of rural deprivation, with the loss of village shops and post offices being another. Anyone considering a major lifestyle change, such as moving to a rural location in retirement, should take time and review all options before coming to a decision.

So-called 'retirement areas' too can mean that you are cut off from a normal cross-section of society, and health services are likely to be overtaxed. After a hard week's wheeling and dealing it is tempting to wax lyrical about exchanging the rat race for a life of rustic solitude. While retiring to the country can be glorious, city dwellers should, however, bear in mind some of the less attractive sides of rural living. Noise, for example low-flying aircraft and church bells, can be an unexpected irritant. If you are not used to it, living near a silage pit or farm can also be an unpleasant experience.

Finally, would a small village or seaside resort offer sufficient scope to pursue your interests once the initial flurry of activity is over? Even if you think you know an area well, check it out properly before coming to a final decision. If possible take a self-catering let for a couple of months, preferably out of season when rents are low and the weather is bad. A good idea is to limit your daily spending to your likely retirement income rather than splurge as most of us do on holiday. This is even more pertinent if you are thinking of moving abroad, where additional difficulties can include learning the language, lower standards of health care and the danger of losing contact with your friends. Another problem for expatriates could be a change in the political climate, resulting perhaps on the one hand in your not being so welcome in your adopted country and, on the other, in a drop in the purchasing power of your pension. For more information on the financial implications of living overseas, see the section 'Retiring abroad'.

Counting the cost

Moving house can be an expensive exercise but, if you can afford to move, some good bargains can be had as desirable purchasers are not plentiful at present. It is estimated that the cost is between 5 and 10 per cent of the value of a new home, once you have totted up extras as search fees, removal charges, insurance, Stamp Duty, VAT, legal fees and estate agents' commission. The rate of Stamp Duty Land Tax (SDLT) or Stamp Duty for short, since 1 January 2010 is 0 per cent on properties up to the value of £125,000. Properties purchased costing £125,001 to £250,000 will incur a rate of 1 per cent Stamp Duty unless you are a first-time buyer when the rate is still 0 per cent. From £250,001 to £500,000 it is 3 per cent for all buyers; rising to 4 per cent for all purchasers on properties costing over £500,001. To find out more about SDLT, including how you pay it and a link to the HM Revenue & Customs' Stamp Duty Land Tax calculator, consult the website: www.direct.gov.uk/moneytaxandbenefits.

When buying a new home, especially an older property, it is essential to have a full building (structural) survey done before committing yourself. This will cost in the region of £500 for a small terraced house but is worth every penny. In particular, it will provide you with a comeback in law should things go wrong. A valuation report, while cheaper, is more superficial and may fail to detect flaws that could give you trouble and expense in the future.

If you are buying a newly built house, there are now a number of safeguards against defects. Most mortgagors will lend on new homes only if they have a National House Building Council (NHBC) warranty or its equivalent. The NHBC operates a 10-year Buildmark residential warranty and insurance scheme under which the builder is responsible for putting right defects during the first two years. It is designed to protect owners of newly built or newly converted residential housing if a problem does occur in a new home registered with NHBC. If the home-owner and builder do not agree on what needs to be done, NHBC can carry out a free independent resolution investigation and, if judged necessary, will instruct the builder to carry out repair works. If a problem becomes apparent after more than two years, the home-owner should contact NHBC, as the Buildmark covers a range of structural aspects as well as double glazing, plastering and staircases. For more information, contact **NHBC**, Tel: 0844 633 1000; website: www.nhbc.co.uk.

Also helpful to home buyers, the Land Registry allows members of the public to seek information directly about the 20 million or so properties held on its register. The details can be accessed through Land Register Online or from one of its 24 local offices in England and Wales. Contact the **Land Registry**, Tel: 0844 892 0456; website: www.landregisteronline.gov.uk.

Home information packs (HIPs)

Home Information Packs (known as HIPs) were suspended from 21 May 2010. Homes marketed for sale since that date no longer require a Home Information Pack. The Energy Performance Certificate (EPC) has been retained. Sellers are required to commission, but won't need to have received, an EPC before marketing their property. For more information on the suspension of HIPs contact the Department for Communities and Local Government on 030 3444 0000; website: www.communities.gov.uk.

Bridging loans

Tempting as it may be to buy before you sell, unless you have the money available to finance the cost of two homes – including possibly two mortgages – you need to do your sums very carefully indeed. Bridging loans are a way of getting over the problem, but can be a very expensive option. As an alternative to bridging loans, some of the major institutional estate agents operate chain-breaking schemes and may offer to buy your property at a discount: normally around 10 or 12 per cent less than the market price. For further information or advice, contact **BridgingLoans.co.uk** on 0800 533 5131; website: www.bridgingloans.co.uk.

Estate agents

Finding your dream house may prove harder than you think. It can take months of exhaustive searching, yet some people catch sight of their perfect future home by casually searching on the internet or scanning the property pages of a local paper.

The **National Association of Estate Agents (NAEA)** runs a service called PropertyLive.co.uk, a network of estate agents working with like-minded professionals committed to making the moving experience straightforward by providing access to a professional, friendly property service. Contact PropertyLive on 01926 417 356; website: www.naea.co.uk.

For protection, there is a Property Ombudsman scheme to provide an independent review service for buyers or sellers of UK residential property in the event of a complaint. As with most Ombudsman schemes, action can be taken only against firms that are actually members of the scheme. The Property Ombudsman also cannot intervene in disputes over surveys of the property. For further information and advice contact **The Property Ombudsman,** on 01722 333 306; website: www.tpos.co.uk.

The 1993 Property Misdescriptions Act prohibits estate agents and property developers from making misleading or inflated claims about a property, site or related matter. If you want to find a qualified local agent, the **Royal Institution of Chartered Surveyors (RICS)** can provide names and addresses of chartered surveyors who are estate agents. Tel: 0870 333 1600; website: www.rics.org.

Retiring abroad

Do you want to move abroad when you retire? A number of people contemplating an adventurous retirement raise funds on their family home in the UK and purchase a small property abroad – becoming what is known as 'residential tourists'. This means they travel to and from their other home without much luggage and spend several months at a time in their overseas home. The property abroad tends to fall into the category of 'lock up and leave' so that travelling to and from it is fairly easy. This bridges the gap between selling up and moving completely from the country you've lived in for years. It allows a certain amount of thinking time before you make a decision on whether or not the foreign property will become your 'forever' home.

Above all, retiring abroad needs a lot of careful planning. If the country is English-speaking no new language skills will be needed. While a pleasure for some people, the thought of having to learn a new language could for others be quite a challenge. Also there are a number of additional costs, besides purchasing the property, which can sometimes get overlooked: legal expenses, notary fees, stamp duty, registration fees and local taxes, costs of a solicitor and surveyor to name a few. The purchase of another car, insuring the vehicle, new furniture, washing machine, dishwasher, fridge and freezer have to be taken into account, and there will be the costs of making a new will. Removal costs from the UK to the new country can be quite heavy too.

So if you are thinking of retiring abroad, be careful. Above all do not get caught unawares by unscrupulous property developers. In particular, don't be rushed into a purchase you may later regret by fast-talking salespeople, or make the mistake of putting down a deposit until you are as certain as you can be that you want to go ahead. As well as all the obvious points such as water and electricity supply, it is essential to get the legal title and land rights thoroughly checked by an independent lawyer with specialist knowledge of the local property and planning laws. Otherwise you could be at risk of later discovering that the property you bought is not rightfully yours.

There are many websites offering advice and information on retiring abroad. Look at:

www.propertyinretirement.co.uk – section on Retiring Abroad;

www.buyassociation.co.uk – section on Advice on Retiring Abroad and Homes Abroad;

www.shelteroffshore.com – lots of information on living abroad including a number of informative Offshore Living Country Guides to various locations;

www.expatfocus.com – provides essential information and advice for a successful move abroad.

Removal

Professional help is essential for anyone contemplating a house move. Whether it is to the next street or half way across the world, using a reputable firm of removers and shippers will take away many of the headaches. A full packing service is something that should be considered, and saves much anxiety and a lot of your time. Costs vary depending on the type and size of furniture, the distance over which it is being moved and other factors, including insurance and seasonal troughs and peaks. Obviously, valuable antiques will cost more to pack and transport than standard modern furniture.

It pays to shop around and get at least three quotes from different removal firms. Some may be able to help reduce costs by arranging part- or return loads. It is also worth asking whether the firm has a 'low-price day', as rates are often cheaper at the start of the week. Remember, however, that the cheapest quote is not necessarily the best. Find out exactly what you are paying for and whether the price includes packing and insurance.

A useful organization to contact is the **British Association of Removers**. Its website has a list of golden rules for anyone moving house. Approved removal firms all work to a rigorous Code of Practice. Contact: 01923 699 480; website: www.bar.co.uk.

Retirement housing and sheltered accommodation

The terms 'retirement housing' and 'sheltered accommodation' cover a wide variety of housing but generally mean property with a resident manager/ caretaker, an emergency alarm system, optional meals, and some communal facilities such as living rooms, garden and laundry. Guest accommodation and visiting services such as hairdressers and chiropodists are sometimes also available. A number of companies offer extra care and nursing facilities in some of their developments. Designed to bridge the gap between the family home and residential care, such housing offers continued independence for the fit and active within a secure environment. Much of it is owned and run by local authorities, housing associations and charities. However, there are a number of well-designed, high-quality private developments of 'retirement homes' now on the market, for sale or rent, at prices to suit most pockets.

Many of the more attractive properties – and among the most expensive – are in converted country houses of architectural or historical merit, or in newly developed 'villages' and 'courtyard' schemes. As a general rule, you have to be over 55 when you buy property of this kind. While you may not wish to move into this type of accommodation just now, if the idea interests you in the long term it is worth planning ahead, as there are often very long waiting lists. Full details of the various types of sheltered accommodation, together with a price guide and some addresses, are given in Chapter 15, Caring for Elderly Parents.

Other options

Caravan or mobile home

Many retired people consider living in a caravan or mobile home that they keep either in a relative's garden or on an established site, possibly at the seaside or in the country. You may already own one as a holiday home that you are thinking of turning into more permanent accommodation. If you want to live in a caravan on land you own or other private land, you should contact your local authority for information about any planning permission or site licensing requirements that may apply.

If, on the other hand, you want to keep it on an established site, there is a varied choice ranging from small fields with just a handful of mobile homes to large, warden-assisted parks with shopping and leisure facilities. Make absolutely sure, whichever you choose, that the site owner has all the necessary permissions. You should check this with the planning and environmental health department of the local authority. It should be noted that many site owners will not accept prospective residents' own mobile homes but require them to buy one from the site or from an outgoing resident. The rights of owners of residential mobile home sites and of residents who own their mobile home but rent their pitch from a site owner are set out in the Mobile Homes Act 1983.

Find out what conditions both the local authority and the site owner attach to any agreement (by law the site owner must provide a written statement setting out terms such as the services provided, charges and maintenance of the site). You should also check your statutory rights (which should be included in the written statement), in particular regarding security of tenure and resale. Under the Act, residents have the right to sell their unit to a person approved by the site owner, who will be entitled to up to 10 per cent commission on the sale price. In the event of a dispute, either party is free to go to court or, with the agreement of both sides, to arbitration. If following a sale the resident is unhappy with the terms of the written agreement, appeal to the court must be within six months of the written terms being received.

It should also be noted that ordinary caravans are not always suitable as long-term accommodation for the over-60s. They can be damp as well as cramped, and what may have been an enjoyable adventure on holiday may soon pall when it is your only option. Modern residential park homes, which are not all that different from bungalows, have the advantage of being more spacious and sturdier but, though usually cheaper than a house of equivalent size, are nevertheless a major expense. Moreover, the law regarding such purchases is complex, and legal advice is very strongly recommended before entering into a commitment to purchase a park home.

Park Home & Holiday Caravan magazine is the UK's original park home magazine. It contains the definitive guide for those who own, or are planning to buy, a park or leisure holiday home. Everything you need to know to discover this new way of life, from reviews of the best parks to legal advice and essential buying tips. Contact: 020 8726 8253; website: www.phhc.co.uk.

Companies that specialize in new homes for sale on residential parks, ready for immediate occupation, are listed below. You could consult the website: www.parkhome-living.co.uk for further information.

> **Berkeley Parks:** With over 55 years of experience in developing bungalow style park home living, Berkeley Parks is Britain's largest park home operator with 45 residential park home estates throughout 20 counties in England and Wales. It has plots on established parks or new developments, parks with 30 homes to 380 homes, easy to run homes of every size and homes from all leading manufacturers. Tel: 01935 862 079; website: www.berkeleyparks.co.uk.

> **Britannia Parks:** For those looking for a secure and safe place to live, Britannia Park Homes could be the right choice. Not only will you be

moving to a welcoming and secure community, you will be living the park home lifestyle. Tel: 01252 408 891; website: www. britanniaparks.com.

Pathfinder Park Homes: Offers individually-designed park homes and leisure lodges, which are ideal for relaxing retirement living. Tel: 01626 833 799; website: www.pathfinderhomes.co.uk.

Regency Park Homes: With 41 sites across the country each of which has its own personality; 16 are within the Cheltenham and Gloucester area. New developments coming soon include Truro Heights in Cornwall. Tel: 01452 855 894; website: www. regencyparkhomes.co.uk.

Tingdene Residential Parks: Choose a Tingdene Residential Park and swap urban sprawl for rural tranquillity. Tel: 01933 230 111; website: www.tingdene.net.

Wessex Park Homes: One of the largest park home and lodge manufacturers in the country, Wessex will design and construct your new home to the very highest standards and equip and finish it exactly as you have specified. Tel: 01258 860 455; website: www. wessexparkhomes.co.uk.

If you do decide to go ahead with the plan, you might like to obtain a copy of *Mobile Homes – A Guide for Residents and Site Owners*, a free booklet available from your housing department or from the **Department for Communities and Local Government,** Tel: 0300 123 1124; website: www. communities.gov.uk.

Self-build

Over 25,000 people a year, including many in their 50s, are now building their own homes and, with typical cost savings estimated at between 25 and 40 per cent, the number has been growing. New building methods have been developed that defy the assumption that you need to be fit or young to undertake such a project, and many older people have successfully become self-builders. No prior building experience is necessary, although this of course helps.

Some building societies offer self-build mortgages to enable borrowers to finance the purchase of land plus construction costs. However, as with any mortgage, it is essential to make sure that you are not in danger of over-committing yourself. It is also as well to be aware that obtaining planning permission from local councils can often be a protracted business and could add to the cost if you have to submit new plans. Most self-builders work in groups and/or employ subcontractors for some of the more specialized work, but individuals who wish to build on their own can make arrangements with an architect or company that sells standard plans and building kits.

Here are some useful websites for you to search:

www.homebuilding.co.uk: Homebuilding and renovating – self-build and house renovation site, featuring house plans, building costs, house design, land for sale, exhibitions and all the information you will need including a self-build cost calculator to help you calculate your self-build costs for building your own home.

www.buildstore.co.uk: Self-build, renovation, plots of land for sale, buying building materials and seeing how others build their own home, including UK map of land for sale, Plot Search and calculator for working out your self-build costs.

www.direct.gov.uk: Raising the money to build your own home – about 20,000 people build their own homes in the UK each year and this number is rising.

www.builditthisway.co.uk: Self-build, building your own home, the ultimate DIY project, using practical examples showing the most cost-effective way to build a small house using time-honoured traditional methods.

www.selfbuildland.co.uk: Self-build land for sale in the UK. A portal for building plots for sale if you are looking to self-build your own home.

www.cat.org.uk: The Centre for Alternative Technology provides a free information and advice service on sustainable living and environmentally responsible building.

How green is your house?

With all the publicity about global warming, recycling, going green, reducing carbon footprints and becoming eco-friendly, it is sensible to set about any home improvement plans as soon as possible with a specific aim of making your home as energy saving, economical and convenient as possible.

Improvements are often easier to afford when you are still earning a regular salary, and any building work is tiresome. So if you are still working, you may find it easier to put up with the mess when you are not living among it 24 hours a day. The sooner you start the earlier you will reap the benefit.

Insulation

When you retire, you may be at home more during the day so are likely to be using your heating more intensively. One of the best ways of reducing those now alarmingly increasing utility bills is to get your house properly insulated. Heat escapes from a building in four main ways: through the roof, walls, floor, and loose-fitting doors and windows. Insulation can not only cut the heat loss dramatically but will usually more than pay for itself within four or five years.

Loft insulation

As much as 25 per cent of heat in a house escapes through the loft. The answer is to put a layer of insulating material, ideally 220 to 270 millimetres thick according to the material used, between and across the roof joists. You may be able to lay this yourself. The materials are readily available from builders' merchants. If you prefer to employ a specialist contractor, contact the **National Insulation Association** for a list of its members, Tel: 01525 383 313; website: www.nationalinsulationassociation.org.uk.

Doors and windows

A further 25 per cent of heat escapes through single-glazed windows, half of which could be saved through double glazing. There are two main types: sealed units and secondary sashes (which can be removed in the summer). Compared with other forms of insulation, double glazing is expensive; however, it does have the additional advantage of reducing noise levels. Since April 2002, any replacement doors and windows installed have to comply with strict thermal performance standards. The work will need to be done by an installer who is registered under the FENSA scheme. For further information contact the **Glass and Glazing Federation,** on: 0870 042 4255; website: www.ggf.co.uk.

Effective draught proofing saves heat loss as well as keeping out cold blasts of air. It is also relatively cheap and easy to install. Compression seals, mounted by a variety of methods and supplied in strip form, are the simplest and most cost-effective way to fill the gap between the fixed and moving edges of doors and windows. For draught proofing older sliding sash windows and doors, wiper seals, fixed with rustproof pins and screws, need to be used. For very loose-fitting frames, gap fillers that can be squeezed from a tube provide a more efficient seal between frame and surround, but this is normally work for a specialist. If you do fit draught seals, make sure you leave a space for a small amount of air to get through, or you may get problems with condensation. If the house is not well ventilated, you should put in a vapour check to slow down the leakage of moisture into the walls and ceiling. For advice on durable products and contractors, contact the **Draught Proofing Advisory Association,** Tel: 01428 654 011; website: www. dpaa-association.org.uk.

Heat loss can also be considerably reduced through hanging heavy curtains (both lined and interlined) over windows and doors. Make sure all curtains cover the windowsill or rest on the floor. It is better to have them too long than too short.

Wall insulation

More heat is lost through the walls than perhaps anywhere else in the house: it can be as much as 50 per cent. If your house has cavity walls – and most houses built after 1930 do – then cavity wall insulation should be considered. This involves injecting mineral wool (rock wool or glass wool), polystyrene beads or foam into the cavity through holes drilled in the outside wall. It is work for a specialist and, depending on what grants are applicable, may be free or could cost upwards of £350. Against this, you could expect a typical saving of around 25 per cent off your heating bill each year, so in most cases the initial outlay should be recovered in under four years. Make sure that the firm you use is registered with a reputable organization, such as the British Standards Institution, or can show a current Agrément Certificate for the system and is approved by the British Board of Agrément (BBA). If a foam fill is used, the application should comply with British Standard BS 5617 and the material with BS 5618.

Solid wall insulation can be considerably more expensive, but well worthwhile, providing similar savings of around 25 per cent off your annual heating bill. Again, this is work for a specialist and involves applying an insulating material to the outside of the wall, plus rendering or cladding. Alternatively, an insulated thermal lining can be applied to the inside. Landlords who install wall insulation can offset up to £1,500 of the cost, per building, against Income Tax. This used only to apply to loft and cavity wall insulation but has now been extended to include solid wall insulation.

The scope of the relief (officially known as the Landlord's Energy Saving Allowance) was further extended to include draught proofing and insulation for hot water systems. Floor insulation is included in the list of energy-saving items that qualify for the allowance. *NB:* the £1,500 cap, which previously applied to the building, now applies per property, so if there are two flats in the building, the £1,500 cap now applies to each one.

For further information and addresses of registered contractors, contact:

British Board of Agrément, Tel: 01923 665 300; website: www.bbacerts.co.uk.

British Standards Institution, Tel: 020 8996 9001; website: www.bsigroup.co.uk.

Cavity Insulation Guarantee Agency (CIGA), Tel: 01525 853 300; website: www.ciga.co.uk.

Eurisol UK Ltd, Tel: 020 7935 8532; website: www.eurisol.com.

Insulated Render & Cladding Association Ltd for solid or defective walls, Tel: 0844 249 0040; website: www.inca-ltd.org.uk.

National Insulation Association for cavity wall and loft insulation, draught proofing and insulated thermal linings applied internally, Tel: 08451 636 363; website: www.nationalinsulationassociation. org.uk.

Floor insulation

Up to 15 per cent of heat loss can be saved through filling the cracks or gaps in the floorboards and skirting. If you can take up your floorboards, rock wool or glass wool rolls can be extremely effective when fixed underneath the joists. Filling spaces with papier mâché or plastic wool will also help, especially if a good felt or rubber underlay is then laid under the carpet. Be careful, however, that you do not block up the underfloor ventilation, which is necessary to protect floor timbers from dampness and rot. Solid concrete floors can be covered with cork tiles or carpet and felt or rubber underlay.

Hot water cylinder insulation

If your hot water cylinder has no insulation, it could be costing you several pounds a week in wasted heat. An insulating jacket around your hot water cylinder will cut wastage by three-quarters. Most hot water tanks now come ready supplied with insulation. If not, the jacket should be at least 80 millimetres thick and will cost from around £25. Jackets come in various sizes, so measure your cylinder before buying and look for one that conforms to BS 5615.

Grants

There are many schemes for helping pensioners with heating bills and insulation costs. Here are some websites that give advice and information on this subject:

www.insulationgrants.info: Home insulation grants – government grants for insulation. Find out if you qualify.

www.freeinsulation.co.uk: Government-backed grants available for cavity wall and loft insulation.

www.getinsulation.co.uk: New cavity wall and loft insulation. Apply for 100 per cent grants.

www.silverhairs.co.uk: The Pensioners page – the Energy Saving Trust can tell you about insulation grants.

www.which.co.uk: Pensioners urged to claim government grants to help meet the cost of insulating their homes.

www.lioninsulation.co.uk: Home insulation grants available for loft and cavity wall insulation and draught proofing. 100 per cent grants are available for those on qualifying benefits.

www.saga.co.uk/money: Home help, grants for home improvements – ask Saga about its home repair assistance grants. Pensioners and people on certain benefits can claim energy-efficiency grants.

www.homeheatingguide.co.uk: Elderly people on pension credit are eligible for grants for home insulation.

www.government-grants.co.uk: Grants for loft and cavity wall insulation available. Further details can be obtained from www.direct.gov.uk or from www.warmfront.co.uk.

Heating

It may be possible to save money by using different fuels or by heating parts of your house off different systems. This could apply especially if some rooms are only occasionally used. Your local gas and electricity offices can advise on heating systems, running costs and energy conservation, as well as heating and hot water appliances.

The **Solid Fuel Association** will give free advice and information on all aspects of solid fuel heating, including appliances and installation. Contact: 0845 601 4406; website: www.solidfuel.co.uk.

The **Building Centre** has a very wide range of building products on display, with information officers on hand to give consumer guidance. Contact: 020 7692 4000; website: www.buildingcentre.co.uk.

Buying and installing heating equipment

When buying equipment, check that it has been approved by the appropriate standards approvals board. For electrical equipment, the letters to look for are BEAB (British Electro-technical Approvals Board) or CCA (CENELEC Certification Agreement), which is the European Union equivalent.

For gas appliances, look for the CE mark, which denotes that appliances meet the requirements of the Gas Appliance (Safety) Regulations Act 1995. Domestic solid fuel appliances should be approved by the Solid Fuel Appliances Approval Scheme; check the sales literature.

When looking for contractors to install your equipment, an important point to note is that new government legislation has come into force placing tighter controls on the standard of electrical and other installation work in households across England and Wales. It is now a legal requirement for electricians as well as kitchen, bathroom and gas installers to comply with Part P of the Building Regulations. You would therefore be well advised to check that any contractor you propose using is enrolled with the relevant inspection council or is a member of the relevant trade association.

Electricians should be approved by the **NICEIC**. All approved contractors are covered for technical work by the NICEIC Complaints Procedure and Guarantee of Standards Scheme and undertake to work to British Standard 7671. Any substandard work must be put right at no extra cost to the consumer. Names and addresses of local approved contractors can be found in the NICEIC Roll of Approved Contractors obtainable from NICEIC: 0870 013 0382; website: www.niceic.org.uk.

An alternative source for finding a reputable electrician is the **Electrical Contractors' Association**. Its members, all of whom have to be qualified, work to national wiring regulations and a published ECA Code of Fair Trading. There is also a work bond, which guarantees that, in the event of a contractor becoming insolvent, the work will be completed by another approved electrician at the originally quoted price, subject to the conditions of the scheme. Contact: 020 7313 4800; website: www.eca.co.uk.

Gas appliances should only be installed by a Gas Safe Register registered installer (Gas Safe Register replaced CORGI as the gas registration body on 1 April 2009). Registration is compulsory by law. As a further safeguard, all registered gas installers carry a Gas Safe Register ID card with their photo, types of gas work they are competent to do, their employer's trading title and the Gas Safe Register logo. After a gas appliance has been installed, you should receive a safety certificate from the Gas Safe Register, proving that it has been installed by a professional. You should keep this safe, as you may need it should you want to sell your home in the future. To find a registered installer in your area, contact the **Gas Safe Register,** Tel: 0800 408 5500; website: www.gassaferegister.co.uk.

Additionally, members of the Heating and Ventilating Contractors' Association can advise on all types of central heating. All domestic installation work done by member companies is covered by a free three-year guarantee. For further information contact the **Heating and Ventilating Contractors' Association,** Tel: 020 7313 4900; website: www.hvca.org.uk.

Tips for reducing your energy bills

Energy can be saved in lots of small ways. Taken together, they could amount to quite a large cut in your bills. You may find some of the following ideas worth considering:

- Set your central heating timer and thermostat to suit the weather. A saving of half an hour or one degree can be substantial. For example, reducing the temperature by 1 degree Celsius could cut your heating bills by up to 10 per cent.

- A separate thermostat on your hot water cylinder set at around 60 degrees Celsius will enable you to keep hot water for taps at a lower temperature than for the heating system.

- If you run your hot water off an immersion heater, have a time switch fitted attached to an Economy 7 meter so that the water is heated at the cheap rate overnight. An override switch will enable you to top up the heat during the day if necessary.

- Showers are more economical than baths, as well as being easier to use when you become older.

- Reflective foil sheets put behind your radiators help to reduce heat loss through the walls.

- Switch off, or reduce, the heating in rooms not being used, and close doors.

- Low-energy light bulbs can save several pounds a year.

- If you have an open fire, a vast amount of heat tends to be lost up the chimney. A wood-burning stove can help reduce heat loss as well as maximize the amount of heat you get from your wood or solid fuel in other ways. If you dislike the idea of losing the look of an open fire, there are now a number of appliances on the market that are open-fronted and fit flush with the fireplace opening. Contact your local office of the **Solid Fuel Association** for further information. If you decide to block up a fireplace, don't forget to fit an air vent to allow some ventilation.

- Some small cooking appliances can save energy in comparison with a full-sized cooker. An electric casserole or slow cooker uses only a fraction more energy than a light bulb and is economical for single households. Similarly, an electric frying pan or multi-cooker can be a sensible alternative for people living on their own. Pressure cookers and microwave ovens can save fuel and time.

- Defrosting fridges and freezers regularly reduces running costs.

- Finally, it is a good idea to get in the habit of reading your electricity and gas meters regularly. This will help you keep track of likely bills. British Gas customers can call the meter reading line, at any time 24 hours a day, for up-to-date readings. You should have your meter reading and account reference number to hand when you ring. The number to call is printed clearly on your gas bill.

You might like to take advantage of one of the British Gas payment options that allows customers to spread their gas or electricity payments over the year in fixed monthly or quarterly instalments, based on an estimate of their annual consumption. Estimates are periodically adjusted up or down, depending on actual meter readings. Price reductions are offered to customers paying by monthly direct debit. For further details, contact **British Gas** (see your gas or electricity bill for the telephone number; website: www. britishgas.co.uk). Many other suppliers have similar budget plans.

If you would like to save money on your water bill, consider having a water meter. You can't switch water provider (as with other forms of energy

– gas and electricity) as the market is privatized but it's not open to competition. This means the most important decision when trying to reduce costs is how you are billed. Only 33 per cent of homes have a water meter; most are still being charged on the 'water bill' system. The price here is fixed on the home's rateable value and the amount of water is irrelevant. It is important to find out whether a meter is financially worthwhile but as a rough rule of thumb, if there are more bedrooms in your house than people, you should check out getting a meter. For further information contact the comparison sites, www.uswitch.com and www.ccwater.org.uk or you could ask your water supplier to provide you with a water meter calculator, which makes it easy for you to work out whether or not you'll save.

Another useful organization to note is the **Energy Saving Trust**, a non-profit organization that provides free impartial advice tailored to suit individuals, including information on available grants and money saving ideas. Tel: 0800 512 012; website: www.energysavingtrust.org.uk.

Consumer Direct is the new statutory organization championing consumers' interests. Tel: 08454 04 05 06; website: www.consumerdirect.gov.uk.

Useful energy saving tips can be found on www.moneysavingexpert.com. You can sign up for an e-newsletter which will be packed full of information and suggestions for helping to reduce your costs in different ways. Similar advice and information but specifically geared to the over-55s is available on www.seniorsdiscounts.co.uk.

Improvement and repair

If your house needs structural repairs, a wise first step would be to contact the **Royal Institution of Chartered Surveyors** to help you find a reputable chartered surveyor. Tel: 0870 333 1600; website: www.rics.org.

Local authority assistance

The Regulatory Reform Order (RRO) gives local authorities greater discretionary powers to provide assistance – such as low-cost loans and grants – to help with renovations, repairs and adaptations to the home, or to help someone move to more suitable accommodation if that is a better solution. Any assistance given, however, must be in accordance with the authority's published policy. For further information contact the environmental health or housing department of your local authority.

Disabled facilities grant (DFG)

This is designed to adapt or provide facilities for a home (including the common parts where applicable) to make it more suitable for occupation by a disabled person. It can cover a wide range of improvements to enable someone with a disability to manage more independently, including, for example, adaptations to make the accommodation safe for a disabled occupant, work to facilitate access either to the property itself or to the main rooms, the provision of suitable bathroom or kitchen facilities, the adaptation of heating or lighting controls, or improvement of the heating system. Provided the applicant is eligible, a mandatory grant of up to £30,000 may be available in England for all the above (local authorities may use their discretionary powers to provide additional assistance), £25,000 in Northern Ireland and up to £36,000 in Wales.

As with most other grants, there is a means test. The local authority will want to check that the proposed work is reasonable and practicable according to the age and condition of the property, and the local social services department will need to be satisfied that the work is necessary and appropriate to meet the individual's needs. The grant can be applied for either by the disabled person or by a joint owner or joint tenant or landlord on his or her behalf. For further information, contact the environmental health or housing department of your local authority. See website: www. direct.gov.uk/disabledpeople.

Do not start work until approval has been given to your grant application, as you will not be eligible for a grant once work has started.

Community care grant

Income Support recipients may be able to obtain a community care grant from the Social Fund to help with repairs; see www.direct.gov.uk/moneytaxandbenefits.

Other help for disabled people

Your local authority may be able to help with the provision of certain special facilities such as a stair lift, telephone installations or a ramp to replace steps. Apply to your local social services department and, if you encounter any difficulties, ask for further help from your local disability group or Age UK group.

Useful contacts

APHC Ltd (Association of Plumbing and Heating Contractors Ltd) maintains a national register of licensed members and can put you in touch with a reputable local engineer. All are carefully vetted every year to ensure they are working to the highest standards. Tel: 0121 711 5030; website: www.competentpersonsscheme.co.uk.

Association of Building Engineers can supply names of qualified building engineers/surveyors. Tel: 0845 126 1058; website: www.abe.org.uk.

Association of Master Upholsterers & Soft Furnishers Ltd has a list of over 500 approved members throughout the country that specialize in all forms of upholstery including curtains and soft furnishings. Names of those operating in your area can be obtained from the Association. Tel: 029 2077 8918; website: www.upholsterers.co.uk.

The Building Centre has displays of building products, heating appliances, bathroom and kitchen equipment and other exhibits and can give guidance on building problems. It has manufacturers' lists and other free literature you can take away, and there is also a well-stocked bookshop covering all aspects of building and home improvement. It is open Monday to Friday, 9.30 am to 6 pm; Saturday, 10 am to 2 pm. Tel: 020 7692 4000; website: www.buildingcentre.co.uk.

Federation of Master Builders (FMB): lists of members are available from regional offices. A warranty scheme, which insures work in progress and gives up to 10 years' guarantee on completion of work, is available from some of its members. Tel: 020 7242 7583; website: www.fmb.org.uk.

Guild of Master Craftsmen can supply names of all types of specialist craftspeople including, for example, carpenters, joiners, ceramic workers and restorers. Tel: 01273 478 449; website: www.guildmc.com.

Institute of Plumbing and Heating Engineering can provide a list of professional plumbers. Tel: 01708 472 791; website: www.ciphe.org.uk.

Royal Institute of British Architects (RIBA) has a free Clients Service, which, however small your building project, will recommend up to three suitable architects. It can also supply you with useful leaflets giving advice on working with an architect. Tel: 020 7580 5533; website: www.architecture.com.

Royal Institution of Chartered Surveyors (RICS) will nominate qualified surveyors in your area, who can be recognized by the initials MRICS or FRICS after their name. It also publishes a number of useful leaflets. Tel: 0870 333 1600; website: www.rics.org.

The Scottish and Northern Ireland Plumbing Employers' Federation (SNIPEF) is the national trade association for all types of firms involved in plumbing and domestic heating in Scotland and Northern Ireland. It has over 800 member firms and operates a Code of Fair Trading, independent complaints scheme and guarantee-of-work scheme. Lists of local members are available on request. Tel: 0131 225 2255; website: www.snipef.org.

Home improvement agencies (HIAs)

Home improvement agencies (sometimes known as 'staying put' or 'care and repair' agencies) work with older or disabled people to help them remain in their own homes by providing advice and assistance on repairs, improvements and adaptations. They also advise on the availability of funding and welfare benefits, obtain prices, recommend reliable builders and inspect the completed job.

Useful contacts

Foundations is the national body for Home Improvement Agencies in England, providing a range of services for agencies. Tel: 08458 645 210; website: www.foundations.uk.com.

Information on Home Improvement Agencies and care and repair in the UK can be found by contacting **EAC (Elderly Accommodation Counsel)** a charity set up to help older and elderly people make informed choices about meeting their housing, support and care needs. Contact the national advice line: 0800 377 7070; website: www.housingcare.org.

Another possibility is the **Anchor Trust,** which offers comprehensive home care for the elderly, including home maintenance services. Tel: 0845 140 2020; website: www.anchor.org.uk.

Safety in the home

Accidents in the home account for 40 per cent of all fatal accidents, resulting in nearly 5,000 deaths a year. Seventy per cent of these victims are over retirement age, and nearly 80 per cent of deaths are caused by falls. A further 3 million people need medical treatment. The vast majority of accidents are caused by carelessness or by obvious danger spots in the home that for the most part could very easily be made safer. Tragically, it is all too often the little things that we keep meaning to attend to but never quite get round to that are the ones that prove fatal.

Steps and stairs should be well lit, with light switches at both the top and the bottom. Frayed carpet is notoriously easy to trip on. On staircases especially, defective carpet should be repaired or replaced as soon as possible. All stairs should have a handrail to provide extra support – on both sides, if the stairs are very steep. It is also a good idea to have a white line painted on the edge of steps that are difficult to see – for instance in the garden or leading up to the front door.

It may be stating the obvious to say that climbing on chairs and tables is dangerous – and yet we all do it. You should keep proper steps, preferably with a handrail, to do high jobs in the house such as hanging curtains or reaching cupboards.

Floors can be another danger zone. Rugs and mats can slip on polished floors and should always be laid on some form of non-slip backing material. Stockinged feet are slippery on all but carpeted floors, and new shoes should always have the soles scratched before you wear them. Remember also that spilt water or talcum powder on tiled or linoleum floors is a major cause of accidents.

The *bathroom* is particularly hazardous for falls. Sensible precautionary measures include using a suction-type bath mat and putting handrails on the bath or alongside the shower. For older people who have difficulty getting in and out of the bath, a bath seat can be helpful. Soap on a rope is safer in a shower, as it is less likely to slither out of your hands and make the floor slippery. Regardless of age, you should make sure that all medicines are clearly labelled. Throw away any prescribed drugs left over from a previous illness.

Fires can all too easily start in the home. If you have an open fire, you should always use a fire-guard and spark guard at night. The chimney should be regularly swept at least once a year, maybe more if you have a wood-burning stove. Never place a clothes horse near an open fire or heater, and be careful of flammable objects that could fall from the mantelpiece. Upholstered furniture is a particular fire hazard, especially when polyurethane foam has been used in its manufacture. If buying new furniture, make sure that it carries a red triangle label, indicating that it is resistant to smouldering cigarettes. Furniture that also passes the match ignition test carries a green label. 'Combustion modified foam' that has passed the BS 5852 test now has to be used instead.

Portable heaters should be kept away from furniture and curtains and positioned where you cannot trip over them. Paraffin heaters should be handled particularly carefully and should never be filled while alight. Avoid leaving paraffin where it will be exposed to heat, including sunlight. If possible, it should be kept in a metal container outside the house.

Gas appliances should be serviced regularly by British Gas or other Gas Safe Register registered installers. You should also ensure that there is adequate ventilation when using heaters. Never block up air vents: carbon monoxide fumes can kill.

If you smell gas or notice anything you suspect could be dangerous, stop using the appliance immediately, open the doors and windows and call the National Grid 24-hour emergency line free: 0800 111 999.

More than one in three fires in the home are caused by accidents with *cookers*. Chip pans are a particular hazard: only fill the pan one-third full with oil and always dry the chips before putting them in the fat or, better still, use oven-ready chips that you just pop into the oven to cook. Pan handles should be turned away from the heat and positioned so you cannot knock them off the stove. If called to the door or telephone, always take the pan off the ring and turn off the heat before you leave the kitchen. Cigarettes left smouldering in an ashtray could be dangerous if the ashtray is full. Smoking in bed is a potential killer.

Faulty electric wiring is another frequent cause of fires, as are overloaded power points. The wiring in your home should be checked every five years and you should avoid using too many appliances off a single plug. Ask an electrician's advice about what is the maximum safe number. Use only plugs that conform to the British Standard 1363. It is a good idea to get into the habit of pulling the plug out of the wall socket when you have finished using an appliance, whether TV or toaster.

All electrical equipment should be regularly checked for wear and tear, and frayed or damaged flexes immediately replaced. Wherever possible, have electric sockets moved to waist height to avoid unnecessary bending whenever you want to turn on the switch. In particular, *electric blankets* should be routinely overhauled and checked in accordance with the manufacturer's instructions. It is dangerous to use both a hot water bottle and electric blanket – and never use an under blanket as an over blanket.

Electrical appliances are an increasing feature of labour-saving *gardening* but can be dangerous unless treated with respect. They should never be used when it is raining. Moreover, gardeners should always wear rubber-soled shoes or boots, and avoid floppy clothing that could get caught in the equipment.

As a general precaution, keep *fire extinguishers* readily accessible. Make sure they are regularly maintained and in good working order. Portable extinguishers should conform to BS EN 3 or BS 6165. Any extinguishers made before 1996 should conform to BS 5423, which preceded BS EN 3. Many insurance companies now recommend that you install a smoke alarm, which should conform to BS 5446-1:2000 or BS EN 14604:2005, as an effective and cheap early warning device.

Here are some useful websites:

www.info.co.uk/HomeSafetyForSeniors

www.home-security-action.co.uk/home-safety-for-the-elderly

www.saferhouses.co.uk/HomeSafetyElderly

www.ageuk.org/home-and-care

www.indobase.com/home/age-lifestyle/home-for-elderly

www.independentliving.co.uk

Home security

Nine out of 10 burglaries are spontaneous and take less than 10 minutes. However, there is much you can do to protect yourself. The crime prevention officer at your local police station will advise you on how to improve your security arrangements. He or she will also tell you whether there is a Neighbourhood Watch scheme and how you join it. This is a free service that the police are happy to provide.

The most vulnerable access points are doors and windows. Simple precautions such as fitting adequate locks and bolts can do much to deter the average burglar. Prices for a good door lock are about £60 to £80 plus VAT, and prices for window locks are about £15 to £20 plus VAT per window.

Doors should have secure bolts or a five-lever mortise lock strengthened by metal plates on both sides, a door chain and a spyhole in the front door. Additionally, you might consider outside lights (ideally with an infra-red sensor) to illuminate night-time visitors and an entry phone system requiring callers to identify themselves before you open the door.

Windows should also be properly secured with key-operated locks. The best advice is to fit locks that secure them when partially open. Install rack bolts or surface-mounted security press bolts on French windows, and draw your curtains at night so potential intruders cannot see in. Louvre windows are especially vulnerable because the slats can easily be removed. A solution is to glue them in place with an epoxy resin and to fit a special louvre lock. An agile thief can get through any space larger than a human head, so even small windows such as skylights need properly fitted locks. Both double glazing and venetian blinds act as a further deterrent. If you are particularly worried, you could also have bars fitted to the windows or install old-fashioned internal shutters that can be closed at night. Alternatively, many DIY shops sell decorative wrought-iron security grilles.

An obvious point is to ensure that the house is securely locked whenever you go out, even for five minutes. If you lose your keys, you should change the locks without delay. Insist that official callers such as meter readers show their identity cards before you allow them inside. If you are going away, even for only a couple of days, remember to cancel the milk and the newspapers. You might also like to take advantage of the **Royal Mail's Keepsafe** service. It will store your mail while you are away and so avoid it piling up and alerting potential burglars to your absence. There is a charge for the service, which starts at £8.95 for up to 17 days. Contact: 0845 7777 888; website: www.royalmail.com/redirections.

If your home will be unoccupied for any length of time, it is sensible to ask the local police to put it on their unattended premises register. Finally, consider a time switch (cost around £15) that will turn the lights on and off when you are away and can be used to switch on the heating before your return.

If you want to know of a reputable locksmith, you should contact the **Master Locksmiths Association,** Tel: 01327 262 255; website: www.locksmiths.co.uk.

Useful reading

The Home Office issues a couple of useful booklets, *Your Practical Guide to Crime Prevention* and *How to Beat the Bogus Caller.* They are available free from your local police station or telephone the Home Office publications line on 0870 2414 680.

Burglar alarms and safes

More elaborate precautions such as a burglar alarm are among the best ways of protecting your home. Although alarms are expensive – they cost from about £450 to well in excess of £1,000 for sophisticated systems – they could be worth every penny. In the event of a break-in, you can summon help or ask the police to do what they can if you are away.

Many insurance companies will recommend suitable contractors to install burglar alarm equipment. The **National Security Inspectorate** website lists approved contractors in your locality that install burglar alarm systems to, among others, British and European standards. There are 700 recognized firms and some 1,000 branches. The National Security Inspectorate will also investigate technical complaints. Tel: 0845 006 3003; website: www.nsi.org.uk.

If you keep valuables or money in the house, you should think about buying a concealed wall or floor safe. If you are going away, it is a good idea to inform your neighbours so that if your alarm goes off they will know something is wrong. Burglar alarms have an unfortunate habit of ringing for no good reason (a mouse or cat can trigger the mechanism), and many people ignore them as a result. It is advisable to give your neighbours a key so that they can turn off and reset the alarm should the occasion arise.

Insurance discounts

According to recent research, seven out of 10 householders are under-insured, some of them unknowingly but some intentionally to keep premiums lower. This could be dangerous because in the event of a mishap they could end up seriously out of pocket. With recent increases in premiums, many readers may feel that this is hardly the moment to be discussing any reassessment of their policy. However, there are two good reasons why this could be sensible. First is because the number of burglaries has risen, so the risks are greater. But, more particularly, you may be able to obtain better value than you are getting at present. A number of insurance companies now give discounts on house contents premiums if proper security precautions have been installed.

Some insurance companies approach the problem differently and arrange discounts for their policyholders with manufacturers of security devices. If you would welcome independent advice on choosing a policy, you might usefully contact the **Institute of Insurance Brokers (IIB)** for details of local IIB brokers; Tel: 01933 410 003; website: www.iib-uk.com. See also the 'Insurance' section, below.

Personal safety

Older people who live on their own can be particularly at risk. A number of personal alarms are now available that are highly effective and can generally give you peace of mind. A sensible precaution is to carry a 'screamer alarm', sometimes known as a 'personal attack button'. These are readily available in department stores, electrical shops and alarm companies.

Age Concern Aid-Call provides a service that enables anyone living alone to call for help simply by pressing a button. The subscriber has a small radio transmitter, worn as a pendant or like a watch, which contacts a 24-hour monitoring centre. The centre alerts a list of nominated relatives and friends, or the emergency services, that something is wrong. There are several ways of paying for Aid-Call based on installation, monitoring and rental. The firm operates a nationwide service and will arrange a demonstration through its head office. Tel: 0800 77 22 66; website: www.aidcall.co.uk.

A telephone can also increase your sense of security. Some families come to an arrangement whereby they ring their older relatives at regular times to check that all is well. Older people feel particularly vulnerable to mugging. While the dangers are often exaggerated, it must be sensible to take all normal precautions. The police are of the view that many muggings could be avoided if you are alert, think ahead and try to radiate confidence.

Insurance

As you near retirement, it is sensible to reassess your building and home contents policy. If the insurance was originally arranged through your building society, it may cease when your mortgage is paid off. In this case it will be essential for you to arrange new cover directly. Similarly, when buying for cash rather than with a mortgage – for instance when moving to a smaller house – it will be up to you to organize the insurance and to calculate the rebuilding value of your home. It is advisable to get a qualified valuer to do this for you.

The value of your home may have increased significantly since you purchased it and the chances are that the cost of replacing the fabric of your house, were it to burn down, would be significantly greater than the amount for which it is currently insured. Remember, you must insure for the full rebuilding cost: the market value may be inappropriate. Your policy should also provide money to meet architects' or surveyors' fees, as well as alternative accommodation for you and your family if your home were completely destroyed by fire.

If you are planning to move into accommodation that has been converted from one large house into several flats or maisonettes, check with the landlord or managing agent that the insurance on the structure of the total building is adequate. All too many people have found themselves homeless because each tenant insured only his or her own flat and the collective policies were not sufficient to replace the common parts.

If when buying a new property you decide to take out a new mortgage, contrary to what many people believe you are under no obligation to insure your home with the particular company suggested by your building society. It is not being recommended here that you should necessarily go elsewhere: the point is that, as with all insurance, policies vary and some are more competitive than others.

About 2 million people live under threat of flooding in the UK – about one in 10 homes – and over 270,000 are at risk. It is highly advisable to check whether you live in a high-risk area and, if so, take steps to protect your property. This could cut your insurance premium by 10 per cent. According to the Association of British Insurers it can cost up to £40,000 to protect your home fully from flood damage. Further information on flood-risk areas can be obtained by calling **Flood-line** on 0845 988 1188; website: www.environment-agency.gov.uk.

Many people are under-insured with regard to the contents of their home. Insurance that simply covers the purchase price is normally grossly insufficient. Instead, you should assess the replacement cost and make sure you have a 'new for old' or 'replacement as new' policy. Most insurance companies offer an automatic inflation-proofing option for both building and contents policies. Don't forget to cancel items on your contents policy that you no longer possess, nor to add new valuables that have been bought or received as presents. In particular, do check that you are adequately covered for any home improvements you may have added, such as a new kitchen or garage, conservatory, extra bathroom, swimming pool or other luxury.

Where antiques and jewellery are concerned, simple inflation-proofing may not be enough. Values can rise and fall disproportionately to inflation and depend on current market trends. For a professional valuation, contact either of the following:

The **British Antique Dealers' Association (BADA)**, Tel: 020 7589 4128; website: www.bada.org.

LAPADA (the Association of Art & Antiques Dealers), Tel: 020 7823 3511; website: www.lapada.org.

Either of these organizations can advise on the name of a specialist. Photographs of particularly valuable items can help in the assessment of premiums and settlement of claims, as well as give the police a greater chance of recovering them in the case of theft. Property marking, for example with an ultraviolet marker, is another useful ploy, as it will help the police trace your possessions should any be stolen.

The **Association of British Insurers** has information on various aspects of household insurance and loss prevention, including *Buildings Insurance for Home Owners* and *Home Contents Insurance*, which give details of what policies you need and advice on how to ensure you have the correct amount of cover. Contact the ABI on 020 7600 3333; website: www.abi.org.uk.

The **British Insurance Brokers' Association** can provide information on registered insurance brokers in your area. Contact the Consumers' helpline: 0870 950 1790; website: www.biba.org.uk.

Some insurance companies offer home and contents policies for older people (age 50 and over) at substantially reduced rates. The rationale behind such schemes is that older people are less likely to leave their homes empty on a regular basis (ie 9 to 5) and are therefore less liable to be burgled. In some cases, policies are geared to the fact that many retired people have either sold or given away many of their more valuable possessions and therefore need to insure their homes only up to a relatively low sum. See the following websites for more information on such policies:

www.rias.co.u

www.castlecover.co.uk

www.ageuk.org.uk

www.staysure.co.uk

www.50plusinsurance.co.uk

www.over50insurance.org

www.saga.co.uk

An increasing number of insurance companies offer generous no-claims discounts. Another type of discount-linked policy that is becoming more popular is one that carries an excess, whereby the householder pays the first chunk of any claim, say the first £100 or £250. Savings on premiums can be quite appreciable, if you check what terms they offer.

Raising money on your home – equity release

The problem for many retired people is that they are 'asset rich, cash poor', with most of their money being tied up in their property. As a result, many retired owner-occupiers struggle to make ends meet on reduced incomes. One way round the dilemma is to sell up and move somewhere smaller in order to provide extra income. For those who prefer to stay put, however, there are schemes that enable people to unlock capital without having to move.

Although house prices have fallen considerably in recent years, they have begun to rally a little and now might be a good time to consider equity release. This is a way of releasing money from the value of your home without actually having to move. It comes in two forms: either a type of mortgage where you pay no interest on the loan until you die (a lifetime mortgage); at this point the property is sold to pay off the debt. Or, you sell a proportion of the property to a company to release a lump sum. This is known as a home reversion scheme. While each has its attractions, neither scheme is without its drawbacks, so it is essential to make sure that you fully understand all the financial implications – including how the plan may affect your estate – before entering into any agreement.

A crucial point to check is that any plan you are considering carries an absolute guarantee of your being able to remain in your home for as long as you need or want to do so. In the past, many elderly people tragically lost their homes as a result of ill-advised and dangerous schemes. Today it is extremely unlikely that you would be offered a high-risk plan, because in October 2004 all lifetime mortgages and home income plans came under the regulation of the FSA. Where your home is concerned you simply cannot afford to take any chances. Since April 2007, reversion schemes have also come under the regulation of the FSA.

The important thing with equity release is to make sure your family knows all about your plans. Since the loan, plus any interest, is paid off when you have died, not letting your family know about the equity release scheme could mean they have a shock at a time when they are least able to cope with it. If you are interested in getting an equity release product, you need to take advice. Make sure you use one of the companies under the **Safe Home Income Plans (SHIP)** scheme, as these companies sign up to a charter guaranteeing that you will not be forced to leave your home at any stage, and the value of the loan will never be more than the property is worth. For further information see website: www.ship-ltd.org.

Home reversion schemes

A home reversion scheme is designed for home owners who wish to release the maximum amount of equity within their property. Unlike an equity release lifetime mortgage scheme, where you retain full ownership of your property using a home reversion plan, you sell some or all of your property to the plan provider.

Home reversion schemes allow home owners to release a lump sum from their property; there is no interest and no concerns over future house prices. The amount of equity you can release under a home reversion plan will depend on your age and the value of your property. With a home reversion scheme, you sell all or part of your property to the plan provider. It is the home reversion scheme provider that takes the risk on future house prices. If you sell 30 per cent of your property to the home reversion plan provider, the home reversion plan provider will be entitled to 30 per cent of the sale price when your property is eventually sold. If you sell 100 per cent of your property to the home reversion scheme provider, the home reversion plan provider will be entitled to 100 per cent of the sale price when your property is eventually sold. You will not be charged any rent, but you will be responsible for maintaining the property and paying for any repairs that are required.

Usually the set-up costs are fairly low. However, the downside is that the money you receive from the sale will be substantially less than the current market value of your home. The price paid will reflect the fact that it could be a great many years before the reversion company can realize its investment. The longer you live, the more value you will get from the scheme. If your life expectancy is not that great, a particular point to query is whether there are any benefit guarantees in the event of early death.

For further information on home reversion schemes, see websites: www.homereversionschemes.co.uk, www.ship-ltd.org or www.sixtyplusonline.co.uk. There is also an FSA fact sheet on equity release schemes available from www.fsa.gov.uk. SHIP members are:

Aviva Equity Release UK	0845 302 0111, www.aviva.co.uk
Bridgewater Equity Release	0845 140 5060, www.bridgewaterequityrelease.co.uk
Hodge Lifetime	0800 731 4076, www.hodgelifetime.com
Home & Capital	01234 321 091, www.homeandcapital.co.uk

Just Retirement Limited	01737 233 296, www.justretirement.com
LV=	0870 609 0616, www.lv.com
More 2 Life	08454 150 150, www.more2life.co.uk
New Life Mortgages Ltd	0121 712 3800, www.newlifemortgages.co.uk
Northern Rock plc	0845 60 50 500, www.northernrock.co.uk
Stonehaven	0800 068 0212, www.stonehaven-uk.com

Lifetime mortgages

A lifetime mortgage is the other type of equity release scheme (sometimes known as 'roll-up loans'). With a lifetime mortgage you continue to own your home and any growth in that property value is yours. Unlike a normal mortgage the interest is added to the amount you have borrowed therefore the debt rises over time. It is this roll-up of interest that makes a lifetime mortgage attractive to retired people, as there are no monthly repayments to make.

There are now options available where some or all of the interest can be paid, thus providing more choice. Some schemes have a drawdown facility where you take just the amount you need now and have the facility to draw down further sums from your lifetime mortgage over the following years. This can mean significant savings in interest. If you want the option to repay your lifetime mortgage you can. If you want to 'ring-fence' some of your property's value to guarantee an inheritance, you can.

While attractive in that clients can spend the money safe in the knowledge that they will not have to make any repayments, the disadvantage is that compound interest can very quickly mount up, leaving little or nothing for their heirs to inherit. To reduce the risk, particular points to check are, first, that the interest is fixed rather than variable and, even more important, that the plan includes a guarantee that there is no danger to your estate of negative equity. Lifetime mortgages are offered by SHIP members, listed above.

Home income plans

Home income plans work on the basis of a mortgage arrangement whereby the loan is used to purchase an annuity to provide a guaranteed income for life. The mortgage interest is fixed and is deducted from the annuity payment before you receive your share. While popular at one time, such plans have largely fallen out of favour owing to the abolition of mortgage interest relief and worsening annuity rates. Few people would derive much value and they should really be considered only by those well into their mid-80s.

Cashing in on the value of your home while continuing to live there for the remainder of your life has attractive advantages, especially if the priority is to generate additional income or to provide you with a lump sum. However, expert advice is essential and you should also consult an independent financial adviser (IFA) with expertise in equity release schemes. A welcome safeguard is that the Financial Services Authority, which regulates lifetime mortgages, extended its powers to include home reversion schemes from April 2007. For further information contact: www.ship-ltd.org or www.sixtyplusonline.co.uk.

Using your home to earn money

Rather than move, many people whose home has become too large are tempted by the idea of taking in tenants. For some it is an ideal plan, for others a disaster. At best, it could provide you with extra income and the possibility of pleasant company. At worst, you could be involved in a lengthy legal battle to regain possession of your property. Before you either rush off to put a card in the newsagent's window or reject the idea out of hand, it is helpful to understand the different options, together with your various rights and responsibilities.

There are three broad choices: taking in paying guests or lodgers, letting part of your home as self-contained accommodation, or renting the whole house for a specified period of time. In all cases for your own protection it is essential to have a written agreement and to take up bank references, unless the let is a strictly temporary one where the money is paid in advance. Otherwise, rent should be collected quarterly and you should arrange a hefty deposit to cover any damage. An important point to be aware of is that there is now a set of strict rules concerning the treatment of deposits, with the risk of large fines for landlords and agents who fail to abide by them.

In a move to encourage more people to let out rooms in their home, the government allows you to earn up to £4,250 a year free of tax. Any excess rental income you receive over £4,250 will be assessed for tax in the normal further information, see leaflet IR 87, *Letting a Room in Your* ⌐ailable from any tax office. If you have a mortgage or are a tenant (even with a very long lease), check with your building society or ⌐ that you are entitled to sublet.

Paying guests or lodgers

This is the most informal arrangement, and will normally be either a casual holiday-type bed and breakfast let or a lodger who might be with you for a couple of years. In either case, the visitor will be sharing part of your home, the accommodation will be fully furnished, and you will be providing at least one full meal a day and possibly also basic cleaning services.

There are few legal formalities involved in these types of lettings, and rent is entirely a matter for friendly agreement. As a resident owner you are also in a very strong position if you want your lodger to leave. Lodging arrangements can easily be ended, as your lodger has no legal rights to stay after the agreed period. A wise precaution is to check with your insurance company that your home contents policy will not be affected, since some insurers restrict cover to households with lodgers. Also, unless you make arrangements to the contrary, you should inform your lodger that his or her possessions are not covered by your policy.

NB: if, as opposed to a lodger or the occasional summer paying guest, you offer regular B&B accommodation, you could be liable to pay Business Rates. Although this is not new, it appears that in recent years the Valuation Office Agency has been enforcing the regulation more strictly against people running B&B establishments.

Holiday lets

It is a good idea to register with your tourist information centre and to contact the environmental health office at your local council for any help and advice.

Useful reading

> *Want to Rent a Room?* Housing leaflet, available from local libraries, housing advice centres and Citizens Advice Bureau.

> *The Complete Guide to Letting Property* by Liz Hodgkinson, published by Kogan Page, £10.99 (website: www.koganpage.com).

Letting rooms in your home

You could convert a basement or part of your house into a self-contained flat and let this either furnished or unfurnished. Alternatively, you could let a single room or rooms. As a general rule, provided you continue to live in the house your tenant(s) have little security of tenure and equally do not have the right to appeal against the rent. Whether you are letting part of the house as a flat or simply a room to a lodger, you would be advised to check your home contents policy with your insurance company. For more details, see the housing booklet *Letting Rooms in Your Home – A Guide for Resident Landlords* available from The **Department for Communities and Local Government (DCLG)**, Tel: 020 7944 4400, website: www. communities.gov.uk/publications/housing.

As a resident landlord, you have a guaranteed right to repossession of your property. If the letting is for a fixed term (eg six months or a year), the let will automatically cease at the end of that fixed period. If the arrangement is on a more ad hoc basis with no specified leaving date, it may be legally necessary to give at least four weeks' notice in writing. The position over notices to quit will vary according to circumstances. For further information, see the housing booklet *Notice That You Must Leave* (see Useful reading, below). Should you encounter any difficulties, it is possible that you may need to apply to the courts for an eviction order.

Tax note

If you subsequently sell your home, you may not be able to claim exemption from Capital Gains Tax on the increase in value of a flat if it is entirely self-contained. It is therefore a good idea to retain some means of access to the main house or flat, but take legal advice as to what will qualify.

Renting out your home on a temporary basis

If you are thinking of spending the winter in the sun or are considering buying a retirement home that you will not occupy for a year or two, you might be tempted by the idea of letting the whole house. In spite of the changes in the Housing Act 1996, there are plenty of horror stories of owners who could not regain possession of their own property when they wished to return.

For your protection, you need to understand the assured short-hold tenancy rules. Unless notified in advance that you need the property back sooner (there are very few grounds on which you can make this notification) or unless earlier possession is sought because of the tenant's behaviour, your tenant has the right to stay for at least six months and must be given two months' notice before you want the tenancy to end.

It is strongly advisable to ask a solicitor or letting agent to help you draw up the agreement. Although this provides for greater protection, you will probably still require a court possession order if your tenant will not leave after you have given the required amount of notice. The accelerated possession procedure may help in some cases to speed up the process.

In most circumstances, by far the safest solution if possible is to let your property to a company rather than to private individuals, since company tenants do not have the same security of tenure. However, it is important that the contract should make clear that your let is for residential, not business, purposes. Before entering into any agreement, you might find it useful to obtain a copy of the booklet *Assured and Assured Shorthold Tenancies – A Guide for Landlords*, available from your local housing department, or from **DCLG**, Tel: 020 7944 4400; website: www.communities. gov.uk. *NB:* the leaflet is about letting to individuals, not companies.

Holiday lets

Buying a future retirement home in the country and renting it out as a holiday home in the summer months is another option worth considering. As well as providing you with a weekend cottage at other times of the year and the chance to establish yourself and make friends in the area, it can prove a useful and profitable investment.

As long as certain conditions are met, income from furnished holiday lettings enjoys most – but not all – of the benefits that there would be if it were taxed as trading income rather than as investment income. In practical terms, this means that you can claim 10 per cent writing-down capital allowances on such items as carpets, curtains and furniture as well as fixtures and fittings, thereby reducing the initial cost of equipping the house. Alternatively, you can claim an annual 10 per cent wear and tear allowance. The running expenses of a holiday home, including maintenance, advertising, insurance cover and Council Tax (or Business Rates – see below), are all largely allowable for tax, excluding that element that relates to your own occupation of the property. Married couples should consider whether the property is to be held in the husband's name or the wife's name, or owned jointly. A solicitor or accountant will be able to advise you.

To qualify as furnished holiday accommodation, the property must be situated in the UK, be let on a commercial basis, be available for holiday letting for at least 140 days during the tax year and be actually let for at least 70 days. Moreover, for at least seven months a year, not necessarily continuous, the property must not normally be occupied by the same tenant for more than 31 consecutive days. This still leaves you with plenty of time to enjoy the property yourself.

There is always the danger that you might create an assured tenancy, so do take professional advice on drawing up the letting agreement. Similarly, if you decide to use one of the holiday rental agents to market your property, get a solicitor to check any contract you enter into with the company. **RICS (Royal Institution of Chartered Surveyors)**, Tel: 0870 3331 600; website: www.rics.org, has a useful set of guidelines for managing agents called *Code of Practice for Management of Residential Property*.

A further point to note is that tax inspectors are taking a tougher line as to what is 'commercial', and loss-making ventures are being threatened with withdrawal of their tax advantages. To safeguard yourself, it is important to draw up a broad business plan before you start and to make a real effort to satisfy the minimum letting requirements. In particular, you should be aware that HMRC has been targeting landlords in the belief that many have been failing to declare their rental income or have over-calculated the amount of tax relief to which they are entitled. Even for innocent mistakes, the likely penalty is the same sum as the amount of tax due – so, if you owe £1,000, it could cost you £2,000.

Tenants' deposits

The Tenancy Deposit Scheme came into force in April 2007 and affects all landlords who let out property under an assured short-hold tenancy. Its purpose is variously to ensure tenants get back the amount owing to them, to make any disputes about the deposit easier to resolve and to encourage tenants to look after the property during the agreed term of their let. The big difference as a result of this new law is that, instead of simply holding the deposit until all or part of it is due to be returned, landlords or agents must now protect it under an approved scheme. Failure to do so within 14 days of receiving the money could result in the landlord being forced to pay the tenant three times the deposit amount.

The two types of tenancy deposit protection schemes available for landlords and letting agents are insurance-based schemes and custodial schemes. All schemes provide a free dispute resolution service. The schemes allow tenants to get all or part of their deposit back when they are entitled to it and encourage tenants and landlords to make a clear agreement from the start on the condition of the property. The schemes make any disputes easier to resolve.

With *insurance-based schemes,* the tenant pays the deposit to the landlord. The landlord retains the deposit and pays a premium to the insurer – the key difference to the custodial scheme. Within 14 days of receiving a deposit, the landlord or agent must give the tenant the details about how their deposit is protected including: the contact details of the tenancy deposit scheme selected; the landlord or agent's contact details; how to apply for the release of the deposit; information explaining the purpose of the deposit; and what to do if there is a dispute about the deposit.

At the end of the tenancy, if an agreement is reached about how the deposit should be divided, the landlord or agent returns all or some of the deposit. If there is a dispute, the landlord must hand over the disputed amount to the scheme for safekeeping until the dispute is resolved. If for any reason the landlord fails to comply, the insurance arrangements will ensure the return of the deposit to the tenant if they are entitled to it.

Custodial schemes are where the tenant pays the deposit to the landlord or agent. The landlord or agent then pays the deposit into the scheme. Within 14 days of receiving a deposit, the landlord or agent must give the tenant details about how their deposit is protected, including the contact details of the tenancy deposit scheme selected; the landlord or agent's contact details; how to apply for the release of the deposit; information explaining the purpose of the deposit; and what to do if there is a dispute about the deposit.

At the end of the tenancy, if an agreement is reached about how the deposit should be divided, the scheme will return the deposit, divided in the way agreed by both parties. If there is a dispute, the scheme will hold the deposit until the dispute resolution service or courts decide what is fair. The interest accrued by deposits in the scheme will be used to pay for the running of the scheme and any surplus will be used to offer interest to the tenant, or landlord if the tenant isn't entitled to it. For further information see www. direct.gov.uk/en/Tenancydepositschemes.

Finally, property that is rented 'commercially' (ie for 140 days or more a year) is normally liable for Business Rates, instead of the Council Tax you would otherwise pay. This could be more expensive, even though partially allowable against tax.

Useful reading

Housing booklets *Letting Rooms in Your Home* and *Notice That You Must Leave*, available from local authority housing departments or DCLG, Tel: 020 7944 4400; website: www.communities.gov.uk.

Benefits and taxes

Housing Benefit

Provided you have no more than £16,000 in savings, you may be able to get help with your rent from your local council. You may qualify for Housing Benefit whether you are a council or private tenant or live in a hotel or hostel. Housing Benefit is fairly complicated and the following outline is intended only as a very general guide. For more detailed advice about your own particular circumstances, contact your local authority or your Citizens Advice Bureau.

The amount of benefit you get depends on five factors: the number of people in your household; your eligible rent (up to a prescribed maximum); your capital or savings; your income; and your 'applicable amount', which is the amount of money the government considers you need for basic living expenses. These are defined roughly as follows.

Eligible rent

This includes rent and some service charges related to the accommodation but excludes meals, water rates and, as a rule, fuel costs. An amount will generally also be deducted for any adult 'non-dependant' (including an elderly relative) living in your household, based on a reasonable contribution on their part towards housing costs. This does not apply to commercial boarders or sub-tenants – but any income from a boarder or sub-tenant will be taken into account.

Capital

Any capital or savings up to £6,000 will be disregarded and will not affect your entitlement to benefit. People with savings or capital between £6,000 and £16,000 will receive some benefit, but this will be on a sliding scale, with every £500 (or part of £500) over £6,000 assessed as being equivalent to an extra £1 a week of their income. (See the paragraph below starting 'If your income is less than your applicable amount …'.) This is called 'tariff income'. If you have savings of more than £16,000, you will not be eligible for Housing Benefit at all. 'Capital' generally includes all savings, bonds, stocks and shares and property other than your own home and personal possessions. The capital limits are the same for a couple as for a single person.

Income

Income includes earnings, social security benefits, pension income and any other money you have coming in after tax and National Insurance Contributions have been paid. While most income counts when calculating your entitlement to Housing Benefit (*NB:* a couple's income is added together), some income may be ignored, for example: all Disability Living Allowance and Attendance Allowance; the first £5 of earnings (single person), £10 of earnings (couple) or £20 of earnings if your 'applicable amount' includes a disability premium or carer's premium; and a £25 disregard for lone parents. War pensions are also ignored in part.

Applicable amount

Your 'applicable amount' will generally be the same as any benefit to cover weekly living expenses you would be eligible for and consists of: your personal allowance, and personal allowances for any younger children (normally those for whom you are receiving Child Benefit), plus any premiums (ie additional amounts for pensioners, the disabled and so on) to which you might be entitled. Details of allowances and premium rates can be found on website: www.direct.gov.uk.

If your income is less than your applicable amount you will receive maximum Housing Benefit towards your eligible rent (less any non-dependant deduction). You may be eligible for Income Support if your capital is less than £8,000, or less than £16,000 if you are aged 60 or over. If your income is equal to your applicable amount you will also receive maximum Housing Benefit. If your income is higher than your applicable amount, a taper adjustment will be made and maximum Housing Benefit will be reduced by 65 per cent of the difference between your income and your applicable amount. If this leaves you with Housing Benefit of less than 50p a week, it is not paid.

How to claim

If you think you are eligible for benefit (see website: www.direct.gov.uk) apply online or ask your council for an application form. It should let you know within 14 days of receiving your completed application whether you are entitled to benefit, and will inform you of the amount.

Special accommodation

If you live in a mobile home or houseboat, you may be able to claim benefit for site fees or mooring charges. If you live in a private nursing or residential care home you will not normally be able to get Housing Benefit to help with the cost. However, you may be able to get help towards both the accommodation part of your fees and your living expenses through Income Support or possibly under the Community Care arrangements. If you make a claim for Income Support you can claim Housing Benefit and Council Tax Benefit at the same time. A claim form for these is included inside the Income Support claim form. When completed, the form is returned to your local authority.

Council Tax

Council Tax is based on the value of the dwelling in which you live (the property element) and also consists of a personal element – with discounts and exemptions applying to certain groups of people.

The property element

Most domestic properties are liable for Council Tax, including rented property, mobile homes and houseboats. The value of the property is assessed according to a banding system, with eight different bands (A to H). The banding of each property is determined by the government's Valuation Office Agency. Small extensions or other improvements made after this date do not affect the valuation until the property changes hands. The planned Council Tax revaluation in England, due to take place in 2007, was postponed.

Notification of the band is shown on the bill when it is sent out in April. If you think there has been a misunderstanding about the valuation (or your liability to pay the full amount) you may have the right of appeal (see 'Appeals', page 202).

Liability

Not everyone pays Council Tax. The bill is normally sent to the resident owner or joint owners of the property or, in the case of rented accommodation, to the tenant or joint tenants. Married couples and people with a shared legal interest in the property are jointly liable for the bill, unless they are students or severely mentally impaired. In some cases, for example in hostels or multi-occupied property, a non-resident landlord or owner will be liable but may pass on a share of the bill to the tenants or residents, which would probably be included as part of the rental charge.

The personal element

The valuation of each dwelling assumes that two adults will be resident. The charge does not increase if there are more adults. However if, as in many homes, there is a single adult, your Council Tax bill will be reduced by 25 per cent. Certain people are disregarded when determining the number of residents in a household. There are also a number of other special discounts or exemptions, as follows:

- People who are severely mentally impaired are disregarded or, if they are the sole occupant of the dwelling, qualify for an exemption.

- Disabled people whose homes require adaptation may have their bill reduced to a lower band.

- People on Income Support should normally have nothing to pay, as their bill will be met in full by Council Tax Benefit.

- Disabled people on higher-rate Attendance Allowance need not count a full-time carer as an additional resident and therefore may continue to qualify for the 25 per cent single (adult) householder discount. Exceptions are spouses or partners and parents of a disabled child under 18 who would normally be living with the disabled person and whose presence therefore would not be adding to the Council Tax.

- Young people over 18 but still at school are not counted when assessing the number of adults in a house.

- Students living in halls of residence, student hostels or similar are exempted; those living with a parent or other non-student adult are eligible for the 25 per cent personal discount.

- Service personnel living in barracks or married quarters will not receive any bill for Council Tax.

Discounts and exemptions applying to property

Certain property is either exempt from Council Tax or is eligible for a discount.

Discounts. Until April 2004, there was a standard 50 per cent discount on second homes and long-term empty property (except in Wales, where councils could charge the full amount on second homes if they wished). However, you can no longer count on this as, in England, councils now have the power to charge owners of second homes up to 90 per cent of the standard rate, and owners of long-term empty property up to 100 per cent.

Exemptions. The most common cases of exemptions include:

- Property that has been unoccupied and unfurnished for less than six months.
- The home of a deceased person; the exemption lasts until six months after the grant of probate.
- A home that is empty because the occupier is absent in order to care for someone else.
- The home of a person who is or would be exempted from Council Tax because of moving to a residential home, hospital care or similar.
- Empty properties in need of major repairs or undergoing structural alteration can be exempt from Council Tax for an initial period of six months, but this can be extended for a further six months. After 12 months, the standard 50 (or possibly full 100) per cent charge for empty properties will apply.
- Granny flats that are part of another private domestic dwelling may be exempt, but this depends on access and other conditions. To check, contact your local Valuation Office.

Business-cum-domestic property

Business-cum-domestic property is rated according to usage, with the business section assessed for Business Rates and the domestic section for Council Tax. For example, where there is a flat over a shop, the value of the shop will not be included in the valuation for Council Tax. Likewise, a room in a house used for business purposes will be subject to Business Rates and not to Council Tax.

Appeals

If you become the new person responsible for paying the Council Tax (eg because you have recently moved or because someone else paid the tax before) on a property that you feel has been wrongly banded, you have six months to appeal and can request that the valuation be reconsidered. Otherwise, there are only three other circumstances in which you can appeal:

1 if there has been a material increase or reduction in the property's value;

2 if you start, or stop, using part of the property for business or the balance between domestic and business use changes;

3 if either of the latter two apply and the listing officer has altered the Council Tax list without giving you a chance to put your side.

If you have grounds for appeal, you should take up the matter with the Valuation Office (see local telephone directory). If the matter is not resolved, you can then appeal to an independent valuation tribunal. For advice and further information, contact your local Citizens Advice Bureau.

Council Tax Benefit

If you cannot afford your Council Tax because you have a low income, you may be able to obtain Council Tax Benefit. The help is more generous than many people realize. For example, people on Pension Credit (Guarantee Credit) are entitled to rebates of up to 100 per cent. Even if you are not receiving any other social security benefit, you may still qualify for some Council Tax Benefit. The amount you get depends on your income, savings, personal circumstances, who else lives in your home (in particular whether they would be counted as 'non-dependants') and your net Council Tax bill (ie after any deductions that apply to your home). If you are not sure whether your income is low enough to entitle you to Council Tax Benefit, it is worth claiming, as you could be pleasantly surprised.

If you disagree with your council's decision, you can ask for this to be looked at again (a revision) or you can appeal to an independent appeal tribunal, administered by the Appeals Service. If you are still dissatisfied, you may apply for leave to appeal to the Social Security Commissioners, but only on a point of law. If you want a revision, you should get on with the matter as soon as possible, as if you delay your request may be out of time.

Apart from Council Tax Benefit for yourself, you may also be able to get help with your Council Tax if you share your home with someone who is on a low income. This is known as 'Second Adult Rebate' or 'Alternative Maximum Council Tax Benefit'. See website: www.direct.gov.uk.

Useful organizations

The following should be able to provide general advice about housing:

- local authority housing departments;
- housing advice or housing aid centres;
- Citizens Advice Bureau;
- local authority social service departments if your problem is linked to disability;
- welfare rights centres if your problem, for example, concerns a landlord who does not keep the property properly maintained;
- leasehold valuation tribunals if there are serious problems with the management of the building;
- local councillors and MPs.

Other organizations that provide a helpful service are as follows:

The Federation of Private Residents' Associations Ltd (FPRA) is a federation of associations of long leaseholders and tenants in private blocks of flats. It advises on setting up residents' associations and provides legal and other advice to its member associations. It issues quarterly newsletters and information sheets, publishes a pack on how to form a tenants' or residents' association (price £15 including postage and packing) and acts as a pressure group seeking to influence legislation regarding leasehold and management of flats in the private sector. FPRA also gives advice on buying the freehold and on management of collectively owned blocks of flats. Tel: 0871 200 3324; website: www.fpra.org.uk.

Shelter. The National Campaign for Homeless People, Shelter provides advice to over 100,000 badly housed and homeless people every year through a national network of housing aid centres and a free 24-hour housing helpline: 0808 800 4444; website: www.shelter.org.uk.

Chapter Nine
Leisure activities

To be able to fill leisure intelligently is the last product of civilization, and at present very few people have reached this level. BERTRAND RUSSELL

Now that retirement is approaching (or has already arrived), you may have been thinking about all the free time available. Perhaps you have already given the matter serious consideration and made lists of all the things you are going to do, once the daily work routine has ceased. Whatever your sphere of interest, there are usually more opportunities than time available. For some, pursuing hobbies, travelling to new places, taking up sporting activities or volunteering becomes a reality rather than a remote possibility. Most recent retirees wonder how they ever found time to go to work. For the leisure industry, the over-55s are a growing section of the population – there are more of them in the UK than under-16 year olds. As a result the choice of leisure pursuits open to pensioners is enormous.

This chapter deals with spare-time activities, sport and holidays, but all are interrelated. Many holidays, for example, involve special interest groups and tours, while other hobbies and pastimes involve short courses or visits to places of interest. Additionally there are volunteering opportunities for retired people who wish to make a valuable contribution within their own community or beyond. You might consider visiting the elderly in their own homes, driving patients to hospital, running a holiday play scheme, helping out at your local Citizens Advice Bureau or becoming a Samaritan. Other ideas that might appeal are conservation work or playing a more active role in local politics. Whatever amount of time you have available, there is almost certainly something suitable on offer. Many organizations have concessionary rates for people of retirement age, as do a number of theatres and other places of entertainment. Given the immense variety of tantalizing options available, it's not surprising that many retired people find they have never been so busy in their lives.

What hobbies do you have? When you are not working, what do you enjoy doing as a leisure activity? Are you looking forward to studying for a degree or trying your hand at an entirely new pastime? You can do anything from basket-weaving to bridge, archery to amateur dramatics. You can join a music-making group, a Scrabble club or a film society, or become a beekeeper. If you are interested in heritage, there are any number of historic homes and beautiful gardens to visit, as well as museums, art galleries, abbeys and castles. Additionally, almost every locality now has excellent sports facilities and there is scope for complete novices to take up bowls, golf, badminton, croquet and many others. Similarly, there are dancing and keep fit classes, railway enthusiasts' clubs and groups devoted to researching their local history.

This chapter is best read in conjunction with Chapter 14, Holidays, as many of the organizations listed there – such as the Field Studies Council – would be equally relevant here. However, to avoid repetition, most are described only once. Those that appear in Chapter 14 either tend in the main to offer residential courses or would probably involve most people in spending a few days away from home to take advantage of the facilities. Any prices that are included are simply to give a guide. In the main they have been omitted because it is impossible to be accurate as most are subject to frequent change. The latest information is always available via websites or from the organization's telephone information line.

Adult education

Have you ever longed to take a degree, learn about computing, study philosophy or do a course in archaeology? Opportunities for education abound, and there are scores of other subjects easily available to everyone, regardless of age or previous qualifications.

There is a website that gives comprehensive information on over 900,000 available courses throughout the UK. These range from self-study (distance learning) to part- or full-time courses. Further information is available from Careers Advice on 0800 100 900; website: www.careersadvice.direct.gov.uk.

Other organizations to consider are:

Home Learning College, the UK's leading home study provider, offers a huge range of home study courses. Over 65,000 students currently enrolled and on average 2,000 new students join each month from all backgrounds and ages. For further information contact: 0800 912 2926; website: www.homelearningcollege.com.

National Extension College (NEC). With a choice of over 150 home study courses, the NEC offers a range of nationally recognized qualifications in a wide variety of subjects. Flexible supported distance learning courses allow you to fit your studies around work or leisure. Contact: 0800 389 2839; website: www.nec.ac.uk.

Open and Distance Learning Quality Council (ODLQC) is the UK guardian of quality in open and distance learning. Set up originally by the government in 1968, it is now an independent organization. Contact ODLQC on: 020 7447 2543; website: www.odlqc.org.uk.

Open University (OU). If you want to learn a subject in depth, or get a qualification, the Open University – voted top for student satisfaction for three year's running – could provide what you desire. For most courses you don't need any previous qualifications, and with a world-leading blend of supported open learning and innovative course materials, the OU provides over 570 courses, with financial support available for some students. For more information contact: 0845 300 60 90; website: www.open.ac.uk.

University extra-mural departments – non-degree and short courses

Many universities have a department of extra-mural studies that arranges courses for adults, sometimes in the evening or during vacation periods; here are a few:

Birkbeck, University of London is a world-class research and teaching institution, and London's only specialist provider of evening higher education. Applications are encouraged from students without traditional qualifications and there is a wide range of programmes to suit every entry level. Over 19,000 students study with Birkbeck every year. Contact Birkbeck on 0845 601 0174; website: www.bbk.ac.uk.

U3A (The University of the Third Age) is a self-help organization for people no longer in full-time employment, providing educational, leisure and creative opportunities in a friendly environment. It consists of local U3As all over the UK, which are charities in their own right and are run entirely by volunteers. For further information contact: 0208 466 6139; website: www.u3a.org.uk.

Workers' Educational Association (WEA) is a democratic, voluntary adult education movement, committed to widening participation and enabling people to realize their full potential through learning. One of the UK's largest charities, the WEA now runs over 10,000 courses each year. For further information contact: 020 7426 3450; website: www.wea.org.uk.

Animals

If you are an animal lover, it is likely that you already have connections with charities and organizations that relate to your favourite animals. But here are some suggestions:

British Beekeepers' Association runs correspondence courses and practical demonstrations and will be glad to put you in touch with one of the 60 local organizations. Tel: 02476 696 679; website: www.britishbee.org.uk.

Our Dogs Publishing has loads of information for dog lovers. The weekly newspaper *Our Dogs* gives details of local shows, rule and registration changes and also news and addresses of canine and breed societies all over the country. Contact Our Dogs on 0844 504 9005; website: www.ourdogs.co.uk.

Wildfowl & Wetlands Trust (WWT) is a leading conversation organization saving wetlands for wildlife and people across the world. WWT is the only UK charity with a national network of specialist wetland visitor centres. For further information contact 01453 891 900; website: www.wwt.org.uk.

Arts

Wherever you live you can enjoy the arts. Whether you are interested in active participation or just appreciating the performance of others, there is an exhilarating choice of events, including theatre, music, exhibitions, film-making and so on. Many entertainments offer concessionary prices to retired people.

Regional Arts Council offices

For first-hand information about what is going on in your area, contact your regional Arts Council office. Most areas have a varied programme offering something of interest to just about everyone. For information and details of each regional office, Tel: 0845 300 6200; website: www.artscouncil. org.uk. The regional offices and the areas each covers are:

Arts Council England, East. Bedfordshire, Cambridgeshire, Essex, Hertfordshire, Norfolk, Suffolk, and the unitary authorities of Luton, Peterborough, Southend-on-Sea and Thurrock.

Arts Council England, East Midlands. Derbyshire, Leicestershire, Lincolnshire (excluding North and North East Lincolnshire), Northamptonshire, Nottinghamshire, and the unitary authorities of Derby, Leicester, Nottingham and Rutland.

Arts Council England, London. Greater London.

Arts Council England, North East. Durham, Northumberland, the metropolitan authorities of Gateshead, Newcastle-upon-Tyne, North Tyneside, South Tyneside and Sunderland, and the unitary authorities of Darlington, Hartlepool, Middlesbrough, Redcar and Cleveland, and Stockton-on-Tees.

Arts Council England, North West. Cheshire, Cumbria, Lancashire, the metropolitan authorities of Bolton, Bury, Knowsley, Liverpool, Manchester, Oldham, Rochdale, St Helens, Salford, Sefton, Stockport, Tameside, Trafford, Wigan and Wirral, and the unitary authorities of Blackburn with Darwen, Blackpool, Halton and Warrington.

Arts Council England, South East. Buckinghamshire, East Sussex, Hampshire, Isle of Wight, Kent, Oxfordshire, Surrey, West Sussex, and the unitary authorities of Bracknell Forest, Brighton and Hove, Medway Towns, Milton Keynes, Portsmouth, Reading, Slough, Southampton, West Berkshire, Windsor and Maidenhead, and Wokingham.

Arts Council England, South West. Cornwall, Devon, Dorset, Gloucestershire, Somerset, Wiltshire, and the unitary authorities of Bath and North East Somerset, Bournemouth, Bristol, North Somerset, Plymouth, Poole, South Gloucestershire, Swindon and Torbay.

Arts Council England, West Midlands. Shropshire, Staffordshire, Warwickshire, Worcestershire, the metropolitan authorities of

Birmingham, Coventry, Dudley, Sandwell, Solihull, Walsall and Wolverhampton, and the unitary authorities of Herefordshire, Stoke-on-Trent, Telford and Wrekin.

Arts Council England, Yorkshire. North Yorkshire, the metropolitan authorities of Barnsley, Bradford, Calderdale, Doncaster, Kirklees, Leeds, Rotherham, Sheffield and Wakefield, and the unitary authorities of East Riding of Yorkshire, Kingston upon Hull, North East Lincolnshire, North Lincolnshire and York.

For those who wish to join in with amateur arts activities, public libraries keep lists of choirs, drama clubs, painting clubs and similar in their locality.

Films

Cinema is a hugely popular art form. Should you enjoy film, you might think of joining a film society or visiting the National Film Theatre. Here are some other ideas:

British Federation of Film Societies (BFFS) is the national organization for the development and support of the film society and community cinema movement in the UK. It offers a wide range of services and resources dedicated to the needs of community cinemas. Contact: 0114 221 0314; website: www.bffs.org.uk.

British Film Institute (BFI) has a world renowned archive, cinemas, festival, films, publications and learning resources. For more information see website: www.bfi.org.uk.

Music and ballet

From becoming a Friend and supporting one of the famous 'Houses' such as Covent Garden to music-making in your own right, here are some suggestions:

Friends of Covent Garden. Friends receive regular mailings of news and information, and free copies of the magazine *About the House*, plus opportunities to attend talks, recitals, study days, master classes and some 'open' rehearsals of ballet and opera. Contact: the Royal Opera House 020 7212 9268; website: www.royalopera.org.

Friends of English National Opera (ENO). As a Friend of ENO, you have the opportunity to apply for tickets for dress rehearsals and to gain an insight into the creation of opera through a variety of special lunchtime and evening events. Contact ENO on 0871 271 5577; website: www.eno.org.

Friends of Sadler's Wells. Sadler's Wells has an ever-changing programme of ballet, opera and contemporary dance. Friends receive discounts and free ticket offers. For further details contact: 0844 412 4300; website: www.sadlerswells.com.

Music-making

Whatever style of music you enjoy, there are associations to suit your taste. Here are some contacts:

Handbell Ringers of Great Britain. The Society, which was formed in 1967, promotes the art of handbell tune ringing and supports handbell, handchime and belleplate players. Concerts, rallies, seminars and workshops are organized. This is a national association with regional branches; for further information contact the National Secretary via the website: www.hrgb.org.uk.

Making Music, The National Federation of Music Societies represents and supports over 2,850 voluntary and amateur music groups throughout the UK. For more information contact: 020 7422 8280; website: www.makingmusic.org.uk.

National Association of Choirs. The NAC represents and supports over 500 choirs and 26,000 voices, all of them amateur and voluntary, throughout the UK. For further information contact: 0844 504 2000; website: www.nationalassociationofchoirs.org.uk.

Society of Recorder Players. The Society has around 1,500 members, is governed by a National Committee and has 53 branches. For further information contact: 01732 456 997; website: www.srp.org.uk.

Poetry

There is an increasing enthusiasm about poetry and poetry readings in clubs, pubs and other places of entertainment. Special local events may be advertised in your neighbourhood.

The mission of **The Poetry Society** is to advance the study, use and enjoyment of poetry. A charitable organization, founded in 1909, it provides support, information and merchandise for specialists and the general public.

There are over 4,000 members worldwide. For further details: 020 7420 9880; website: www.poetrysociety.org.uk.

Television and radio audiences

The BBC aims to reflect the nations, regions and diverse communities it serves and to involve all sections of the audience in making shows. It also wants to encourage people of all ages, backgrounds and abilities to apply to participate as members of studio audiences and contributors to programmes. The BBC regularly audits its buildings to ensure accessibility for all visitors with disabilities and will, where possible, make reasonable adjustments for disabled people wishing to take part in BBC activities. Contact: 0370 901 1227; website: www.bbc.co.uk.

For independent television channels, information can be obtained by contacting:

Channel 4 Viewers Enquiries	0845 076 0191; website: www.channel4.com
ITV Viewer Enquiries	0844 881 4150; website: www.itv.com
Ulster TV	028 9032 8122; website: www.ulstertv.com

Theatre

Details of current and forthcoming productions, as well as theatre reviews, are well advertised in the press and on the internet. Preview performances are usually cheaper, and there are often concessionary tickets for matinees. Listed here are some theatres and organizations that offer special facilities of interest, including priority booking and reduced price tickets. Also included is an association for enthusiasts of amateur dramatics:

Ambassador Theatre Group is the largest theatre group in the UK with 39 venues in London and across the country. It sells tickets for all West End shows and is the leading booker of senior groups into London. Contact (for individuals) 0870 060 6615 (for groups) 0844 871 7644; website: www.ambassadortickets.com.

Barbican Centre is the largest multi-arts centre in Europe, featuring art, film, music, theatre, dance and education all under one roof and all under one creative director. Reduced price tickets for senior citizens are available for many concerts and theatre performances, as well as the art gallery and cinema. Contact: 020 7382 7211; website: www.barbican.org.uk.

National Theatre stages over 20 theatre productions each year in three auditoriums – the Lyttleton, Cottesloe and Olivier theatres. The National also offers free exhibitions and restaurant facilities. There are group price reductions, and pensioners can also buy midweek matinee tickets at concessionary prices. Contact: 020 7452 3500; website: www.nationaltheatre.org.uk.

Scottish Community Drama Association (SCDA) is a community-based organization and operates through 24 district committees throughout Scotland. Membership gives access to the Association's libraries, training courses and script discounts. The Association also runs playwriting competitions and can put you in touch with local dramatic societies. Contact: 01786 440 077; website: www.scda.org.uk.

Official London Theatre is the capital's only official theatre website. It is run by the Society of London Theatres, the trade association for the London Theatre industry. It has a wealth of information and listings, what's on, how to buy tickets, and events. See website: www. officiallondontheatre.co.uk.

Theatre Network is a social network and online magazine for the performing arts industry. It carries news and features, as well as national and regional theatre listings and review guides. For more information check the website: www.uktheatre.net.

TKTS has half-price theatre tickets for sale every day. There are two booths – one in Leicester Square and the other in Brent Cross. Each is open to personal callers only on the day of the performance. For further details see website: www.tkts.co.uk.

Visual arts

If you enjoy attending exhibitions and lectures, membership of some of the arts societies offers a good choice:

Art Fund is an independent charity committed to saving art for everyone to enjoy. With over 80,000 members the Art Fund has offered over 860,000 works of art to more than 600 museums and galleries throughout the UK. These range from priceless masterpieces which were under threat of being sold abroad to works costing a few hundred pounds. There are art tours at home and abroad led by experts. For further information contact: 0870 8482 003; website: www.artfund.org.

Contemporary Art Society promotes the collecting of contemporary art and aims to acquire works by living artists for gift to public galleries. Members can take part in an extensive programme of events including visits to artists' studios and private collections, previews and parties at special exhibitions, and trips outside London and overseas. Contact 020 7831 1243; website: www.contemporaryartsociety.org.

National Association of Decorative & Fine Arts Societies (NADFAS) is an arts-based charity with over 340 local decorative and fine arts societies in UK and mainland Europe. NADFAS promotes the advancement of arts education and appreciation and the preservation of our artistic heritage. Many local societies have volunteer groups working in museums, libraries and historic houses, and there are also church-recording groups that make detailed records of the interiors of churches. There are many day events and tours organized both in the UK and abroad. Contact: 020 7430 0730; website: www.nadfas.org.uk.

Royal Academy of Arts. Friends of the Royal Academy receive many benefits including unlimited access to the world-renowned exhibition programme with guests, and the award-winning *RM* quarterly magazine. For further details contact: 020 7300 5664; website: www.royalacademy.org.uk.

Tate is a public institution, owned by and existing for, the public. Tate's mission is to increase public knowledge, understanding and enjoyment of British modern and contemporary art through its collection and programmes in and beyond its galleries. For further information, contact 020 7887 8888; website: www.tate.org.uk.

Painting as a hobby

If you are interested in improving your own painting technique, art courses are available at your local adult education institute. Your library may have details of painting groups and societies in your area, or you could contact **The Society for All Artists (SAA)**, which exists to inform, encourage and inspire all who want to paint, whatever their ability, and provides all that you need to enjoy this hobby – instruction, materials and information. Contact: 0800 980 1123; website: www.saa.co.uk.

Crafts

The majority of suggestions are contained in Chapter 14, Holidays, variously under 'Arts and crafts' and 'Special interest holidays', since many organizations offer residential courses and painting holidays. However, if you are interested in a particular form of craft work many of the societies and others listed in Chapter 14 should be able to help you. Here are a few additional possibilities:

Basket-makers' Association promotes classes, courses, exhibitions, lectures and discussions on all aspects of basket-making, chair seating and allied crafts. It arranges day schools, residential courses, demonstrations and exhibitions. See website: www.basketassoc.org.

Crafts Council's aim is to make the UK the best place to make, see, collect and learn about contemporary craft. It believes that everyone should have the opportunity to excel at the craft of their choice and visit markets, fairs, galleries, shops and other outlets for craft work. For further information contact: 020 7806 2500; website: www.craftscouncil.org.uk.

Open College of the Arts (OCA), which is affiliated to the Open University, is an educational charity established to widen participation in arts education. It offers home study courses for those wishing to acquire or improve skills or gain a higher education qualification. For further information contact 0800 731 2116; website: www.oca-uk.com.

Dance/keep fit

Clubs, classes and groups exist in all parts of the country, offering ballroom, old time, Scottish, folk, ballet, disco dancing and others. Additionally, there are music and relaxation classes, aerobics and more gentle keep fit sessions. Many of the relaxation and keep fit classes are particularly appropriate for older people. Your local library may help you find out what is available in your area. Listed here are some of the national organizations that can advise you and put you in touch with local groups. (There are further suggestions in Chapter 13, Health, 'Keeping fit'):

British Dance Council is the governing body of all competition dancing in the UK. It can put you in touch with recognized dance schools in your area. Contact 020 8545 0085; website: www.british-dance-council.org.

CCPR – One Voice for Sport and Recreation is the national alliance of governing and representative bodies of sport and recreation. For more information contact 020 7976 3900; website: www.ccpr.org.uk.

English Folk Dance and Song Society is one of the leading folk development organizations in the UK. It is a membership society with over 4,000 members, an arts venue and provides classes and workshops in all styles of folk and dance for people of all abilities. Contact: 020 7485 2206; website: www.efdss.org.

Imperial Society of Teachers of Dancing aims to educate the public in the art of dancing in all its forms. There are some 7,000 teachers offering instruction in virtually all forms of dancing. For further details contact 020 7377 1577; website: www.istd.org.

Keep Fit Association (KFA) offers 'Fitness through Movement, Exercise and Dance' classes. There are hundreds of classes throughout the UK for all ages and abilities. (See also 'Extend', p. 310 in Chapter 13, Health.) For more information, contact 01403 266000; website: www.keepfit.org.uk.

Royal Scottish Country Dance Society has 170 branches worldwide with members from 16 to 80-plus. The branches offer instruction at all levels, and members join in dance events. For further information contact: 0131 225 3854; website: www.rscds.org.

Games

Many local areas have their own bridge, chess, whist, dominoes, Scrabble and other groups that meet together regularly in a club, hall, pub or other social venue to enjoy friendly games. Competitions are organized and district and county teams are usually taken very seriously. Your library should have information on any clubs or regular group meetings. Alternatively, you can contact these national organizations:

English Bridge Union is a membership organization committed to promoting the game of duplicate bridge. Members receive a wide range of services including details of tournaments and bridge holidays at home and abroad. For further information contact: 01296 317 200; website: www.ebu.co.uk.

English Chess Federation can provide information about chess clubs and tournaments throughout England. Contact: 01424 775 222; website: www.englishchess.org.uk.

Scrabble Clubs UK is the association that co-ordinates all the Scrabble tournaments in the UK. For details of your nearest club or how to join see the website: www.absp.org.uk.

Gardens and gardening

Courses, gardens to visit, special help for people with disabilities, and how to run a gardening association; these and other interests are all catered for by the following organizations:

English Gardening School teaches all aspects of gardening. Courses ranging in length from a day to an academic year are held in its new home on the Thames in Chelsea Wharf. For further information, Tel: 020 7352 4347; website: www.englishgardeningschool.co.uk.

Garden Organic is Europe's largest organic gardening organization and has been at the forefront of organic gardening for over half a century. It has over 40,000 supporters and reaches over 3 million across the world through its expert advice and information. Based at Garden Organic Ryton in Warwickshire, the organization celebrated its 50th anniversary in 2008. To join, contact: 024 7630 3517; website: www.gardenorganic.org.uk.

Gardening for Disabled Trust provides practical and financial help to disabled people who want to garden actively. The Garden Club publishes a quarterly newsletter, gives answers to horticultural questions and encourages gardeners with disabilities to meet. For more information contact the Secretary via the website: www.gardeningfordisabledtrust.org.uk.

National Gardens Scheme has over 3,700 gardens to choose from, mostly privately owned. Over half a million visitors each year enjoy visiting gardens that open to the public a few days a year. Money is raised for a variety of nursing, caring and gardening charities including Macmillan Cancer Relief, Marie Curie Cancer Care and the Queen's Nursing Institute. To join, contact: 01483 211 535; website: www.ngs.org.uk.

National Society of Allotment & Leisure Gardeners Ltd aims to protect, promote and preserve allotments for future generations. It acts as a national voice for allotment and leisure gardeners. For further information contact 01536 266 576; website: www.nsalg.org.uk.

Royal Horticultural Society's mission statement is 'to be the leading organization demonstrating excellence in horticulture and promoting gardening', delivering benefit to all those interested and involved in horticulture and gardening in the UK. For further information, contact: 0845 0621 111; website: www.rhs.org.uk.

Scotland's Gardens Scheme facilitates the opening of large and small gardens in Scotland that are of interest to the public. Most are privately owned and thus normally inaccessible to the public at other times. For membership contact: 0131 226 3714; website: www.gardensofscotland.org.

Thrive is a small national charity that uses gardening to change lives. It champions the benefits of gardening, carries out research and offers training and practical solutions so that anyone with a disability can take part in, benefit from and enjoy gardening. Contact: 0118 988 5688; website: www.thrive.org.uk.

History

People with an interest in the past have so many activities to choose from – visit historic monuments, including ancient castles and stately homes, in all parts of the country; explore the City of London; study genealogy; research the history of your local area; and attend lectures and receptions. Here are some suggestions:

Age Exchange is the UK's leading charity working in the field of reminiscence and works to improve the quality of life for older people through reminiscence-based creative workshops. The Centre is fully equipped for disabled access and has a café. Contact: 020 8318 9105; website: www.age-exchange.org.uk.

Architectural Heritage Society of Scotland promotes the protection of Scottish architecture and encourages the study of Scottish buildings, their furniture and fittings, urban design and designed landscapes. There are six regional groups, covering all of Scotland, which arrange regular events including talks, visits and study trips. For membership information contact: 0131 557 0019; website: www.ahss.org.uk.

Bekonscot Model Village is a miniature wonderland where nobody grows up. Established in 1929, it captures 1930s rural England and is an unforgettable day out, including Bekonscot's historic Gauge 1 line, one of the largest, most exciting and complex model railways in the country. Contact: 01494 672 919; website: www.bekonscot.co.uk.

British Association for Local History exists to promote the study of local history as an academic discipline and as a rewarding leisure pursuit for individuals and groups. For membership information contact: 01283 585 947; website: www.balh.co.uk.

City of London Information Centre acts as a tourist office for the area, giving advice and guidance. Among the many attractions, all of which are open to the public at varying times, are: St Paul's Cathedral, the Guildhall, Dr Johnson's House, the Monument, Barbican, the Central Criminal Court and several museums. Additionally, there are interesting examples of London's architecture. For more information contact: 020 7332 1456; website: www.cityoflondon.gov.uk.

English Heritage manages over 400 historic attractions throughout England. Members receive a colour handbook with map and enjoy free admission to all English Heritage properties. Further details on: 0870 333 1182; website: www.english-heritage.org.uk.

Federation of Family History Societies is an umbrella organization for more than 160 societies throughout the world that provide assistance if you are interested in tracing your ancestors. For further information contact: 01455 203 133; website: www.ffhs.org.uk.

Garden History Society is dedicated to the conservation and study of historic designed gardens and landscapes. With only 1,500 members it is a small but influential charity. For membership details contact: 020 7608 2409; website: www.gardenhistorysociety.org.

Georgian Group exists to preserve Georgian buildings and to stimulate public knowledge and appreciation of Georgian architecture and town planning. Activities include day visits and long weekends to buildings and gardens, private views of exhibitions and a programme of evening lectures in London. For membership information contact: 0871 750 2936; website: www.georgiangroup.org.uk.

Historic Houses Association (HHA) has nearly 300 member houses and gardens in England, Scotland and Wales, which members of the HHA are welcome to visit. There are also invitations to lectures, concerts, receptions and other events. To join, contact: 01462 896 688; website: www.hha.org.uk.

Historical Association supports the study and enjoyment of history. With over 6,000 members the HA is the major national organization bringing together people of all ages and backgrounds who share an interest in and love for the past. There are over 50 local branches nationwide offering a programme of social events and monthly talks by top historians. For more information, contact 020 7735 3901; website: www.history.org.uk.

Monumental Brass Society encourages the preservation and appreciation of monumental brasses. There are many brass-rubbing centres around the country where facilities are provided for the craft. Contact the membership secretary via the website: www.mbs-brasses.co.uk.

National Trust exists to protect historic buildings and areas of great natural beauty in England, Wales and Northern Ireland. Membership gives you free entry to the Trust's many properties and to those of the National Trust for Scotland. You also receive an annual handbook, magazines and details of activities in your own region. To join, contact: 0844 800 1895; website: www.nationaltrust.org.uk.

National Trust for Scotland cares for over 100 properties and 183,000 acres of countryside. Members also enjoy free admission to any of the National Trust properties in England, Wales and Northern Ireland. To join, contact: 0844 493 2100; website: www.nts.org.uk.

Northern Ireland Tourist Board has a free information bulletin, *Visitor Attractions*, listing historic sites and other places of interest. Many sites are free, and others offer reduced rates for pensioners. For information contact: 028 9023 1221; website: www.discovernorthernireland.com.

Oral History Society promotes the collection, preservation and use of recorded memories of the past for projects in community history, schools, reminiscence groups and historical research. It welcomes the help of older people in all these activities. Contact: 01442 879 097; website: www.ohs.org.uk.

Society of Genealogists promotes the study of genealogy and heraldry. Lectures are arranged throughout the year, and there is also a variety of courses, including day and weekend seminars. For further information on how to join contact: 020 7251 8799; website: www.sog.org.uk.

Victorian Society campaigns to preserve fine Victorian and Edwardian buildings in England and Wales. It organizes walks, tours, lectures and conferences through its national office and eight regional groups. For further information contact: 020 8994 1019; website: www.victorian-society.org.uk.

Magazines

Over 65 Magazine is a new online publication launched in January 2010 aimed at mature readers who are young at heart. Available monthly to download, the magazine is free, to view online or print off. The online magazine has the advantage that you can find out more about services featured simply by clicking on to the provided links to the sponsor's websites. Contact: 01539 723 799; website: www.over65magazine.co.uk.

Retirement Today is a lifestyle magazine aimed at the active retired or those contemplating retirement. The magazine is produced bi-monthly and a wide range of subjects is covered including culture, gardening and travel, as well as informative topics on finance, tax, health and more. Contact: 01296 632 700; website: www.retirement-today.co.uk.

Museums

Most museums organize free lectures, guided tours and sometimes slide shows on aspects of their collections or special exhibitions. As with art galleries and theatres, an increasing trend is to form a group of 'Friends' who pay a membership subscription to support the museum and in return enjoy certain advantages, such as access to private views, visits to places of interest, receptions and other social activities:

British Association of Friends of Museums (BAFM) is an umbrella organization that acts as a national forum for Friends and volunteers who support museums around the UK. Many museums offer the opportunity, through membership of a Friends group, of rewarding voluntary activity. For further information contact the administrator or membership department via the website: www.bafm.org.uk.

British Museum Friends enjoy free entry to exhibitions and evening openings as well as information about lectures, study days and 'visits behind the scenes'. For joining information contact: 020 7323 8195; website: www.britishmuseum.org.

Friends of the Fitzwilliam Museum receive regular mailings with information about museum events, including exhibitions, concerts, lectures and parties. There are visits to other museums and historic houses in the Cambridge area and throughout the UK, and trips to overseas cities are also arranged. For membership information contact: 01223 332 900; website: www.fitzmuseum.cam.ac.uk.

Friends of the National Maritime Museum enjoy the Museum complex, housed in Greenwich Park, which comprises the largest maritime museum in the world, Wren's Royal Observatory and Inigo Jones's Queen's House. There are reciprocal free entry arrangements with many other maritime organizations. For further information contact: 020 8312 6678; website: www.nmm.ac.uk.

Friends of the V&A (Victoria and Albert Museum) have free admission to V&A exhibitions, members' previews, a programme of events and a free subscription to *V&A Magazine*. For further information contact: 020 7942 2271; website: www.vam.ac.uk.

Membership of the National Museums of Scotland gives regular mailings and the *Explorer* magazine, invitations to lectures and other events, and free admission to exhibitions and some sites. There is also a UK and overseas travel programme. For further information contact: 0131 247 4191; website: www.nms.ac.uk.

Nature and conservation

Many conservation organizations are very keen to recruit volunteers and are, therefore, listed in Chapter 12, Voluntary Work. Also, many of those concerned with field studies arrange courses and other special activity interests where there is usually a residential content, so others are listed in Chapter 14, Holidays. The potential list is enormous but a few are listed here:

Amenity organizations:. if you are interested in conservation and the environment, you might like to join your local amenity society. You should be able to contact it through your public library, or for a comprehensive list contact: 01302 388 883; website: www.btcv.org.uk.

Field Studies Council is an environmental educational charity committed to helping people understand and be inspired by the natural world. Fieldwork and cross-curricular courses inspire thousands of students each year through their countrywide network of 17 centres. Contact: 0845 345 4071; website: www.field-studies-council.org.

Forestry Commission offers thousands of walks and trails, forest drives, picnic places, wildlife watching and visitor centres. Contact: 0845 367 3787; website: www.forestry.gov.uk.

Inland Waterways Association is a national charity run by over 17,500 volunteers, which campaigns for the use, maintenance and restoration of Britain's inland waterways. Contact: 01494 783 453; website: www.waterways.org.uk.

Wildlife Trusts is the largest UK voluntary organization dedicated to conserving the full range of the UK's habitats and species. There are 47 local Wildlife Trusts caring for 2,500 nature reserves and campaigning for the future of our threatened wildlife. Contact: 01636 677711; website: www.wildlifetrusts.org.

Public library service

Britain's public library service issues over 600 million books free a year, lends CDs and DVDs and is a source of masses of information about both local and national activities. Additionally, the reference sections contain newspapers and periodicals as well as a wide selection of reference books covering any subject.

Among the many facilities on offer, large print books are available at most libraries, as are musical scores, leaflets on state benefits, consumer information and details of local community activities. Major libraries have computer databases and can provide specialized information from Europe and North America. If the information you require is not available in the library itself, the trained staff will normally do their best to tell you where you might find it. There is an excellent online public library service if you are interested in searching the internet.

Sciences and other related subjects

If astronomy or meteorology fascinates you, there are several societies and associations that may be of interest:

British Astronomical Association is open to all people interested in astronomy. Members' work is coordinated in such sections as Sun, Moon, terrestrial planets, meteors, Jupiter, asteroids, historical, telescope making and so on. Contact: 020 7734 4145; website: www.britastro.org.

Geologists' Association organizes lectures, field excursions and monthly meetings at Burlington House, and members also receive a quarterly magazine. Contact: 020 7434 9298; website: www.geologists.org.uk.

Royal Meteorological Society, which includes among its membership both amateurs and professionals, exists to advance meteorological science. Contact: 0118 956 8500; website: www.rmets.org.

Special interests

Whether your special enthusiasm is stamp collecting or model flying, most of the associations listed organize events, answer queries and can put you in contact with kindred spirits:

British Association of Numismatic Societies (BANS) is an umbrella organization that helps to coordinate the activities of some 65 local societies. Its members are those interested in the study or collection of coins, medals or similar. Contact: 020 8523 6351; website: www.numis.co.uk.

British Jigsaw Puzzle Library is a lending library with puzzles (mostly wooden) usually exchanged by post. They vary in difficulty, style and size, and the library tries to suit each member. Postal charges are extra. Contact: 01227 742 222; website: www.britishjigsawpuzzlelibrary.co.uk.

British Model Flying Association (BMFA) is responsible nationally for all types of model flying. It organizes competitions and fun-fly meetings, provides advice and guidelines on model flying, and can put you in touch with clubs in your area from its list of over 700 clubs. Contact: 0116 244 0028; website: www.bmfa.org.

Miniature Armoured Fighting Vehicle Association (MAFVA) is an international society that provides advice and information on tanks and other military vehicles and equipment and issues a bi-monthly magazine, *Tankette*. Contact: 01477 535 373; website: www.mafva.net.

National Association of Flower Arrangement Societies (NAFAS) can put you in touch with local clubs and classes, and can offer individual affiliated membership through a yearly subscription. The Association has over 70,000 members who receive the magazine *Flower Arranger*, newsletters, NAFAS events, information on the National Show, and details of NAFAS courses in floral art and design. Contact: 020 7247 5567; website: www.nafas.org.uk.

National Philatelic Society for those interested in stamp collecting, buying and selling stamps through the Society's auctions or postal packet scheme. Contact via website: www.ukphilately.org.uk.

Railway Correspondence and Travel Society is among the leading railway enthusiast groups, with nearly 4,000 members all over the country. There are regular meetings at about 30 centres, and the Society has a library with a postal loan facility. Contact via website: www.rcts.org.uk. *Railway Modeller* is a magazine for railway enthusiasts. It lists railway preservation events and gives information about local railway societies – including how to contact them.

Sport

Retirement is an ideal time to get fit and take up a sporting hobby. To find out about opportunities in your area, contact your local authority recreational department or your local sports or leisure centre.

Angling

Angling Trades Association promotes the interests of anglers and angling, including educational and environmental concerns, where to find qualified tuition, local tackle dealers and similar information. Contact: 024 7641 4999; website: www.anglingtradesassociation.com.

Badminton

Badminton England is the sport's governing body in England. Many categories of membership are available, from supporters, through club and county players to the World Class squad. Most sports and leisure centres have badminton courts and give instruction. Contact: 01908 268 400; website: www.badmintonengland.co.uk.

Bowling

Bowls Development Alliance is the united body of Bowls England, English Indoor Bowling Association, English Short Mat Bowling Association and British Crown Green Bowling Association. Supported by Sport England to develop and promote Bowls, it is a game that is available to everyone from 8 to 80. Contact: 01664 481 900; websites: www.esmba.co.uk, www.bowlsengland.com, www.eiba.co.uk, www.crowngreenbowls.org.

English Bowling Association has 2,600 local clubs, many of which provide instruction for beginners by qualified coaches. Some clubs have reduced rates for senior citizens. A national competition for 55-plus singles and pairs is organized through clubs each year. Contact: 01903 820 222; website: www.bowlsengland.com.

Clay pigeon shooting

Clay Pigeon Shooting Association (CPSA) is an association of individual shooters and a federation of clubs. As a member you have public liability insurance of £5 million, your scores are recorded in the national averages and you can compete in national events. For further information on all aspects of the sport, contact: 01483 485 400; website: www.cpsa.co.uk.

Cricket

Brit Oval is home to the Surrey County Cricket Club and one of the main venues for international and county cricket. Club membership entitles you to a number of benefits, including free or reduced price tickets for the Members' Pavilion to watch international matches as well as county events. Contact: 0207 820 5700; website: www.britoval.com.

England and Wales Cricket Board (ECB). To play, watch or help at cricket matches, contact your local club or contact the ECB to get in touch with your county cricket board. It also organizes an over-50 County Cricket Championship. Contact: 020 7432 1200; website: www.ecb.co.uk.

Lord's Cricket Ground offers a conducted tour of Lord's that includes the Long Room, the futuristic Media Centre and the MCC Museum, where the Ashes urn is on display. There are three tours per day during the summer and two per day during the winter: times subject to variation so please check beforehand. Senior citizens can attend County Championship matches and the National League matches for half-price. Contact: 020 7616 8500; website: www.lords.org.

Croquet

Croquet Association – a number of local authorities as well as clubs now offer facilities for croquet enthusiasts, and this association runs coaching courses and can advise about clubs, events, purchase of equipment and other information. Contact: 01242 242 318; website: www.croquet.org.uk.

Cycling

CTC (Cyclists' Touring Club) is the largest national cycling organization, offering members free third-party insurance, free legal aid, colour magazines, organized cycling holidays and introductions to 200 local cycling groups. There is also a veterans' section. Contact: 0844 736 8451; website: www.ctc.org.uk.

Darts

British Darts Organisation – opportunities for playing darts can be found almost anywhere in clubs, pubs and sports centres. Contact: 020 8883 5544; website: www.bdodarts.com.

Golf

> **English Golf Union** is one of the largest sports governing bodies in England, looking after the interests of over 1,900 golf clubs and 740,000 members. It is a not-for-profit organization run for the benefit of the game and its players. Contact: 01526 354 500; website: www.englishgolfunion.org.
>
> **Golfing Union of Ireland:** 00 353 1 505 4000; website: www.gui.ie.
>
> **Scottish Golf Union:** 01334 466 477; website: www.scottishgolfunion.org.
>
> **Welsh Golfing Union:** 01633 436 040; website: www.golfunionwales.org.

National Golf Unions can provide information about municipal courses and private clubs, of which there are some 1,700 in England alone. Additionally, many adult education institutes and sports centres run classes for beginners.

Swimming

British Swimming is the new name for the Amateur Swimming Federation of Great Britain Ltd. The organization is a federation made up of three members – England, Scotland and Wales:

> England: ASA – Amateur Swimming Association 01509 618 737; website: www.sportcentric.com.
>
> Scotland: SASA – Scottish Amateur Swimming Association 01786 466 520; website: www.scottishswimming.com.
>
> Wales: WASA – Welsh Amateur Swimming Association 01792 513 636; website: www.openwaterswimming.eu.

Table tennis

> **English Table Tennis Association** – ETTA is the association for this sport, which can be enjoyed by people of all ages and all levels of

competence. Contact: 01424 722 525; website: www.englishtabletennis.org.uk.

Veterans English Table Tennis Society – VETTS holds regional and national championships including singles and doubles events for various ages over 40, attracting increasing numbers of men and women who enjoy playing socially and competitively well into their retirement. Contact: 01462 671 191; website: www.vetts.org.uk.

Tennis

Lawn Tennis Association – LTA facilities have been greatly improving, and your local authority recreation department should be able to provide more details. The LTA can give you information about anything to do with tennis, from advice on choosing a racket to obtaining tickets for major tournaments. Contact: 020 8487 7000; website: www.lta.org.uk.

Vets Tennis GB promotes competitions for older players in various age groups from 35 to 80 years. There are many affiliated clubs, and information is available on club, county and international events. Contact: 020 8875 1773; website: www.vetstennisgb.org.

Veteran rowing

British Rowing has enthusiasts aged from 31 to well past 80, and for those who enjoy a competitive edge, there are special races and regattas, with types of boat including eights, fours and pairs, as well as single, double and quadruple sculling. Touring rowing is also on the increase. Contact: 020 8237 6700; website: www.britishrowing.org.

Walking

Ramblers' Association – anything from a gentle stroll to an action-packed weekend trek with stout boots and a rucksack comes under the heading of Rambling. The Association provides a comprehensive information service on all aspects of walking and can advise on where to walk, clothing and equipment and organized walking holidays, as well as details of the 450 local groups throughout the country. Contact: 020 7339 8500; website: www.ramblers.org.uk.

Windsurfing

Seavets, affiliated to the Royal Yachting Association, aims to encourage the not-so-young of all abilities to enjoy the challenge of windsurfing. Events are organized throughout the country from March to October, providing recreational windsurfing and racing for enthusiasts aged 35-plus. Further information from the membership secretary via the website: www.seavets.co.uk.

Yachting

Royal Yachting Association – RYA has 2,200 affiliated clubs and more than 1,500 recognized training centres. The Association also provides a comprehensive information service for boat owners and can give advice on everything from moorings to foreign cruising procedure. Contact: 02380 604 100; website: www.rya.org.uk.

Women's organizations

Although today women can participate in almost any activity on equal terms with men, women's clubs and organizations continue to enjoy enormous popularity. Here are some:

Mothers' Union (MU) is an international Christian charity that seeks to support families worldwide. In 81 countries with over 4 million members, the association promotes the well-being of families through practical work, policy and prayer. Contact: 020 7222 5533; website: www.themothersunion.org.

National Association of Women's Clubs has 212 clubs with a membership of 7,250 throughout the country, open to women of all ages, faiths and interests. Typical activities include crafts, drama, keep fit and talks from guest speakers covering a wide variety of subjects, and there are outings to theatres and exhibitions and visits to places of interest. Contact: 020 7837 1434; website: www.nawc.org.uk.

National Women's Register (NWR) is an organization of 400 groups of 'lively minded women' who meet informally in members' homes to enjoy challenging discussions. The groups choose their own topics and many also arrange a varied programme of social activities. Contact NWR, Tel: 0845 450 0287; website: www.nwr.org.uk.

Scottish Women's Rural Institutes (SWRI) is one of the largest women's organizations in Scotland and has around 22,000 members of all ages who enjoy social, recreational and educational activities. There are talks and demonstrations, classes in arts and crafts, and discussions on matters of public interest. Contact: 0131 225 1724; website: www.swri.org.uk.

If you live in Northern Ireland, contact the **Federation of Women's Institutes of Northern Ireland,** Tel: 028 9030 1506; website: www.wini.org.uk.

Townswomen's Guilds is one of the UK's leading women's organizations, providing fun, friendship and a forum for social change since 1929. Over 34,000 women nationwide have joined Townswomen to enjoy national events, informative conferences and organized travel packages and to learn new skills. Contact: 0121 326 0400; website: www.townswomen.org.uk.

The WI (Women's Institute) is the largest national organization for women, with nearly 205,000 members in 6,500 WIs. It plays a unique role in providing women with educational opportunities and the chance to build new skills, take part in a wide variety of activities and campaign on issues that matter to them and their communities. Contact: 020 7371 9300; website: www.thewi.org.uk.

For people with disabilities

Facilities for the disabled have improved dramatically in recent years so there are fewer activities from which disabled people are now excluded. This section deals with one topic – the enjoyment of books – which for many blind or partially sighted people can be a special problem:

Calibre Audio Library has audio books that bring the pleasure of reading to people who have sight problems, dyslexia or other disabilities that prevent them from reading a print book. With a wide choice of fiction and non-fiction on standard cassettes, MP3 discs and USB memory sticks for both children and adults, this service is entirely free. Contact: 01296 432 339; website: www.calibre.org.uk.

Listening Books is a UK charity providing a large collection of audio books to over 11,000 people nationwide who find it difficult or impossible to read due to illness or disability. Audio books are sent through the post on CD or they can be downloaded on the internet. Contact: 020 7407 9417; website: www.listening-books.org.uk.

RNIB's Talking Book Service offers over 16,000 audio books, paid for by annual subscription, and delivered direct to your door. Talking books are recorded in DAISY format, which makes them easy to navigate. Six books can be chosen at a time. Contact: 0303 123 9999; website: www.rnib.org.uk.

Public transport

One of the big gains of reaching retirement age is the availability of cheap travel. Local authorities are now required to offer men, as well as women, concessionary bus fares from the age of 60 instead of men having to wait till 65 before being able to benefit. Bus travel, for the moment, is free out of peak hours, anywhere in the country. Coaches very often have special rates for older people, and Senior Rail cards, available to men and women over 60, offer wonderful savings. Details of these are given in Chapter 14, Holidays.

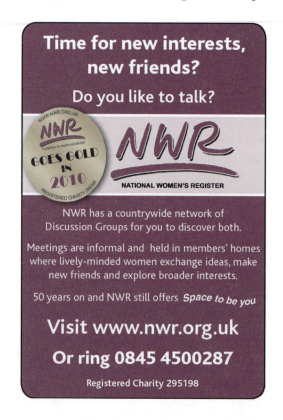

Chapter Ten
Starting your own business

Success in business requires training and discipline and hard work. But if you're not frightened by these things, the opportunities are just as great today as they ever were.

DAVID ROCKERFELLER (1915 –)

Have you ever thought of running your own business? Maybe after years of working for someone else the idea of continuing to work is not high on your list of priorities. For some people however, being their own boss can be one of the most satisfying retirement occupations. Self-employment is regarded as the top employment option in retirement, according to Aviva's recent Real Retirement Report. Its research indicated that seven out of ten adults intend working beyond their current standard retirement age, and 61 per cent of the over-55s feel self-employment offers freedom and flexibility, and highlights a growing trend of gradual retirement or 'part-retirement'. While financially rewarding, this is not the only reason people want to continue working past retirement age. Social and emotional benefits also feature; keeping the mind active and interacting with other people are important too.

Anyone thinking about going self-employed in their 50s and 60s has a number of advantages: they probably have a specialist area of knowledge or expertise they have gained over a good number of years of working experience, and they would rather continue to use it (than lose it). They may have been longing for an opportunity to do something different – possibly related to a lifelong interest that has been kept firmly on the back burner due to restrictions of time while they were employed. Perhaps they have a desire to do something useful and regard working as a vocational thing rather than being profit-driven, so are not motivated entirely for financial reasons. Good advice is to assess what skills you have; make sure you work on all your existing contacts; be prepared to re-skill if necessary; and if you have a hobby or spare-time interest that could possibly provide a source of self-employed income, be prepared to stick your toe in the water.

There are hundreds of success stories about those who took the plunge post-retirement to build a company that provided involvement, fun and income, plus a legacy for their children. Whether you graduated from Oxbridge or the University of Life, nothing should stop you from accumulating wealth if you are hungry for success. But if you intend to make it to the ranks of the super-rich, building an empire does take time and effort. Whatever your choice, for whatever reason, with government proposals for increasing retirement age, it seems likely that many in their 50s and 60s will be working well past the traditional cut off age and going for gradual or part-retirement.

For every success story, however, there is a failure, and your money could disappear fast if you set up in big-company style. Running a small business successfully in its early stages is all about keeping costs down, handling the finances intelligently and doing it yourself until you have a positive cash flow and are making profits. If you are married, your partner's attitude is a crucial one. Even if not directly involved, he or she will have to accept (at least) the loss of a room in the house being used as an office. There will be the added distractions of out-of-hours phone calls and suddenly cancelled social engagements. If you have a skill to offer, the drive to sell it and the health to support your ambition, this chapter will give you the information you need to set up or buy into a small concern and join the ranks of other successful entrepreneurs.

It is an exciting prospect but best not to make things too complicated in the beginning: keep things small and simple. This will leave you time to get on with the work you obviously want to do – whether that is acting in a consultancy capacity, or doing something you love (and getting paid for it). Here is some straightforward and simple advice about getting started if you are thinking of going self-employed.

Legal structure of the business

When thinking of starting a business, you have three main choices as to the legal form it can take. You can operate as a sole trader, a partnership or a limited company.

Sole trader

This is the simplest form of trading, with virtually no start-up expenses and minimal bureaucracy involved. If you trade under your own name then, apart from informing HM Revenue & Customs (HMRC), there are no legal formalities. If you use another name, you must indicate on documents such as letterheads that you are the owner. Even if you employ others, you will be treated as self-employed for both tax and National Insurance purposes and will be liable to pay personal Income Tax on your profits, after deducting allowable expenses.

HMRC simplified the main tax return for self-assessment in 2008 by including fewer self-employment pages for businesses with a turnover of less than £30,000. Such small enterprises are now able to submit a three-line statement showing income, expenses and profit. Proper records will nevertheless need to be kept in the event of a query or investigation by the tax office.

The main disadvantage of operating as a sole trader is that it carries unlimited liability, so you are personally liable for all business debts. Should the business fail, your own assets (including your home) as well as your business ones would be at the disposal of your creditors – and, if the worst came to the worst, you could be made personally bankrupt.

Partnership

A partnership is a business with two or more proprietors. It is similar to a sole trader in that it can be formed without any legal formalities or documentation other than informing HMRC. To avoid any possible future misunderstanding, however, it is advisable to have a formal partnership agreement drawn up at the outset, covering such points as distribution of profits (equal or unequal shares), voting rights, control of the bank account and arrangements for admitting new partners. While it is a simple matter to form a partnership, it can be very irksome to settle the affairs of one that has gone wrong. A few legal expenses at the beginning could prove a worthwhile investment.

As with sole traders, partners are treated as self-employed for both tax and National Insurance purposes. Profits are divided and taxed as the personal income of individual partners. However, if one partner fails to pay his or her share the other partners will be called upon to meet the shortfall. Similarly, each partner carries unlimited liability for all the debts of the business.

An exception to this rule – although rare today – is that of a limited partnership. This has to be registered at Companies House and at least one partner has to incur unlimited liability. The limited partners (sometimes known as 'sleeping partners') cannot take part in the running of the business in any way, and their liability is limited to their share of the partnership capital. Accounts need to be prepared at least once a year, but they do not need to be published.

Limited company

A limited company is a legal entity in its own right. As the name implies, liability for the company's debts in the event of insolvency is limited to the amount invested in the business by each shareholder. As a director of a limited company, you will be treated for tax and National Insurance purposes as an employee of the business, paying Income Tax under the PAYE system. Corporation Tax will also be payable on the profits of the company.

The main disadvantage of a limited company is the bureaucracy. A limited company must be registered by Companies House (or, in Scotland, by the Registrar of Companies for Scotland): this involves the filing of both a Memorandum of Association and the Articles of Association. The company's accounts have to be audited once a year by a firm of qualified accountants, and a set, showing among other details a profit and loss account, must be filed annually with Companies House, together with basic information about the company and its directors, all of which are open to public inspection.

Another disadvantage of a limited company as compared to a partnership or sole trader is that sole traders and partnerships can set off any losses they incur during the first four years' trading retrospectively against the owners' Income Tax on earnings in the three preceding years. This may enable you to recover tax already paid in earlier years of ordinary employment. Losses can only be set off against a company's Corporation Tax when it makes a profit.

Registering a limited company

Although you can register a limited company yourself, it is advisable to get a professional accountant, solicitor or company registration agent to do it for you.

To register a limited company, you need to fill in Form 10, Notification of First Directors and Secretary and Location of Registered Office, and Form 12, Declaration of Compliance. These must be sent to the Registrar of Companies together with the Memorandum of Association (stating the company's name, registered office, share capital and nature and scope of the business arrangements, including the extent of liability) and the Articles of Association (stating the internal rules of the company). All the necessary forms can be obtained either from law stationers or from Companies House in Cardiff. Specimen memoranda and articles can only be obtained from law stationers.

There are two scale rates: the normal service, which costs £20 to register and the same-day incorporation service, which costs £50. To take advantage of the same-day service, it is necessary to present the completed documents at Companies House by 3 pm. If you use the standard service, registering a new company will take five working days from the receipt of correct documents at Companies House.

'Off the shelf'

Another possibility, if you are not too fussy about the company name, is to buy a previously registered company 'off the shelf' from a company registration agent. This will cost, on average, about £150 for all the documentation, including the company books. There will be a further charge of around £75 should you decide to change the name and a charge of around £25 to change the Articles of Association. If you simply need to change the name, which is not a difficult matter, you could do it direct with the Registrar. Forms, guidance notes and other information are available from **Companies House Contact Centre**, Tel: 0303 1234 500; website: www.companieshouse.gov.uk.

Business names

It is no longer necessary to register a business name. However, where a sole trader uses a business name that is different from his or her real name, or where a partnership trades under a name that differs from those of all the partners, or a limited company trades other than under its full corporate name, then certain legal requirements have to be met. All business stationery – including letterheads, order forms, invoices and receipts – must contain the real name(s) of the sole trader, partner or company, together with the official address of the business. These details must also be prominently displayed on all business premises. Failure to do so is a criminal offence, punishable by a fine.

There are also certain regulations governing the words that may be used in a business or company name 'without justification'. Prohibited words include those considered offensive or those that imply connection with the Crown, the government or a local authority, for instance 'British', 'National' and 'European'. Other prohibited categories are titles like 'Society' and

'Institute' that suggest a representative status, or words that imply a specific function such as insurance or banking. In all such cases, approval must be sought from the appropriate government department or governing body that the use of such words is justified. For more information see *Company Names* (GBF 2) and *Business Names* (GBF 3), available from **Companies House Contact Centre**, Tel: 0303 1234 500; website: www.companieshouse.gov.uk.

Domain names

Now that businesses rely so heavily on the internet, an important first step, should you be considering setting up a new business in retirement, is what domain name to have and how to register it. There are two basic steps for getting your website online. Registering or reserving the domain name is the first. For those of you who are unfamiliar with this process, the domain name makes up the address of your website, and can end with .co.uk, .com, .net, .org, .info, .us, .biz, etc. This name, once registered, will require a web host. The web host is the 'nuts and bolts' of your website, because this is where you design and publish your web pages, add and improve them and operate your site.

Depending on what sort of business you are running it may be important to you to be found easily and quickly in the major search engines (such as Google). If so, you should try to register a name that contains key words as to what you do, rather than your company name. Use a company name that includes a word that your target audience would be likely to use when they start searching. You can still list your company name on your web pages. It is, however, essential that the domain name includes your 'search-friendly' key words if you want customers to find you easily.

Top tips on choosing the best domain name include: don't make it too long or complicated, it needs to be easy to remember (for you and your customers). Use hyphens if your name is long; it makes it easier to understand, and it looks better. It is very important to protect your name by registering multiple extensions (such as .net, .org, etc); this prevents people from copying your name. It doesn't mean you have to have multiple websites, but by reserving them it stops people infringing your territory or copying your name and ideas. Your business could become valuable, and this step will prevent predatory competitors from encroaching.

Reserving a domain name is easy and remarkably low-cost. It doesn't matter where you register your domain. Every registrar provides similar services. You should take steps, when registering, to protect your privacy. This means keeping your domain name private, which will stop your information (name, e-mail address, etc) from becoming part of the global internet database. It is also essential for preventing loads of spam from reaching your e-mail box. This tip is highly recommended, as it comes from many people who wish it had been available when they first created their sites.

A huge number of companies offer domain name registration and ongoing support. Search 'domain names and how to register them' on Google and you will find over 18 million offers of advice. Best suggestion: ask friends who are already 'web savvy', or small business owners who you know operate their business using a website. Don't ignore help that is right in front of your nose: young friends or relatives, especially the grandchildren, will know more than you ever will about this subject. They may even prove keen to help and can design your website for you if you want.

As with all new things, take advice and think carefully before committing yourself. But if you are going to be taken seriously in business, having a well designed and user-friendly website is essential.

Alternative ways of getting started

Rather than start a new business, you could buy into one that is already established, or consider franchising.

Buying a business

Buying an established business can be an attractive route to becoming your own boss, as it eliminates many of the problems of start-up. The enterprise is likely to come equipped with stock, suppliers, an order book, premises and possibly employees. It is also likely to have debtors and creditors. Take professional advice before buying any business, even one from friends. In particular, you should consider why the business is being sold. It may be for perfectly respectable reasons – for instance, a change of circumstances such as retirement. But equally, it may be that the market is saturated, that the rent is about to go sky-high or that major competition has opened up nearby.

Before parting with your money, make sure that the assets are actually owned by the business and get the stock professionally valued. You should also ensure that the debts are collectable and that the same credit terms will apply from existing suppliers. Get an accountant to look at the figures for the last three years and have a chartered surveyor check the premises. It is also advisable to ask a solicitor to vet any legal documents, including staff contracts: you may automatically inherit existing employees.

The value of the company's assets will be reflected in its purchase price, as will the 'goodwill' (or reputation) that it has established. For more information, contact the agents specializing in small businesses, **Christie & Co**, Tel: 020 7227 0700; website: www.christie.com.

Franchising

Franchising has become an increasingly popular form of business, with attractions for both franchisor and franchisee. The franchisor gains in that an ambitious group is able to expand very quickly. The advantage to the franchisee is that there are normally fewer risks than starting a business from scratch.

A franchisee buys into an established business and builds up his or her own enterprise under its wing. In return for the investment plus regular royalty payments, he or she acquires the right to sell the franchisor's products or services within a specified geographic area and enjoys the benefits of its reputation, buying power and marketing expertise. As a franchisee you are effectively your own boss. You finance the business, employ the staff and retain the profits after the franchisor has had its cut. You are usually expected to maintain certain standards and conform to the broad corporate approach of the organization. In return, the franchisor should train you in the business, provide management support and give you access to a wide range of back-up services.

Cost

The amount of capital needed to buy a franchise varies enormously according to the type of business, and can be anywhere between £3,000 and £500,000 or more. The franchisee is normally liable to pay an initial fee, covering both the entry cost and the initial support services provided by the franchisor, such as advice about location and market research. Advice should be taken as to whether the fee will be partially or wholly allowable for tax purposes.

Length of agreement

The length of the agreement will depend both on the type of business involved and on the front-end fee. Agreements can run from three to 20 years, with five years being average. Many franchisors include an option to renew the agreement, which should be treated as a valuable asset.

Raising the finance

Franchising has now built up a good track record with a relatively low rate of business failures, so raising the money for a franchising venture is rarely a major difficulty. Most of the leading high street banks operate specialist franchise loan sections. Franchisors may also be able to help in raising the money and can sometimes arrange more advantageous terms through their connections with financial institutions.

The **British Franchise Association** (BFA) represents 'the responsible face' of franchising, and its members have to conform to a stringent code of practice. The BFA publishes a *Franchisee Guide*, which provides comprehensive advice on buying a franchise, together with a list of BFA member franchisors and affiliated advisers. It is well worth attending a franchise seminar to find out more and compare the various franchise options on offer.

A good franchisor will provide a great deal of invaluable help. However, some franchisors are very casual in their approach, lacking in competence, or even downright unethical. Make careful enquiries before committing any money: as basic information, you should ask for a bank reference together with a copy of the previous year's accounts. Also check with the BFA whether the franchisor in question is a member and talk to some of the other franchisees to find out what their experience has been. Before signing, seek advice from an accountant or solicitor. For more information, contact the British Franchise Association on: 01235 820 470; website: www.thebfa.org.

Developing an invention

If you have a clever idea that you would like to market, you should ensure that your intellectual property is protected. For information about patenting an invention and much more, contact the **UK Intellectual Property Office**, Tel: 0845 9 500 505; website: www.ipo.gov.uk.

Taxation

Taxation arrangements vary considerably according to whether you are operating as a sole trader, partnership or limited company. As you will know, tax rates, bands and allowances are revised annually and take effect at the beginning of the financial year in April.

Sole trader or partnership

As soon as you start work on your own account, you should inform your local Inspector of Taxes. To do so, you should obtain form CWF1 from your local tax office and return it, when completed, together with your form P45, which your employer will have given you when you left. For further information see website: www.hmrc.gov.uk.

Income Tax

As a sole trader or member of a partnership, you are treated as self-employed for tax purposes. Profits are aggregated with any other personal income and are taxed at the normal rates of Income Tax. From April 2011, the basic rate of 20 per cent applies to the first £37,400 of taxable income, with all income in excess of this subject to the higher rate of 40 per cent.

Not all your income is taxable. In common with everyone else, you get a personal tax allowance (from 6 April 2011, £7,475); and if you qualify for the married couple's allowance you will also receive the minimum £2,670 allowance (or more if the husband's income is below the income threshold). Additionally, as a self-employed person (Schedule D), you are allowed certain other reliefs. Ask your accountant, but the following expenses and allowances are tax deductible:

- *Business expenses.* These must be incurred 'wholly and exclusively' for the purposes of the trade. Professional publications will probably qualify; however, your 'wages', National Insurance Contributions and any business entertaining will not. Bad debts are usually allowable. Certain expenses incurred in advance of getting the business started are also permitted, for example necessary travelling, printing costs and telephoning.

- *Partially allowable expenses.* These mainly apply if you are working from home. They include such items as that part of your rent, heating, lighting and telephone usage that you devote to business purposes, and also possibly some of the running expenses on your car, if you use your car for your business. Remember that your business equipment and premises are capital items. These cannot be counted as an expense. Instead they must be categorized under fixed assets and writing-down allowances are calculated at the year end, to reduce your profits (see below).

- *Spouse's wages.* If you employ your partner in the business, his or her pay (provided this is reasonable) qualifies as a legitimate expense, in the same way as any other employee's, but must of course be accounted for through the PAYE system.

- *Pension contributions.* Since April 2006, everyone is free to invest up to 100 per cent of annual earnings into a pension plan with the benefit of tax relief, up to a maximum figure (known as the 'annual allowance') of £255,000. There is also a lifetime limit of £1.8 million for total pension funds including fund growth.

- *Capital allowances.* These were overhauled in April 2008. There is a new annual investment allowance for the first £50,000 of expenditure (except on certain items such as cars), and the writing-down allowance for plant and machinery in the general pool is reduced from 25 to 20 per cent. The rate of writing-down allowances on long-life assets expenditure increases from 6 to 10 per cent.

- *Research and development.* There are generous reliefs available if you can meet the stringent qualifying conditions. Best advice is to check with an accountant.

- *Interest on loans.* Tax relief is given on money borrowed to invest in a small firm, in most normal circumstances.

- *Tax losses.* Any tax losses in the first four years may enable you to recover PAYE from your last three years in employment. A tax loss made by the business can also be set against any other income the proprietor may have.

Because of these reliefs, being a sole trader or partner can offer substantial tax advantages. As a result, HMRC has become increasingly strict about the definition of self-employed. If you work as a consultant or freelance and most of your income derives from one employer, your Inspector of Taxes may argue that you are an employee of that firm – and not a self-employed person. For more information, see leaflet IR 56 *Employed or Self-Employed? A Guide to Employment Status for Tax and National Insurance* on the website: www.hmrc.gov.uk.

Capital Gains Tax (CGT)

On 23 June 2010 CGT was increased to a flat 28 per cent rate for all individuals, personal representatives and trustees. New entrepreneurs' relief was increased to allow the first £5 million of lifetime gains to be taxed at an effective rate of 10 per cent. Since the introduction of independent taxation, in the case of a married couple both husband and wife are taxed independently on their capital gains and each enjoys his or her own separate annual exemption. Tax may not be payable if the proceeds are reinvested within three years in another business (or business assets). Assets bought the previous year might also qualify. This is normally referred to as 'roll-over relief'.

Another valuable relief allows trading losses to be offset against Capital Gains Tax. Proprietors of unincorporated businesses who make a loss (and do not have enough income in the year to offset that loss in full) can make a claim to set the unused loss against capital gains of the same year – with any excess of loss carried forward against capital gains of the following years.

When calculating your likely gains, you should be aware that the definition of business assets has been tightened up by HMRC and, for a business relief to apply, the assets must be solely relevant to the business and not include, for example, unrelated property or other investments. In all instances, consult your accountant before deciding on a particular course of action.

Inheritance Tax

Most small family-owned businesses can be passed on to the next generation free of Inheritance Tax. Although in recent years tax planning has become much easier for small business owners, you would nevertheless be strongly advised to speak to an accountant.

Preparation of accounts

Since self-assessment, sole traders and partners are no longer required to submit accounts to HMRC. Very small businesses – that is, those with a turnover of less than £30,000 – are required to submit only a three-line account on their tax return to provide HMRC with the following information:

- details of their total takings;
- details of their expenses;
- their profits.

Larger businesses will need to provide more detail, with accounts normally in two parts, in line with HMRC's standard format: a trading account and profit and loss account, which provide a summary of the year's trading transactions; and the balance sheet, which shows the assets and liabilities of the business at the end of the year.

The accounts of a sole trader, partnership or limited company with a turnover of less than £5.6 million do not have to be audited by an independent qualified accountant, provided it has either fewer than 50 employees or a balance sheet total of less than £2.8 million. However, whether you draw up the accounts yourself or engage professional help, full and accurate records must be kept from the start. While not essential, there is a very strong argument for having a qualified accountant to help you, since his or her advice is likely to prove invaluable on a whole range of matters.

Making a tax return

As an employee, you will have had Income Tax deducted from your gross pay automatically under the PAYE system. When you become self-employed, you become responsible for the payment of tax and are required by law to make a true return of your income each year.

Self-assessment

As an employer, self-assessment might both affect you personally and also affect some of your employees and/or co-directors. People who work for (or with) you who receive a tax return will require certain information from you, mainly about PAYE, benefits in kind and expenses payments. For further information contact **HMRC Self-assessment helpline:** 0845 900 0444; website: www.hmrc.gov.uk.

There is a requirement to keep records of all your sources of income and capital gains for at least 22 months, or five years and 10 months in the case of a business. If you intend to file your tax return online the deadline is 31 January. Paper returns must be filed by 31 October. If you submit your return online, the calculation will be made automatically. The dates are important, as there is an automatic penalty of £100 if your tax return arrives after 31 January. For further information contact HMRC Self-assessment helpline: 0845 900 0444; website: www.hmrc.gov.uk.

Useful reading

Three excellent books that have comprehensive information on starting and running your own business are: *Working for Yourself* (an entrepreneur's guide to the basics) by Jonathan Reuvid; *Start Up and Run Your Own Business* (the essential guide to planning, funding and growing your new enterprise) and *Forming a Limited Company* (a practical guide to legal requirements and procedures) by Patricia Clayton – all published by Kogan Page – website: www.koganpage.com.

Limited company

HMRC will be automatically notified when a limited company is formed, and will contact the directors in due course. However, to avoid delays it is sensible for you to contact HMRC as soon as the company is incorporated.

Corporation Tax

A company pays Corporation Tax on its taxable profits. The main rate is 27 per cent for the 2011/12 tax year. The small companies' rate is 20 per cent for the 2011/12 tax year. The main rate of Corporation Tax applies to companies with taxable profits over £1.5 million. The small companies' rate applies to businesses with taxable profits of £300,000 or less.

If you are a director of a limited company, the business will pay your salary (which will be subject to PAYE) out of its trading income. Allowable expenses, similar to those for sole traders and partnerships, are also deductible before Corporation Tax is charged. Directors' expenses may, however, be disallowed, in whole or in part, if HMRC takes the view that these benefited directors personally – as opposed to being a legitimate business expense. Such expenses may be taxed as a personal benefit.

Relief for losses

If your company makes a loss, the directors cannot offset this against their personal taxable income. The losses can, however, be offset against both future and past profits made by the company, with trading losses carried back for up to one year.

Relief for pre-trading expenditure

The period for tax relief for expenditure incurred before the start of trading is seven years.

Preparation of accounts

Limited companies are required to file annual accounts within 10 months of their year-end. These accounts will normally form the basis of HMRC's tax assessment. As stated earlier, however, small companies can take advantage of an abbreviated form of accounts for filing provided they can meet two of the following criteria:

1 fewer than 50 employees;
2 turnover of less than £5.6 million;
3 a balance sheet total of less than £2.8 million.

Capital Gains Tax

When a company sells an asset such as a building at a profit, it will pay Corporation Tax on the chargeable gain. If the company itself is subsequently sold, the shareholders will have CGT at the flat rate of 28 per cent to pay on the gain realized from the sale of the shares.

Venture capital relief

Many entrepreneurs wishing to defer paying tax on gains arising from the sale of shares in their own companies used to think in terms of reinvestment relief. Reinvestment relief, as such, has been abolished and is now merged with the *Enterprise Investment Scheme (EIS)* to create a unified system of venture capital reliefs. Consult your tax adviser or accountant about this.

Tax offset

If your company makes a trading loss, this can be used as an offset against profits made on the sale of assets, provided the sale takes place in the same or the previous year.

Inheritance Tax

Since 1992 most small family-owned businesses have been taken out of the Inheritance Tax net and can be passed on to the next generation free of tax. There are certain cases, however, where IHT could still be a factor; these are where the controlling shares are in a fully quoted company, and where certain assets are owned by partners or by controlling shareholders and are used in their respective businesses. In such cases, there is tax relief of 50 per cent. Although IHT planning has now become much easier for small business owners, you would nevertheless be strongly advised to speak to an accountant.

Value Added Tax (VAT)

VAT is imposed on most business transactions. The legal structure of the enterprise does not in general affect the issue.

Registration Registration is required if your sales are over £70,000 in any period of 12 months or less, or if you expect it to exceed the threshold in a future period of 30 days. You may register for VAT voluntarily if your turnover is below this figure.

Charging and paying VAT You collect VAT from your customers by including it in, or adding it to, the price you charge (output tax). Similarly, you will be charged VAT by your suppliers on the goods and services you buy (input tax). When you receive a VAT return, your input tax is subtracted from your output tax and the difference is paid to HMRC. If the input tax is greater than the output tax, you can claim a refund on the difference.

Small businesses with a taxable turnover of up to £150,000 can opt to take advantage of a flat-rate scheme for calculating their VAT liability. Instead of keeping detailed records of the VAT charged on every purchase and sale, they can calculate the amount due by applying a flat-rate percentage to their total turnover.

Businesses with an annual turnover of less than £1.35 million can opt to submit a VAT return once a year instead of quarterly. A condition is that they must make monthly payments by direct debit, based on estimates agreed with HMRC, with a balancing adjustment made when the annual return is submitted. This is allowable for all businesses until their taxable turnover reaches £1.6 million.

Any business with an annual turnover of less than £1.35 million can opt for cash accounting for VAT, enabling them to delay paying the VAT on their sales to HMRC until they have actually received payment for them. However, you cannot issue invoices in advance of supply or for sales where payment is not due for more than six months after the date of the invoice. The scheme is designed to help the cash flow of small firms with slow-paying clients and provide automatic VAT relief for bad debts. Bad debts can be written off for the purpose of claiming VAT relief after six months. A debtor no longer has to be declared formally insolvent for relief to be allowed. This scheme can be operated by businesses until their taxable turnover reaches £1.6 million.

Taxable supplies and exempt supplies Most transactions are liable to VAT at either the standard rate (20 per cent since 4 January 2011) or the zero rate (nil). Zero-rated supplies include most foodstuffs, children's clothing and books. Reduced rate VAT supplies include children's car seats, domestic supplies of fuel and power.

Exempt supplies include education, health and financial services. If all the supplies you make are exempt from VAT, you will not be required to register for VAT but you will not be able to reclaim the VAT you pay on goods and services for your business. If some of the supplies are exempt, you would probably still need to be registered. Your accountant should be able to advise, or check with your local HMRC office.

Below the VAT registration limit If you are not registered for VAT, any expenditure you incur that includes a charge for VAT should be entered in your records, inclusive of VAT. Even if you do not have to register at present, you may have to do so in the future if your taxable turnover increases. There could be an argument for early registration, as you would be able to offset the VAT the business has to pay to its suppliers. Another advantage is that VAT usually helps in establishing well-kept accounts. For more information see website: www.hmrc.gov.uk.

How to register It is important that you notify HMRC within the 30-day limit once you are liable to be registered. Should you forget to do so, you may have to account for tax that you have not collected, together with penalties for late registration. You should start keeping VAT records and charging VAT to your customers from the date of your registration, which will be notified to you on the certificate of VAT registration that will be sent to you after your registration application has been processed and approved by HMRC. You will have to account for VAT from this date, whether or not you have included VAT in your prices.

Helpful reforms The government has tried to make VAT simpler and less onerous for business. In the event of a bad debt, firms are no longer required to notify their debtors in writing that they are claiming relief. Even more welcome, businesses with turnover up to £150,000 that are late with their VAT payments can expect to be offered help and advice rather than get an automatic fine. For further information, contact **HM Revenue & Customs National Advice Service,** Tel: 0845 010 9000; website: www.hmrc.gov.uk.

Benefits in kind

The rules affecting benefits in kind apply to all directors and to employees earning £8,500 or more a year (including the value of benefits in kind). Any tax payable is deducted via the PAYE system. A particular item of interest to many smaller businesses is company cars. Other possible items that you may need to check are company computers and mobile phones loaned to employees for their private use.

Computers and mobile phones The rules concerning the loan of computers and mobile phones to employees for private use have recently been revised. The benefit for computers is now liable for tax and National Insurance in the same way as other benefits in kind. While mobile phones still largely escape the tax, there is now a limit on the number of mobile phones that employers can loan to employees, tax-free, for private use. The figure is one per employee, and the benefit is no longer extended to the employee's family or members of the household. In both cases, where the equipment is solely provided for business purposes, no tax and National Insurance are due.

National Insurance

As with tax, your liability for National Insurance Contributions will depend on whether you are self-employed (sole trader or partner) or whether you are a director of a limited company.

Self-employed

If you are self-employed, you will have to pay flat-rate *Class 2* contributions, currently £2.40 a week, unless:

- you are over 65 (men) or 60 (women) (even if you have not retired from work);
- you are entitled to pay married women's or widow's reduced-rate Class 1 contributions;
- you have been granted 'a certificate of exception' because your earnings are likely to be less than £5,075 a year.

You must register to pay Class 2 contributions within three months of becoming self-employed or you risk incurring a £100 penalty.

If your annual taxable profits or profit share are above £5,715, you will also have to pay *Class 4* contributions of 8 per cent on profits between £5,715 and £43,875, plus 1 per cent on profits above this amount, unless you are in one of the following categories:

- not resident for income tax purposes in the UK;
- trustee, executor or administrator of wills and settlements (there are, however, exceptions);
- sleeping partner, taking a profit and supplying capital, but not active in the business.

How to pay

Class 2 contributions can be paid either by direct debit from your bank or by the quarterly billing system that has replaced the traditional NI stamps. If you prefer quarterly billing, the National Insurance Contributions Office should automatically advise you of the amount owing for the previous quarter, which is payable through banks or at all post offices via Girobank. Class 4 contributions are normally assessed and collected by HMRC, together with PAYE or Schedule D income tax. As they will be paid retrospectively, remember to keep the necessary cash ready and not spend it as part of your monthly salary.

Husband and wife

As with independent taxation, husband and wife are assessed separately for Class 4 contributions. Further information about Schedule D tax assessments and related Class 4 National Insurance Contributions can be obtained from your local Inspector of Taxes. For help on deferment or refund of Class 4 contributions, contact the **National Insurance Contributions Office, general helpline: 0845 915 4515** or see website: www.hmrc.gov.uk.

Double income

If you are self-employed but also receive a salary you may have to pay NIC on both incomes. If too much has been deducted in total you can reclaim the excess or ask for a reduction of Class 2 and/or Class 4 contributions.

Limited company

If you trade as a limited company, the company will pay employer's Class 1 contributions and you will suffer the same deductions from your salary as any other employee. If you control the company, you will in effect be paying both the employer and the employee's share of NIC on your own account. If you are a director of several companies, you may be liable for multiple NI Contributions. See leaflet CA 44, *National Insurance for Company Directors*, available from HMRC offices, website: www.hmrc.gov.uk.

National Insurance benefits

Different classes of contributions qualify you for different types of benefit.
Class 2 Contributions count for:

- incapacity benefit;
- basic retirement pension;
- bereavement benefits;
- basic maternity benefit.

Class 1 Contributions entitle you to all the above and additionally to the Jobseeker's Allowance, should the need ever arise. They also count towards the additional State pension.

Class 3 Contributions may be paid voluntarily to help you qualify for, or improve your entitlement to, certain benefits. A flat rate of £12.05 a week is payable. See leaflet CA 5603, *To Pay Voluntary National Insurance Contributions*, available from any HMRC office, website: www.hmrc.gov.uk.

Pensions

Sole traders and partners are self-employed for pension, as well as tax, purposes and must make their own arrangements, which might variously be a personal pension, SIPP or stakeholder pension. Directors of limited companies are treated as employees and may be included in their company's pension scheme or may run their own self-administered pension schemes. See Chapter 3 for more detail.

Your responsibilities as an employer

Should you consider employing staff, you will immediately increase the complexity of your business. Sole traders who need to take on staff would be sensible to take advice before doing so on what roles and responsibilities this will involve. Many people starting a business wisely limit recruitment to the minimum in the early days, until they are sure that they can afford the cost of having permanent staff.

Once you become an employer, you take on responsibilities. As well as paying salaries, you will have to account for PAYE, keep National Insurance records and conform to the multiple requirements of employment legislation. While this may sound rather daunting, two recent measures should hopefully reduce much of the complexity. First, the Contributions Agency has been transferred to HMRC, with the advantage that employers now need to go through only a single organization to sort out tax and National Insurance matters. Second, the government provides a service, staffed by new business advisers, to help small businesses employing staff for the first time get to grips with the tax and National Insurance systems. For telephone advice or to arrange a visit by an adviser, ring the **New Employer Helpline: 0845 607 0143**; website: www.hmrc.gov.uk.

If you are still worried or don't want the bother of doing the paperwork yourself, your bank and possibly your accountant are likely to offer a full payroll service, which will cost you money but will take the burden off your shoulders. Here is some brief information on the main points you should consider.

PAYE

If you employ someone in your business (including your spouse) you are responsible for deducting Income Tax under the PAYE arrangements and accounting for it to the Collector of Taxes. You will be provided with tax tables and working sheets. The tax office will then notify you of the various PAYE tax codes in respect of your employees and explain how to use the tax table to work out the deductions. If an employee does not have an existing P45, you should ask him or her to complete a starting certificate, form P46, obtainable from the tax office.

An individual is liable for tax after deduction of his or her personal allowance and various reliefs. If your business has fewer than 50 employees, you could save £250 in tax by filing your PAYE return online. If you have any queries or need advice, call the **HMRC Online Services Helpdesk:** 0845 6055 999; website: www.hmrc.gov.uk.

Working Tax Credit

If you employ any low-income members of staff, they may be entitled to an earnings top-up known as Working Tax Credit. All recipients receive the money direct from HMRC.

Personnel records

Many businesses find it useful to keep personnel records covering such information as National Insurance numbers, tax codes, merit appraisal reports and so on. You should contact the **Information Commissioner** for advice about your obligations under the Data Protection Act; Tel: 0845 630 6060; website: www.ico.gov.uk.

Employment legislation

As an employer, you have certain legal obligations in respect of your staff. The most important cover such issues as health and safety at work, terms and conditions of employment and the provision of employee rights including, for example, parental leave, trade union activity and protection against unfair dismissal. Very small firms are exempt from some of the more onerous requirements and the government is taking steps to reduce more of the red tape. However, it is important that you understand in general terms what legislation could affect you.

Minimum wage

There are now three levels of minimum wage. For all workers under the age of 18 who are no longer of compulsory school age, the minimum hourly rate from 1 October 2010 is £3.64; for those aged 18 to 20, the minimum is £4.92; and for those aged 21 and above, the minimum is £5.93 an hour.

Health and safety at work

The Health and Safety at Work Act applies to everyone in a business, whether employer, employee or self-employed. It also protects the general public who may be affected by your business activity. The Health and Safety Executive publishes a number of useful free leaflets and also has a public enquiry point that is open between 8 am and 6 pm. Ring the **HSE Information Line**: 0845 345 0055 or consult HSE's website: www.hse.gov.uk.

Discrimination

An employer, however small the business, may not discriminate against someone on the grounds of sex, race, disability, religion, marital status, sexual orientation or, since October 2006, age. This applies to all aspects of employment, including training, promotion, recruitment, company benefits and facilities.

In particular, following the 1995 Disability Discrimination Act, there is a duty to make any necessary changes – known as 'reasonable adjustments' – to the workplace and employment arrangements, so that a disabled person is not at any substantial disadvantage. Until recently, companies with fewer than 15 employees were exempt from this requirement, but now even the smallest companies are required to comply with the legislation.

As stated above, the recent age discrimination legislation now equally makes it illegal for employers to discriminate against older candidates or employees on account of age. Provided individuals are still physically and mentally capable of doing their job, an employer can no longer force them to retire before the 'default' retirement age. The Government plan to scrap this in October 2011. Employers now also have a duty to consider requests by employees to postpone their retirement and need to give those they wish to retire at least six months' notice of their decision in writing.

The Equality and Human Rights Commission is a non-departmental public body, founded in 2007, that works to eliminate discrimination, reduce inequality, protect human rights and build good relations within society. Its website has details of the most significant piece of equality legislation for years, The Equality Act, effective since October 2010. For further information see the **Equality and Human Rights Commission** website: www.equalityhumanrights.com or contact the telephone helplines: England: 0845 604 6610; Wales: 0845 604 8810; Scotland: 0845 604 5510.

Contract of employment

A contract of employment is an agreement entered into between an employer and an employee under which they have certain mutual obligations. It comes into being as soon as an employee starts work, when it is taken that he or she accepts the job on the terms offered. Within two months of the job starting, the employer must normally give the employee a written statement highlighting the key terms and conditions of the job, together with a general description of the duties.

Entitlement to a written statement applies to all staff, including part-timers and employees working on fixed-term contracts. By law, they are required to be treated no less favourably than comparable full-timers or permanent employees in respect of their terms and conditions of employment, including access to training, holiday entitlement and benefits.

For further information and advice consult your local Citizens Advice Bureau or your solicitor, or ring the **ACAS** helpline on 08457 47 47 47; website: www.acas.org.uk.

Disputes

If you find yourself with a potential dispute on your hands, it is sensible to approach **ACAS,** which operates an effective information and advisory service for employers and employees on a variety of workplace problems, including employment legislation and employment relations. It also has a wide range of useful publications, giving practical guidance on employment matters. Contact: 08457 47 47 47; website: www.acas.org.uk.

Licences

Certain types of business require a licence or permit to trade; these include pubs, off-licences, nursing agencies, pet shops, kennels, mini-cabs or buses, driving instructors, betting shops, auction sale rooms, cinemas, hairdressers, street traders and, in some cases, travel agents and tour operators. You will also require a licence to import certain goods. Your local authority planning office will advise you whether you require a licence, and in many cases your council will be the licensing authority.

Permissions

Depending on the nature of your business, other permissions may need to be obtained, including those of the police, the environmental health department, licensing authorities and the fire prevention officer. In particular, there are special requirements concerning the sale of food and safety measures for hotels and guest houses. Your local authority will advise you on what is necessary.

Working from home

Many people quietly 'set up shop' from home and there are no questions asked. There could, however, be trouble if in consequence of the business there is an increase in traffic, noise, smells or other inconvenience caused to neighbours. Even more likely, unless you own the freehold of your home, you could have problems with your landlord if the tenancy agreement states that the accommodation is for domestic use only. If you simply use your home as a telephone base, this will probably not be an issue, but if you have a stream of callers and a van parked outside, you could be accused of violating the lease. You may have to pay Business Rates (in addition to your Council Tax) on that part of your home you use as business premises.

Another possible downside of working from home is that this could have Capital Gains Tax implications should you ever want to sell the property. As working out the various financial pros and cons has become rather a complex matter, before taking any decision you would be advised to take professional advice.

Insurance

Insurance is more than just a wise precaution. It is essential if you employ staff, have business premises or use your car regularly for commercial purposes. Many insurance companies now offer 'package insurance' for small businesses that covers most of the main contingencies in a single policy. This usually works out cheaper than buying a collection of individual policies. If you buy a package, check that it contains whichever of the following are relevant to your needs:

- *Employers' liability.* This is compulsory if you employ staff. It provides indemnity against liability for death or bodily injury to employees and subcontractors arising in connection with the business. Exceptionally, companies that employ only the owner of the business are not obliged to buy employers' liability insurance.

- *Product and public liability.* This insures the business and its products against claims by customers or the public. It could also cover legal expenses and the cost of complying with enforcements or judgements.

- *Professional indemnity.* This is now essential for all businesses offering investment advice in whatever form. It is also highly recommended for doctors, architects, consultants and other professionals who might be sued personally – or whose business might be sued – if a client suffered a mishap, loss or other damage in consequence of advice or services received. With the recent growth in litigation, many professional bodies are recommending that cover should continue after retirement in the event of an individual, or his or her estate, being sued for work done some years previously.

- *Material damage risk.* This covers against fire or other risk to the property, damage to equipment and theft. You can also be insured against loss of money or goods in transit.

- *Loss of profits or business interruption risk.* This insures the business against loss of profits in the event of your having to cease or curtail trading for a time, owing to material damage. The two policies are normally linked. It should also cover the risk of breakdown of a key item of machinery.

- *Motor risks.* This is compulsory for all motor vehicles.

- *Life assurance.* This is essential should you wish to provide for your own family or key employees' families or to ensure that funds are available to pay off any debts or to enable the business to continue in the event of your death.

- *Permanent health insurance.* Otherwise known as 'income protection', it provides insurance against long-term loss of income as a result of severe illness or disability. Most income protection plans are pretty flexible and can be tailored to individual needs.

- *Key person insurance.* This applies to the loss of a key person through prolonged illness as well as death. In small companies where the success or failure of the business is dependent upon the skills of two or three key executives, key person insurance is increasingly being written into investment deals as part of the necessary security demanded by banks, financial institutions and private investors. Remember, however, that whereas life insurance benefits your family, key person insurance benefits only the company.

- *Jury service insurance.* Businesspeople cannot seek automatic exemption from jury service even though prolonged absence from work could severely disrupt their business. Insuring against the risk of being called for jury service is therefore worth considering.

Insurance when working from home

If you are self-employed, you may need to extend your existing private policies to cover your commercial activities. A fire at home could destroy business products as well as your domestic possessions. Likewise, your motor insurance may not be sufficient for business purposes, if the loss of your car could cause serious interruption to your trading. You should discuss these points with your insurance company or a broker.

To find an insurance broker, contact the **British Insurance Brokers' Association,** Tel: 0870 950 1790; website: www.biba.org.uk, or contact the **Association of British Insurers,** Tel: 020 7600 3333; website: www.abi.org.uk.

Marketing

Unless you were employed in sales or marketing, this could be a weak point in your business plan. The essence of good marketing is very simple: find out what the customer wants and then try to supply it. This is far easier than designing a product or service and hoping that buyers will come flocking to your door. The points you need to consider are:

- what kinds of individuals (or companies) are likely to be your customers, including their age group and sex;
- whether you are competing with existing suppliers or are offering a genuinely new concept (including, for example, a delivery service that other local shopkeepers do not supply);
- whether the market is expanding or contracting, with particular emphasis on how many potential customers live close by;
- finally, how you can inform the potential market that your new product or service is available.

This sort of preliminary thinking is essential. The organizations outlined below may be able to help you formulate a realistic marketing plan.

Your local council will have information on the population and demographic profile of the area and will be able to give you details of any development plans that could affect customer potential. Your local Enterprise Agency and Business Link exist to help small businesses and should be able to offer valuable marketing advice. Approved Chambers of Commerce should be able to offer practical advice and training in marketing techniques and may be able to assist with useful contacts. There is also a wealth of information and sources of help available on the internet.

National organizations that offer help include the following:

The Chartered Institute of Marketing runs courses for non-members who need general marketing advice. Tel: 01628 427 120; website: www.cim.co.uk.

The Chartered Management Institute runs an extensive management information centre, which non-members can visit with the agreement of the Institute. Tel: 01536 204 222; website: www.managers.org.uk.

The Market Research Society (MRS) is a leader in the provision of market, social and opinion research, business intelligence, market analysis, customer insight and consultancy. For more information, Tel: 020 7490 4911; website: www.mrs.org.uk.

The Office for National Statistics holds information on many aspects of the economy, including sales by UK manufacturers. Tel: 0845 601 3034; website: www.ons.gov.uk.

Promotion

Once you have assessed where your market lies, you have to decide how to promote yourself. Methods of advertising your product or service might include:

- direct mailshots and leaflet drops;
- advertising in specialist publications or local newspapers with a potentially high readership among your target market;
- a good website that is user-friendly;
- exhibitions and local displays at functions such as school prize-givings, agricultural shows or local sporting events;
- telephone sales, perhaps with the help of a small team;
- editorial coverage in the press, on local radio programmes or on TV.

You are likely to succeed better with any of these techniques if you discuss your plans with a professional consultancy. The names of local practitioners should be available from:

The Chartered Institute of Marketing, Tel: 01628 427 120; website: www.cim.co.uk.

The Chartered Institute of Public Relations Tel: 020 7631 6900; website: www.cipr.co.uk.

Public Relations Consultants Association Ltd, Tel: 020 7233 6026; website: www.prca.org.uk.

Competitors

It is useful to know who your competitors are and what they are doing. Obtaining copies of their annual reports or finding out information via their websites are two simple methods. Contact **Companies House,** Tel: 0303 1234 500; website: www.companieshouse.gov.uk.

It is also sensible to attend trade shows of the industries or sectors within which you are planning to operate. For a list of major UK trade shows, check the website: www.exhibitions.co.uk.

Raising finance

Before you approach anyone for money, you must have a proper business plan. This means that you are bound to spend some time researching your business ideas and producing a realistic projection of cash flow needs. Your business plan should be brief and to the point but must contain the following items:

- a clear statement of what product or service you plan to offer;
- sales and marketing projections based, if possible, on some research or knowledge of the market;
- your initial investment plus ongoing cash flow requirements;
- basic information concerning premises, staff, equipment and development plans;
- profit and loss projections, showing when you expect the business to start making money.

It is a good idea to ask an accountant to vet your business plan. Some high street banks offer this service for a fixed fee and may also offer other help, such as a period of free banking. The different types of finance now available to small businesses through traditional sources such as banks and other institutions are more extensive than most people realize.

Advice and training

Small business is very well served when it comes to general help and training. A number of organizations offer free advice and low-cost consultancy, as well as a variety of training schemes, ranging from general information on setting up and developing a business to more specialized courses.

Business Links

A network of Business Links exists throughout England to provide small businesses with access to the full range of advisory and support services in their area. They can provide help and guidance across a wide range of topics, including business planning, financial management, employment issues, marketing and e-commerce. For further information, contact **Business Link**, Tel: 0845 600 9006; website: www.businesslink.gov.uk.

Adult education centres

Short courses in specific business skills are run by business schools and colleges of higher and further education. Various trade and professional associations also run courses. Further information is available from www. learndirect.co.uk and www.direct.gov.uk.

Regional agencies

Throughout the UK there are a number of organizations designed to assist the development of industrial activity in their local areas, and all have small business divisions that will be only too glad to offer any assistance they can. In Scotland, you could consult the following:

Scottish Enterprise operates through a network of 12 Local Enterprise Companies in lowland Scotland, offering a wide range of services to start-up and expanding businesses. Tel: 0845 607 8787; website: www.scottish-enterprise.com.

Highlands and Islands Enterprise (HIE) network covers the northern and western parts of Scotland, as well as the Scottish islands. It offers a free counselling service to small firms and to those considering setting up in these areas. Financial assistance may be given to meet start-up and training expenses. Tel: 01463 234 171; website: www.hie.co.uk.

Non-government sources of advice and training

Many enterprise agencies, Chambers of Commerce, business institutes and small business clubs, scattered around the country, provide counselling services, together with, in some cases, more formal training.

Useful organizations

Lawyers for Your Business is a network of 1,000 solicitor firms in England and Wales offering specialist advice to small and medium-sized businesses. To help firms access business-related legal advice, Lawyers for Business offer a free half-hour initial consultation with a lawyer in your area who is a member of the scheme. Advice can be sought on a range of issues. Contact Lawyers for Your Business for a list of members; Tel: 020 7405 9075; website: www.lawsociety.org.

PRIME (The Prince's Initiative for Mature Enterprise) helps people over the age of 50 set up in business for themselves. PRIME offers free information, workshops and business networking events. It can refer people to accredited advisers for free business advice, and in some parts of the country can also offer free mentoring and other services. Should you be interested in self-employment, PRIME Business Club is full of practical ideas and helpful business information. Tel: 0800 783 1904; website: www.primebusinessclub.co.uk.

Enterprise UK is the government-funded organization set up in 2004 to encourage entrepreneurial endeavour. It is the only independent enterprise body founded and governed by the four leading business organizations – the CBI, IOD, BCC and FSB. The following are the key organizations representing small business interests. Some act as pressure groups and conduct research as well as provide a service to their members:

- **British Chambers of Commerce,** Tel: 020 7654 5800; website: www.britishchambers.org.uk
- **CBI,** Tel: 020 7379 7400; website: www.cbi.org.uk
- **Federation of Small Businesses,** Tel: 0808 2020 888; website: www.fsb.org.uk
- **Forum of Private Business,** Tel: 0845 612 6266; website: www.fpb.org
- **Institute of Directors,** Tel: 020 7766 8866; website: www.iod.com

Useful reading

An extensive list of books is available for small and start-up businesses published by Kogan Page; Tel: 020 7278 0433; website: www.koganpage.com.

Chapter Eleven
Looking for paid work

" Work saves us from three great evils: boredom, vice and need. VOLTAIRE (1694–1778)

F ar from thinking of putting your feet up when you retire from your present job, you may, like many others, need seriously to consider carrying on working. The economic downturn has affected tens of thousands of people, many of whom had thought their savings more than adequate to finance their retirement. Government plans to scrap the default retirement age in the UK from October 2011 are seen by many as a 'victory' against ageism. It has long been regarded by many as unfair that people were forced out of jobs because of their age. The charity, Age UK, which campaigns for older people's rights has welcomed the government's proposal. It is hardly surprising that a large proportion of retirees are keen to carry on working and play an active part in the labour market. After all, they possess years of experience, dedication and knowledge; these resources are of great value to the economy and should not be overlooked. Friends' Provident carried out research last year that suggested that by 2020 there will be 2 million more over-55s in the workforce as demand grows for their talent, skills and experience.

Working in your 50s, 60s and beyond can be rewarding in ways other than just financial. The growing number of options available to mature workers are as interesting as they are challenging. Rushing straight into the first job you find, which you may not particularly like, could be a mistake, so it makes sense to take time to think about what kind of work would suit you best. The good news for mature people is that it's more than 80 per cent likely that your next job will come from someone you know, and that over 72 per cent of people hired are known to the company that employs them.

If you had the choice, instead of seeking a new job, would you for example rather remain in your existing one? You may find that, contrary to past practice, your employer is willing to continue to employ you. Also, thanks to a recent change in the pension rules, people in occupational schemes are no longer prevented from drawing their pension benefits while continuing to work for their existing employer. If you have already left or are shortly about to do so, what is your main motive in wanting to work? Is it to augment your income? Is it for the social aspects? Do you fear boredom if you don't work? Or do you enjoy the mental stimulation you derive from working? Some people admit they like having a sense of purpose, something to get them up in the morning, which is why they wish to continue to work. Others have a lurking suspicion that, if they don't have a job, their friends and acquaintances will be less interested in them.

Whatever your reason for wanting to continue actively working, it should be a valid one and something you've thought through and talked about with family and friends. The answer may well be a combination of factors, but you should at least try to pinpoint your priorities to avoid taking on work that does not suit your lifestyle. There are many stories of people whose prime reason for seeking work was to get out of the house to make new friends, who ended up working from home in solitary state. Likewise, there are numerous cases of people whose real purpose was financial but who somehow signed up for unpaid voluntary work.

Another fundamental consideration is how much work to do. Have a serious think about the number of hours per week you would like to work. Is it a full working week, Monday to Friday? Or would just a couple of half-days be sufficient? While on the subject of time, is working a long-term goal, or do you see it as a pleasant occupation to fill in the next year or so? Consider travel for a moment: would you be prepared to commute? If not, perhaps you are seeking a job that is strictly local. Was there anything – for example, the requirement to take part of your holiday at specified times – that you particularly disliked about your previous employment? If so, make sure that you bear it in mind to avoid a similar situation occurring in the future.

One of the most important things is deciding what you are going to do. Are you looking for an opening in a similar field, where your experience and contacts would come in useful? Or do you want to do something entirely different? If you want a complete change, would you be willing to learn a new skill and undertake some training?

Finally, do the sums. Factors such as your age, your total weekly earnings, your pension and other income, as well, of course, as any out-of-pocket expenses you incur need to be thought through. Whatever your reasons for seeking paid work, you need to consider what advantages there are.

Financial considerations

Since the abolition of the earnings rule, no matter what age you are or how much you earn there is no longer any forfeit to your State pension, although of course you may have to pay tax on your additional income. If you are working close to a full-time week and/or have enough money to live on, there could still be an advantage in asking the DWP to defer your pension, as this will entitle you to a bigger pension in the future. Each year of deferral earns an increment of about 10.4 per cent of the pension. Another advantage is that, if you choose to defer your pension by at least a year, you will have the option of taking the money as a taxable lump sum instead of in higher weekly pension payments.

Decisions concerning your occupational pension

These could also arise, particularly if you are looking not so much for a retirement job as for a last big move before you retire. Most (though not all) pension schemes apply actuarial reductions for early retirement. Joining a new pension scheme in late middle age, though not impossible, can present difficulties or impose certain limitations. One of the reasons for this is because many employers are revising their pension schemes, with rather less generous benefits for new members.

National Insurance (NI)

NI is another consideration. If you are over state retirement age or have earnings of £110 a week or less (2010/11), you can forget about NIC. Otherwise you are liable for the normal Class 1 contributions. If, as many early retirees do, you work for two or more different employers, you will have to pay Class 1 in respect of each. Should you obtain work through an agency (eg catering, nursing or exhibition work), you are usually regarded as an employee of the agency for NI purposes, and the agency is responsible for the payment of Class 1 contributions on your behalf. However, this does not apply if you do the work from home, are not subject to anyone's direct supervision, or are in the entertainment business.

If you are over retirement age and have a job, the only requirement is that you obtain an exemption card to give to your employer; see form CF 384 (Certificate of Exception). If you do freelance or other assignment work (unless virtually all your earnings come from one employer, in which case

HM Revenue & Customs (HMRC) would argue that you are an employee of the organization), you are officially considered to be self-employed for both NI and taxation purposes (see Chapter 10, Starting Your Own Business). For further information, you might find it helpful to read leaflet IR 56, *Employed or Self-Employed? A Guide to Employment Status for Tax and National Insurance*, available from any tax office.

Tax rules

HMRC has tightened up the rules in order to clamp down on what it sees as the avoidance of PAYE and Class 1 NIC in respect of the provision of services, including for example consultancy and contract work. Those most likely to be affected are individuals who: 1) offer their services via small limited companies; 2) work over a period of time for a sole organization; or 3) work for a client or clients who have the right to control and supervise how the work is performed, as opposed to leaving the initiative to the individual concerned. If you are thinking of operating in an independent capacity – as opposed to becoming a bona fide employee – it would be sensible to discuss the tax implications with an accountant before determining whether you should operate as self-employed, sole trader, partnership or limited company.

Jobseeker's Allowance (JSA)

You can claim JSA provided you:

- are under State pension age;
- are unemployed or working on average less than 16 hours a week;
- have paid, or have been treated as having paid, sufficient National Insurance Contributions; or
- have a low income.

To qualify, you must be capable of, available for and actively seeking work, and must enter into a jobseeker's agreement with your local Jobcentre. The essence of the agreement is an action programme aimed at maximizing your chances of finding a job. You will receive help and advice, and there is also a fortnightly Jobsearch review to give you and your adviser an opportunity to assess your progress and to discuss any potential openings that might be suitable.

Claimants are not allowed to turn down a job offered to them via their Jobcentre without good reason. Lower pay would not normally be accepted as a reason although, that said, there is a 'permitted period' up to a maximum of 13 weeks when individuals may be allowed to restrict their job search to openings that take advantage of their skills, experience and reasonable salary expectations. A particularly welcome feature of JSA is that it makes it more worthwhile for recipients to do part-time work. For further information about JSA and other benefits, contact your local **Jobcentre Plus** office on 0800 055 66 88; website: www.direct.gov.uk/employment.

Working Tax Credit

If you have a job but are not earning very much, you may be able to boost your income by claiming Working Tax Credit. In certain circumstances, including in particular households with three or more dependent children or where a member of the family has a disability, those with slightly higher incomes could still be eligible to apply. HMRC advises that the easiest way to check is to complete the form listed under 'Tax credits' on its website. To qualify, you would usually be expected to work at least 30 hours a week. However, those with a disability and/or dependent children are required to work only 16 hours. All recipients now receive the payment direct from HMRC. Contact: **HMRC Tax Credits Helpline:** 0845 300 39 00; website: www.hmrc.gov.uk.

Redundancy

If you have just been made redundant, or fear this is a possibility, see the information in Chapter 2, Money in General.

Special measures to assist disabled people to work

If you can't work because of illness or disability (and this happened before 27 October 2008) you may be able to get Employment and Support Allowance (which replaced Incapacity Benefit). This is a weekly payment for people who become incapable of work while under State Pension age. For details on eligibility go to the website: www.direct.gov.uk/DisabledPeople.

Age discrimination

Age discrimination legislation came into force in October 2006, making it illegal for employers to discriminate against older candidates on account of age, as regards recruitment, training and promotion. In particular, provided individuals are still physically and mentally capable of doing their job, an employer can no longer oblige them to retire before a 'default' retirement age. Employers also now have a duty to consider requests by employees who want to postpone their retirement and will need to give those they want to retire at least six months' written notice of their decision.

Assessing your abilities

Some people know exactly what job they want. They have planned their action campaign for months beforehand, done their research, prepared a CV and followed up selective openings. They are ready, waiting for their present employment to come to an end, to embark on their next career phase. But, if you are not one of those few, having announced your intention to find a job, then comes a moment of truth when the big question is: what to do?

Knowing what you have to offer is an essential first step. Make a list of everything you have done, in both your formal career and ordinary life, including your outside interests. In particular, consider adding any practical or other skills, knowledge or contacts that you have acquired over the years. These could now prove especially useful. If you, for example, have done a lot of public speaking, fund-raising, committee work, or conference organization, these would be excellent transferable skills that would make you attractive to a prospective employer. As a result of writing everything down, most people find that they have far more to offer than they originally realized.

In addition to work skills, you should include your personal attributes and any special assets that would attract an employer. The list might include health, organizing ability, a good telephone manner, communication skills, the ability to work well with other people, use of a car and willingness to do flexible hours. Maturity can also be a positive asset. Many employers prefer older people: they can be more reliable and less likely to be preoccupied with family and social demands. Also, in many newly established companies, run by young directors, a senior person's accumulated experience is often rated as especially valuable.

If you spend some time working on your personal branding, how to market yourself and to whom, you will become much more focused. It will help you form a clearer idea of the sorts of jobs that would suit you. Although it's sensible to keep a fairly open mind and not limit your applications too narrowly, the worst mistake you can make is to answer scores of advertisements indiscriminately – and end up with a sack load of rejections, or worse, no response at all to your applications. As a general rule when job hunting, the more accurate and targeted you can be in the application process, the more likely you are to succeed.

Many people find this extraordinarily difficult. After years of working in one occupation, it takes quite a leap in imagination to picture yourself in another role, even if it is in the same or a related area. If you intend to do something completely different, it will be harder still, as your knowledge of what the job entails will probably be second-hand. Also, quite apart from the question of what you would enjoy, in many parts of the country the issue may be more a matter of what is available.

Talking to other people helps. Friends, family, work colleagues or business acquaintances may have useful information and moreover will quite likely be able to appraise your abilities more objectively than you can yourself. It could also be sensible to consult outside experts who specialize in adult career counselling and whose advice may be more realistic than that of friends in the context of the current job market.

Jobcentre Plus

Jobcentre Plus brings together the former Benefits Agency and Employment Service to provide a one-stop shop where jobseekers can get help and advice about work and training opportunities and also about any benefits for which they might be eligible. Jobcentre Plus provides a network of offices and telephone contact centres. For further information, contact your local Jobcentre or Tel: 0845 606 0234; website: www.direct.gov.uk/employment.

Travel to interview scheme

This provides financial assistance in meeting travel costs to long-distance interviews. The scheme is available to people who have been unemployed and are receiving JSA or help with NI Contributions.

Job counselling

This is usually a mixture of helping you to identify your talents in a vocational sense combined with practical advice on successful job-hunting techniques. Counsellors can assist with such essentials as writing a CV, preparing for an interview and locating job vacancies. They can also advise you of suitable training courses. There are numerous companies offering this service if you search the internet. The best advice is to ask for recommendations from other people before signing up with a company. If you want to make really certain they can help, you could ask to speak to one or two of their former clients, to find out whether they found the service useful. These may be worth contacting:

Career Counselling Services offers individual career counselling sessions to help you become clearer about what you want to do and how to be focused in getting it. A service to help with job hunting is also available. Contact 020 3178 5261; website: www.career-counselling-services.co.uk.

Grey Hair Management exists to help professionals find new opportunities, and employment. It provides professional coaching to managers and executives to help them win the jobs race. Contact 01242 210 212; website: www.greyhairmanagement.com.

Training opportunities

Knowing what you want to do is one thing, but before starting a new job you may want to brush up existing skills or possibly acquire new ones. Most professional bodies have a full programme of training events, ranging from one-day seminars to courses lasting a week or longer. Additionally, adult education institutes run a vast range of courses or, if you are still in your present job, a more practical solution might be to investigate open and flexible learning, which you can do from home.

Open and flexible learning

Open and flexible learning is successfully helping to provide a greater range and flexibility of vocational education and training opportunities for individuals of all ages. In particular, it is designed to increase the scope for participants to learn at a time, place and pace best suited to their own particular circumstances.

The following organizations offer advice and an excellent range of courses:

Learn Direct courses are flexible; many can be done at local centres, at work or from home. Courses are broken down into bite-sized chunks so that you can learn at your own pace, whenever and wherever it suits you. Contact: 0800 101 901; website: www.learndirect.co.uk.

Home Learning Courses offers home learning solutions to its clients, to fit with their circumstances and location. For more information contact: 0800 138 77 80; website: www.homelearningcourses.com.

IT skills

If you are considering a change in direction, some new qualifications may be advantageous. Good IT skills are desirable in most organizations, so if you are not confident about your computer literacy and don't have much IT experience or specialist knowledge, there are lots of good courses you could look at.

Affordable Training is the leading source for affordable IT training and certification. Contact: 0800 612 6572; website: www.affordabletraining.co.uk.

Computer Literacy can provide the right learning solution whatever your needs. It offers IT training in London and the South East, and its courses are carefully chosen to maximize the value and enjoyment delegates receive from them. Contact: 0870 240 6160; website: www.computerliteracy.co.uk.

Skills Train is the UK's largest specialist home study and distance learning provider of IT courses. Courses allow you to learn at your own pace, to fit around the life you lead. Contact 0800 181 076; website: www.skillstrainuk.com.

Help with finding a job

The ideal is to find a job for your retirement while you are still at work. Prospective employers may prefer applicants who are busy and actively working rather than those who have had a period of non-employment for whatever reason. However, whether you are hoping to go straight from one job to another or have had an enforced period of not working, this should not affect the way you approach your job search. If you have been retired for some time and want to return to work, you might consider doing some voluntary work in the meantime (see Chapter 12 – Voluntary Work). This would provide a ready answer to the inevitable interview question: what have you been doing?

There are four basic ways of finding a job: through your own personal contacts, by following up advertisements, by applying to an agency for suitable introductions, or by direct approaches to suitable employers. As with most other things, the more ways you try, the better your chances of success. For a start, make sure you tell your friends and acquaintances that you are in the market for work – and include on the list your present employer. Some firms actually encourage consultancy links with former executives, or at least are prepared to respond to a good idea. A greater number are more than happy to take on previous employees over a rush period or during the holiday season.

Another obvious move, if you are a member of a professional institute, is to inform this organization of your availability. Many institutes keep a register of members wanting work and, encouragingly, receive a fair number of enquiries from firms seeking qualified people for projects, part-time or temporary work, interim management or sometimes even permanent employment. Other sources of useful contacts include your local Chamber of Commerce, the CBI or the Institute of Directors. Any clubs to which you belong could provide useful leads, as well as any committee you sit on or any other group with which you are involved. Often someone you know will be the perfect link between you and your next employer.

If you intend to follow up advertisements, selectivity is the name of the game. Limit your applications to those that sound genuinely promising. You will save yourself a lot of time this way. Many vacancies are advertised on the internet, so be prepared to have a CV and covering letter ready for submitting your application electronically. Sign on to a select number of sites that will keep you posted about work opportunities. Agencies usually have more applicants than vacancies, except where skill shortages exist. When applying, please note that enthusiasm counts. Keep in regular contact, by telephone, e-mail or personal visit. Sometimes being on the spot and available at the right time is the key to success.

A direct approach to likely employers is another option. Do your research carefully on the internet, and amongst your local and personal network. Ask your colleagues, contacts and friends for their advice on which organizations might be interested in employing someone with your abilities. If possible find out the name of the appropriate person to contact and the best method to reach him or her. If someone you know can prepare the ground in advance by way of introduction, and act as referrer, this is far more likely to get you noticed.

The following websites may be useful:

Laterlife will help you with your job search and working in later life. The job search section of its website is geared to assist you with all the information and services you need. Website: www.laterlife.com.

Redundancy Expert was formed to provide comprehensive information and advice on redundancy. The section of its website dedicated to finding work and getting a job is both useful and helpful. See website: www.redundancyexpert.co.uk.

TAEN (The Age and Employment Network) works to promote an effective labour market that serves the needs of people in mid and later life, employers and the economy. TAEN directs individuals looking for employment, who want to change direction, develop their careers or undertake training, to relevant organizations and a number of useful resources. See website: www.taen.org.uk.

Wise Owls provides information about older people and workers alongside a comprehensive one-stop-shop for both employers who have vacancies and individuals who are looking for work. See website: www.wiseowls.co.uk.

CV writing

Regardless of whether you use contacts, advertisements or agencies – or preferably all three – a prime requirement will be to have a well-presented CV. This is your personal sales document. It should contain:

- your name and address;
- contact numbers – land line and mobile;
- e-mail and website address;
- date of birth;
- key achievements to date;
- qualifications and work experience, past employers, position held and responsibilities;
- referees.

Your CV should not be longer than two pages of A4. While some CVs are highly professional, a common fault tends to be that they are over-long, which is often counterproductive. It should be targeted to the job on offer, emphasizing those elements of your experience and skills that are relevant.

Interview technique

If you have worked for the same employer for a number of years, your interview skills may be a little rusty. It is a good idea to list all the questions you expect to be asked (including those you hope won't be brought up) and then get a friend to rehearse you in your answers. In addition to questions about your previous job, have answers prepared for the following: what you have done since leaving employment; whether your health is good; why you are interested in working for this particular employer; and, given the job requirements, what you think you have of special value to offer. You may also be asked what you know about the organization, so make sure you do your research. Obvious mistakes to avoid are claiming skills or knowledge that you do not possess; giving the impression that you have a series of stock answers to problems; and criticizing your former employer.

Be prepared to have an answer to the question: how much money would you expect? With the economy still struggling, you may have to take a reality check and strike a balance between what you would like and what is realistic in the current market.

Useful reading

Preparing the Perfect CV (5th edition), *Preparing the Perfect Job Application* (5th edition), and *Successful Interview Skills* (5th edition), all by Rebecca Corfield and published by Kogan Page; website: www.koganpage.com.

Part-time openings

Part-time work may for some people be the ideal solution; others may regard it as second best. With the job market still so difficult, many part-time or temporary assignments offer the perfect way into employment that may develop into full-time work in future. This is especially true of small firms, which may be cautious about recruitment while the business is relatively young.

With the average job now lasting between 1.8 and three years, temporary or project-based professional and executive assignments that last a specific time are becoming increasingly common. People with specialist expertise are actively sought, so it is important to be aware of the growth areas in employment. Over a fifth of all new jobs are now on a contract basis, the average being for six months or a year. Mature candidates have everything to gain here because of the greater turnover of jobs. Serial part-time or freelance work can easily develop into a full-time occupation. Many retired businesspeople take on two or three part-time jobs and then find themselves working as hard as they have ever done in their life.

Employment ideas

Consultancy

A number of retired executives hire themselves back to their former employer in a consultancy guise. As opposed to being paid a regular salary and working full time, they undertake specific projects for which they are paid a fee. This may be structured as a lump sum or, as many consultants do, they may negotiate a day-rate. Consultancy, by definition, is not limited to a single client. By using your contacts judiciously plus a bit of marketing initiative, it is quite possible to build up a steady list of assignments on the basis of your particular expertise.

Marketing skills are always in demand, as is knowledge of website design, accountancy, HR issues and, increasingly today, public relations experience and fund-raising. Small firms are often a good bet for consultants, as they cannot afford to employ specialists full time and normally buy in expertise as and when it is required. Many established consultancies retain a list of associates – a sort of freelance register – whom they call on, on an 'as needed' basis, to handle suitable assignments.

The Institute of Business Consulting (IBC) is the professional body for management consultants and business advisers. It encompasses the entire profession of consultants and advisers with a membership touching on all areas of the UK economy. It has several thousand members and over 20 branches nationwide, and has contacts with all business advice centres, enterprise agencies and similar organizations seeking businesspeople qualified to advise small, start-up and medium-sized businesses. Contact: 020 7497 0580; website: www.ibconsulting.org.uk.

A new organization is **Grey4Gold**, a free to access and use, web-based search and recruitment service. It has been designed to bring together mature experienced directors, managers and professionals with newer SMEs (small and medium-sized enterprises) and start-ups. Both individuals seeking positions and businesses or start-ups looking for skills can register with the Grey4Gold website: www.Grey4Gold.com.

Interim management

Interim management represents a huge growth area in recruitment over the past few years. In essence it is an outside specialist recruited short term to implement a particular assignment. The growth is largely due to two factors: organizations downsizing and small companies needing specialist skills that they cannot afford to employ full time. Many of the best jobs go to those who have recently taken early retirement or been made redundant. Fees vary enormously and typical assignments last between six and nine months. They could be full time or involve just one or two days' work a week.

The Interim Management Association, (IMA) can put you in touch with its accredited members in a location suitable to you. See website: www.interimmanagement.uk.com.

Openings via a company or other reference

Secondment from your current employer to another organization is something worth considering. This can be part time for a few hours a week or full time for anything from a few weeks to two years. It can also often lead to a new career. Normally only larger employers are willing to consider the idea since, as a rule, the company will continue to pay your salary and other benefits during the period of secondment. If you work for a smaller firm it could still be worth discussing the suggestion, as employers benefit from the favourable publicity the company attracts by being seen to support the local community.

Business in the Community works with businesses to build a sustainable future for people and the planet. For information on secondment opportunities for both employers and individuals, contact: 020 7566 8650; website: www.bitc.org.uk.

Public appointments

Opportunities regularly arise for individuals to be appointed to a wide range of public bodies, such as tribunals, commissions and consumer consultative councils. Many appointments are to local and regional bodies throughout the country. Some are paid but many offer an opportunity to contribute to the community and gain valuable experience of working in the public sector on a part-time, expenses-only basis.

These opportunities are now advertised on a website that provides a single source of information about public appointments vacancies at local and regional levels across England as well as those with a national remit. You can search the site by subject area, government department and location to find vacancies that are of interest to you. You can view detailed information about each vacancy and how to apply. See www.appointments.org.uk or www.direct.gov.uk.

Non-executive directorships

Many retiring executives see this as the ideal solution; however, these appointments carry heavy responsibilities made more onerous by recent legislation. If you are able and committed and have the necessary experience, you could contact the following:

The NED Exchange provides expert help to individuals seeking non-executive director jobs and recruitment services to companies seeking to recruit a non-executive director. For further information contact: 01494 483 728; website: www.nedexchange.co.uk.

First Flight Placements is a specialist provider of non-executive directors and chair people to start-up, early stage and developing companies. It also puts together management-buy-in teams to facilitate an exit strategy for a company owner looking to retire. For further information contact: 01797 270 271; website: www.nonexecutivedirector.co.uk.

NER (Non-Executive Register) places exceptional candidates for FTSE 250 and Fortune 500 companies wishing to strengthen their boards. Contact: 0207 105 2962; website: www.nonexecutive.com.

Market research

In addition to the normal consultancy openings in marketing, there is also scope for those with knowledge of market research techniques. The work covers a very broad spectrum, from street or telephone interviewing to data processing, designing questionnaires, statistical analysis and sample group selection.

The Research Buyer's Guide is a directory of market research providers and support services. It is published by **The Market Research Society.** Contact: 020 7490 4911; website: www.mrs.org.uk.

Survey interviewing

National Centre for Social Research (NatCen) is Britain's leading centre for independent social research. Its research covers all aspects of social policy and its findings have direct, practical applications in terms of understanding social behaviour and informing policy. Contact: 020 7250 1866; website: www.natcen.ac.uk.

Paid work for charities

Although charities rely to a very large extent on voluntary workers, most charitable organizations of any size have a number of paid appointments. Other than particular specialists that some charities may require for their work, the majority of openings are for general managers or administrators, fund-raisers and those with financial skills. Salaries have been improving but in general are still considerably below the commercial market rate. Anyone thinking of applying for a job in a charity must be in sympathy with its aims and style.

Agencies specializing in charity recruitment advise that it is a good idea to work as a volunteer before seeking a paid appointment, as this will provide useful experience. The following organizations may be useful:

CF Appointments helps charities and not-for-profit organizations fill their key jobs and also finds trustees, who are unpaid. Contact: 020 7220 0180; website: www.cfappointments.com.

CharityJob.co.uk helps candidates, charities and agencies in their search to find work or personnel or place people. Contact: 020 8939 8430; website: www.charityjob.co.uk.

Harris Hill recruits senior and middle managers for charities and other not-for-profit organizations. Harris Hill also helps charities to find trustees who can offer skills and experience on a voluntary basis. Contact: 020 7833 0770; website: www.harrishill.co.uk.

Sales

Almost every commercial firm in the country needs good sales staff. Many people who have never thought of sales could be excellent in the job because of their specialist knowledge in a particular field combined with their enthusiasm for the subject. Educational and children's book publishers, for example, are often keen to recruit ex-teachers to market their books to schools and libraries. There is an almost insatiable demand for people to sell advertising space, and if you are an avid reader of a particular publication, for example a specialist motoring or gardening magazine, you might find the work fun and be very successful.

Additionally, many firms employ demonstrators in shops or at exhibitions for special promotions. The work is usually temporary or freelance by definition, and while pay is normally good the big drawback is that you could be standing on your feet for long periods of the day.

If the idea of selling appeals and it fires you with enthusiasm, you could actually find yourself making more money in your retirement than ever before.

Tourist guide

Tourist guide work is something that will appeal to extroverts, the super-fit with oodles of stamina and a liking for people. If you do not possess these qualities, this may not be the line of work for which you are best suited. It requires an academic mind as well, since you will need to put in some fairly concentrated study. While there are various possible qualifications (some easier than others), training for the coveted Blue Badge takes 15 months. The Blue Badge itself is no guarantee of steady work, since openings are largely seasonal. In fact most tourist guides are self-employed and the field is highly competitive, but opportunities are greatest in London, especially for those with fluency in one or more foreign languages. For more information contact the **Guild of Registered Tourist Guides,** on 020 7403 1115; website: www.blue-badge-guides.com.

Another possibility is to sign on as a lecturer with one of the growing number of travel companies offering special interest holidays. To be eligible you need real expertise in a subject, the ability to make it interesting and an easy manner with people. Pay is fairly minimal, although you may receive tips – plus of course the bonus of a free holiday. See Chapter 14 for the names of tour operators that may be worth contacting.

Other tourist work

If you live in a popular tourist area, there is a whole variety of seasonal work, including jobs in hotels, restaurants, shops and local places of interest. Depending on the locality, the list might also include jobs as deckchair attendants, play leaders for children, caravan site staff, extra coach drivers and many others.

Teaching and training skills

If you have been a teacher at any stage of your career, there are a number of part-time possibilities.

Coaching

With examinations becoming more competitive, demand has been increasing for ex-teachers with knowledge of the public examination system to coach youngsters in preparation for A and AS levels, GCSE and common entrance. Contact local schools, search the internet or contact a specialist educational consultancy.

Gabbitas Educational Consultants provides a wide range of recruitment and consultancy services to independent schools in Great Britain and to English-speaking schools overseas. It also maintains an extensive register of teachers seeking appointments, as well as a register for tutors. Contact: 020 7734 0161; website: www.gabbitasrecruitment.com.

Specialist subjects

Teachers are in demand for mathematics, physics, chemistry, technology and modern languages. People with relevant work experience and qualifications may be able to teach or give tuition in these subjects. A formal teaching qualification is, however, required to teach in state-maintained schools. Contact the **Training and Development Agency for Schools**; Tel: 0845 6000 991; website: www.tda.gov.uk.

English as a foreign language

There is an ongoing demand for people to teach English to foreign students. Opportunities are concentrated in London and the major academic cities such as Oxford, Cambridge, Bath and York. Good English-language schools require teachers to have an initial qualification in teaching English to those who have a different first language. See the following websites for more information: www.global-english.com; www.intesolinternational.com; www.tefl.net.

Working in developing countries

There are various opportunities for suitably qualified people to work in the developing countries of Africa, Asia, the Caribbean and the Pacific on a semi-voluntary basis. Skills most in demand include civil engineering, mechanical engineering, water engineering, architecture, urban, rural and regional planning, agriculture, forestry, medicine, teaching English as a foreign language, maths and physics training, and economics. All air fares, accommodation costs and insurance are usually covered by the organizing agency, and pay is limited to a 'living allowance' based on local levels. As a general rule, there is an upper age limit of 65 (VSO accepts volunteers up to 75), and you must be willing to work for a minimum of two years. The following are the major agencies involved in this kind of work (fuller details are contained in Chapter 12, Voluntary Work):

International Service	01904 647799; website: www.internationalservice.org.uk
Progressio	020 7354 0883; website: www.progressio.org.uk
Skillshare International:	0116 254 1862; website: www.skillshare.org
Voluntary Service Overseas (VSO)	020 8780 7500; website: www.vso.org.uk

Publishing

Publishers are increasingly using freelance staff with appropriate experience for proofreading, copy-editing, design, typography, indexing and similar work as well as for writing specialist copy. For a list of firms that could be interested, see website: www.thebookseller.com.

Caring for other people

There are a number of opportunities for paid work in this field. If you are considering working with vulnerable people (young or old), you will be required to have a full Criminal Records Bureau (CRB) check with enhanced disclosure, designed to protect those who need to rely on other people and to ensure that no one unsuitable is appointed to a position of trust who is likely to abuse it. These checks are extremely thorough and can take several weeks or even months to process. Please be patient and as accurate as possible when asked to provide information by prospective employers, charities or not-for-profit organizations. For further information about CRB checks and why they are required, see the **Criminal Records Bureau** website: www.crb.gov.uk.

Domestic work

A number of private domestic agencies specialize in finding temporary or permanent companions, housekeepers and extra-care help for elderly and disabled people or for those who are convalescent. Pay rates vary depending on which part of the country you live in and the number of hours involved. The following agencies may be of interest:

Anchor Care	0845 140 2020; website: www.anchor.org.uk
Consultus Care & Nursing Agency Ltd	01732 355 231; website: www.consultuscare.com
Country Cousins	0845 601 4003; website: www.country-cousins.co.uk
Universal Aunts Ltd	020 7738 8937; website: www.universalaunts.co.uk

Check on the internet for other agencies – search under 'Domestic', 'Employment' or 'Care Agencies' or look in *The Lady* magazine, published every Wednesday.

Home helps

Local authorities sometimes have vacancies for home helps, to assist disabled or elderly people in their own home by giving a hand with the cleaning, light cooking and other chores. Ask at your local social services department.

Child-minding

If you already look after a grandchild during the day, you might consider caring for an additional couple of youngsters. You will need to be registered with the local social services department, which will explain all the requirements including details of any basic training – such as first aid – that you may first need to do.

Nursing

Qualified nurses are in great demand in most parts of the country and stand a good chance of finding work at their local hospital or through one of the many nursing agencies. Family planning clinics could also be worth approaching. Those with suitable experience, although not necessarily a formal nursing qualification, could apply to become a care support worker for the charity **Crossroads,** which provides regular short-term relief for carers of sick or disabled people in their own homes. Contact: 0845 450 0350; website: www.crossroads.org.uk.

Home-sitting

Taking care of someone else's home while they are away on holiday or business trips is something mature, responsible people, usually non-smokers with no children or pets, can do. It is a bit like a paid holiday, and you get paid every week (extra if care of pets is involved), depending on the responsibilities and on the size of the house or flat. Food and travelling expenses are normally also paid. It is useful to have your own car. Firms specializing in this type of work include:

Absentia	01279 777 412; website: www.home-and-pets.co.uk
Homesitters Ltd	01296 630 730; website: www.homesitters.co.uk
Universal Aunts Ltd	020 7738 8937; website: www.universalaunts.co.uk

Cashing in on your home interests

Cooking, gardening, home decorating, dressmaking and DIY skills can all be turned into modest money-spinners.

Bed and breakfast

Tourist areas, in particular, offer scope for taking in B&B visitors. However, unless you want to make a regular business of it, it is advisable to limit the number of guests to a maximum of five; otherwise you will be subject to stringent fire regulation precautions requiring special doors and other expensive paraphernalia. To be on the safe side, contact the local environmental health officer who will advise you of anything necessary you should do. You should also register with your local tourist information centre. See the section 'Letting rooms in your home' in Chapter 8, Your Home.

Cooking

Scope includes catering other people's dinner parties, selling home-made goodies to local shops and cooking for corporate lunches. Other than top-class culinary skills, requirements are a large deep freeze, a car (you will normally be required to do all the necessary shopping) and plenty of stamina. Notify your friends, advertise locally and via your website.

Gardening

Small shopkeepers and florists sometimes purchase flowers or plants direct from local gardeners, in preference to going to the market. Alternatively, you might consider dried flower arrangements or herbs, for which there has been a growing demand. However, before spending any money, check around to find out what the sales possibilities are. If you are willing to tend someone else's garden, the likelihood is that you will be inundated with enquiries. Spread the word among friends and acquaintances as well as local advertising.

Dressmaking and home decorating

If you are happy to do alterations, the chances are that you could be kept busy from dawn to dusk. Many shops are desperate for people who sew. Likewise, many individuals and families would love to know of someone who could alter clothes, as well as dress-make properly. Perhaps to a slightly lesser extent, the same goes for curtains, chair covers and other soft furnishings. Often a good move is to approach firms selling materials for the home, which might be only too glad to put work out to you. Advertising your services locally will often yield a number of clients.

Agencies and other useful organizations

Job hunting through agencies is very much a question of luck. So many vacancies are advertised via the internet, there is no need to be out of work for long if you are proactive. Work for the over-50s and 60s varies and if you are seeking challenging opportunities, it might be worth checking the following organizations:

The Corps offers full- or part-time employment across a wide range of occupations, including security guards, concierges, receptionists, post-room staff, and commissionaires who provide an usher service at corporate functions and sporting events. Contact: 0800 028 6303; website: www.the-corps.co.uk.

Executive Stand-By Ltd specializes in placing executives of proven competence in management or similar posts in industry, commerce and voluntary organizations. These are mainly temporary or part-time but can lead to permanent positions. Contact: 01244 323 600; website: www.esbpeople.co.uk.

Extend runs recreational exercise-to-music classes for the over-60s and for people with disabilities of all ages. The organization is constantly looking for potential group teachers. Training courses last approximately 12 days spread over several weeks; there are written and practical assessments on completion. Contact: 01582 832 760; website: www.extend.org.uk.

Manpower UK is a major supplier of temporary, contract and permanent staff. Skills in particular demand include secretarial and clerical experience, driving and assembly or manufacturing, and finance and accountancy. Contact: 01895 205 200; website: www.manpower.co.uk.

Officers' Association provides a job-finding service for managerial, professional and senior technical people who are either leaving the armed services or who, having served as officers, are currently unemployed. Contact: 0845 873 7140; website: www.officersassociation.org.uk.

Parity specializes in all types of IT contract and permanent work, with openings nationwide for, among others, senior project managers, analysts, programmers and network and software engineers. Contact: 0845 873 0790; website: www.parity.net.

Quality Assurance Design Services caters for both permanent and contract (part- and full-time) personnel, specializing in the engineering, technical and construction sectors. Assignments cover both the UK and overseas. Contact: 01244 323 100; website: www.qads.co.uk.

Wrinklies Direct is a network of recruitment agencies around the country that specialize in finding work for older people. Vacancies vary across a very broad range. To find your local agency, contact: 08452 601 117; website: www.wrinklies.org.

Chapter Twelve
Voluntary work

> *We make a living by what we get, we make a life by what we give.* SIR WINSTON CHURCHILL (1874–1965)

Have you reached the stage in your life where you would like to put something back into your community? Can you work with other ordinary people to achieve amazing things and make a real difference for those less fortunate than yourself? If so, perhaps volunteering is for you. If you haven't had the time or opportunity before, you may find that it is one of the most satisfying things you've ever done. There are probably as many different kinds of voluntary work that need to be done as there are organizations that need your help. The range of tasks and the variety of groups are enormous. Perhaps this is one reason why some people simply steer clear of the whole area, fearing that the commitment may get out of control and that they may find themselves getting far too involved. Although this can sometimes happen, there are probably many thousands more who, starting in a small way, find themselves caught up in the enthusiasm for their cause. They soon find they are immensely rewarded by the contribution they make and by the new friends volunteering brings them. Very broadly, volunteers are usually enlisted to help with the following roles: clerical and administrative, fundraising, committee work, and direct work with the public.

Clerical

Any active group is likely to need basic administrative help, from typing and stuffing envelopes to answering the telephone and organizing committees. This may involve a day or so a week or occasional assistance at peak times. Many smaller charities in particular would also greatly welcome hearing from individuals with IT expertise to assist with setting up databases, a website, etc.

Fund-raising

Every voluntary organization needs money, and when donations are static or falling, more creativity and ingenuity are required to help bring in funds. Events are many and varied, but anyone with energy and experience of organizing fund-raising events would be welcomed with open arms as a volunteer.

Committee work

This can cover anything from very occasional help to virtually full-time commitment as branch treasurer or secretary. People with business skills or financial or legal backgrounds are likely to be especially valuable, and those whose skills include minute taking are always in demand.

Direct work

Driving, delivering 'meals on wheels', counselling, visiting the housebound, working in a charity shop, helping with a playgroup, respite care for carers: the list is endless and the value of the work incalculable. While certain qualifications and experience – financial, legal, nursing and social work – have particular value in some circumstances, there is also a multitude of interesting and useful jobs for those without special training or with abilities like driving or computer skills. Similarly, the time commitment can vary to suit both helper and organization. It is far better to give just one morning a month and be reliable, than to promise more time than you can spare and end up cancelling or letting people down. Equally, as with a paid job, before you start you should be absolutely clear about all the terms and conditions:

- What sort of work is involved?
- Who will be working with you?
- What is expected?
- When will you be needed?
- Are expenses paid? What for? How much? (See 'Tax note', below.)

If you have all this mapped out in the beginning there will be less chance of any misunderstandings. You will find that voluntary work is not only very rewarding in its own right but also allows you to make a real contribution to the community.

You will be required to have a full Criminal Records Bureau (CRB) check with enhanced disclosure if you are considering working with vulnerable people (young or old). This was covered in Chapter 11, Looking for Paid Work, and applies to many jobs these days, both paid and unpaid. The purpose is to protect those who rely on other people from anyone unsuitable being appointed to a position of trust. These checks are extremely thorough and can take several weeks or even months to process. Patience is needed and the more accurate the information you provide when requested to do so by prospective employers, charities or not-for-profit organizations, the less tedious the process will be. For further information about CRB checks and why they are required, see the **Criminal Records Bureau** website: www.crb.gov.uk.

Tax note

Volunteer drivers who receive a motor mileage allowance and who make a small profit, in that the allowance exceeds their actual incurred expenses (ie petrol and maintenance), are taxed on any profit they make. For further information, see leaflet IR 122, *Guidance – Volunteer Drivers* available from **HMRC**; see website: www.hmrc.gov.uk.

Choosing the right voluntary work

Once you've decided that you might take on some volunteering, the next question is what to do. You will need to find out where the opportunities are in your local area and what particular outlet would suit your talents. You may have friends or neighbours who are already involved in volunteering locally. Asking their advice would be a start, as they may well have some good suggestions or know which organizations are in need of extra pairs of hands. However, if you don't know where to start, here is a list of organizations, arranged in broad categories of interest, indicating the types of activities for which they are seeking volunteers. As there are literally thousands of voluntary groups, national and local, which need help in some way or other, don't regard this list as exhaustive.

For further information on needs and opportunities in the charity and not-for-profit sector, here are some sources you could explore:

REACH finds voluntary, part-time opportunities for experienced managers and professional people of all ages who would like to use their skills working for a voluntary organization. Out-of-pocket expenses are paid, and the service, which is free, is available throughout the UK. Many openings are waiting to be filled, so there is a good chance of finding one that makes real use of your skills, as well as giving you the opportunity of acquiring new ones. Contact: 020 7582 6543; website: www.reachskills.org.uk.

Volunteer centres. Most towns have a body of this kind that seeks to match up volunteers with local organizations seeking help.

Volunteer Development Scotland can help you find out about volunteering opportunities anywhere in Scotland by putting you in touch with a local organization. Contact: 01786 479 593; website: www.vds.org.uk.

Volunteering England can help you find out about volunteering opportunities anywhere in England by putting you in touch with a local organization. Contact: 0845 305 6979; website: www.volunteering.org.uk.

Wales Council for Voluntary Action is the umbrella body for voluntary activity in Wales. It will put you in contact with an organization that would welcome your help. Contact: 0800 2888 329; website: www.wcva.org.uk.

General

The scope of the work of the British Red Cross, WRVS and Citizens Advice Bureau is so broad that they almost justify a category to themselves:

British Red Cross is the world's largest humanitarian organization. It needs volunteer help from men and women for first aid, staffing medical loan depots, fire victim support, emergency response and vital community services. Training is always provided. National Headquarters will provide local branch information. Contact: 0844 871 11 11; website: www.redcross.org.uk.

Citizens Advice Bureau was founded in 1939, and has continued giving invaluable help and advice for 70 years. It deals with millions of enquiries a year and has thousands of volunteers working from over 4,000 locations, interviewing and advising clients on a wide range of questions, including welfare benefits and legal rights. Language skills are also urgently needed to help local people for whom English is a second language. Contact: 08451 264 264; website: www.citizensadvice.org.uk.

Community Service Volunteers (CSV) operates a UK-wide programme called the Retired and Senior Volunteer Programme (RSVP) for people aged 50 and over who want to be involved in their community. Each local group plans its own activities, which include befriending frail older people, helping children with reading and numeracy in schools, and working with health centres on primary care projects. Contact: 020 7643 1385; website: www.csv.org.uk.

Lions Clubs International is the largest voluntary organization in the world with over 1.3 million members and over 18,000 members in the UK. Their groups raise funds providing financial support for worldwide projects. Contact: 0845 833 9502; website: www.lionsmd105.org.uk.

Toc H has branches in all parts of the country involved in a wide range of good neighbour schemes within their local community. Volunteers are needed for such activities as hospital visiting, giving a day out to children in inner cities and providing a helping hand to people with disabilities. Contact: 01296 640 055; website: www.tochparticipation.co.uk.

WRVS works in partnership with many organizations, including local authorities and hospitals, to cover a wide range of needs in the community. It particularly welcomes offers of help from men and women with time during the working day. Activities include meals on wheels, home support for older people, providing transport in rural areas, helping in hospital shops and assisting with catering and welfare services in emergencies. Contact: 0845 601 4670; website: www.wrvs.org.uk.

Animals

The Cinnamon Trust is a registered charity that seeks to relieve the problems of elderly pet owners who, owing to illness or some other emergency, are temporarily unable to care for their pets. It also offers a long-term haven to animals whose owners have died and who had registered their pets with the Trust. Animal lovers throughout the country assist in a voluntary capacity, either by fostering a pet in their own home or by helping out on a daily basis, for example walking a dog, feeding it, cleaning out a bird cage or similar. Contact: 01736 757 900; website: www.cinnamon.org.uk.

Pet Fostering Service Scotland provides short-term foster care for the pets of elderly people who, owing to some emergency such as going into hospital, are temporarily unable to manage. Volunteers may either look after a pet in their own home until the owner is able to take it back or provide some other caring service, such as walking a dog. Contact: 0844 811 9909; website: www.pfss.org.uk.

Pets As Therapy (PAT) is a national charity that originated the PAT visiting scheme to give those in hospitals, care homes and other establishments the important contact with animals that many may miss. It is essential that the dogs and cats are well behaved and fully vaccinated. At present, there are around 4,000 volunteers throughout the country making regular visits. Contact: 01844 345 445; website: www.petsastherapy.org.

The Royal Society for the Prevention of Cruelty to Animals (RSPCA) works to promote kindness and prevent cruelty to animals. Operating through its team of inspectors, it is concerned with the welfare of all animals and with education of the general public by campaigning in the media and through its range of promotional material. It also works for the cause of animal welfare abroad. Contact: 0300 1234 555; website: www.rspca.org.uk.

The Wildfowl & Wetlands Trust (WWT) works to conserve threatened wetland birds and their habitats. As well as Slimbridge, there are visitor centres in Lancashire, Sussex, Tyne and Wear, the Cambridgeshire/Norfolk border, London, Dumfriesshire, South Wales and Northern Ireland. All have a network of volunteers who give valuable help. Contact: 01453 891 900; website: www.wwt.org.uk.

Bereavement

Cruse Bereavement Care has 150 branches throughout the UK and is the national organization for people who have been bereaved. It provides support, information and advice. Volunteers are needed in the branches to help with all these services. Contact: 020 8939 9530; website: www.crusebereavementcare.org.uk.

Children and young people

Action for Sick Children is a charity that supports sick children and their families and advocates that health services be planned to cater for their special needs. Local branches give practical help to parents and professionals in the hospitals. Work is organized through local branches that can be contacted through the head office. Contact: 01663 763 004; website: www.actionforsickchildren.org.

Barnardo's provides services for children who face disability or disadvantage. Projects throughout the country include work with families, day care centres, community projects, playgroups, play buses and holiday schemes. Two major areas require help – fund-raising and the childcare programme. This could involve helping a child with reading or befriending a young person with a disability, to give the parent a much-needed break. Contact: 0208 551 0011, website: www.barnardos.org.uk.

Children's Society runs projects for highly vulnerable children and young people in England, including children at risk on the streets, young refugees, disabled children and those in trouble with the law. Every local branch would be grateful for more fund-raisers. There are also charity shops throughout the country that need volunteers. Contact: 0845 300 1128; website: www.childrenssociety.org.uk.

The Children's Trust Tadworth helps children with multiple disabilities, complex health needs and acquired brain injury. It relies on the support of over 400 volunteers to help the children and their families by providing care, education, therapy and rehabilitation. Contact: 01737 365 000; website: www.thechildrenstrust.org.uk.

Save the Children UK fights for children in the UK and around the world who suffer from poverty, disease, injustice and violence, working with them to find long-term answers to their problems. Volunteers are very much welcomed to assist with fund-raising, campaigning, working in a shop or becoming involved in a specialist assignment. Contact: 020 7012 6400; website: www.savethechildren.org.uk.

Scout Association provides an enjoyable programme of activities for young people aged 6 to 20. Volunteers are needed in many roles, for example as leaders running weekly meetings or as commissioners overseeing several different groups. Other openings include becoming administrators or fellowship members who help with managing the property, fund-raising, contribute to training and edit newsletters. Contact: 0845 300 1818; website: www.scouts.org.uk.

Sea Cadet Corps is a youth organization that offers boys and girls aged 10 to 18 challenging new experiences and adventure. Emphasis is placed on water-borne activities, with encouragement given to those who wish to pursue a career at sea. Units exist throughout the UK and welcome volunteer help either as administrators or as specialist instructors. Contact: 020 7654 7000; website: www.ms-sc.org.

Volunteer Reading Help (VRH) recruits and trains volunteers to work with children who find reading difficult. The volunteers then work in a primary school with the same children every week, helping them to improve their literacy skills and increase their confidence. No formal qualifications are needed, but you would be asked to give up to three hours a week during term-time for at least a year. Contact: 020 7729 4087; website: www.vrh.org.uk.

Conservation

Architectural Heritage Society of Scotland promotes the study and protection of Scottish architecture. As well as enjoying events such as talks and visits, members can join case panels, for which volunteers are always needed. The work involves visiting and assessing listed buildings and conservation and planning applications. Contact: 0131 557 0019; website: www.ahss.org.uk.

British Trust for Conservation Volunteers (BTCV) plays a leading role in encouraging volunteers from both town and country to improve the environment. Over 500 working holidays are organized nationally, and over 1,600 local groups run community projects at weekends and during the week. Typical projects include planting trees, cleaning ponds, restoring footpaths, protecting valuable habitats for wildlife, creating urban nature areas and assisting with woodland management. A reasonable degree of fitness is required. Volunteers are also needed to help the local offices with administration, fund-raising and publicity. Contact: 01302 388 883; website: www.btcv.org.uk.

Campaign to Protect Rural England (CPRE) works to protect and enhance the countryside. Volunteers act as local watchdogs within CPRE's county branches, assessing and reporting unsightly development projects and threats to the environment, and sometimes representing CPRE at enquiries. Contact: 020 7981 2800; website: www.cpre.org.uk.

Friends of the Earth is one of the leading environmental pressure organizations in the UK, aiming to conserve and protect the resources of the planet. Over 200 groups run local campaigns and fund-raising projects. Contact: 020 7490 1555; website: www.foe.co.uk.

Greenpeace is an international environmental pressure group that campaigns to protect the natural environment. Volunteers are needed both to help in the London office and also for campaigning by local groups across the country. Contact: 020 7865 8100; website: www.greenpeace.org.uk.

Ramblers' Association aims to encourage walking, to defend and improve access to the outdoors and to protect the beauty of the countryside throughout the UK. Nearly all the work is carried out by volunteers, who keep an eye on footpaths, check maps of access areas, campaign on countryside matters, compile guidebooks, organize walks, help with administration and perform many other tasks. Contact: 020 7339 8500; website: www.ramblers.org.uk.

Royal Society for the Protection of Birds (RSPB) works to secure a healthy environment for birds and wildlife. It has over a million members and a network of over 180 nature reserves around the UK. Volunteers have a valuable contribution to make and are regularly needed to undertake biological surveys, help with management work on nature reserves, assist visitors and young people, and carry out administrative tasks in offices around the country. Volunteer opportunities range from a few days to a few weeks. Contact: 01767 680 551; website: www.rspb.org.uk.

The elderly

The Abbeyfield Society needs local volunteers to perform a number of roles to help support older people in family-style residential homes.

The aim is to achieve a friendly atmosphere and to support the independence of each resident. There are also registered residential care houses for older people who need a high degree of support. Contact: 01727 737 971; website: www.abbeyfield.com.

Age UK: Age Concern and Help the Aged merged in 2010 to become Age UK, the leading national charity for everyone later in life. Local groups, using volunteer helpers, operate all over the country, and services can include day care, lunch clubs, home visiting, over-60s clubs and, in some areas, specialist services for physically and mentally frail elderly people. Fund-raising activities in all their variety are also organized locally. Contact: 0800 169 65 65; website: www.ageuk.org.uk.

Carers UK is a mine of information for family, partners or friends who need help because they look after an ill, frail or disabled person at home. With around 80 local branches, it provides information and advice through a CarersLine, and campaigns for a better deal for carers. Contact: 020 7378 4999; website: www.carersuk.org.

Contact the Elderly offers a way of making new friends while at the same time providing much needed companionship for lonely elderly people living nearby. Contact volunteers keep a personal link with isolated elderly people by taking them on one Sunday afternoon each month to have tea in the home of a volunteer host. Contact: 0800 716 543; website: www.contact-the-elderly.org.uk.

Independent Age helps older people on low incomes to remain independent by giving practical and financial support. Local volunteers keep in touch with beneficiaries through regular visits and telephone calls and by offering friendship to alleviate loneliness. Volunteers are also very much welcomed to participate in local fund-raising events. Contact: 020 7605 4200; website: www.independentage.org.uk.

The Princess Royal Trust for Carers is the largest provider of carers' support services in the UK. It gives information, advice and support to carers of all ages through its network of 130 independently managed carers' centres and two interactive websites. Volunteers are wanted to run aromatherapy and relaxation sessions. Help is also needed to provide telephone and administrative help in the centres. Contact: 0844 800 4361; website: www.carers.org.

The family

Marriage Care runs pre-marriage courses and also provides a professional counselling service for anyone with relationship problems. Help is required in running and administering its 56 centres. New potential counsellors are also sought. Contact: 020 7371 1341; website: www.marriagecare.org.uk.

Relate works to support marriage and family life. There are about 88 local Relate centres, which offer counselling to anyone with relationship problems; some also undertake education work in schools. Volunteers who would like to become counsellors receive training. There are also openings to serve on committees and help in the office. Contact: 0300 100 1234; website: www.relate.org.uk.

SSAFA Forces Help provides a welfare and advisory service for the families of Service and ex-Service men and women. There are 7,000 volunteers in branches throughout the UK and overseas, as well as professionals wherever service families are stationed. Case workers deal with every kind of problem – domestic, financial, legal and compassionate. Training is given, and although there is no minimum time commitment it is obviously critical to see a case through to the end. Help is particularly needed in inner cities. A Service background is not necessary. Contact: 0845 1300 975; website: www.ssafa.org.uk.

Health

Attend (formerly the National Association of Hospital and Community Friends) is the representative body for Friends groups throughout the UK. Each group is autonomous, and all work to improve the comfort and dignity of patients in both hospitals and the community. Volunteers, of whatever age, are always welcomed. Attend can put new volunteers in touch with their local Friends group. Contact: 0845 450 0285; website: www.attend.org.uk.

BackCare funds research into the causes and treatment of back pain. It teaches children and adults how to use their bodies sensibly and runs a network of local self-help branches. Volunteer activities include organizing exercise and hydrotherapy classes, arranging talks and demonstrations, and running social and fund-raising events. Contact: 0845 130 2704; website: www.backcare.org.uk.

British Heart Foundation (BHF) funds research into the causes, prevention, diagnosis and treatment of heart disease. Its educational role includes promoting training in simple life-saving skills, informing the medical and scientific community about the results of its research and making the information known to the general public. BHF also provides life-saving cardiac care equipment to hospitals and other health providers, and helps support rehabilitation courses and heart support groups. Contact: 020 7554 0000; website: www.bhf.org.uk.

Calibre is a national lending library of recorded books on ordinary standard cassette tapes for use by anyone with sight problems, dyslexia and other disabilities that prevent them from reading a book. Volunteers are needed to help run the library, which is maintained entirely from donations. Publicity and fund-raising help are also required. Contact: 01296 432 339; website: www.calibre.org.uk.

Cancer Research UK aims to bring hope to all those touched by cancer through pioneering research into the prevention, treatment and cure of the disease. It is almost entirely dependent on the generosity of the general public, and your support, whether helping to raise funds or sparing a few hours of your time, will contribute towards the work of its scientists in their efforts to conquer cancer. Thousands of volunteers organize local fund-raising events, help in Cancer Research UK's shops or assist with general work in its office. Contact: 020 7121 6699; website: www.cancerresearchuk.org.

Disability Snowsport UK, the skiers and boarders charity, provides opportunities for people with a disability to participate in skiing and snowboarding. Its goal is to help individuals improve their quality of life and transfer the benefits that they can derive from taking part to their everyday life. Contact: 01479 861 272; website: www.disabilitysnowsport.org.uk.

Leonard Cheshire Disability is the UK's largest voluntary sector provider of support services to disabled people, helping them to live their lives as they choose. Its many services throughout the UK are supported by local people via regional offices, who make an enormous contribution. There are endless ways in which you can lend a hand, including driving, gardening, befriending individuals and fund-raising, or you might like to help on the campaigning side. Contact: 020 3242 0200; website: www.lcdisability.org.

Mind (The National Association for Mental Health) works for a better life for people with experience of mental distress. It has offices in England and Wales and more than 200 local associations. Their activities include running social clubs and day centres, befriending schemes, an advocacy service and self-help groups. Contact: 0845 766 0163; website: www.mind.org.uk.

RDA (Riding for the Disabled Association) aims to help provide opportunities for riding for disabled children and adults. You can help in one of the 520 local groups. Legal and financial knowledge is particularly valuable, and for those with experience of horses, leading or walking beside the ponies while they are being ridden and accompanying parties on riding holidays. Contact: 0845 658 1082; website: www.riding-for-disabled.org.uk.

Royal National Institute of Blind People (RNIB) aims to help blind and partially sighted people lead full and independent lives. Among many other initiatives, it runs schools for blind children, provides careers advice, offers training and assists with finding suitable employment. It also manages some rehabilitation centres and special homes, has a welfare advisory service, and sells specially designed or adapted goods to make life easier and safer for blind or partially sighted people. Contact: 0303 123 9999; website: www.rnib.org.uk.

St Dunstans is a charity providing lifelong support to blind and visually impaired ex-Service men and women, promoting and enabling them to regain their independence, meet new challenges and achieve a better quality of life. Contact: 020 7616 8365; website: www.st-dunstans.org.uk.

St John Ambulance is best known for its first aid role at public events. Its volunteers also carry out care within the community, and receive special induction training, tailored to their needs according to their chosen activity: care, transport, communications, support work at public events, the library service or first aid. Contact: 08700 10 49 50; www.sja.org.uk.

Scope works to promote equality and create education and employment opportunities for people with cerebral palsy and related disabilities. There are also over 250 local groups offering information, confidential support and advice. Volunteers are particularly needed for helping in Scope shops, supporting local groups and participating in fund-raising events. Contact: 0808 800 3333; website: www.scope.org.uk.

Heritage and the arts

If you wish to volunteer in the arts, there are numerous opportunities through community arts projects, arts centres, local arts councils and other arts activities associated with special groups such as the youth services or people with disabilities. All kinds of volunteer abilities are needed, from painting and other creative skills to accounting and clerical know-how. Further information should be obtainable through your local authority, library or local arts centre.

> **Council for British Archaeology** organizes archaeological excavations that take place throughout the UK, mainly from March to September. The work will probably involve lifting, stooping and wheeling barrows, so fitness and stamina are desirable. A two-week stay is the average with accommodation varying according to the site. Contact: 01904 671 417; website: www.britarch.ac.uk.

> **National Trust Central Volunteering** involves volunteers in many aspects of the work of conservation in the great houses open to the public and on 248,000 hectares of coast and countryside properties. Inevitably, the needs will vary according to the location and time of the year. Over 40,000 volunteers a year work alongside Trust staff in the regions. Contact: 01793 817 400; website: www.nationaltrust.org.uk.

> **SPAB (Society for the Protection of Ancient Buildings)** promotes the sensitive repair of old buildings. Volunteers are needed in London and around the country to help with organizing events, administration, and cataloguing the archive. SPAB would also very much like to hear from qualified architects, building surveyors and structural engineers to assist with specific projects. Contact: 020 7377 1644; website: www.spab.org.uk.

The needy

> **Alexandra Rose Charities,** founded in 1912 by Queen Alexandra, works with charities and community organizations across the country helping

them to raise funds. More than 250 people-caring groups benefit from their national profile, expertise and organizational support. Contact: 01252 726 171; website: www.alexandrarose.org.uk.

Elizabeth Finn Care has been helping people overcome the worst effects of poverty for over a century. Volunteers meet regularly with beneficiaries and applicants in their own home, both to ensure that they are receiving the right help and to maintain links between the charity and those in its care. Contact: 0208 834 9200; website: www.elizabethfinncare.org.uk.

Oxfam works with others to overcome poverty and suffering. Over 22,000 volunteers are involved in all parts of Great Britain. One of the main areas of need is help with the running of Oxfam shops. Help is also needed to organize fund-raising events, give administrative assistance and support the educational and campaigning aspects of Oxfam's work. Contact: 0300 200 1300; website: www.oxfam.org.uk.

Royal British Legion was founded to help needy ex-Service men and women and also their dependants. Today it runs care homes, maintains sheltered workshops for the disabled, gives pension counselling, provides training for job-seekers, and offers advice and friendship. It also organizes pilgrimages to war graves overseas and has a small business advice service. The Royal British Legion's most important fund-raising activity is the Poppy Appeal, in the fortnight before Remembrance Day on the second Sunday in November. Contact: 08457 725 725; website: www.britishlegion.org.uk.

Samaritans offers 24-hour confidential, non-judgemental emotional support for people experiencing distress or despair. Much of the work is done on the telephone and complete reliability is an essential quality in a volunteer. Training is given; the minimum time commitment is about four hours a week plus one night duty a month. Contact: 08457 90 90 90; website: www.samaritans.org.

Offenders and the victims of crime

Nacro strives to make society safer by finding practical solutions to reducing crime. It provides housing, training and resettlement services for prisoners and ex-offenders, supports disadvantaged families and communities, and steers young people away from crime. Contact: 020 7840 7200; website: www.nacro.org.uk.

New Bridge Foundation offers friendship and support to people in prison and on their release, with the aim of giving them the encouragement and practical skills to lead responsible and law-abiding lives in the future. It achieves this by running vocational and parenting courses, as well as managing a 'befrienders' scheme. This involves hundreds of volunteers who visit offenders in prison and keep in touch through letter writing. Contact: 0207 976 0779; website: www.newbridgefoundation.org.uk.

Supporting Others through Volunteer Action (SOVA) works in England and Wales with the Prison Service and many other organizations by involving local volunteers in strengthening communities and reducing crime. It is organized on a regional basis. Contact: 020 7793 0404; website: www.sova.org.uk.

Victim Support offers information, support and practical help to over a million people affected by crime every year. Volunteers play a crucial role in this delicate work. Victim Support also very much welcomes volunteers with IT expertise to work in its offices, as well as enthusiasts able to assist with publicity, fund-raising and interpreting. No qualifications are necessary to become a volunteer but a CRB check will be carried out. Contact: 0800 840 4207; website: www.victimsupport.org.uk.

Politics

You may not immediately think of political parties in the context of voluntary work, but all of them use vast numbers of volunteer helpers. Between elections the help is mostly required with fund-raising, committee work and staffing the constituency offices. At election time, activity is obviously intense: delivering literature, addressing and stuffing envelopes, recording canvass returns, driving elderly and disabled people to the polls and, for the politically informed, canvassing. Contact details for the major parties are:

Conservative Party	020 7222 9000; website: www.conservatives.com
Green Party	020 7272 4474; website: www.greenparty.org.uk
Labour Party	08705 900 200; website: www.labour.org.uk
Liberal Democrats	020 7222 7999; website: www.libdems.org.uk
Plaid Cymru	029 20 472 272; website: www.plaidcymru.org
Scottish National Party	0131 525 8928; website: www.snp.org
Social Democratic and Labour Party (SDLP)	028 90 247 700; website: www.sdlp.ie
UKIP	01626 831 290; website: www.ukip.org.uk
Ulster Unionist Party	028 9046 3200; website: www.uup.org

Work after work

British Chambers of Commerce, the organizations representing the local business community, are highly active in a wide range of projects to promote local economic development and renewal in the wider community. Many take the lead in initiatives for inner-city regeneration, crime prevention, industry-education links, training schemes and similar activities. Contact: 020 7654 5800; website: www.britishchambers.org.uk.

The National Federation of Enterprise Agencies: for those in England who would like to continue to work in business after retirement, an enterprise agency may be the answer. Set up as a partnership between government, employers, trade unions and the voluntary sector, it aims to encourage the greater local involvement of businesses in the communities in which they operate. In practice the work will involve advising and helping new small firms at the start-up stage and as they further develop. Contact: 01234 831 623; website: www.nfea.com.

For those in **Scotland** who are interested in Enterprise Trusts, which are similar partnerships, contact: 0131 451 1100; website: www.sbcscot.com.

Long-term volunteering

If you are thinking of a long-term, probably residential, commitment there are a number of organizations both in the UK and abroad in need of voluntary help for a wide variety of projects. Some require specialist skills, such as engineering or medicine; others essentially need people with practical qualities, common sense and enthusiasm. All require a two-year minimum period of service. General conditions are similar for all of them; travel is paid, plus a living allowance or salary that is based on local levels rather than on expatriate rates. Couples without dependent children are welcome, as long as both have the necessary skills. National Insurance Contributions are provided, and a resettlement grant is paid on completion of the tour.

Overseas

There are four main organizations for overseas volunteering: Voluntary Service Overseas (VSO), Skillshare International, Progressio and International Service, details of which have already been provided in Chapter 11 (Looking for Paid Work – Working in developing countries).

Volunteering abroad for the over-50s is referred to as 'grey gapping'. It is gaining popularity amongst many 50–75 year olds. Over 200,000 mature people have taken gap years recently and the number is growing. If a life-changing experience and doing some voluntary work abroad before or just after you retire appeals to you, **Gap Year Advice For All** should be able to help. Contact: 01494 673 448; website: www.gapadvice.org. (This is further described in Chapter 14, Holidays.)

In the UK

Although the groups that we have listed in this section are primarily concerned with schemes requiring volunteer help for between two weeks and six months, they would also welcome shorter-term help with administration and fund-raising:

Sue Ryder Care centres provide hospice and neurological care. They are run as far as possible as family homes in the true sense of the word. Volunteers are needed for work in a variety of jobs, including the general running of the 17 care centres and help in the 430 Sue Ryder Care charity shops. Contact: 0845 050 1953; website: www.suerydercare.org.

Vitalise needs volunteers of all ages all months of the year at the five accessible residential centres. Volunteers support and provide companionship to the guests. No formal qualifications are required. Stay is for one or two weeks. Board and lodging are free and fares are refunded for UK travel. Volunteers are also needed in the charity's two day centres, and to act as sighted guides for visually impaired people on holidays. Contact: 0845 330 0148; website: www.vitalise.org.uk.

Chapter Thirteen
Health

Be careful about reading health books. You may die of a misprint. **MARK TWAIN (1835–1910)**

Keeping fit

Retirement should be a time for positive good health. For the first time in years possibly you have the opportunity to make lifestyle changes that can prevent illness and help you retain fitness, mobility and independence into your 80s and 90s. For some people the chance to be out in the fresh air and take up sport again is something they may have been looking forward to for a while. For others, not having to eat 'on the hoof', attend business lunches or have sandwiches day after day, comes as a pleasant change. A big plus for most people is not having to make regular journeys to and from work in the rush hour. In winter particularly there is often little choice but to travel with or sit near people coughing and sneezing, and suffer the inevitable uncomfortable delays on public transport or in traffic. All of these could adversely affect anyone's blood pressure but once free of the strain and stress that are part of any job, you should feel less harassed and look more relaxed.

People can get aches and pains, of course, as they become older. Doctors advise that this is far less likely if you remain physically and mentally active. Since people retiring today are often younger in looks and behaviour than previous generations, they should be able to enjoy many healthy years ahead. However, bodies do require care and attention if they are to function at their best. Just as you regularly service your car, routine checks for eyes and teeth are obviously sensible. Also if habits can be moderate, rather than excessive, this is generally a wiser policy. It means you can enjoy small vices without paying the penalty for over-indulgence. There is no need to get out of shape: you will have time to make changes that help you to look good and keep alert, which should mean you are likely to have a far longer and more enjoyable retirement.

Exercise is important if you are to keep healthy whatever age you are. It tones up muscles and improves the circulation, reduces flab, helps ward off illnesses and can be good fun. For those not accustomed to regular exercise, it is essential to build up gradually. Trying to recapture the sporting feats of your youth could be unwise. If you are planning to run a marathon or win the local tennis competition, start gently.

Training in a whole range of sports is available around the country, with beginners in their 50s and older especially welcomed. Details of some of the many facilities, together with other keep fit options, are listed in Chapter 9, Leisure Activities. In addition to some of the more exotic choices, swimming has long been recognized as one of the best forms of exercise. Some people say there is nothing to beat a good brisk walk. Gardening is also recommended. With the explosion of sports clubs, leisure centres and adult keep fit classes run by local authorities and other organizations, opportunities have never been greater.

At the top end of the market, there are deluxe health clubs located in hotels, sports clubs and other venues. These offer, amongst other things, facilities such as a fitness centre, swimming pool, massage and beauty salon. They have qualified staff who can advise on – and supervise – personal fitness programmes. However, at a fraction of the price, many local authority leisure centres offer a marvellous range of sports. They also usually run regular classes in everything from self-defence to badminton.

Emphasis on, and availability of, every type of keep fit activity is on the increase. It is a welcome innovation, as there are a growing number of opportunities for older people and those with disabilities. Information should be available on nearby facilities in your local newspaper or library, or you can search the internet. Otherwise the following organizations may be able to help you:

Extend, which celebrated its 30th year in 2009, provides gentle exercise to music for older people and anyone of any age who has a disability, throughout the UK. Contact: 01582 832 760; website: www.extend.org.uk.

Fitness League is a well established nationwide exercise network, supported by Sport England. Emphasis is on exercise and movement to music, with special regard to individual ability. Contact: 01344 874 787; website: www.thefitnessleague.com.

Medau Movement encourages the body to move with energy, strength, stamina, suppleness and co-ordination. Classes are held throughout the country. Contact: 01403 266 000; website: www.medau.org.uk.

Pilates

Pilates is an invigorating form of exercise for your mind and body that can improve your strength, flexibility and overall mobility. It helps restore your body to balance. As a result your posture will change and you will move more efficiently. Pilates is a safe and effective exercise method that will enable you to look and feel your very best. **The Pilates Foundation** has qualified teachers across the UK. Contact: 020 7033 0078; website: www.pilatesfoundation.com.

Yoga

Yoga is popular with all ages and it is a means of improving fitness and helping relaxation. Classes are provided by many local authorities and there are also a number of specialist organizations.

British Wheel of Yoga is a registered charity and is the largest yoga organization in the country. With over 3,000 qualified teachers it promotes yoga classes, workshops and events for its members and the public. Contact: 01529 306 851; website: www.bwy.org.uk.

Iyengar Yoga Institute runs classes at all levels, including remedial for those with medical conditions. Of special interest is the 59-plus class for people who would like to start gently. Contact: 020 7624 3080; website: www.iyi.org.uk.

Sensible eating

Excess weight and being out of condition tend to add years to anyone's age. So a trim, well-kept body is one of the secrets of a youthful appearance. Regular exercise is important but so is sensible eating. With about one in four adults in Britain being obese, it is a worrying trend that so many people are seriously overweight. The more excess weight that you carry the greater the risks to your health. In particular there is an increased risk of a heart attack, as well as operations being made more difficult. As age increases, the greater the likelihood of restricted mobility.

It is important to consult your doctor before embarking on serious dieting. But medical advice does not need to be sought should you plan to cut out or cut down on sweets, cakes, sticky buns, deep-fried foods, alcohol and rich sauces. Healthy foods that most people (except of course those on a special doctor's diet) can eat in almost unlimited quantities are fruit, salad, vegetables, fish and white meat, such as chicken.

Cholesterol levels are important to watch. Excess cholesterol (fatty deposits that collect in the arteries) is a great concern; slimmer people can also suffer from it. The basic health message is to eat low-fat, healthy food and include plenty of roughage such as wholemeal bread in the diet. It is important to cut down on dishes with a high sugar, salt and animal fat content – this particularly includes cream, butter and red meat.

As every health magazine advises, crash diets are no solution for long-term fitness. Many people need a boost to get started, and whatever method you choose is fine as long as it works. So if a short stay at a health spa is what you need to kick start your new healthier lifestyle, go for it. If nothing else, the experience is relaxing, though not cheap. There are many places to choose from but if you have friends who can give a recommendation, so much the better.

Cheaper and arguably more successful for long-term slimmers are **Weight Watchers** meetings, held across the UK. Their aim is to help members establish a healthy, balanced approach to weight loss, with emphasis on making small, lifetime changes that can be maintained for the long term. Contact: 0845 345 1500; website: www.weightwatchers.co.uk.

The **Natural Health Advisory Service** maintains that many women's problems associated with the menopause can be alleviated by healthy eating and exercise. Contact: 01273 609 699; website: www.naturalhealthas.com.

Some single people tend to get weight problems because they find it a bore to cook for one, so get into bad habits by snacking on the wrong kind of foods. Elderly women are often at risk from malnourishment, so not only do they undermine their health but because of their general frailty they are more susceptible to falls and broken bones. Self-help to avoid trouble is one thing, but those who suspect that they could have something wrong with them should not hesitate to consult their doctor.

Food safety

As most readers will know, basic rules on food safety are important. It is inadvisable for anyone to eat raw eggs, whether consumed steak tartar fashion or used in uncooked dishes such as mayonnaise and mousses. Elderly people as well as the very young should probably also avoid eating lightly cooked eggs. Seafood can present problems but when it comes to food poisoning, eggs and seafood are far from being the only culprits.

'Cook-chill' foods in particular, including ready-cooked chickens and pork pies, are a breeding ground for bacteria, especially in the summer when many foods – even vegetables – are liable to deteriorate more quickly. Storage and cooking also play a major part in warding off the dangers of food poisoning. The government leaflet *Preventing Food Poisoning* gives the following basic advice:

- Keep all parts of your kitchen clean.
- Aim to keep your refrigerator temperature at a maximum of 5°C.
- Keep raw and cooked foods separate and use within the recommended dates.
- Cook foods thoroughly.
- Do not reheat food more than once and don't keep cooked food longer than two days.

Drink

Most doctors cheerfully maintain that 'a little bit of what you fancy does you good'. Retirement is no reason for giving up pleasures and in moderate quantities alcohol can be a very effective nightcap and can also help to stimulate a sluggish appetite. However, bear in mind that alcoholism is the third greatest killer after heart disease and cancer. The condition is far more likely among those who are bored or depressed and drift into the habit of having a drink to cheer themselves up or to pass the time. Because the early symptoms appear fairly innocuous, the danger signs are apt to be ignored.

Whereas most people are sensible enough to be able to control the habit themselves, others may need help. The family doctor will be the first person to check with for medical advice. But additionally, for those who need moral support, the following self-help groups may be the answer:

Al-Anon Family Groups UK & Eire offers support and understanding to anyone whose life has been affected by someone else's drinking. There are over 800 support groups in the UK and Eire. Contact: 020 7403 0888; website: www.al-anonuk.org.uk.

Alcohol Concern is the national agency on alcohol misuse, campaigning for effective alcohol policy and improved services for people whose lives are affected by alcohol-related problems. Contact: 020 7264 0510; website: www.alcoholconcern.org.uk.

Alcoholics Anonymous has over 3,000 autonomous groups all over the country, designed to help those with a serious alcohol problem learn how to stay sober. Through friendship and mutual support, sufferers assist each other in coping, which is made easier by meeting others with the same problem. Contact: 0845 769 7555; website: www.alcoholics-anonymous.org.uk.

Smoking

Any age is a good one to cut back on smoking or preferably to give up altogether. Smokers are 20 times more likely to contract lung cancer; they are at more serious risk of suffering from heart disease and they are more liable to chronic bronchitis and other ailments. Most people agree that it is easier to give up completely than attempt to cut back. Every habitual smoker knows that after the first cigarette of the day you can always think of a thousand excuses for lighting another. Aids to willpower include the ban on smoking in restaurants, bars and pubs and other designated areas.

Many hardened smokers swear by nicotine patches, but working out how much money you could save in a year and promising yourself a holiday or other reward on the proceeds could help. Thinking about your health in years to come should be an even more convincing argument. Dozens of organizations concerned with health publish leaflets about giving up smoking. Here are three of them:

NHS Smoking Helpline offers help and advice to smokers who want to quit, gives information about local services, including nicotine replacement therapy, and group support. Contact 0800 022 4 332; website: www.nhs.uk/gosmokefree.

Quit is the independent charity whose aim is to save lives by helping smokers to stop. Smokers wanting to quit should contact: 0800 00 22 00; website: www.quit.org.uk.

Smokeline (Scotland only) offers free advice, counselling and encouragement to those wishing to give up smoking. It is available noon to midnight, seven days a week. Contact: 0800 84 84 84; website: www.canstopsmoking.com.

Accident prevention

One of the most common causes of mishap is an accident in the home. In particular this is due to falling and incidents involving faulty electrical wiring. The vast majority of these could be avoided by taking normal common sense precautions, such as repairing or replacing worn carpets and installing better lighting near staircases. For a list of practical suggestions, see 'Safety in the home', in Chapter 8, Your Home.

If you are unlucky enough to be injured in an accident, whether in the street or elsewhere, the Law Society offers a free service called the Accident Line to help you decide whether you can make a claim. You will be entitled to a free consultation with a local solicitor specializing in personal injury claims. A similar service is offered by the National Accident Helpline. For further details contact:

Accident Line	0800 19 29 39; website: www.accidentlinedirect.co.uk
National Accident Helpline	0800 376 0185; website: www.national-accident-helpline.co.uk

Aches, pains and other abnormalities

There is nothing about becoming 50, 60 or even 70 that makes aches and pains inevitable. Age itself has nothing to do with the vast majority of ailments. Many people ignore the warning signs when something is wrong yet treatment when a condition is still in its infancy can often cure it altogether, or at least help to delay its advance. The following should always be investigated by a doctor:

- any pain that lasts more than a few days;
- lumps, however small;
- dizziness or fainting;
- chest pains, shortness of breath or palpitations;
- persistent cough or hoarseness;
- unusual bleeding from anywhere;
- unnatural tiredness or headaches;
- frequent indigestion;
- unexplained weight loss.

Health insurance

If you were covered by private health insurance during your career, and you wish to continue this benefit, you will normally be welcomed as an individual client by most of the main groups if you are under 70. You can then renew your membership when you do reach 70. Even if you have not previously been insured, it is not too late to consider doing so.

The terms and conditions of the different schemes offered by health insurance groups vary. All the major ones offer to pay, if not all, at least the greatest part of the costs. These include inpatient accommodation, treatment and medical fees, as well as outpatient charges for specialists, X-rays and similar services. They do not normally cover GPs' costs. Subscription levels depend on the area in which you live and on the type of hospital to which you choose to be admitted.

Other factors that can substantially affect the price are your age, the extent of the cover offered and the various restrictions or exclusions that may apply. Many insurers have recently introduced a range of budget policies, which while they have the advantage of being less costly are naturally also less comprehensive. There may be an annual cash limit or the policy may include an excess. As with all types of insurance, the small print matters, so look carefully at all the plans available before selecting the scheme that best suits your needs.

The NHS has, generally, an excellent record in dealing with urgent conditions and accidents. However, it sometimes has a lengthy waiting list for the less urgent and more routine operations. By using health insurance to pay for private medical care you will probably get faster treatment, as well as greater comfort and privacy in hospital. Here are some major organizations that provide cover:

AXA PPP Healthcare	0800 783 1279; website: www.axappphealthcare.co.uk
BUPA	0800 600 500; website: www.bupa.co.uk
Exeter Friendly Society	0300 123 3209; website: www.exeterfriendly.co.uk

Two other groups that offer health insurance plans relevant to people over retirement age are:

| Saga Services Ltd | 0800 857 857; website: www.saga.co.uk |
| Simplyhealth | 0800 980 7890;
 website: www.simplyhealth.co.uk |

Help with choosing a scheme

With so many plans on the market, selecting the one that best suits your needs can be quite a problem. An independent financial adviser or specialist insurance broker could advise you, such as:

| Medibroker | 0800 980 1082;
 website: www.medibroker.co.uk |
| The Private Health Partnership | 01274 588 862;
 website: www.php.co.uk |

Private patients – without insurance cover

If you do not have private medical insurance but want to go into hospital in the UK as a private patient, there is nothing to stop you, provided your doctor is willing and you are able to pay the bills. The choice if you opt for self-pay lies between the private wings of NHS hospitals, hospitals run by charitable or non-profit-making organizations (such as the Nuffield Hospitals; **Nuffield Health,** Tel: 0845 602 9262; website: www.nuffieldhealth.com), and those run for profit by private companies.

An interesting alternative

Have you ever thought of taking a holiday and having an operation at the same time? Sounds curious, but you could investigate one of the latest growth areas in health care – health tourism. Health and medical tourism is where you travel to take advantage of less expensive health treatments. These include cosmetic, dental and spa treatments and medical procedures (including joint replacement, heart surgery and other elective procedures). You can usually save over 50 per cent on the fees that you would pay for private treatment in the UK – and have a holiday as well. The destinations are extensive and sometimes exotic. Leading health tourism destinations include Eastern Europe, the Baltic region, Malta, Cyprus, Turkey, the Middle East, India, Malaysia, Singapore, South Korea, Costa Rica and Argentina. One way to find out about this new and growing market and to meet some of the providers of such services is to visit the annual Health Tourism Show held at Olympia:

The Health Tourism Show	01372 743 837; website: www.healthtourismshow.com
Treatment Abroad	01442 817 817; website: www.treatmentabroad.com

Long-term care insurance (LTCI)

An emergency operation is one thing; long-term care because an individual can no longer cope unaided is quite another. A number of insurance companies have policies designed to help meet the costs in the event of people needing to stay long term in a nursing home or requiring a carer to look after them in their own home. Increasingly people are having to contribute towards the costs of their own care and many have to support themselves from their savings. (*NB:* a married couple will not be forced into selling their home if the other partner is still living there.)

Nursing home fees are rising and good homes increasingly expensive. Care in your own home, if you were ever to become seriously incapacitated, is likely to be at least as expensive. It is advisable, if you can, to make some provision against long-term care. The big advantages of insurance cover of this type are that it buys peace of mind and helps safeguard your savings should care ever become a necessity in the future.

Cover normally applies only if an illness is diagnosed after joining and, while some plans cover a wide range of eventualities, others specifically exclude some of the critical illnesses, such as cancer. The premiums, which can be paid on a regular annual basis or as a lump sum, vary considerably. In all cases, the charges are largely determined by the subscriber's age at the time of first joining and, as you would expect, are very much cheaper at 55 than 75.

Although pre-funded insurance is the cheapest way of buying care cover, a disadvantage is that if you never claim you lose all the money you have paid over the years. Some policies link the insurance with an investment, providing a payout on death if no claim has been made. Though initially more expensive, you can take your money out of the plan at any time. However, if the investment growth is poor you could lose some of your capital.

A possible alternative to a conventional long-term care policy is *critical illness insurance,* which pays a lump sum if you are unfortunate enough to suffer from cancer or have a stroke. Rather than pay into a policy ahead of time, an alternative solution that has been growing in popularity is to buy a *care fee annuity* (sometimes known as an 'immediate-needs annuity') as and when the need arises. An advantage is that you buy a care plan only at the time it would actually be useful.

Care fee annuities do require you to invest a sizeable chunk of capital, which, depending on your life expectancy, may or may not prove good value in the long term. Also, prices quoted by different companies to provide exactly the same annual income often differ by many thousands of pounds. You are strongly advised to shop around and to read the small print extremely carefully before signing, or you could ask an independent financial adviser (IFA) to recommend what would be your best choice.

However good the advice, only you can decide whether some form of long-term care cover would be a sensible precaution. As with most major items of expenditure, there will inevitably be arguments for and against. All LTCI products and services now come under the compulsory jurisdiction of the Financial Ombudsman Service and the Financial Services Compensation Scheme. If you choose to seek the advice of an IFA, the **Financial Services Authority (FSA)** has a helpful fact sheet, *Choosing a Financial Adviser – How Key Facts Can Help You,* available from the FSA Consumer Helpline: 0845 606 1234; website: www.fsa.gov.uk.

Permanent health insurance (PHI)

PHI should not be confused with other types of health insurance. It is a replacement-of-earnings policy for people who are still in work and who, because of illness, are unable to continue with their normal occupation for a prolonged period and in consequence suffer loss of earnings. While highly recommended for the self-employed, many employees have some protection under an employer's policy. Either way, if you are close to retirement, PHI is unlikely to feature on your priority list.

Health screening

Prevention is better than cure, and most of the provident associations offer a diagnostic screening service to check general health and to provide advice on diet, drinking and smoking if these are problem areas. These tests show that roughly a quarter of patients aged over 55 have an unsuspected problem that can often be treated quickly and easily. Screening services normally recommend a check-up every two years, and centres are usually available to members of insurance schemes and others alike:

BMI Healthcare: 0808 101 0337; website: www.bmihealthcare.co.uk.

BUPA: 0800 600 3458; website: www.bupa.co.uk/wellness.

National Health Service offers several different screening services of particular relevance to those aged 50-plus. See website: www.nhs.uk/livewell/screening.

Hospital care cash plans

These are inexpensive insurance policies that provide cover for everyday healthcare costs. Claims are made after the customer has paid for the treatment and reimbursed within a week. For further information contact: British Health Care Association: 01343 544 841; website: www.bhca.org.uk.

National Health Service

Choosing a GP

If you move to a new area, the best way to choose your new GP is to ask for a recommendation. Otherwise your local primary care trust or strategic health authority can assist, or search the NHS website: www.nhs.uk.

Additional points you may want to consider are: how close the doctor is to your home; whether there is an appointments system; and whether it is a group practice and, if so, how this is organized. All GPs must have practice leaflets, available at their premises, with details about their service.

Having selected a doctor, you should take your medical card to the receptionist to have your name registered. This is not automatic as there is a limit to the number of patients any one doctor can accept. Also, some doctors prefer to meet potential patients before accepting them on their list. If you do not have a medical card, you will need to fill in a simple form.

Changing your GP

If you want to change your GP, you go about it in exactly the same way. If you know of a doctor whose list you would like to be on, you can simply turn up at his or her surgery and ask to be registered; or you can ask your local primary care trust, or health board in Scotland, to give you a copy of its directory before making a choice. You do not need to give a reason for wanting to change, and you do not need to ask anyone's permission.

NHS Direct

If you need medical advice when you are on holiday or at some other time when it may not be possible to contact your doctor, you could ring NHS Direct, which offers a 24-hour free health advice service, staffed by trained nurses. The number to call is 0845 46 47; website: www.nhsdirect.nhs.uk. *NB*: the government has announced that this service is to be replaced with a new 111 helpline.

Help with NHS costs

If you or your partner are in receipt of Income Support, income-based Jobseeker's Allowance or the Pension Credit Guarantee Credit, you are both entitled to free NHS prescriptions, NHS dental treatment, NHS wigs and fabric supports and an NHS sight test. You are both equally entitled to the maximum value of an optical voucher to help towards the cost of glasses or contact lenses and payment of travel costs to and from hospital for NHS treatment. You are also entitled to help if you and/or your partner are entitled to, or named on, a current tax credit NHS exemption certificate.

Even if you are not automatically entitled to help with the above costs, you and your partner may be entitled to some help on the grounds of low income. To find out, fill in claim form HC1 – obtainable from social security or Jobcentre Plus offices as well as many NHS hospitals, dentists, opticians and GPs – and send it to the Health Benefits Division in the prepaid envelope provided with the form. If you are eligible for help, you will be sent a certificate that is valid for up to 12 months according to your circumstances. Depending on your income, you may receive an HC2 certificate, which entitles you to full help with NHS costs, or alternatively an HC3 certificate, which will entitle you to partial help. For further information contact: **NHS Response Line:** 0300 123 1002; website: www.dh.gov.uk.

Benefits

If you are on Income Support and have a disability, you may be entitled to certain premiums on top of your ordinary allowance. Various social security benefits are also available to those with special problems because of illness. These include:

Attendance Allowance (see leaflet DS 702);

Disability Living Allowance (see leaflet DS 704);

Employment and Support Allowance (ESA), which replaced Incapacity Benefit in October 2008. ESA is a new integrated contributory and income-related allowance.

For further information, including the special concessions for voluntary and permitted work, see the **Department for Work and Pensions** website: www.dwp.gov.uk/esa.

Prescriptions

Both men and women aged 60 and over are entitled to free NHS prescriptions. Certain other groups are also entitled to free prescriptions, including those on low income. If you are not sure if you qualify, you should pay for your prescription and ask the pharmacist for an NHS receipt form FP57, which tells you how to claim a refund. For further information, see leaflet HC11, *Help with Health Costs*, obtainable from some pharmacies and GP surgeries.

People who do not qualify but who require a lot of prescriptions could save money by purchasing a prescription prepayment certificate. A prepayment certificate will work out cheaper if you are likely to need more than four prescription items in three months, or more than 14 items in 12 months, as there is no further charge regardless of how many prescription items you require. For further information contact **NHS Help With Health Costs:** 0845 850 0030; website: www.nhsbsa.nhs.uk.

Going into hospital

There are now improved schemes to cut waiting lists for those in need of operations. Many patients are unaware that they can ask their GP to refer them to a consultant at a different NHS trust or even, in certain cases, help make arrangements for them to be treated overseas. Before you can become a patient at another hospital, your GP will need to agree to your being referred. A major consideration will be whether the treatment would be as clinically effective as the treatment you would receive locally.

Those likely to need help on leaving hospital should speak to the hospital social worker, who will help make any necessary arrangements. Help is sometimes available to assist patients with their travel costs to and from hospital. If you receive Income Support, income-based Jobseeker's Allowance or Pension Credit Guarantee Credit, you can ask for repayment of 'necessary travel costs'. For further information contact **NHS Help With Health Costs:** 0845 850 0030; website: www.nhsbsa.nhs.uk.

If you go into hospital, you will continue to receive your pension as normal. Your pension – as well as Employment and Support Allowance, Severe Disablement Allowance, Income Support and Pension Credit Guarantee Credit – will continue to be paid in full, without any reductions, for the duration of your stay. For further information, see leaflet GL12, *Going into Hospital?* obtainable from social security or Jobcentre Plus offices and NHS hospitals. See website: www.jobcentreplus.gov.uk, or www.dwp.gov.uk.

Complaints

The NHS has a complaints procedure if you are unhappy about the treatment you have received. In the first instance, you should speak to someone close to the cause of the problem, such as the doctor, nurse, receptionist or practice manager. If, for whatever reason, you would prefer to speak to someone who was not involved in your care, you can speak to the complaints manager at your local NHS trust or strategic health authority instead; addresses will be in the telephone directory. In jargon terms, this first stage is known as *local resolution*.

If you are not satisfied with the reply you receive, you can ask the NHS trust or strategic health authority for an *independent review*. The complaints manager will be able to tell you whom to contact about arranging this. If you are still dissatisfied after the independent review, then the Health Service Ombudsman (known formerly as the Health Service Commissioner) might be able to help. The Ombudsman is independent of both government and the NHS and investigates complaints of failure or maladministration across the whole range of services provided by, or for, the NHS, including pharmacists, opticians and dentists, as well as private hospitals and nursing homes if these are paid for by the NHS. The Ombudsman cannot, however, take up legal causes on a patient's behalf. Contacts are:

Health Service Ombudsman for England	0345 015 4033; website: www.ombudsman.org.uk
Health Service Ombudsman for Wales	01656 641 150; website: www.ombudsman-wales.org.uk.
Scottish Public Services Ombudsman	0800 377 7330; website: www.spso.org.uk

If you wish to make a complaint, there is a time limit. You should register complaints within 12 months of the incident or within 12 months of your realizing that you have reason for complaint. If you need further advice on the complaints procedure, contact the independent complaints advisory service, **POhWER:** 0300 456 2370; website: www.pohwer.net.

Rather than proceed through the formal channels described above, an alternative approach is to contact the independent advice centre that offers guidance to patients in the event of a problem with the health service, the **Patients Association:** 0845 608 4455; website: www.patients-association.com.

Useful reading

Your Guide to the NHS, obtainable from the Department of Health Publications Orderline: 0870 155 5455; website: www.dh.gov.uk.

Alternative medicine

Alternative medicine is dismissed by some doctors out of hand, while many patients claim that it is of great benefit. Here are some of the better-known organizations:

British Acupuncture Council (BAcC). Treatment, using fine needles, is claimed to be effective for a wide range of illnesses, including arthritis, rheumatism, high blood pressure and depression. For qualified acupuncture practitioners in your local area contact: 020 8735 0400; website: www.acupuncture.org.uk.

British Chiropractic Association. Practitioners specialize in mechanical disorders of the spine and joints and the effects on the nervous system. For a list of members in your area, contact: 0118 950 5950; website: www.chiropractic-uk.co.uk.

British Homeopathic Association. Homeopathy is essentially natural healing that follows the principle of looking at the whole person rather than just the illness. The Association can supply a list of practising GPs as well as the names and addresses of pharmacies that stock homeopathic medicines. Contact: 01582 408 675; website: www.trusthomeopathy.org.

British Hypnotherapy Association. Hypnotherapy may help people with phobias, emotional problems, anxiety, migraine, psoriasis or relationship difficulties. For details of the nearest registered trained hypnotherapist contact: 020 8579 5533; website: www.hypnotherapy-association.org.

Incorporated Society of Registered Naturopaths. Naturopaths are concerned about the underlying conditions that may cause illness, including, for example, diet, general fitness, posture, stress and the patient's mental outlook on life. Contact: 0131 664 3435; website: www.naturecuresociety.org.

National Institute of Medical Herbalists. The practice of herbal medicine aims to offer the sufferer not just relief from symptoms but an improved standard of general health and vitality. Contact: 01392 426 022; website: www.nimh.org.uk.

Osteopathic Information Service. Osteopathic treatment is often appropriate for those with back problems or with muscle or joint disorders. It can also provide pain relief from arthritis. Contact: 020 7357 6655; website: www.osteopathy.org.uk.

Wessex Healthy Living Centre is a non-profit-making registered charity which runs a clinic where all natural therapies are available under one roof. Contact: 01202 422 087; website: www.wessexhealthylivingcentre.org.

Eyes

It is advisable to have your sight checked at least every two years. Did you know that regular sight tests can pick up conditions such as glaucoma, cataract, macular degeneration, dry eye and inflammation of the cornea? But in addition they can also detect signs of other diseases including diabetes, hypertension (high blood pressure), thyroidtoxicosis, auto immune disorders, pituitary tumours, raised cholesterol and shingles.

You will qualify for a free NHS sight test if you are aged 60 and over; you live in Scotland, you or your partner receive income support, family credit, income based Job Seekers Allowance, Pension Credit Guarantee Credit and are entitled to or named on a valid NHS tax credit exemption certificate or are named on a valid HC2 certificate. For details, see leaflet HC11 – website: www.direct.gov.uk.

Even if you do not belong to any of these groups but are on a low income, you may be entitled to a free, or reduced-cost, sight test. To find out if you qualify for help, you should fill out claim form HC1, which you can get from social security or Jobcentre Plus offices – website: www.dwp.gov.uk.

People with mobility problems who are unable to get to an optician can ask for a domiciliary visit to have their eyes examined at home. This is free for those with an HC2 certificate or who are in receipt of one of the benefits listed above. People with a (partial help) HC3 certificate can use this towards the cost of a private home visit by their optician. The going rate for private sight tests if you do have to pay is about £25.

You do not need a doctor's referral to have your eyes tested. Whether you have to pay or not, the optician must either give you a prescription identifying what type of glasses you require or give you a statement confirming that you have no need of spectacles. The prescription is valid for two years. If you do not use it straight away, you should keep it safe so that it is handy when you need to use it. When you do decide to buy spectacles or contact lenses, you are under no obligation to obtain them from the optician who tested your eyes but can buy them where you like.

There is a voucher system for helping with the purchase of glasses or contact lenses. If you or your partner are in receipt of Income Support, income-based Jobseeker's Allowance or Pension Credit Guarantee Credit, you will receive an optical voucher, with a cash value. The amount you get will depend on your optical prescription. If you do not get any of the above benefits but are on a low income, you may still be entitled to help. To find out, fill in claim form HC1, as explained above; see websites: www.adviceguide.org.uk and www.dwp.gov.uk.

The voucher might be sufficient to pay for your contact lenses or spectacles outright, or it may make only a small contribution towards the cost. Part of the equation will depend on the frames you choose. You will not be tied to any particular glasses: you can choose spectacles that cost more than the value of the voucher and pay the difference yourself.

People who are registered blind are entitled to a special tax allowance of £1,890 a year. A great deal of practical help can be obtained by contacting the **Royal National Institute of Blind People (RNIB)**. In addition to giving general advice and information, it can supply a range of special equipment, details of which are listed in a free catalogue. Contact: 0303 123 9999; website: www.rnib.org.uk.

Do any of the following apply to you: Are you over 40? Do you have a family history of glaucoma? Are you short-sighted? Do you have diabetes? Are you of African-Caribbean origin? If the answer to any of these is yes, then you could be at risk. There are various types of glaucoma, but the most common is primary open angle glaucoma (POAG). It has no symptoms in the early stages but slowly and painlessly destroys sight if not detected and treated. For more information **The International Glaucoma Association** can help. Contact: 01233 64 81 64; website: www.glaucoma-association.com.

Many elderly people with failing sight suffer from macular degeneration, which affects their ability to distinguish detail. Although there is no known cure, individuals can be helped to make the most effective use of their sight by special magnifiers and other aids, such as clip-on lenses that fit over normal spectacles. Contact the **Partially Sighted Society:** 0844 477 4966; website: www.partsight.org.uk.

British Wireless for the Blind is a national independent charity, providing specially adapted radio sets. Nearly 1 million radio sets have been issued across the UK to blind and partially-sighted people in need. Sets are issued, repaired or replaced as necessary. Their mission is to keep blind people in touch with the world through radio. Contact: 01622 754 757; website: www.blind.org.uk.

It is worth knowing that all the main banks will provide statements in Braille; and Barclaycard now also issues credit card statements in Braille, on request. Additionally, several institutions offer large-print chequebooks or templates for chequebooks, as well as other facilities, such as a taped version of their annual report. There is no extra charge for these services.

Finally, **BT** has a free directory enquiry service for customers who cannot read or handle a phone book. To use the service you first need to register with BT, which will issue you with a personal identification number. Contact: 0800 800 150; website: www.bt.com/inclusion

Feet

Many people forget about their feet until they begin to give trouble. Corns and bunions, if neglected, can become extremely painful, and ideally everyone, especially women who wear high heels, should have podiatry treatment from early middle age or even younger. One of the problems of which podiatrists complain is that because many women wear uncomfortable shoes they become used to having painful feet and do not notice when something is more seriously wrong. The result can sometimes be ingrowing toenails or infections.

Podiatry is available on the National Health Service without referral from a doctor being necessary, but facilities tend to be very oversubscribed, so in many areas it is only the very elderly or those with a real problem who can get appointments.

The **Society of Chiropodists and Podiatrists,** which is the professional association for registered chiropodists and podiatrists, has information on its members. Contact: 020 7234 8620; website: www.feetforlife.org.

Hearing

A great many people suffer some deterioration in their sense of hearing as they age. Although eyes and teeth are routinely checked, hearing is often taken for granted. But it is one of the most important senses, and is responsible for safety and awareness; conversation and interaction; enjoyment and entertainment. Because hearing works 'invisibly', it isn't always given as much attention as it should. Changes happen so gradually, hearing loss can often go undetected. Signs to look out for:

- not hearing the doorbell or a telephone ring;
- turning up the television too loud for the comfort of others;
- not hearing people come into the room;
- misunderstanding what has been said;
- not speaking clearly or speaking in a monotonous tone;
- uncertainty about where sounds are coming from;
- difficulty in hearing at a distance or in public gatherings.

If you have noticed any of these, talk to your GP who may refer you to an audiologist or hearing care professional. They will be able to advise on the best course of action to help your hearing.

You can obtain a hearing aid and batteries free on the NHS or buy them privately. There are many other aids on the market that can make life easier. BT, for example, has a variety of special equipment for when a standard phone becomes too difficult to use. Contact: 0800 800 150 and ask for a free copy of *Communications Solutions;* website: www.bt.com/inclusion.

There are also a number of specialist organizations that can give you a lot of help, on hearing aids and on other matters:

British Deaf Association (BDA) works to protect the interests of deaf people and also provides an advice service through its regional offices. Contact: 02476 550 393; website: www.bda.org.uk.

British Tinnitus Association (BTA). Tinnitus is a condition that produces a sensation of noise, such as hissing or ringing, in the ears or head. The BTA helps to form self-help groups and provides information. Contact: 0800 018 0527; website: www.tinnitus.org.uk.

Hearing Concern LINK provides support and information to people with hearing loss, as well as their families. Contact: 01323 638 230; website: www.hearingconcernlink.org.

RNID publishes a comprehensive range of free leaflets and fact sheets for deaf and hard-of-hearing people. Titles include: *The Facts: Hearing Aids*; *The Facts: Losing Your Hearing* and *The Facts: Equipment*. Contact: 0808 808 0123. The charity also aims to promote hearing health, prevent hearing loss and cure deafness. Contact: 020 7296 8001; website: www.rnid.org.uk.

Friends and family can do a great deal to help those who are deaf or hard of hearing. One of the essentials is not to shout but to speak slowly and distinctly. You should always face the person, so he or she can see your lips, and avoid speaking with your hand over your mouth or when smoking. It could also be helpful if you, as well of course as deaf people themselves, were to learn British Sign Language. In case of real difficulty, you can always write down your message.

Teeth

Everyone knows the importance of having regular dental check-ups. Many adults, however, slip out of the habit, which could result in their having more trouble with their teeth as they become older. Dentistry is one of the treatments for which you have to pay under the NHS, unless you have a low income. If you or your partner are in receipt of Income Support, income-based Jobseeker's Allowance or Pension Credit, you are entitled to free NHS dental treatment. You may also receive some help if you are in receipt of the Working Tax Credit; for details, see leaflet HC11.

Even if you do not belong to any of these groups, you may still get some help if you have a low income. To find out if you qualify, fill in claim form HC1 (obtainable from social security or Jobcentre Plus offices, NHS hospitals and NHS dentists). To avoid any nasty surprises when the bill comes along, it is important to confirm with your dentist before he or she treats you whether you are being treated under the NHS. This also applies to the hygienist, should you need to see one. The best advice is to ask in advance what the cost of your treatment is likely to be.

Help with the cost is all very well, but for many an even bigger problem than money is the difficulty of finding an NHS dentist in their area. The best advice is to call the British Dental Health Foundation's helpline (see below) or, if you are thinking of going private, ask friends and acquaintances for recommendations.

For those who like to be able to budget ahead for any dental bills, **Denplan** could be of interest. It offers two plans: Denplan Care, which for a fixed monthly fee entitles you to all routine and restorative treatment including crowns and bridges; and Denplan Essentials, for a lower monthly fee covers just normal routine care including examinations, X-rays and hygienists' visits. In both cases, patients' actual monthly fees are calculated by their own dentist after an initial assessment of their oral health. Registration must be with a Denplan member dentist, but as around a third of UK dentists participate this should not be a problem. Contact: 01962 828 000; website: www.denplan.co.uk.

Prevention is always better than cure. If you want free, independent and impartial advice on all aspects of oral health and free literature on a wide range of topics, including patients' rights, finding a dentist and dental care for older people, contact the **British Dental Health Foundation**: 0845 063 1188; website: www.dentalhealth.org.uk.

Personal relationships

Retirement, for couples, involves a major lifestyle change. With it comes fresh opportunities, and inevitably, a few compromises are needed. Many women continue to work once their husbands retire. Couples can sometimes find it difficult to adjust to spending longer together while others may feel they have little left in common. There has been a recent increase in the over-60s divorce rate so it is important in the early stages of retirement that couples work out the best way of living out their retirement together. Normally, with goodwill and understanding on both sides, difficulties are quickly resolved to allow the relationship to flourish. However, for some couples it does not work out so easily, and it may be helpful to seek skilled guidance:

Albany Trust offers counselling for people facing change and with difficulties in relationships, depression or psychosexual problems. Contact: 020 8767 1827; website: www.albanytrust.org.

Marriage Care offers a similar service, plus a confidential telephone helpline, for those who are having problems with their marriage or other close personal relationship. Contact: 020 7371 1341; website: www.marriagecare.org.uk, or **Scottish Marriage Care**: 0845 271 2711; website: www.scottishmarriagecare.org.

Relate offers a counselling service to people who are experiencing difficulties in their marriage or other personal relationships. Sometimes couples come together; sometimes either the husband or the wife comes alone. Each counselling centre operates an independent pricing policy, and counsellors will discuss with clients what they can reasonably contribute. Contact **Relate England**: 0300 100 1234; website: www.relate.org.uk; **Relate Scotland**: 0845 119 2020; website: www.relatescotland.org.uk.

Help for grandparents

A sad result of today's divorce statistics is the risk to grandparents of losing contact with their grandchildren. While some divorcing parents lean over backwards to avoid this happening, others – maybe through force of circumstance or hurt feelings – deny grandparents access or even sever the relationship completely.

Recourse to the law is never a step to be taken lightly and should obviously be avoided if there is the possibility that a more conciliatory approach could be successful. An organization that has considerable experience of advising grandparents and that can also offer a mediation service in London, as well as practical help and support with legal formalities, is the **Grandparents' Association**. Contact: 0845 434 9585; website: www.grandparents-association.org.uk.

There is another association, **BeGrand.net – the website for grandparents,** which has been created especially for grandparents. Being a grandparent can be rewarding but it is not always easy. If you are worried that your children aren't making the right decisions for your grandchildren, or just concerned that you might not be seeing enough of them, this website is for you. It has articles on everything to do with grandparenting and information about benefits and rights. Online advisers give free confidential advice on issues that affect grandparents and there is an online community where grandparents can share ideas and talk about things that matter. To find out more, contact: 0845 434 6835; website: www.BeGrand.net.

Depression

Depression is a condition that is often akin to problems in a marriage and other personal crises. A number of retired people find it develops as a result of loneliness, boredom or general lack of purpose. Usually people manage to deal with it alone. If the condition persists for more than a few days, a doctor should always be consulted, as depression can create sleeping difficulties.

Another reason for consulting a doctor is that depression may be due to being physically run down. If you've recently suffered from flu, maybe all that is required is a good tonic – or perhaps a holiday. Sometimes, however, depression persists. In these cases it may be that, rather than medicines or the stimulus of a new activity, individuals need to talk to someone. There are several organizations that may be able to help:

Depression Alliance offers assistance to anyone affected by depression. As well as a nationwide network of groups where individuals can meet to provide mutual support, the Depression Alliance has a pen friend scheme. Contact: 0845 123 23 20; website: www.depressionalliance.org.

Mind (The National Association for Mental Health) works for a better life for people with experience of mental distress. It has offices in England and Wales and more than 200 local associations that offer a wide range of special facilities and services, including housing with care, day centres, social clubs, advocacy and self-help groups. Contact: 0845 766 0163; website: www.mind.org.uk.

Samaritans are available at any time of the day or night, every single day of the year. They are there to talk or listen for as long as an individual needs or wants to be able to speak to another person. You do not need to feel actively suicidal before contacting the Samaritans; if you are simply depressed, they will equally welcome your call. Contact: 08457 90 90 90; website: www.samaritans.org.

Sane is a mental health charity which, in addition to initiating and funding research, operates a helpline to give individuals in need of emotional support or practical information the help they require. Contact: 0845 767 8000; website: www.sane.org.uk.

Some common afflictions

You may be one of the lucky ones and the rest of this chapter will be of no further interest to you. It deals with some of the more common afflictions, such as back pain and heart disease, as well as with disability. However, if you are unfortunate enough to be affected, or have a member of your family who is, then knowing which organizations can provide support could make all the difference in helping you to cope.

Aphasia

Aphasia is a condition that makes it hard to speak, read or understand language. It typically affects individuals after a stroke or a head injury. **Speakability (Action for Dysphasic Adults)** is the national charity offering information and support to people with aphasia, their families and their carers. Contact: 080 8808 9572; website: www.speakability.org.uk.

Arthritis and rheumatism

Although arthritis is often thought of as an older person's complaint, it accounts for the loss of an estimated 70 million working days a year in Britain.

Arthritis Care is a registered charity working with, and for, people with arthritis. It encourages self-help and has over 400 local branches offering practical support and social activities. Contact: 0808 800 4050; website: www.arthritiscare.org.uk.

Arthritis Research is the charity leading the fight against arthritis. For further information contact: 01246 558 033; website: www.arthritisresearchuk.org.

Back pain

Four out of five people suffer from back pain at some stage of their lives. While there are many different causes, doctors agree that much of the trouble could be avoided through correct posture, care in lifting heavy articles, a firm mattress, and chairs that provide support in the right places. The following two organizations could be helpful:

The Back Shop is a shop and mail-order business that sells ergonomically approved products that help prevent back trouble or may provide relief for those who suffer. Contact: 020 7935 9120; website: www.thebackshop.co.uk.

BackCare is a registered charity that funds research into the causes and treatment of back pain and also publishes a range of leaflets and fact sheets to help back pain sufferers. It has local branches around the country that organize talks, lectures and exercise classes, as well as social activities and fund-raising events. Contact: 0845 130 2704; website: www.backcare.org.uk.

Blood pressure

Unlike most illnesses or diseases, high blood pressure can be symptomless. Yet it is the leading cause of strokes in the UK and can lead to heart attack and heart failure. One in three adults has high blood pressure but a third of those will be completely unaware of it. Anyone over the age of 50 should keep a check on their blood pressure as it tends to rise with age. Post-menopausal women also see an increase in their blood pressure. The good news is that blood pressure can be successfully managed with medication and some simple lifestyle changes. In brief:

- watch your salt intake;
- eat at least five portions of fruit and vegetables per day;
- watch your weight;
- cut down on alcohol;
- take regular exercise;
- laughter – watch a funny movie;
- be sociable – lonely people are more likely to suffer from high blood pressure.

The **Blood Pressure Association** can provide more help and information. Contact: 0845 241 0989; website: www.bpassoc.org.uk.

Cancer

Cancer is now a subject that is often discussed openly, and with continuing research and improved treatments many people make a complete recovery. Early diagnosis can make a vital difference. Doctors recommend that all women should undergo regular screening for cervical cancer, and women over 50 are advised to have a routine mammography to screen for breast cancer at least once every three years.

Computerized cervical screening systems for women aged 25 to 64 and breast cancer screening units for women aged 50 to 70 are available nationwide. In both cases, older women can have access to the services on request. It also goes without saying that anyone with a lump or swelling, however small, should waste no time in having it investigated by a doctor. There are a number of excellent support groups for cancer sufferers:

Bowel Cancer UK aims to save lives by raising awareness of bowel cancer, campaigning for best treatment and care, and providing practical support and advice. For information about the symptoms and risks of bowel cancer and advice on how to take preventative steps to help reduce your risk of the disease, contact: 0800 840 3540; website: www.bowelcanceruk.org.uk.

Breast Cancer Care offers practical advice, information and emotional support to women who have, or fear they have, breast cancer or benign breast disease. Its services include a helpline, free leaflets, a prosthesis-fitting service, and one-to-one support from volunteers who have themselves experienced breast cancer or whose partner has been affected. Contact: 0808 800 6000; website: www.breastcancercare.org.uk.

Macmillan Cancer Support offers a free and confidential telephone information service to help people affected by cancer. Calls are answered by a qualified nurse who has the time, knowledge and understanding to answer your questions and listen to how you may be feeling. Contact: 0808 808 00 00; website: www.macmillan.org.uk.

Chest and heart diseases

The earlier sections on smoking, diet, drink and exercise list some of the most pertinent 'dos and don'ts' that can help prevent heart disease. The advice is not to be taken lightly. Latest statistics reveal that UK death rates from coronary heart disease are among the highest in the world, killing almost 120,000 people a year and responsible for one in five of all deaths. Although people tend to think of heart attacks as particularly affecting men, over four times as many women die from heart disease as from breast cancer. In an effort to reduce the casualty rate, the **British Heart Foundation** publishes a range of 'help yourself' booklets, designed to create greater awareness of how heart disease can best be prevented through healthy living. Contact: 0300 330 3311; website: www.bhf.org.uk.

Diabetes

Diabetes occurs when the amount of glucose in the blood is too high for the body to use properly. It can sometimes be treated by diet alone; sometimes pills or insulin may also be needed. Diabetes can be diagnosed at any age, although it is common in the elderly and especially among individuals who are overweight. **Diabetes UK** aims to improve the lives of people with diabetes. Contact: 0207 424 1000; website: www.diabetes.org.uk.

Migraine

Migraine affects over 10 million people in the UK. It can involve severe head pains, nausea, vomiting, visual disturbances and in some cases temporary paralysis. The **Migraine Trust** funds and promotes research, holds international symposia and runs an extensive support service. Contact: 020 7462 6601; website: www.migrainetrust.org.

Osteoporosis and menopause problems

Osteoporosis is a disease affecting bones, which become so fragile that they can break very easily, with injuries most common in the spine, hip and wrist. It affects one in two women (and one in five men) and often develops following the menopause, when body levels of oestrogen naturally decrease. The following may be useful:

Menopause Exchange produces a quarterly newsletter and number of fact sheets with the aim of providing reliable and easily understood information about the menopause and other health issues of concern to women in mid-life. Contact: 020 8420 7245; website: www.menopause-exchange.co.uk.

National Osteoporosis Society offers help, support and advice on all aspects of osteoporosis. There is a medical helpline staffed by specialist nurses, a range of leaflets and booklets, and also a network of over 120 local support groups throughout the UK. Contact: 0845 450 0230; website: www.nos.org.uk.

Women's Health Concern (WHC) provides an independent service to advise, reassure and educate women about their health concerns, to enable them to work in partnership with their own medical practitioners and health advisers. Contact: 01628 478 473; website: www.womens-health-concern.org.

Stroke

Over 130,000 people suffer a stroke every year in England and Wales. A stroke is a brain injury caused by the sudden interruption of blood flow. It is unpredictable in its effects, which may include muscular paralysis or weakness on one side, loss of speech or loss of understanding or language, visual problems or incontinence. Prevention is similar to the prevention of heart disease.

The **Stroke Association** works to prevent strokes and helps stroke patients and their families. It produces a range of publications and provides advice and welfare grants to individuals through its London office and regional centres. Its Community Services, Dysphasia Support and Family Support help stroke sufferers through home visits, and over 400 stroke clubs provide social and therapeutic support. Contact: 0303 303 3100; website: www.stroke.org.uk.

Disability

Disability is mainly covered in Chapter 15, Caring for Elderly Parents, so if you or someone in your family has a problem you may find the answer you need there. In this section, there are simply one or two points that may be useful for younger people.

Local authority services

Social services departments (social work departments in Scotland) provide many of the services that people with disabilities may need, including:

- practical help in the home, perhaps with the support of a home help;
- adaptations to your home, such as a ramp for a wheelchair or other special equipment for your safety;
- meals on wheels;
- provision of day centres, clubs and similar;
- the issue of badges for cars driven or used by people with a disability (in some authorities this is handled by the works department or by the residents' parking department);
- advice about other transport services or concessions that may be available locally.

In most instances, you should speak to a social worker, who will either be able to make the arrangements or point you in the right direction. He or she will also be able to tell you of any special facilities or other help provided by the authority.

Occupational therapists, who can advise about special equipment and help teach someone with a disability through training and exercise how best to manage, also come within the orbit of the social services department.

Health care

Services are normally arranged through either a GP or the local authority health centre. Key professional staff include:

- health visitors (who are qualified nurses), who rather like social workers will be able to put you in touch with whatever specialized services are required;
- district nurses, who will visit patients in their home;
- physiotherapists, who use exercise and massage to help improve mobility, for example after an operation;
- medical social workers, employed in hospitals, who will help with any arrangements before a patient is discharged.

Council Tax

If someone in your family has a disability, you may be able to claim a reduction on your Council Tax. If you have a blue badge on your car, you may get a rebate for a garage. You would normally apply to the housing benefits officer, but different councils employ different officers to deal with this; see website: www.dwp.gov.uk.

Chapter Fourteen
Holidays

When you travel, remember that a foreign country is not designed to make you comfortable. It is designed to make its own people comfortable. CLIFTON FADIMAN (1904–1999)

Holidays are big business, particularly for the over-50s. Baby boomers are largely responsible for driving the travel industry out of recession because there are millions of them, and they have the time and money to take trips when and where they choose. Once you have retired, you no longer need to plan months ahead in order to fit in with colleagues. You can avoid peak periods, which are usually more expensive and crowded. You can enjoy flexibility that is impossible while you are working. A great thing about retirement is the availability of concessionary prices. You can research cheaper fares and reduced charges for hotel accommodation.

The fact that you've retired makes very little difference to what you do or where you go. Many people combine holidays with a special interest, such as painting or music. There is ample opportunity for you to enrol for summer school, exchange homes with someone in another country or sign on for a working holiday, such as voluntary conservation activity or home- and pet-sitting, for which you get paid. The choice is enormous. If you wish to go somewhere exotic, it is likely the prices will be high. But some holidays can be extremely reasonable in cost. Whether you are fit and active or require special care, there are plenty of options. Retirement is a time for experimentation, so don't be afraid to try something different.

For ease of reference, entries are listed under sub headings, for example 'Arts and crafts', 'Sport', 'Self-catering and other low-budget holidays'. To avoid repetition, the majority are featured only once in the most logical place. There is a general information section with brief details about insurance, concessionary fares and other travel tips at the end of the chapter.

Website addresses and contact numbers are as up to date as possible at the time of going to press.

Art appreciation

Many tour operators, clubs and other organizations that arrange group holidays include visits to museums, churches and other venues of artistic interest along with their other activities such as walking, bridge and general sightseeing. Alternatively, if you enjoy the performing arts, you could spend several glorious days attending some of the music and drama festivals held in many parts of the country, as well as some of the famous festivals overseas.

> **Specialtours** arranges accompanied cultural tours in association with numerous organizations, including the Art Fund. Contact: 020 7386 4690; website: www.specialtours.co.uk.

> **Kirker Holidays** has been organizing carefully crafted tailor-made short breaks to Europe and beyond for nearly 25 years. Over 140 destinations are featured with particular emphasis on art, architecture, gardens, archaeology, history and music, including opera holidays and escorted tours to Europe's leading music festivals and events. Contact: 020 7593 2284; website: www.kirkerholidays.com.

Festivals

There is a feast of music, drama and the arts. The most famous festivals in the UK are those held at Edinburgh and Aldeburgh. Over the years the number of festivals has been growing, and are now a regular feature in many parts of the country. To find out what is going on where, contact the Arts Council or your regional Arts Council office. Look in the national press or search the internet for lists of major festivals at home and overseas.

> **Aldeburgh Music,** world-renowned as an outstanding year-round performance centre, has a varied programme of classical and contemporary music. There are also exhibitions, talks, walks and films. Contact: 01728 687 100; website: www.aldeburgh.co.uk.

> **Edinburgh International Festival** is held every August. Details of music, theatre, dance, opera and other events are available from early April. For further information see website: www.edinburghfestivals.co.uk.

Three Choirs Festival is the oldest classical music festival in Europe, originating in the early 1700s. It takes place in August each year by rotation in the Cathedral cities of Gloucester, Hereford and Worcester. Choral music at its best, in a quintessentially English setting. Contact: 0845 652 1823; website: www.3choirs.org.

Arts and crafts

The focus is on taking courses or just participating for pleasure, rather than viewing the works of others. Further suggestions are also given in Chapter 9, Leisure Activities.

Benslow Music Trust provides exciting opportunities for music making and appreciation, with a year-round programme of weekend and midweek courses for adult amateur musicians of all standards. The programme includes chamber music, choral and solo singing, music appreciation, beginner courses, jazz, solo and ensemble wind, orchestras, big band and early music. Contact: 01462 459 446; website: www.benslow.org.

The Crafts Council aims to position the UK as the global centre for the making, seeing and collecting of contemporary craft. This is a growing industry and contributes to the UK's reputation as a world leader in creativity. Contact: 020 7806 2500; website: www.craftscouncil.org.uk.

West Dean College, housed in a beautiful mansion surrounded by landscaped gardens and parkland, organizes short residential courses in contemporary and traditional crafts, the visual arts, photography, music and gardening – variously lasting from one to seven days. There are also full-time diploma programmes all of which are validated by the University of Sussex. Contact: 01243 811 301; website: www.westdean.org.uk.

Coach holidays

Some coach companies organize holidays, as distinct from simply offering a mode of transport. Before embarking on a lengthy coach tour, try a few shorter excursions to see how you cope with the journey.

National Express is Britain's largest scheduled coach service provider in the UK. It operates to 1,000 destinations and carries over 16 million customers a year. Passengers aged 60-plus, or who are registered disabled, travel for half-price, but this does not include any hotel costs. Contact: 08717 818 181; website: www.nationalexpress.com.

Historical holidays

Holidays with a particular focus on history are becoming increasingly popular.

Holts Tours – Battlefields & History offers a choice of over 40 battlefield, historical and archaeological tours throughout the world. All are accompanied by a specialist guide-lecturer, and local experts are also used. Most tours are half-board in good-standard hotels with private facilities. Special group tours can be arranged. Contact: 01293 865 000; website: www.holts.co.uk.

Kentwell Hall offers a glimpse into both past and present of this unique house if you visit during one of the award-winning recreations of Tudor, Victorian or WWII everyday life. Kentwell pioneered domestic living history events in the UK. Contact: 01787 310 207; website: www.kentwell.co.uk.

Mike Hodgson Battlefield Tours has over 25 years' experience in organizing guided coach tours for small groups (about 25 people) to visit European battlefields. For details of available tours see website. Contact: 01526 342 249; website: www.mhbattlefieldtours.co.uk.

Should you wish to visit a particular grave, the **Commonwealth War Graves Commission** will help you identify the exact location. Contact: 01628 634 221; website: www.cwgc.org.

Poppy Travel is the official travel division of The Royal British Legion. It has been providing uniquely personalized and memorable journeys of remembrance since 1927. Its worldwide programme of 65 fully escorted Remembrance and Battlefield Tours to 28 countries spans 250 years of British and Commonwealth history. Contact: 01622 716 729; website: www.poppytravel.org.uk.

Language courses

If you are hoping to travel more when you retire, being able to speak the language when abroad will greatly add to your enjoyment. The quickest and easiest way to learn is in the country itself. There are attractive opportunities for improving your French, German, Italian, Spanish and even Japanese.

British Institute of Florence is situated in the historic centre of Florence, offering courses in Italian language and art history as well as in life drawing, watercolour painting, Tuscan cooking and Italian opera. A regular programme of events including lectures, concerts and films is held in the Institute's library overlooking the River Arno. Contact: 00 39 055 267 781; website: www.britishinstitute.it.

Goethe-Institut London offers a variety of German-language courses, from beginners to examination level, at 16 centres in Germany. The instruction is designed so that you can follow from one level to another in all centres. Contact: 020 7596 4000; website: www.goethe.de.

Instituto Cervantes provides courses for studying Spanish in London and also discovering the cultures of Spain and Latin America. Contact: 0207 235 0353; website: www.londres.cervantes.es.

Other people's homes

Living in someone else's home free is one of the cheapest ways of enjoying a holiday. There are two ways of doing this: exchange your home with another person in this country or abroad, or become a home-sitter and mind someone else's property while they are away.

Home exchange

Exchanges are normally arranged direct between the two parties concerned, who agree the terms between themselves. Some people even exchange their cars and pets. Here are some organizations that may be useful:

Home Base Holidays operates an international home exchange agency. Accommodation varies from small city apartments to large country homes complete with swimming pool. Your own exchange offer is included on the website, and you can search the other homes registered on the site. Contact: 020 8886 8752; website: www.homebase-hols.com.

HomeLink International offers around 14,000 home exchange possibilities in nearly 70 countries. Register, and your home is included on the website with a photo and is entered in the twice-yearly directory. Contact: 01962 886 882; website: www.homelink.org.uk.

Home-sitting

Retired people are generally considered ideal home-sitters: you provide a caretaking service and get paid for doing so. Duties variously involve light housework, plant watering, care of pets and sometimes tending the garden. First-class references are required.

Absentia sitters variously offer a holiday care service, provide long-term specialized care (as, for example, when a property is vacant during probate) or care for a home and any pets if owners have to go into hospital. Pay varies, depending on duties. Contact: 01279 777 412; website: www.home-and-pets.co.uk.

Homesitters are looking for mature, responsible people who are non-smokers with no children or pets and have their own car. Payment rates vary depending on responsibilities. The houses can be anything from a city centre apartment to an isolated country mansion. Contact: 01296 630 730; website: www.homesitters.co.uk.

Universal Aunts organize a home- and pet-sitting service for absent owners. All applicants for the home-sitters' panel are interviewed before acceptance. Contact: 020 7738 8937; website: www.universalaunts.co.uk.

Overseas travel

Many big tour operators make a feature of offering special holidays designed for the over-55s. Also included here are companies that specialize in arranging cruises and packaged motoring holidays, and information on timesharing.

Explore Worldwide arranges more than 400 tours to over 130 countries. Accommodation varies from camping to modest hotels and rustic lodges. Contact: 0845 013 1537; website: www.explore.co.uk.

Relais du Silence is a French group of independently owned hotels with a network of about 230 hotels throughout Europe, including Britain. It offers tranquil, rural settings in two-, three- and four-star comfort at reasonable prices, with good food and a family-like atmosphere. Contact: 0033 1 44 49 90 00; website: www.relaisdusilence.com.

Saga Holidays are exclusively for people aged 50 and over. There is a large range of options worldwide including, among others, ocean and river cruising (including Saga's own cruise ships, *Saga Rose* and *Saga Ruby*), safaris, short- and long-stay resort holidays and multi-centre tours. There is also a selection of special interest holidays. Contact: 01303 774 176; website: www.saga.co.uk/travel.

Cruises

Some 1.5 million people in the UK take a cruise holiday every year and that figure is expected to rise to 2 million by 2012. Cruise operators have been making cruising more accessible, exciting, varied and affordable. **The Leading Cruise Agents** have their own website: www.thelca.com, or contact: 0870 122 5511. The following are also recommended:

Fred Olsen Cruise Lines	01473 746 175; website: www.fredolsencruises.com
NCL (Norwegian Cruise Line)	0845 201 8912; website: www.ncl.co.uk
P&O Cruises	0845 678 0014; website: www.pocruises.com
Page & Moy	0844 567 6633; website: www.pageandmoy.com
Princess Cruises	0845 3555 800; website: www.princess.com

Cargo ship cruises

If price is one of the main considerations, travelling via cargo ship could be the solution. Accommodation and facilities (there is often a swimming pool) vary according to the size and type of vessel. A few of the best are:

Andrew Weir Cruises	020 7575 6000; website: www.aws.co.uk
Cargo Ship Voyages	0800 804 7086; website: www.cargoshipvoyages.co.uk
Strand Voyages	020 7921 4340; website: www.strandtravel.co.uk

Motoring holidays abroad

A number of organizations, including in particular some ferry operators, offer packages for the motorist that include ferry crossings, accommodation and insurance. While these often provide very good value, some people prefer to make all their own arrangements in order to get exactly what they want.

Automobile Association (AA) offers several helpful products and services for motoring at home and abroad, including route planning, maps, AA Five Star Europe Breakdown Assistance and travel guides. Contact: 0870 600 0371; website: www.theaa.com.

Brittany Ferries offers short-break holidays in France and Spain including accommodation, breakfast and return car ferry crossings. There is also a selection of gite holidays in France. Contact: 0871 244 0744; website: www.brittany-ferries.co.uk.

RAC Motoring Services offers a range of overseas single trip or annual travel insurance, plus international driving permits, camping cards and other essential documents in addition to roadside assistance. Contact: 08705 722 722; website: www.rac.co.uk.

Tips when motoring abroad

- Have your car thoroughly serviced before you go.
- Take the following with you: a tool kit, the manual for your car, a rented spares kit, a fuel can, a mechanic's light that plugs into the cigarette lighter socket, at least one extra set of keys, and any extras required by local laws such as a reflective tabard and warning triangles.
- Always lock your car and park it in a secure place overnight (nearly 75 per cent of luggage thefts abroad are from cars).
- Unless you are taking one of the packages that include insurance, you should contact your insurance company or broker well ahead of time

to arrange special insurance cover. Contact either the AA or the RAC overseas travel department. Both have facilities for helping you if you become stranded, and welcome non-members.

Other sources of advice and services are:

Association of British Insurers	020 7600 3333; website: www.abi.org.uk
Europ Assistance	0800 138 2468; website: www.europ-assistance.co.uk
Green Flag	0845 246 2766; website: www.greenflag.com

Advice from seasoned travellers is to have information about garages, spare parts and the legal rules of the country, or countries, through which you are driving. The requirements – and documents you need to carry – are not the same for all European countries, and failure to have the right bond, special permit or spares could mean a fine, or even imprisonment.

If your main purpose in taking your car is to enjoy the freedom it offers when you reach your destination, rather than the journey itself, it is worth looking at the Motorail facilities to Southern France and Italy and the long-range ferries to Spain and Portugal, which save on wear and tear and may be no more expensive than the extra cost of petrol plus overnight stays.

If, instead of taking your own car, you plan to hire a vehicle overseas, you will probably have to buy special insurance at the time of hiring the vehicle. Make sure that this is properly comprehensive (check for any excesses or exclusions) and that at the very least it gives you adequate third-party cover. If in any doubt, you would be recommended to seek advice from the local motoring organization as to the essential requirements, including any foreign words or terms you particularly need to understand before signing.

Short breaks

Many organizations offer short-break holidays all year round, with special bargain prices in spring and autumn. British hotels have winter breaks from November to April, and overseas travel operators slash prices during the off-peak seasons. Advertisements on TV, in the press and on the internet give the latest offers.

Timesharing

Timesharing is an investment in long-term holidays. The idea is that you buy the use of a property for a specific number of days each year, either for an agreed term or in perpetuity. Your timeshare can be lent to other people, sublet or left eventually in your will. Most timeshare schemes allow you to swap your week(s) for one in other developments throughout the world for your annual holiday, via one of the exchange companies.

A week's timeshare will vary in price – from £8,000 to over £50,000 depending on the location, the size of the property, the time of year and the facilities of the resort. Maintenance charges could cost another £250-plus a week, and you should always check that these are linked to some form of cost-of-living index such as the RPI. Another useful point to check is that there is an owners' association linked to the property.

While the great majority of people enjoy very happy experiences, stories about unscrupulous operators still occur. You should beware timeshare scratch cards and fraudulent holiday clubs that are not protected by the Timeshare Directive. Also be wary of such enticing promotional gifts as a 'free' holiday flight to visit the property. You might also like to check whether the operator is a member of the Resort Development Organization.

Thanks to the 1994 Timeshare Directive, all EU member countries must provide a 10-day minimum cooling-off period and a full prospectus to residents of EU member countries in their own language. In the UK, there is now also a ban on timeshare providers taking a deposit during the cooling-off period. Among the terms you need to be especially careful about are the future management and maintenance charges and the potential resale value of a property.

The **Resort Development Organization (RDO)** is the regulatory body dedicated to promoting the interests of all with a legitimate involvement in the industry. It offers potential buyers free advice and information and also has an arbitration scheme, run in conjunction with the Chartered Institute of Arbitrators, to handle complaints that are not resolved through its standard complaints-handling procedure. Website: www.rdo.org. Most reputable companies belong to one of two worldwide exchange organizations:

RCI Europe	0845 60 86 363; website: www.rci.com
Interval International Ltd	0844 701 4444; website: www.intervalworld.com

Existing owners wishing to sell their property should be on their guard against unknown resale agents contacting them 'on spec' and offering, in exchange for a registration fee, to act on their behalf. While some may be legitimate, the RDO has received complaints about so-called 'agents' taking money and doing nothing further. A telephone call to the RDO will establish whether the company is a member body. If not, leave well alone.

Holiday Property Bond

Although it has been in existence for more than 25 years, the **Holiday Property Bond** remains one of the best kept secrets in the holiday industry. It is a uniquely flexible alternative to fixed-week time share and villa ownership. The Bond is a life assurance bond that invests, after initial charges, in a combination of securities and carefully chosen holiday properties throughout the UK and Europe. By securing a financial interest in HPB's entire portfolio of villas, cottages and apartments, Bondholders and their family and friends are entitled to use any Bond property at any time – rent free. (It is a privilege that can be passed on, without charge, to their children and grandchildren too.) To request your free DVD or information pack, contact: 0800 230 0391; website: www.hpb.co.uk.

Retreats

If peace and quiet is what you seek when you are on holiday, a retreat might be the answer. The **Retreat Association** gives details of 240 retreat centres in Britain and Ireland, together with its programmes. Contact: 01494 433 094; website: www.retreats.org.uk.

Self-catering and other low-budget holidays

If you cannot quite manage to survive on a tenner a day, some of the suggestions in this section need hardly cost you much more. Camping, caravanning or renting very simple accommodation with friends as well as farm cottages, hostels, university accommodation and other rentals of varying degrees of sparseness or comfort are listed here:

Camping and Caravanning Club: 0845 130 7632; website: www.campingandcaravanningclub.co.uk.

English Country Cottages: 0845 268 0785; website: www.english-country-cottages.co.uk.

Farm Stay UK Ltd: 024 7669 6909; website: www.farmstayuk.co.uk.

Holiday Cottages in Scotland: 01738 451 610; website: www.scottish-holiday-cottages.co.uk.

Landmark Trust restores historic buildings and lets them for holidays, ranging from castles, timber and thatched cottages and moated properties, to towers and follies. Contact: 01628 825 925; website: www.landmarktrust.org.uk.

Lee Abbey is a holiday, retreat and conference centre, run by a Christian community, set in a 280-acre coastal estate. There is a Christian content to the holidays and there are reductions for clergy and their families. Contact: 01598 752 621; website: www.leeabbey.org.uk.

National Trust Holiday Cottages has a wide variety of holiday cottages and flats in many areas of England, Wales and Northern Ireland. Contact: 0844 800 2070; website: www.nationaltrustcottages.co.uk.

National Trust for Scotland has a large number of holiday cottages available in all areas, as well as cruises. Contact: 0844 493 2108; website: www.nts.org.uk.

Venuemasters is a consortium of university and college venues that let residential accommodation during the vacation periods and some other times of the year. Contact: 0114 249 3090; website: www.venuemasters.co.uk.

Villas4you offers a large range of self-catering holidays in France, Italy, Sicily, Spain, Majorca, Portugal and New England. Contact: 0845 604 3877; website: www.villas4you.co.uk.

YHA (England and Wales) Ltd welcomes people of all ages. There are over 200 youth hostels in England and Wales and over 4,000 worldwide. Overnight prices vary according to the location and facilities. Contact: 01629 592 700; website: www.yha.org.uk.

Special interest holidays

This section includes weekend courses and more formal summer schools, between them offering a huge variety of subjects including crafts, computer studies, drama, archaeology, creative writing, photography and many others. It also includes holidays in the more conventional sense, both in Britain and abroad, but with the accent on a hobby such as bridge, dancing, yoga, photography, antiques and other pastimes. Many of the organizations offer a wide range of choices.

Centre for Alternative Technology features interactive displays and working examples of sustainable living, renewable energy, environmentally responsible building and organic gardening. Short residential courses are held frequently, ranging from two to five days, and subjects covered include renewable energy systems, organic gardening, environmental building and green sanitation. Contact: 01654 705 981; website: www.cat.org.uk.

City & Guilds offers special interest day, weekend and summer school courses at many colleges and universities throughout the country. Contact: 0844 543 0000; website: www.cityandguilds.com.

Denman College is the WI's residential adult education college. It runs over 500 short courses each year that are open to both WI and non-members. Courses cover art, antiques, IT, dance, drama, literature, crafts, aromatherapy and many others. Contact: 01865 391 991; website: www.thewi.org.uk.

Earnley Concourse is a residential centre near Chichester that holds weekend and week-long courses throughout the year on such subjects as arts and crafts, music, wildlife, computer studies, keep fit, yoga and others. Contact: 01243 670 392; website: www.earnley.co.uk.

Field Studies Council (FSC) offers over 600 leisure and special interest courses at its 14 centres throughout the UK. Centres are based in the Lake District, Yorkshire Dales, Snowdonia, Shropshire, Pembrokeshire, Exmoor, South Devon, Suffolk, the North Downs, Epping Forest, County Fermanagh and the Scottish Highlands. Contact: 0845 345 4071; website: www.field-studies-council.org.

HF Holidays Ltd offers walking and special interest holidays in a wide range of locations throughout Britain and abroad. The choice includes golf, bridge, bowls, ballroom dancing, yoga, painting, photography, music making and birdwatching. Contact: 0845 470 7558; website: www.hfholidays.co.uk.

Mercian Travel Centre Ltd specializes in arranging bridge and bowling holidays to over 15 countries throughout the world, lasting from four nights to a fortnight and also arranges a wide choice of cruises. Contact: 01562 883 795; website: www.merciantravel.co.uk.

The Peak District National Park Centre for Environmental Learning offers weekend and week-long special interest breaks, including painting and illustration, natural history, birdwatching, navigation, photography and rambling at Losehill Hall. Contact: 01433 620 373; website: www.peakdistrict.gov.uk.

Vegi-Ventures is a holiday tour company that specializes in catering for vegetarians, offering an attractive range of destinations in Britain, Europe and wider afield. Accommodation is chosen very much with the food in mind; destinations range from relaxing to challenging. Contact: 01760 755 888; website: www.vegiventures.com.

Sport

Holidays with on-site or nearby sporting facilities exist all over the country. The list that follows is limited to organizations that can advise you about organized residential courses or can offer facilities. For wider information, see Chapter 9, Leisure Activities, which lists some of the national sports associations.

Sportscotland runs three national sports centres that offer courses for all levels in sports such as golf, hill-walking, skiing and sailing. Contact: 0141 534 6500; website: www.sportscotland.org.uk.

Boating

Blakes Holiday Boating offers holiday boating throughout all the main waterways of Britain and also in France and Ireland. Basic boating tuition is provided for novices. Contact: 0845 604 3985; website: www.blakes.co.uk.

Hoseasons Boating Holidays. Choose from the Norfolk Broads, the Cambridgeshire waterways, the Thames, and the canals of England, Scotland and Wales, as well as boating holidays in France, Belgium, Holland, Italy and Ireland. Contact: 0844 847 1356; website: www.hoseasons.co.uk.

Phoenix Holidays are dedicated River Cruise professionals who use their experience to offer quality river cruise holidays along Europe's waterways. Modern ships with air conditioning, outside cabins and en suite facilities. Contact: 08444 129 900; website: www.phoenixholidays.co.uk.

Royal Yachting Association (RYA) can supply a list of recognized schools that offer approved courses in sailing, windsurfing, motor cruising and power boating. Contact: 023 8060 4100; website: www.rya.org.uk.

Cycling

CTC organizes cycling tours in Britain and overseas and can also provide a great deal of extremely helpful information for cyclists wishing to arrange their own holiday, including advice on accommodation and scenic routes. CTC also offers members free third-party insurance, free legal aid and introductions to local cycling groups. Contact: 0845 045 1121; website: www.cyclingholidays.org.

Cycling for Softies. Susi Madron's Cycling Holidays offer over 50 holiday options in 10 regions of France from three to 14 nights, cycling between a network of small country hotels, with terrain varying from very easy to quite a few hills. Contact: 0161 248 8282; website: www.cycling-for-softies.co.uk.

Railways. Cycles are allowed on some trains. However, it is normally necessary to make an advance reservation, and there is usually a small charge to pay. Contact: 0845 7484 950; website: www.nationalrail.co.uk.

Golf

Some clubs will allow non-members to play on weekdays when the course is less busy, on payment of a green fee. Many hotels around the country offer special golfing weekends and short-break holidays.

Lotus Supertravel Golf offers a wide choice of golfing holidays overseas. Favourite destinations include Florida, Spain and the Algarve in Portugal. Contact: 020 7459 2984; website: www.golf.supertravel.co.uk.

Rambling

Rambling features on many special interest and other programmes as one of the options on offer. Three organizations that specialize in rambling holidays are:

ATG Oxford. Walking ATG Oxford style means staying in the most comfortable hotels in the area, having your luggage transported and enjoying the option of a ride on days when you feel like taking it easy. The emphasis is on visiting places of historical, cultural or artistic interest, exploring the scenic highlights and dining out on the best local cuisine. Destinations: Italy, France, Turkey, Spain, the Czech Republic, India, South Africa and many others. Contact: 01865 315 678; website: www.atg-oxford.co.uk.

Exodus offers a wide choice of graded walking holidays in Europe throughout the year. Accommodation is in hotels and guest houses and includes half-board. Cross-country skiing holidays are also offered during the winter. Contact: 0845 863 9600; website: www.exodus.co.uk.

Ramblers Holidays Ltd organizes guided walking tours worldwide. Some trips focus on a special interest such as birdwatching or flowers. Contact: 01707 33 11 33; website: www.ramblersholidays.co.uk.

Skiing

Disability Snowsport UK provides opportunities for people with a disability to participate in skiing and snowboarding. It is the goal of Disability Snowsport to help individuals improve their quality of life and transfer the benefits that they can derive from taking part to their everyday life. Contact: 01479 861 272; website: www.disabilitysnowsport.org.uk.

Ski Club of Great Britain runs skiing holidays in Austria, France, Italy, Switzerland, Canada and the United States for over-50s who have some skiing experience. Qualified leaders accompany each group and will ski with you and offer advice, if wanted. Contact: 0208 410 2000; website: www.skiclub.co.uk.

Tennis

The **Lawn Tennis Association (LTA)** can provide details of residential courses at home and abroad. Contact: 020 8487 7000; website: www.lta.org.uk.

For other sporting holidays, see 'Tourist boards', below. Their websites give information on golfing, sailing and fishing holidays, pony trekking in Wales, skiing in Scotland and many others.

Wine tasting

Wine-tasting holidays are popular with many people and ensure plenty of variety with visits, talks, convivial meals, free time for exploring as well as memorable tastings.

Arblaster & Clarke Wine Tours visit France, Spain, Portugal, Italy, California, Australia, Hungary, Chile, South Africa and New Zealand. Most of the chosen regions are places of interest in their own right, famous for their historic buildings or picturesque scenery. Guides accompany every tour. Contact: 01730 263 111; website: www.winetours.co.uk.

Winetrails offers wine-tasting holidays, combined with walking or cycling, in France, Italy, Spain, Hungary and many other countries. Most last between 6 and 12 days, and groups are limited to a maximum of 14 people. Contact: 01306 712 111; website: www.winetrails.co.uk.

Working holidays

There is scope for volunteers who would like to engage in a worthwhile project during their holidays. Activities vary from helping run play schemes to conservation work. A few are listed here but most are mentioned in Chapter 12, Voluntary Work.

The British Trust for Conservation Volunteers (BTCV) welcomes anyone who would like a working holiday in conservation. BTCV organizes over 500 conservation holidays each year throughout the UK. Projects usually last either a week or a weekend, and the work can vary from hedge-laying to repairing dry-stone walls. Contact: 01302 388 888; website: www.btcv.org.uk.

BTCV Scotland offers training in conservation skills and opportunities to work as a conservation volunteer for as much or as little time as you can spare. The type of work varies – dry-stone diking, fencing, footpath conservation, historic building restoration and habitat management. Contact: 01786 479 697; website: www.btcv.org.uk.

National Trust Working Holidays organizes around 450 week and weekend working holidays each year on Trust properties in England,

Wales and Northern Ireland. Full guidance and instruction is given by Trust wardens, and many of the projects are suitable for the reasonably fit and active of all ages. Contact: 0844 800 3099; website: www.nationaltrust.org.uk.

Toc H organizes short residential events throughout the year, normally lasting between a weekend and three weeks. Scope for volunteers includes running play schemes, activities with disabled people, conservation and manual work. Contact: 01296 640 055; website: www.tochparticipation.co.uk.

Grey gapping

Increasing numbers of middle-aged Britons are taking gap years: this is a popular trend amongst baby boomers (the 55–65 year-olds born after the end of WWII). Research carried out by Halifax shows that 59 per cent of this age group would take a gap year despite recent economic uncertainty. Taking a year out, it seems, is no longer the preserve of the young.

Most people think of gappers as young, backpack-laden people hiking around the world, communicating only when their credit card doesn't work or their mobile phone has been lost or stolen. But it's now big business for the 50-plus age group. For a lot of people a career break is not as crazy as it sounds. After years of working in a high-pressure environment, taking a year out rather like a sabbatical to experience a complete contrast of culture and work ethic can be revitalizing. Leaving a job in the city to work as a volunteer with an AIDS charity in Africa – there's no greater contrast.

An online survey published by the *Independent* in 2009 showed that, of 1,500 people aged over 65, a staggering 57 per cent wished they had travelled more and 45 per cent regretted that they had never given up their jobs or changed profession. But things are changing. Whether or not they are getting a good press (they are known in the travel industry as 'denture venturers' or 'Saga louts'), there are a lot of grey gappers out there. There are an estimated 200,000 pre-retirement gappers in the UK alone. Some of these people are both wealthy and adventurous. They were hippies in the 1960s and now have good earnings behind them. They have financial security, children who are now adults themselves and mortgage-free properties. No wonder the younger generation refer to them as SKINs – spending kids' inheritance now.

If you are interested in escaping on a gap year, **Gapadvice.org**, can help you. Contact: 01494 673 448; website: www.gapadvice.org.

Holidays for singles

There are a number of people, who, if being completely honest, admit they would rather not go on holiday if it means travelling alone. It wasn't all that long ago that single people, especially women over 50, were virtually ignored by the holiday industry. However, things have been improving and now many of the special interest holidays listed on previous pages are ideal for those without a partner, as are some of the working holidays. Additionally, a few organizations now cater specifically for solo holidaymakers:

Companions2Travel is about travel and friendship and more holiday for your money. All applicants complete a form online listing their special interests and the type of destination they have in mind, as well as other requirements. (This is not a dating service.) Website: www.companions2travel.co.uk.

Just You organizes worldwide escorted holidays, including cruises, for single travellers. Groups usually include around 20 to 30 people, with ages ranging from approximately mid-30s to 70-plus. Contact: 0844 567 8844; website: www.justyou.co.uk.

Solo's Holidays specializes in arranging group holidays for single people, including a good selection for those aged 45-plus. A vast choice of special interests is catered for, including opera, golf, cruises, walking holidays and many others. Contact: 0844 815 0005; website: www.solosholidays.co.uk.

Holidays for those needing special care

Over the past few years, facilities for infirm and disabled people have been improving. More hotels are providing wheelchairs and other essential equipment. Transport has become easier. Specially designed self-catering units are more plentiful and of a higher standard. Also, an increasing number of trains and coaches are installing accessible loos. Many people with disabilities can now travel perfectly normally, stay where they please and participate in entertainment and sightseeing without disadvantage.

Travel and other information

If you need help getting on and off a train or plane, inform your travel agent in advance. Arrangements can be made to have staff and, if necessary, a wheelchair available to help you at both departure and arrival points. If you are travelling independently, you should ring the airline and/or local station: explain what assistance you require, together with details of your journey, so that facilities can be arranged at any interim points, for example if you need to change trains.

Age UK can put individuals in touch with organizations that can assist with transport or that organize special care holidays. Contact: 0800 169 65 65; website: www.ageuk.org.uk.

ATS Travel specializes in planning tailor-made holidays for people with disabilities. Among other services, it will arrange the journey from door to door. This includes booking suitable accommodation according to your requirements. It will also organize the provision of special equipment and generally take care of any other details to make your holiday as enjoyable and trouble-free as possible. Contact: 01708 860 514; website: www.assistedholidays.com.

Tourism for All/Vitalise is the UK voice for accessible tourism. It can provide details about a wide range of suitable accommodation, facilities and services both in the UK and overseas and has information about hiring equipment for holiday use, accessible attractions and respite care centres. Contact: 0845 124 9971; website: www.tourismforall.org.uk.

Virgin Holidays has been much recommended, especially for holidays in the United States. For travellers with disabilities, it offers a wide range of hotels with wheelchair-accessible rooms, will arrange transport including adapted cars for hire and (subject to availability) will also book whatever medical equipment may be needed in-flight and during the holiday stay. Contact the Special Assistance Team: 0844 557 3998; website: www.virginholidays.co.uk.

Another source to contact is your local social services department. Some local authorities arrange holidays or give financial help to those in real need.

Tourist boards

If you plan to holiday within the British Isles, and are looking for hotels and accommodation in Britain, or are simply after UK travel, attractions or event information, you will find everything you need to know at **Visit Britain,** website: www.visitbritain.com.

Regional tourist boards

England's regional tourist boards cover the following areas; the boards for Scotland and Wales are also listed:

East of England Tourism: Bedfordshire, Cambridgeshire, Essex, Hertfordshire, Norfolk and Suffolk. Contact: 01284 727 470; website: www.visiteastofengland.com.

East Midlands Tourism: Derbyshire, Leicestershire, Lincolnshire, Northamptonshire, Nottinghamshire and Rutland. Contact: 0115 988 8546; website: www.eastmidlandstourism.co.uk.

Heart of England Tourism: Birmingham, Herefordshire, Shropshire, Staffordshire, Warwickshire, the West Midlands and Worcestershire. Contact:www.heartofengland.com.

North East Tourist Board: Durham, Northumberland, the Tees Valley, and Tyne and Wear. Contact: 0844 249 5090; website: www.visitnortheastengland.com.

North West Regional Development Agency: Cheshire, Cumbria, Greater Manchester, Lancashire and Merseyside. Contact: 01925 400 100; website: www.nwda.co.uk.

South West Tourism: Bath, Bristol, Cornwall, Devon, Dorset, Gloucestershire, the Isles of Scilly, Somerset and Wiltshire. Contact: www.swtourism.co.uk.

Tourism South East: Berkshire, Buckinghamshire, East Sussex, Hampshire, the Isle of Wight, Kent, Oxfordshire, Surrey and West Sussex. Contact: 023 8062 5400; website: www.visitsoutheastengland.com.

Visit London: Greater London area. Contact: 020 7234 5800; website: www.visitlondon.com.

Visit Scotland: 0845 22 55 121; website: www.visitscotland.com.

Visit Wales: 0870 830 0306; website: www.visitwales.co.uk.

Yorkshire Tourist Board: Northern Lincolnshire and Yorkshire. Contact: www.yorkshire.com.

Long-haul travel

The specialist organizations listed below can offer a great deal of practical information and help, as well as assist in obtaining low-cost fares, if you are planning to travel independently. Round-the-world air tickets are an excellent buy. Travel agents may also achieve savings by putting together routes using various carriers. Most airlines offer seasonal discounts that sometimes include a couple of nights' concessionary hotel stay, if you want to break your journey or visit another country at minimum extra travel cost.

Trailfinders Travel Centre will plan a tailor-made itinerary for you to any destination worldwide; book hotels, car hire and low-cost flights; and arrange comprehensive travel insurance. Contact: 0845 058 5858; website: www.trailfinders.com.

Voyages Jules Verne has over 30 years' experience in tours that span the globe, following carefully devised itineraries by air, road, river and rail that capture the true essence of your chosen destination. Contact: 0845 166 7060; website: www.vjv.com.

WEXAS offers a variety of trips to long-haul destinations, including such places as the Antarctic, China and the Nile Valley. Those booking a long-haul flight economy class, plus at least two nights' accommodation through WEXAS, are entitled to VIP lounge access with their family at 23 UK airports. Contact: 0845 643 6568; website: www.wexas.com.

Visa and passport requirements

All too many people get caught out at the airport by not keeping up to date with the visa and other requirements of the country to which they are travelling. These sometimes change without much warning and, at worst if you get it wrong, can result in you being turned away on arrival.

Health and safety advice

This sometimes changes, and travel agents are not always as good as they should be about keeping customers informed. The best advice, especially if you are travelling out of Europe, including to the United States, is to check the **Foreign Office** website (www.fco.gov.uk) several weeks before departure, to allow time for inoculations, and again just before you leave.

Insurance

Holiday insurance, once you are over the age of 65, is not only more difficult to obtain but also tends to be considerably more expensive. However, were you unfortunate enough to fall ill or experience some other mishap, it would almost certainly cost you very much more than paying a bit extra for decent insurance. Age UK offers insurance policies for the over-60s and other firms who cater for people in their 60s and 70s are American Express and Saga.

Many tour operators try to insist that, as a condition of booking, you either buy their inclusive insurance package or make private arrangements that are at least as good. While this suggests that they are demanding very high standards, terms and conditions vary greatly. Before signing on the dotted line, you should read the small print carefully. Be sure to check that the package you are being offered meets all the eventualities and provides you with adequate cover should you make a claim.

If you are travelling independently, it is even more important to be properly insured. Under these circumstances you will not be protected by the normal compensation that the reputable tour operators provide for claims for which they could be held liable in the event of a mishap.

Holiday insurance should cover you for:

- medical expenses, including hospital treatment and the cost of an ambulance, an air ambulance and emergency dental treatment, plus expenses for a companion who may have to remain overseas with you should you become ill;
- personal liability cover, should you cause injury to another person or property;
- personal accident leading to injury or death (check the small print, as some policies have reduced cover for older travellers);
- additional hotel and repatriation costs resulting from injury or illness;

- loss of deposit or cancellation (check what emergencies or contingencies this covers);
- the cost of having to curtail your holiday, including extra travel expenses, because of serious illness in the family;
- compensation for inconvenience caused by flight cancellations or other travel delays;
- cover for baggage and personal effects and for emergency purchases should your baggage be delayed;
- cover for loss of personal money and documents.

If you are planning to take your car abroad you will need to check your existing car insurance to ensure that you are properly covered. Alternatively, if you are planning to hire a vehicle overseas, you will need to take out fully comprehensive insurance cover (which you may need to purchase while on holiday).

Before purchasing new insurance, check whether any of the above items are already covered under an existing policy. This might well apply to your personal possessions and to medical insurance. Even if the policy is not sufficiently comprehensive for travel purposes, it will be better and cheaper in the long run to pay a small supplement to give you the extra cover you need than to buy a holiday insurance package from a tour operator. A cost-effective plan may be to extend any existing medical insurance to cover you while abroad. Then take out a separate policy (without medical insurance) to cover you for the rest of your travel needs.

The Association of British Insurers suggests the following guidelines in respect of the amount of cover holidaymakers should be looking for in their policy:

- *Cancellation or curtailment of holiday:* the full cost of your holiday, as well as the deposit and any other charges paid in advance, plus cover for any extra costs should you be forced to return early. Depending on the policy, cover is normally limited to a maximum of £5,000 per person.
- *Money and travel documents:* £500. Some companies offer additional cover for lost or stolen documents. Normally there is a limit of £200 to £300 for cash.
- *Luggage/belongings:* £1,500 (NB: check the limit on single articles).
- *Delayed baggage:* £100 for emergency purchases in the event that luggage is lost en route and arrives late.

- *Delayed departure:* policies vary greatly. A number pay around £20 to £30 if departure is delayed by more than a certain number of hours. Some will allow you to cancel your holiday once departure has been delayed by over 12 hours, with cover normally limited to the same as for cancellation. If risk of delay is a serious concern, you should check the detail of your policy carefully.
- *Personal liability:* up to £2 million.

It is essential that you take copies of the insurance documents with you, as losses or other claims must normally be reported immediately. You will also be required to quote the reference number and/or other details given on the docket. Additionally, there may be particular guidelines laid down by the policy. For instance, you may have to ring a helpline before incurring medical expenses. Failure to report a claim within the specified time limit could nullify your right to compensation. The best advice is to check that you have the 24-hour helpline number and to keep it with you at all times.

Be sure to get a receipt for any special expenses you incur – extra hotel bills, medical treatment, long-distance phone calls and so on. You may not get all the costs reimbursed, but if your insurance covers some or all of these contingencies you will need to produce evidence of your expenditure.

The Association of British Insurers has information on holiday insurance and motoring abroad. Contact: 020 7600 3333; website: www.abi.org.uk.

The Association of British Travel Agents (ABTA) operates a Code of Conduct for all travel agents and tour operators that are ABTA members and helps holidaymakers seek redress if they are dissatisfied with their travel company. Contact: 0901 201 5050; website: www.abta.com.

Compensation for lost baggage

If the airline on which you are travelling loses or damages your baggage, you should be able to claim compensation up to a maximum value of about £850. (The figure may vary slightly up or down, depending on currency fluctuations.)

Cancelled or overbooked flights

Also useful to know about is the *Denied Boarding Regulation,* which entitles passengers who cannot travel because their flight is overbooked to some immediate cash payment. This applies even if the airline puts them up in a hotel or books them on to an alternative flight a few hours later. To qualify, passengers must have a confirmed reservation and have checked in on time. Also, the airport where they were 'bumped off' must be in an EU country. (It may sometimes also be possible to get compensation in the United States.)

If, as opposed to being overbooked, your flight is cancelled, you are entitled to get a refund if you decide not to travel. Alternatively, you can request to be re-routed. You may, additionally, get compensation of between £125 and £600, depending on the length of your journey and how long you are delayed. If the delay is more than two hours, you will also be entitled to meals or refreshments plus two free telephone calls, e-mails or faxes. If it is overnight and you have more than five hours' wait, you will be put up in a hotel and given free transfers. Compensation is not, however, obligatory if the cancellation is due to 'extraordinary circumstances which could not have been avoided'. For further information, or if you have trouble in obtaining your compensation, contact the **Air Transport Users Council**: 020 7240 6061; website: www.caa.co.uk.

If you miss your flight or have to cancel your trip, you may be able to get a refund on at least a small part of the ticket cost. Most airlines will reimburse non-fliers for the air passenger duty and overseas government taxes. This applies even to normal non-refundable tickets. However, you have to make a claim, and in most cases there is an administration charge. This may vary somewhere between £15 and £20. If you booked through a travel agent, there could be a second administration charge. Even so, especially for long-haul travel and family holidays, the savings could be quite considerable.

Medical insurance

This is one area where you should never skimp on insurance. Although many countries now have reciprocal arrangements with the UK for emergency medical treatment, these vary greatly in both quality and generosity. Some treatments are free, as they are on the National Health Service; others, even in some EU countries, may be charged for as if you were a private patient.

The Department of Health leaflet *Health Advice for Travellers* (T7) explains what is entailed and what forms you should obtain. In particular you should get a European health insurance card (EHIC). This card entitles you to free or reduced-cost emergency medical treatment throughout EU countries, as well as in Switzerland, Norway, Iceland and Liechtenstein.

Each person, including members of the same family, requires his or her own individual card. To obtain one, phone 0845 606 2030.

However, even the very best reciprocal arrangements may not be adequate in the event of a real emergency. Moreover, they certainly will not cover you for any additional expenses you may incur. In the United States the cost of medical treatment is astronomical. For peace of mind, most experts recommend cover of £1 million for most of the world and up to £2 million for the United States. Some policies offer higher, or even unlimited, cover. Although theoretically there is no upper age limit if you want to take out medical insurance, some insurance companies are very difficult about insuring older travellers. Many request a note from a qualified medical practitioner stating that you are fit to travel if you are over 75, or require you to confirm that you are not travelling against medical advice.

Another common requirement is that the insured person should undertake not to indulge in any dangerous pursuits, which is fine in theory but in practice (depending on the company's interpretation of 'dangerous') could debar you from any activity that qualifies as 'strenuous'.

Book through a reputable operator

Many of the sad tales of woe one hears could have been avoided, or at least softened by compensation. It is essential that holidaymakers check to ensure that their travel agent or tour operator is affiliated to either ABTA or the Association of Tour Operators (ATO). Both organizations have strict regulations that all member companies must follow, and both run an arbitration scheme in the event of complaints. No one can guarantee you against every mishap, but a recognized travel company plus adequate insurance should go a long way towards giving you at least some measure of protection.

Travel and other concessions

Buses, coaches, some airline companies and especially the railways offer valuable concessions to people of retirement age.

Trains

Some of the best-value savings that are available to anyone aged 60 and over are provided by train companies. These include:

Disabled Persons Railcard: costs £18 for one year or £48 for three years and entitles the holder and one accompanying adult to reduced train fares. Contact: 0845 605 0525; website: www.disabledpersons-railcard.co.uk.

Family Friends Railcard: costs £26 for a whole year and entitles up to four adults and four children to travel on one card. Adults get one-third off and children get 60 per cent off the normal child fare. Contact: 08448 714 036; website: www.familyandfriends-railcard.co.uk.

Network Railcard: costs £25 and is valid for 12 months, available only in London and the South-East. It gives a one-third reduction on most standard-class fares after 10 am, Monday to Friday. Up to three adults can travel with you and they will also get one third off their fares, and you can take four children with you and save 60 per cent on their fares. Contact: 08448 714 036; website: www.railcard.co.uk.

Senior Railcard: for those aged 60 plus, costs £26 for one year and entitles you to a third off standard and first class fares. Discounts on hotels, restaurants and days out. Contact: 08448 714 036; website: www.senior-railcard.co.uk.

Buses and coaches

Over 11 million people over 60 in the UK use buses for free travel around the country. Make the most of this while you can: it is reported that the government has plans to raise the eligible age gradually to 65.

If you live in **England,** over-60s and disabled people can travel free on local buses anywhere in England between 9.30 am and 11 pm on weekdays and all day weekends and public holidays.

If you live in **Scotland,** over-60s and disabled people can travel free on local buses and scheduled long distance coach services in Scotland at any time – no time restrictions.

If you live in **Wales,** over-60s and disabled people can travel free on local buses in Wales at any time. People living in Wales can also use their passes to travel free on cross-boundary journeys in and out of England, providing the journey starts or finishes in Wales.

Wherever you live you can go where you want. It's free and easy. Bus passes are usually issued free by local authorities. **Arriva** has further information. Contact: 0844 800 44 11; website: www.arrivabus.co.uk.

There are often reduced rates for senior citizens on long-distance buses and coaches. For example, discounts of 33 per cent apply on **National Coaches** on both ordinary and Rapide services. If you are planning to travel by coach, readers have advised that it is worth shopping around to find out what bargains are available.

Airlines

Several of the airlines offer attractive discounts to older travellers. The terms and conditions vary, with some carriers offering across-the-board savings and others limiting them to selected destinations. Likewise, in some cases the qualifying age is 60; in others, it is a couple of years older. A particular bonus is that concessions are often extended to include a companion travelling at the same time. To find out more, best advice is to ask your travel agent or the airline at the time of booking what special discounts, if any, are offered.

Overseas

Many countries offer travel and other reductions to retired holidaymakers including, for example, discounts for entry to museums and galleries, day excursions, sporting events and other entertainment. As in Britain, provisions are liable to change, and for up-to-date information probably the best source to contact is the national tourist office of the country to which you are travelling. All EU countries – as well as most lines in Switzerland – give 25 per cent reductions on international rail fares. These are available to holders of a Railplus Card purchasing international rail travel tickets and are applicable to both first- and second-class travel.

Airport meet-and-greet services

If you hate the hassle of parking your car in the long-term car park and collecting it again on your return after a long journey, **BCP** offers a better choice for parking. It operates a meet-and-greet service at six airports (Heathrow, Gatwick, Stansted, Birmingham, Manchester and Edinburgh). It will arrange for a rep to meet you at the terminal at both ends of your journey, park the car, deliver it back and valet it while you are on holiday. Contact: 0800 316 0169; website: www.parkbcp.co.uk.

A number of firms offer a similar service but, at the time of booking, enquire where your car will be parked and, when dropping it off it would be sensible to ask for a 'conditions form' to complete, to avoid disputes if you find any damage on your return.

Health tips for travellers

- Remember to pack any regular medicines you require: even familiar branded products can be difficult to obtain in some countries.
- Take a mini first aid kit, including plasters, disinfectant, tummy pills and so on.
- If you are going to any developing country, consult your doctor as to what pills (and any special precautions) you should take.
- One of the most common ailments among British travellers abroad is an overdose of sun. In some countries it really burns, so take it easy, wear a hat and apply plenty of protective lotion.
- The other big travellers' woe is 'Delhi belly', which unhappily can occur in most hot countries, including Italy and Spain. Beware the water, ice, salads, seafood, ice cream and any fruit that you do not peel yourself. Department of Health advice is only to eat freshly prepared food that is thoroughly cooked and still piping hot.
- Always wash your hands before eating or handling food, particularly if you are camping or caravanning.
- Travelling is tiring and a sudden change of climate more debilitating than most of us admit. Allow plenty of time during the first couple of days to acclimatize before embarking on any activity programme.
- Have any inoculations or vaccinations well in advance of your departure date.
- When flying, wear loose clothes and above all comfortable shoes, as feet and ankles tend to swell in the air.
- To avoid risk of deep vein thrombosis, which can be fatal, medical advice is to do foot exercises and walk around the plane from time to time. For long-haul travel especially, wear compression stockings, which can be bought at most chemists. Unless advised otherwise by your doctor, taking an aspirin before flying is also recommended.
- On long journeys, it helps to drink plenty of water and remember the warning that 'an alcoholic drink in the air is worth two on the ground'. If you have a special diet, inform whoever makes your

booking. Most airlines, especially on long-distance journeys, serve vegetarian food.

- Department of Health leaflet T7, *Health Advice for Travellers*, contains essential information and advice on what precautions to take when you travel abroad and how to cope in an emergency. Contact: 020 7210 4850; website: www.dh.gov.uk.

- Finally, the old favourite: don't drink and drive.

Chapter Fifteen
Caring for elderly parents

Age is not a particularly interesting subject. Anyone can get old. All you have to do is live long enough.

GROUCHO MARX (1890–1977)

The greatest population increase recently has been in those aged 85 and over: the 'oldest old'. In 1984 there were around 660,000 people of this age group living in the UK. Since then the numbers have more than doubled, reaching 1.4 million in 2009. By 2034, it is projected that the number of people aged over 85 will have reached 3.5 million, representing 5 per cent of the total population, according to the Office for National Statistics (www.statistics.gov.uk.)

Figures such as these make startling reading. With so many more people living longer, sooner or later most of us are likely to have to shoulder some responsibility for the care of elderly parents. The vast majority can fortunately manage, with a little help, to remain in their own homes for a long time. This is the undoubted preference of most older people themselves. The main bias of this chapter is towards helping aged parents remain as independent as possible, for as long as possible, until a care home or nursing home becomes necessary.

Knowing what facilities are available and what precautions your parents can take against a mishap occurring is an important factor. Being aware of whom they can turn to in an emergency can make all the difference. There is now much greater awareness of the needs of the elderly and this has been much highlighted and publicized, mostly in regard to the financial implications of funding older people's care. In line with this, many provisions for the elderly have enormously improved. Simple gadgets such as personal alarm systems can buy peace of mind, and full-scale nursing care is available, if you know where to find it. Familiarizing yourself (on your parent's behalf) with how to source funding or access equipment and aids is half the battle.

Many families face the difficult choice between moving parents in to live with them or allowing them to continue to live on their own. While the decision will depend on individual circumstances, in the early stages at least the majority choice on all sides is usually to 'stay put'. Later in the chapter we cover sheltered housing, which some people see as the best of all worlds. Meanwhile, to avoid a move the best solution for most elderly people is to adapt their home to make it safer and more convenient.

Ways of adapting a home

Many elderly people will not require anything more complicated than a few general improvements. These could include better lighting, especially near staircases, a non-slip mat and grab-rails in the bathroom, and safer heating arrangements. For some a practical improvement might be to lower kitchen and other units to place them within easy reach and make cooking less hazardous.

Another fairly simple option is to convert a downstairs room into a bedroom and en suite bathroom, should managing the stairs be proving difficult. These and other common sense measures are covered in more detail in Chapter 8, Your Home.

For some people, however, such arrangements are not really sufficient. In the case of a physically handicapped or disabled person, more radical changes will usually be needed. Today it involves accessing help from the GP and local authority.

Local authority help

The state system is designed to support the elderly in their own home for as long as possible. Local authorities have a legal duty to help people with disabilities and, depending on what is required and the individual's ability to pay, may assist with the cost. Your parents can either approach their GP or contact the social services department direct. A sympathetic doctor will be able to advise what is needed and supply any prescriptions, such as for a medical hoist. Your parents' GP will also be able to suggest which unit or department to approach as well as make a recommendation to the housing department, should rehousing be desirable. If your parents can afford it, they will have to pay for the services they need themselves. If their income and savings are low, the council may pay part or all of the cost.

Personal budgets

Increasingly, councils no longer provide services themselves. Instead your parents will be offered cash, so that they can choose and buy in the services they need. The council will provide contact details for local providers. Local councils are also in the process of putting in place a system of 'personal budgets'. Under this system, the cash allocated to your parents is paid into an account in their name. While they choose the services they need, either they or the local authority can commission and pay for them from that account. If they need medical care in their own home, for example visits from the district nurse to change dressings or administer drugs, this is free on the NHS.

In Scotland, personal care up to £153 a week (2009–10) is provided free for anyone aged 65 whose local authority assessment finds they need it. This is paid direct to the care provider and can be used for help with, for example, bathing, toileting, feeding, help taking medication and so on.

Help with home repair and adaptations

Disabled facilities grant

This is a local council grant to help towards the cost of adapting a home to enable a disabled or elderly person to live there. It can cover a wide range of improvements to enable the occupants to manage more independently. This includes work to facilitate access either to the property itself or to the main rooms, the provision of suitable bathroom or kitchen facilities, the adaptation of heating or lighting controls, improvement of the heating system, and various other works where these would make a home safe for a disabled person. Provided the applicant is eligible, currently a mandatory grant of up to £30,000 in England, £25,000 in Northern Ireland and £36,000 in Wales may be available. Contact: 0303 444 0000; website: www.direct.gov.uk/DisabledPeople.

Home improvement agencies (HIAs)

Depending on where your parents live, **Foundations** is the national body for Home Improvement Agencies in **England.** Home Improvement Agencies help older and vulnerable people maintain their independence by providing housing-related support. For more information about how home improvement agencies can help, contact: 08458 645 210, website: www. foundations.uk.com; in **Wales**: Care and Repair Cymru: 029 2057 6286, website: www.careandrepair.org.uk; in **Scotland**: Care and Repair Scotland: 0141 221 9879, website: www.careandrepairscotland.co.uk.

Other sources of help

Age UK (Tel: 0800 00 99 66; website: www.ageuk.org.uk) and **British Red Cross** (Tel: 0844 871 11 11; website: www.redcross.org.uk) can loan equipment in the short term and may also be able to advise on local stockists. Larger branches of Boots, for example, sell a wide range of special items for people with disabilities, including bath aids, wheelchairs and crutches.

Assist UK heads up a UK-wide network of locally situated disabled living centres. Each centre includes a permanent exhibition of products and equipment, giving people opportunities to see and try products and equipment and get information and advice from professional staff. There are over 325 advisers working at over 60 member centres. Contact: 0161 238 8776; website: www.assist-uk.org.

CAE (Centre for Accessible Environments) offers a range of access consultancy services customized to the needs of clients. Contact: 020 7840 0125; website: www.cae.org.uk.

DEMAND (Design & Manufacture for Disability) is an independent charity that transforms the lives of disabled people through the provision of bespoke equipment. It does not charge clients for its services. Contact: 01923 681 800; website: www.demand.org.uk.

Disability Wales/Anabledd Cymru is another helpful source of advice. Contact: 029 2088 7325; website: www.disabilitywales.org.

Disabled Living Foundation (DLF) is a national charity that provides impartial advice, information and training on daily living aids. It does not sell products but helps clients find the people who do. Contact: 0845 130 9177; website: www.dlf.org.uk.

Hearing and Mobility has a range of mobility aids and equipment that are available online or through a number of outlet stores nationwide. Contact: 0844 888 1338; website: www.hearingandmobility.co.uk.

REMAP is a special charity working through volunteers who use their ingenuity and skills to enable people with disabilities to achieve much-desired independence, often helping design or adapt goods to suit individuals where there is no commercially available product to meet their particular needs. Contact: 0845 130 0456; website: www.remap.org.uk.

Alarm systems

Alarm systems for the elderly are many and varied, but the knowledge that help can be summoned quickly in the event of an emergency is reassuring in its own right to many elderly or disabled people. Having a personal alarm can enable many people to remain independent far longer than would otherwise be sensible. Some alarm systems allow people living in their own homes to be linked to a central control, or have a telephone link, enabling personal contact to be made. Others simply signal that something is wrong. Sometimes a relative or friend who has been nominated will be alerted. Your parents' local authority social services department will have information. See website: www.direct.gov.uk/Help/SocialServices.

Commercial firms

A number of firms install and operate alarm systems. Price, installation cost and reliability can vary quite considerably.

For advice on choosing an alarm, plus a list of suppliers, the **DLF (Disabled Living Foundation)** can assist you. Contact: 0845 130 9177; website: www.dlf.org.uk.

Contact4me is an identification, next of kin and medical alert notification service. It ensures that if anything should happen to an elderly person, the emergency services on the scene receive fast and secure access to the person's identity, next of kin and vital medical alerts. Contact: 0800 124 4521; website: www.contact4me.com.

Community alarms

Telephone alarm systems operated on the public telephone network can be used by anyone with a direct telephone line. The systems link into a 24-hour monitoring centre and the individual has a pendant that enables help to be called even when the owner is some distance from the telephone. Grants may be available in some cases to meet the costs.

Age Concern Personal Alarm Service is highly recommended, as the subscriber wears a pendant or a watch which is connected to a 24-hour monitoring centre. Contact: 0800 77 22 66; website: www.aidcall.co.uk.

SeniorLinkEldercare operates a social alarm system. Contact: 0808 100 2435; website: www.seniorlinkeldercare.com.

Main local authority services

Quite apart from any assistance with housing, local authorities supply a number of services that can prove invaluable to an elderly person. The two most important are meals on wheels and home helps. Additionally, there are social workers and various specialists concerned with aspects of health. Since the introduction of Community Care, local authority social services departments have taken over all responsibility for helping to assess and coordinate the best arrangements for individuals according to their particular requirements.

Meals on wheels

The meals on wheels service is sometimes run by local authorities direct and sometimes by voluntary organizations, such as WRVS, acting as their agents. The purpose is to deliver a hot lunch (or batch of frozen lunches) to individuals in their own homes. Different arrangements apply in different areas, and schemes variously operate from two to seven days a week, or possibly less frequently when frozen meals are supplied. Cost also varies. For further information, contact the local social services department.

WRVS also runs a private frozen meals scheme that delivers complete frozen meals direct to customers' doors. Contact: 029 2073 9000; website: www.wrvs.org.uk.

Home helps

Local authorities have a legal obligation to run a home help service to help frail and housebound elderly people with such basic household chores as shopping, tidying up, a little light cooking and so on. In many areas the service is badly overstretched, so the amount of help actually available varies considerably, as does the method of charging. A health and social care assessment with the social services department of your local council is often the first step towards getting the help and support your parents need. The assessment is also known as an 'assessment of need'. See website: www.direct.gov.uk/DisabledPeople.

Specialist helpers

Local authorities employ a number of specialist helpers, variously based in the social services department or health centre, who are there to assist:

Social workers are normally the first people to contact if your parents have a problem. They can put them in touch with the right person, if they require a home help or meals on wheels, or have a housing difficulty or other query and are not sure whom to approach. Contact the local social services department or, in Scotland, the social work department.

Occupational therapists have a wide knowledge of disability and can assist individuals via training, exercise, or access to aids, equipment or adaptations to the home. Contact the local social services department.

Health visitors are qualified nurses with a broad knowledge both of health matters and of the various services available through the local authority. Rather like social workers, health visitors can put your parents in touch with whatever specialized facilities are required. Contact is through the local health centre.

District nurses are fully qualified nurses who will visit a patient in the home, change dressings, attend to other routine nursing matters, monitor progress and help with the arrangements if more specialized care is required. Contact is through their health centre.

Physiotherapists use exercise and massage to help improve mobility and strengthen muscles, for example after an operation or to alleviate a crippling condition. They are normally available at both hospitals and health centres.

Medical social workers (MSWs) (previously known as almoners) are available to consult, if patients have any problems – whether practical or emotional – on leaving hospital. MSWs can advise on coping with a disablement, as well as such practical matters as transport, after-care and other immediate arrangements. They work in hospitals, and an appointment should be made before the patient is discharged.

Good neighbour schemes

A number of areas of the country have an organized system of good neighbour schemes. In essence, these consist of volunteers agreeing to act as good neighbours to one or several elderly people living close by. Depending on what is required, they may simply pop in on a daily basis to check that everything is all right, or they may give more sustained assistance such as providing help with dressing, bathing, shopping or preparing a light meal. To find out whether such a scheme exists locally, enquire at the social services department.

Key voluntary organizations

Voluntary organizations complement the services provided by statutory health and social services in making life easier for elderly people living at home. The range of provision varies from area to area but can include:

- lunch clubs;
- holidays and short-term placements;
- day centres and clubs;
- friendly visiting;
- aids such as wheelchairs;
- transport;
- odd jobs and decorating;
- gardening;
- good neighbour schemes;
- prescription collection;
- advice and information;
- family support schemes.

The particular organization providing these services depends on where your parents live, but the Citizens Advice Bureau – website: www.citizensadvice. org.uk – will be able to advise you whom to contact. The following are the key agencies:

Age UK: 0800 169 6565; website: www.ageuk.org.uk.

Age Scotland: 0845 125 9732; website: www.ageuk.org.uk/scotland.

Age Wales: 0800 169 65 65; website: www.ageuk.org.uk/cymru.

Age Northern Ireland: 0808 808 7575; website: www.ageuk.org.uk/northern-ireland.

British Red Cross (Tel: 0844 871 1111; website: www.redcross.org.uk) supplies some important services to elderly people such as:

- helping sick, disabled or frail people make essential journeys;
- loaning medical equipment for short-term use at home and on holiday;
- providing home-from-hospital support: easing the transition of patients to their own home after discharge;
- 'signposting' vulnerable people towards the statutory or voluntary services by which their needs may best be met.

St John Ambulance has over 45,000 volunteers who provide first aid and care services, helping in hospitals, and in people's homes to assist with various practical tasks such as shopping, collecting pensions, staying with an elderly person for a few hours or providing transport to and from hospital. National Headquarters can advise on what services are available. Contact: 08700 10 49 50; website: www.sja.org.uk.

WRVS runs many local projects: books on wheels; social transport; meals on wheels; good neighbour schemes; lunch clubs; a meal delivery service for those not qualifying for meals on wheels. Contact: 029 2073 9000; website: www.wrvs.org.uk.

Other sources of help and advice

Age UK runs SeniorLine, a free advice and information service, available throughout the UK for older people and their carers. Contact: 0800 169 6565; website: www.ageuk.org.uk.

Civil Service Retirement Fellowship runs a network of social groups across the country and aims to enable people to have a better and more fulfilling retirement. Contact: 020 8691 7411; website: www.csrf.org.uk.

Counsel and Care is a national charity working with older people, their families and carers to get the best care and support. It provides personalized, in-depth help and advice. Contact: 0845 300 7585; website: www.counselandcare.org.uk.

Disability Alliance is a national registered charity that produces a number of publications including the *Disability Rights Handbook,* containing information on benefits and rights for the disabled. Contact: 020 7247 8776; website: www.disabilityalliance.org.

Jewish Care provides services for elderly Jewish people, including those who are mentally ill, in London and the South-East of England. Principal facilities include: special day care centres; residential and nursing homes; community centres; a home care service for the housebound; and short-term respite care. Contact: 020 8922 2222; website: www.jewishcare.org.

Transport

Difficulty in getting around is often a major problem for elderly and disabled people. In addition to the facilities run by voluntary organizations already mentioned, there are several other very useful services:

Forum of Mobility Centres provides information on a network of independent organizations throughout England, Scotland, Wales and Northern Ireland to help individuals who have a medical condition or are recovering from an accident or injury that may affect their ability to drive. Contact: 0800 559 3636; website: www.mobility-centres.org.uk.

London Taxi Card Service is a scheme whereby disabled people can use a taxi on weekdays and weekends at a much reduced rate, subsidized by their local authority. Prices may vary depending on the borough in which the person is resident. Contact: 020 7934 9791; website: www.taxicard.org.uk.

Motability is a registered charity set up to assist recipients of the war pensioners' mobility supplement and/or the higher-rate mobility component of Disability Living Allowance to use their allowance to lease or buy a car or a powered wheelchair or scooter. Contact Motability: 0845 456 4566; website: www.motability.co.uk.

Driving licence renewal at age 70

All drivers aged 70 are sent a licence renewal form to have their driving licence renewed. The entitlement to drive will need to be renewed by the **DVLA** and this will be valid for three years. Contact: 0870 240 0009; website: www.direct.gov.uk/Motoring.

Holidays

Many people in their late 70s and older travel across the world, go on activity holidays and see the great sights in the UK and abroad without any more difficulty than anyone else. They will find plenty of choice in Chapter 14, including information about how to obtain assistance at airports and railway stations. However, some elderly people need special facilities if a stay away from home is to be possible. A number of organizations can help:

Able Travel: accessible African safaris and worldwide adventure travel advice for wheelchair users and physically disabled people. Website: www.able-travel.com.

Accessible Travel and Leisure: specialist travel service offering holidays and related services for disabled people. Website: www.accessibletravel.co.uk.

ATS Travel: tour operator arranging holidays for disabled people (wheelchair users) and their families in Britain and abroad. Contact: 01708 860 514; website: www.assistedholidays.com.

Can be done: tour operator specializing in accessible holidays worldwide. Website: www.canbedone.co.uk.

Chalfont Line: escorted holidays for people with limited mobility and wheelchair users. Website: www.chalfont-line.co.uk.

Enable holidays: accessible holidays in Florida, Spain, Majorca, Canary Islands, Portugal, Cyprus and the Greek Islands. Website: www.enableholidays.com.

Holiday Access Direct: accessible accommodation and holiday service. Website: www.holidayaccessdirect.com.

Tourism for All: provides details about a wide range of suitable accommodation, facilities and services both in the UK and overseas, including information about hiring equipment for holiday use, accessible attractions and respite care centres. Contact: 0845 124 9971; website: www.tourismforall.org.uk.

A number of the specialist **voluntary** organizations run holiday centres or provide specially adapted self-catering accommodation. In some cases, outings and entertainment are offered. In others, individuals plan their own activities and amusement. Guests requiring assistance usually need to be accompanied by a companion, although in a few instances care arrangements are inclusive. Most of the organizations can advise about the possibility of obtaining a grant or other financial assistance.

Grooms Holidays: accessible holidays. Website: www.johngrooms.org.uk.

Holidays for all: group of organizations providing holidays for disabled people: website: www.holidaysforall.org.uk.

Holiday with Help: respite care breaks for disabled people and their carers: website: www.holidayswithhelp.org.uk.

Leonard Cheshire: the charity has an accessible hotel and cottage. Website: www.leonard-cheshire.org.

Vitalise: short breaks for disabled adults and their carers. Website: www.vitalise.org.uk.

There are also a couple of useful publications, listing a wide choice of holiday venues where disabled travellers can go in the normal way but with the advantage of having special facilities provided.

Disabled Travellers' Guide, by the **AA**, gives information on holiday accommodation suitable for disabled individuals and their families, together with advice on travelling in Europe. Contact: 0800 262 050; website: www. theaa.com. *Holidays in Britain and Ireland* is available from **RADAR** (Royal Association for Disability and Rehabilitation), Contact: 020 7250 3222; website: www.radar.org.uk.

Power of Attorney

Giving another person Power of Attorney authorizes someone else to take business and other financial decisions on their behalf. A Lasting Power of Attorney continues, regardless of any decline, throughout the individual's life. To protect the donor and the nominated attorney, the law clearly lays down certain principles that must be observed, with both sides signing a declaration that they understand the various rights and duties involved. The law furthermore calls for the power to be formally registered with the Public Trust Office in the event of the donor being, or becoming, mentally incapable.

Lasting Powers of Attorney (LPA) have replaced Enduring Powers of Attorney. This coincided with the implementation of the Mental Capacity Act 2005. LPAs enable individuals to give their attorney power to make decisions about their personal welfare, including health care, and their finances, when they lack the capacity to make such decisions themselves. Enduring Powers of Attorney set up before October 2007 are still effective. However, if your parents have not yet set one up but are planning to do so, they will now need to apply for the new LPA instead.

The right time to give Power of Attorney is when the individual is in full command of his or her faculties, so that potential situations that would require decisions can be properly discussed and the donor's wishes made clear. For the Lasting Power of Attorney to be valid, the donor must in any event be capable of understanding what he or she is agreeing to at the time of making the power.

If your parents are considering setting up an LPA, it is advisable that they consult their GP and the family solicitor.

Temporary living-in help

Elderly people living alone can be more vulnerable to flu and other winter ailments; they may have a fall; or, for no apparent reason, they may go through a period of being forgetful and neglecting themselves. Equally, as they become older, they may not be able to cope as well with managing their homes or caring for themselves. In the event of an emergency or if you have reason for concern – perhaps because you are going on holiday and will not be around to keep a watchful eye on them – engaging living-in help can be a godsend. Most agencies tend inevitably to be on the expensive side, although in the event of a real problem they often represent excellent value for money. A more unusual and interesting longer-term possibility is to recruit the help of a Community Service Volunteer.

Community Service Volunteers (CSV)

CSV has volunteers who are aged over 16 and are involved in a variety of projects nationwide. The volunteers are untrained and work for periods of four to 12 months away from home. They take their instructions from the people for whom they are working, but are not substitutes for professional carers. They provide practical assistance in the home and also offer companionship. Usually a care scheme is set up through a social worker, who supervises how the arrangement is working out. Volunteers are placed on a one-month trial basis. Contact your parents' local social services department, or approach CSV direct for further information, Tel: 020 7278 6601; website: www.csv.org.uk.

Agencies

The agencies listed specialize in providing temporary help, rather than permanent staff. Charges vary, but in addition to the weekly payment to helpers there is normally an agency booking fee. As a rule payment is gross, so your parents will not be involved in having to work out tax or National Insurance:

Consultus Care & Nursing Agency Ltd	01732 355 231; website: www.consultuscare.com
Country Cousins	0845 601 4003; website: www.country-cousins.co.uk
Universal Aunts Ltd	020 7738 8937; website: www.universalaunts.co.uk

For a further list of agencies, see *The Lady* magazine, or search the internet under the heading 'Employment agencies' or 'Care agencies'.

Nursing care

If one of your parents needs regular nursing care, the GP may be able to arrange for a community or district nurse to visit him or her at home. This will not be a sleeping-in arrangement but simply involves a qualified nurse calling round when necessary. If you want more concentrated home nursing you will have to go through a private agency. Some of those listed above can sometimes supply trained nurses. Additionally, there are many specialist agencies that can arrange hourly, daily or live-in nurses on a temporary or longer-term basis.

Terms of employment vary considerably. Some nurses undertake nursing duties only – and nothing else – and may even expect to have their meals provided. Others will do light housework and act as nurse-companions. Fees vary throughout the country, with London inevitably being most expensive. Private health insurance can sometimes be claimed against part of the cost, but this is generally only in respect of qualified nurses. Your local health centre or social services department should be able to give you names and addresses of local agencies, or search the internet under the heading 'Nursing agencies'.

Permanent living-in help

There may come a time when you feel that it is no longer safe to allow one of your parents to live entirely on his or her own. One possibility is to engage a companion or housekeeper on a permanent basis, but such arrangements are normally very expensive. However, if you want to investigate the idea further, many domestic agencies supply housekeeper-companions. Alternatively, you might consider advertising in *The Lady* magazine, which is probably the most widely read publication for these kinds of posts. Contact: 020 7379 4717; website: www.lady.co.uk.

Permanent help can also sometimes be provided by agencies, which will supply continuous four-weekly placements. This is an expensive option, and the lack of continuity can at times be distressing for elderly people, particularly at the changeover point. The three agencies listed above may be worth contacting.

Au pairs are cheaper but a drawback is that most au pairs speak inadequate English (at least when they first arrive). As they are technically students living *en famille,* they must by law be given plenty of free time to attend school and study. An alternative solution for some families is to engage a reliable daily help who, in the event of illness or other problem, would be prepared to stay overnight.

Flexible care arrangements

One of the problems for many elderly people is that the amount of care they need is liable to vary according to the state of their health. There are other relevant factors including, for example, the availability of neighbours and family. Whereas after an operation the requirement may be for someone with basic nursing skills, a few weeks later the only need may be for someone to act as a companion. Under normal circumstances it may be as little as simply popping in for the odd hour during the day to cook a hot meal and check all is well. Few agencies cater for all the complex permutations that may be necessary in caring for an elderly person in his or her own home, but here are three that offer a genuinely flexible service:

Anchor Care workers can be engaged by the hour, or nightly, for temporary or longer periods, or on a more permanent residential basis. All staff are personally interviewed, their references are taken up, and training is given. Contact: 0845 140 2020; website: www.anchor.org.uk.

Cura Domi – Care at Home is a specialist organization able to provide care and support seven days a week, 52 weeks of the year, as much or as little as required. Contact: 01483 420 055; website: www.curadomi.co.uk.

UKHCA (United Kingdom Home Care Association) works for quality in home care and represents over 1,500 member branches throughout the country that specialize in providing care for elderly and/or disabled people in their own home. Contact: 020 8288 5291; website: www.ukhca.co.uk.

Although any of these suggestions can work extremely well for a while, with many families it may sooner or later come down to a choice between residential care and inviting a parent to live with you. Sometimes, particularly in the case of an unmarried son or daughter or other relative, it is more practical to move into the parent's (or relative's) home if the accommodation is more suitable.

Emergency care for pets

For many elderly people a pet is a very important part of their lives. It provides companionship and fun as well as stimulating them into taking regular outdoor exercise. But in the event of the owner having to go into hospital or through some other emergency being temporarily unable to care for the pet, there can be real problems. Two organizations that can help under these circumstances are listed here:

The Cinnamon Trust offers permanent care for pets whose owners have died, as well as respite care while the owners are in hospital. Some animals stay at the Trust's havens in Cornwall and Devon. Others are found alternative loving homes with a new owner. Contact: 01736 757 900; website: www.cinnamon.org.uk.

Pet Fostering Service Scotland focuses on temporary care. The only charges are the cost of the pet's food, litter (in the case of cats) and any veterinary fees that may be incurred during fostering. Contact: 0844 811 9909; website: www.pfss.org.uk.

Practical help for carers

If your parent is still fairly active – visits friends, does his or her own shopping, or enjoys some hobby that gets him or her out and about – the strains and difficulties may be fairly minimal. This applies particularly if your parent is moving in with you and your home lends itself to creating a granny flat, so everyone can retain some privacy and your parent can continue to enjoy maximum independence. However, this is not always possible, and in the case of an ill or very frail person far more intensive care may be required. It is important to know what help is available and how to obtain it.

The many services provided by local authorities and voluntary agencies, described earlier in the chapter, apply as much to an elderly person living with a family as to one living alone. If there is nothing in the list that solves a particular problem you may have, it could be useful to contact the following:

Age UK	0800 169 65 65; website: www.ageuk.org.uk
British Red Cross	0844 87 11 11; website: www.redcross.org.uk
St John Ambulance	08700 10 49 50; website: www.sja.org.uk
The Princess Royal Trust for Carers	0844 800 4361; website: www.carers.org
WRVS	029 2073 9000; website: www.wrvs.org.uk

Most areas now have, or are planning, respite care facilities to enable carers to take a break from their dependants from time to time. Depending on the circumstances, this could be for just the odd day or possibly for a week or two to enable carers who need it to have a real rest. A particularly welcome aspect of respite care is that many schemes specially cater for, among others, elderly people with dementia.

Another service well worth knowing about is **Crossroads – Caring for Carers**, which arranges for helpers to care for very frail or disabled people in their own home while the regular carer is away. The helpers will come in during the day, or stay overnight, and provide whatever practical help is required. Arrangements are planned very much on an individual basis and are tailored to meet particular family circumstances. Contact: 0845 450 0350; website: www.crossroads.org.uk.

Holiday breaks for carers

There are various schemes to enable families with an elderly relative to go on holiday alone or simply to enjoy a respite from their caring responsibilities. A number of local authorities run *fostering schemes,* on similar lines to child fostering. Elderly people are invited to stay in a neighbour's home and live in the household as an ordinary family member. Lasting relationships often develop. There may be a charge, or the service may be run on a voluntary basis (or be paid for by the local authority). Some voluntary organizations arrange *holidays for older people* to give relatives a break. Different charities take responsibility according to the area where you live: the Citizens Advice Bureau, volunteer centre or social services department should know whom you should approach.

Another solution is a *short-stay home,* which is residential accommodation variously run by local authorities, voluntary organizations or private individuals, catering specifically for elderly people. The different types of home are described in more detail under the heading 'Residential care homes' further on in this chapter. For information about local authority provision, ask the social services department. If, as opposed to general care, proper medical attention is necessary, you should consult your parent's GP. Many *hospitals and nursing homes* offer short-stay care arrangements as a means of relieving relatives, and a doctor should be able to help organize this for you.

Carers UK was set up to support and campaign for those caring for an ill, frail or disabled relative at home. It has around 80 self-help branches that are run for and by carers. Contact: 0808 808 7777; website: www.carersuk.org.

Jewish Care runs a number of carers' groups, mostly in London. Contact: 020 8922 2222; website: www.jewishcare.org.

Useful reading

Caring for Someone? (SD4), available free from social security or Jobcentre Plus; website: www.jobcentreplus.gov.uk.

Benefits and allowances

There are a number of benefits or allowances available to those with responsibility for the care of an elderly person and/or to elderly people themselves.

If you are caring for someone, Directgov is the place to turn to for the latest and widest range of online public information. There is a section for *carers* covering support services and assessments, carer's rights, working and caring, carer's allowance and much more. For clearly written, useful and easy to find information, visit www.direct.gov.uk/carers.

Directgov is also the place to turn to for online public information for *disabled people*. This covers employment, financial support, independent living, disability rights, health and support and much more. For information and services local to you, and links to charities and other helpful organizations supporting disabled people, go to www.direct.gov.uk/disability.

Entitlements for carers

Home Responsibilities Protection

This is a means of protecting your state pension if you are unable to work because of the necessity to care for an elderly person. For further details, see under 'State pensions' at the start of Chapter 3, or ask for leaflet CF411 at any pension centre.

Carer's Allowance

If you spend at least 35 hours a week caring for someone who is getting attendance allowance or the middle or highest rate of the disability living allowance care component, you may be able to claim carer's allowance (£53.10 a week in 2009/10). You cannot get this if you are already getting the State pension or work and earn over £95 per week. For more information, **Benefit Enquiry Line** contact: 0800 882 2000; website: www.direct.gov.uk/caringforsomeone.

Entitlements for elderly or disabled people

Higher personal tax allowance

People over 65 receive a higher personal allowance – £9,490 for those aged 65–74 and £9,640 for those aged 75 and over. The full amount is given only to people whose income does not exceed £22,900. People with higher incomes will have the age-related element of their personal allowance reduced by £1 for every £2 of income above the income limit. These figures are valid to April 2011. For further information, see IR leaflet 121, *Income Tax and Pensioners*. See website: www.hmrc.gov.uk.

Higher married couple's tax allowance

A higher married couple's allowance is similarly available to those couples where the older partner is over 75. The current amount is £6,965, compared with the normal minimum of £2,670. The full amount is given only to those whose income does not exceed £22,900. These figures are valid to April 2011. All married couple's allowances are restricted to 10 per cent tax relief.

Attendance Allowance

This is paid to people aged 65 or over who are severely disabled, either mentally or physically, and have needed almost constant care for at least six months. (They may be able to get the allowance even if no one has actually given them that help.) An exception to the six months' qualifying period is made in the case of those who are terminally ill, who can receive the allowance without having to wait.

There are two rates of allowance: £71.40 a week for those needing 24-hour care, and £47.80 for those needing intensive day- or night-time care. The allowance is tax-free and is generally paid regardless of income (although payment might be affected by entering residential care). For more information: **Benefit Enquiry Line** contact 0800 882 2000; website: www.direct.gov.uk.

Disability Living Allowance (DLA)

This benefit is paid to people up to the age of 65, inclusive, who become disabled. It has two components: a mobility and a care component. A person can be entitled either to one or to both components. The level of benefit depends on the person's care and/or mobility needs. There are two rates for the mobility component and three rates for the care component. DLA is tax-free and is generally paid regardless of income (although payment may be affected by entering residential care). Except in the case of people who are terminally ill, who can receive the higher-rate care component of DLA immediately, there is a normal qualifying period of three months. For more information: **Benefit Enquiry Line** contact 0800 882 2000; website: www.direct.gov.uk.

Cold weather payments

These are designed to give particularly vulnerable people extra help with heating costs during very cold weather. Anyone aged 60 and over who is in receipt of the guaranteed element of Pension Credit, Income Support or income-based Jobseeker's Allowance qualifies automatically. The payment is made by post as soon as the temperature in an area is forecast to drop – or actually drops – to zero degrees Celsius (or below) for seven consecutive days, so people can turn up their heating secure in the knowledge that they will be receiving extra cash help. The amount paid is £25.00. Those eligible should receive it without having to claim. For more information: **Benefit Enquiry Line** contact 0800 882 2000; website: www.direct.gov.uk.

Winter fuel payments

This is a special annual tax-free payment of between £125 to £400, given to all households with a resident aged between 60 and 80 and over. For more information: **Benefit Enquiry Line** contact 0800 882 2000; website: www. direct.gov.uk.

Free off-peak bus travel

People over the age of 60 and also disabled people can travel free on any bus service in the country. See Chapter 14, section on 'Travel and other concessions'.

Free TV licence

People aged 75 and older no longer have to pay for their TV licence.

Financial assistance

A number of charities give financial assistance to elderly people in need. These include the following:

> **Counsel and Care** gives advice on ways to fund care, whether this is for nursing or other residential care, or for care in the home. Single needs payments are sometimes available to help towards holidays, special

equipment, telephone installations and other priority items. Contact: 0845 300 7585; website: www.counselandcare.org.uk.

Elizabeth Finn Care gives grants to enable British and Irish people to remain in their own home and can also provide weekly grants to top-up private care homes fees. Contact: 020 8834 9200; website: www.elizabethfinncare.org.uk.

Guild of Aid for Gentlepeople can assist those 'of gentle birth or good education' who want to stay in their own home and who cannot call on any professional or trade body. Contact: 020 7255 4480; website: www.aco.uk.net.

Independent Age helps older people to remain independent by providing small lifetime annuities, financial help in times of crisis, and equipment to aid mobility. It provides residential and nursing care and assistance with fees. Contact: 020 7605 4200; website: www.independentage.org.uk.

Independent Living Fund (ILF) is a trust fund set up with government backing to assist people aged 16 to 65 with severe disabilities to pay for domestic or personal care to enable them to remain in their own homes. To become eligible, applicants must first approach their local authority for assistance under the Community Care scheme and be successful in obtaining care services. Contact: 0845 601 8815; website: www.ilf.org.uk.

Motability is a registered charity set up to assist recipients of the war pensioners' mobility supplement or the higher-rate mobility component of DLA to use their allowance to lease or buy a car, a powered wheelchair or a scooter. Contact: 0845 456 4566; website: www.motability.co.uk.

RABI (Royal Agricultural Benevolent Institution) supports retired disabled or disadvantaged members of the farming community and their families, in England, Wales and Northern Ireland. Contact: 01865 724 931; website: www.rabi.org.uk.

SSAFA Forces Help is restricted to those who have served in the armed forces (including reservists and those who have done National Service) and their families. Contact: 0845 1300 975; website: www.ssafa.org.uk.

Wireless for the Bedridden Society loans radios and televisions on a permanent basis to elderly housebound people who cannot afford sets. Application should be made through a health visitor, social worker or officer of a recognized organization. Contact: 01708 621 101; website: www.w4b.org.uk.

Useful reading

For other sources of financial help, ask your library for *A Guide to Grants for Individuals in Need*, published by the Directory of Social Change, and *The Charities Digest*, published by Waterlow Professional Publishing.

Helpful guidance

For many people, one of the main barriers to getting help is knowing which of the many thousands of charities to approach. **Charity Search** exists to help elderly people in need overcome their problem by putting them in contact with those charities most likely to be able to assist. Contact: 0117 982 4060; website: www.charitysearch.org.uk.

Another organization that helps people to access money that is available to them through charities, welfare grants and benefits is **Turn2Us,** which is part of Elizabeth Finn Care. Contact: 0808 802 2000; website: www.turn2us.org.uk.

Special accommodation

Retired people who need particular support, assistance or care may choose or need to move to accommodation where special services are provided. This can be either sheltered housing or a care home. Both kinds of accommodation cover an enormous spectrum, so anyone considering either of these options should make a point of investigating the market before reaching a decision. Choosing the right accommodation is critically important, as it can make all the difference to independence, lifestyle and general well-being. It can also of course lift a great burden off families' shoulders to know that their parents are happy and comfortable, in congenial surroundings and with on-the-spot help, should this be necessary.

Sheltered housing

Sheltered housing is usually a development of independent, purpose-designed bungalows or flats within easy access of shops and public transport. It generally has a house manager and an alarm system for emergencies, and often some common facilities. These could include a garden, possibly a launderette, a sitting room and a dining room, with meals provided for residents, on an optional basis, either once a day or several days a week.

Residents normally have access to all the usual range of services – home helps, meals on wheels and so on – in the same way as any other elderly people. Sheltered housing is available for sale or rental through private developers, housing associations or local authorities. It is occasionally also provided through gifted housing schemes, or on a shared ownership basis.

Sheltered housing for sale

Good developments are always sought after and can require you to join a waiting list. Although this is emphatically not a reason for rushing into a decision you might regret, if you were hoping to move in the fairly near future it could be as well to start looking sooner rather than later. There are many companies offering sheltered housing for sale, with standards and facilities varying enormously. Some also provide personal care services as an adjunct to their retirement home schemes. Flats and houses are usually sold on long leases (99 years or more) for a capital sum, with a weekly or monthly service charge to cover maintenance and resident support services. Should a resident decide to move, the property can usually be sold on the open market, either through an estate agent or through the developer, provided the prospective buyer is over 55 years of age.

Occupiers normally have to enter into a management agreement with the house builder, and it is important to establish exactly what the commitment is likely to be before buying into such schemes. Factors that should be considered include: who the managing agent is; the house manager's duties; what the service charge covers; the ground rent; the arrangements for any repairs that might prove necessary; whether there is a residents' association; whether pets are allowed; what the conditions are with regard to reselling the property – and the tenant's rights in the matter.

Although the rights of sheltered housing residents have been strengthened over the years, you would nevertheless be strongly recommended to get any contract or agreement vetted by a solicitor before proceeding.

Prices The range of prices is very wide, depending on size, location and type of property. Weekly service charges vary widely too. Additionally, there is usually an annual ground rental – and Council Tax is normally excluded.

The service charge usually covers the cost of the house manager, alarm system, maintenance, repair and renewal of any communal facilities (external and internal) and sometimes the heating and lighting costs. It may also cover insurance on the building (but not the contents). A particular point to watch is that the service charge tends to rise annually, sometimes well above the inflation level. Be wary of service charges that seem uncommonly reasonable in the sales literature, as these are often increased sharply following purchase. Owners of sheltered accommodation have the same rights as other leaseholders, and charges can therefore be challenged by appeal to a leasehold valuation tribunal.

A further safeguard is the Sheltered Housing Code operated by the **NHBC**, which is mandatory for all registered house builders selling sheltered homes. The Code, which applies to all new sheltered dwellings in England and Wales registered on or after 1 April 1990, has two main requirements. One is that all prospective purchasers should be given a purchaser's information pack (PIP), clearly outlining all essential information that they will need to enable them to decide whether or not to buy. The second is that the builder and management organization enter into a formal legal agreement giving purchasers the benefit of the legal rights specified in the Code. Contact: 0844 633 1000; website: www.nhbc.co.uk.

The following can provide information about sheltered housing for sale:

Elderly Accommodation Counsel maintains a nationwide database of all types of specialist accommodation for elderly people and gives advice and detailed information to help enquirers choose the support and care most suited to their needs. Contact: 020 7820 1343; website: www.eac.org.uk.

Retirement Homesearch is an estate agent that specializes in retirement homes for sale. It operates nationwide and deals in all types of property including flats, houses and bungalows, in all price ranges. For properties in England and Wales contact: 0845 880 5560; for properties in Scotland: 0141 248 2846; website: www.retirementhomesearch.co.uk.

Private companies with sheltered housing for sale New developments are constantly under construction. Properties tend to be sold quickly soon after completion, so it pays to find out about future developments and to get on any waiting lists well in advance of a prospective purchase. Firms specializing in this type of property include the following:

Beechcroft Developments offers one-, two- and three-bedroom cottages and apartments located in towns and villages in Southern England: Berkshire, Dorset, Gloucestershire, Hampshire, Hertfordshire, Surrey and Wiltshire. Contact: 01491 825 522; website: www.beechcroft.co.uk.

Bovis Homes Retirement Living offers one- and two-bedroom apartments in Cambridgeshire, Hertfordshire, Suffolk, Surrey and Wiltshire. Developments include 24-hour staffing. Contact: 01474 876 200; website: www.bovishomes.co.uk.

Churchill Retirement Living apartments give you independent, safe and secure retirement living. Development locations in the South East and Midlands. Contact: 0800 458 1847; website: www.churchillretirement.co.uk.

English Courtyard Association (ECA) offers architecturally award-winning 'courtyard-style' schemes throughout England, with two- and three-bedroom houses, cottages and flats for sale on 150-year leases. Contact: 01491 615 960; website: www.englishcourtyardassociation.org.uk.

McCarthy & Stone Retirement Living builds over 2,000 new retirement apartments a year in all parts of England, Scotland and Wales. Contact: 0800 919 132; website: www.mccarthyandstone.co.uk.

Pegasus Retirement Homes plc offers one-, two- and three-bedroom apartments in the Midlands and South-East and South-West of England. Contact: 0800 583 8844; website: www.pegasus-homes.co.uk.

Housing associations with sheltered housing for sale Housing associations build sheltered housing for sale and also manage sheltered housing developments on behalf of private construction companies:

Anchor has nearly 200 estates of mainly one- and two-bedroom flats, bungalows and cottages, comprising almost 7,000 properties countrywide. Contact: 0845 140 2020; website: www.anchor.org.uk.

RLHA Group is a not-for-profit provider of housing and care services to elderly people and others. It offers a leasehold retirement scheme, shared ownership and domiciliary care services. Contact: 01252 356 000; website: www.rlha.org.uk.

Rented sheltered housing

This is normally provided by local authorities, housing associations and certain benevolent societies. As with accommodation to buy, quality varies.

Local authority housing is usually only available to people who have resided in the area for some time. There is often an upper and lower age limit for admission, and prospective tenants may have to undergo a medical examination, since as a rule only those who are physically fit are accepted. Should a resident become infirm or frail, alternative accommodation will be found. Apply to the local housing or social services department or via a housing advice centre.

Housing associations supply much of the newly built sheltered housing. Both rent and service charges vary around the country. In case of need, Income Support or Housing Benefit may be obtained to help with the cost. Citizens Advice Bureau and housing departments often keep a list of local housing associations. There are hundreds to choose from; here are just a few:

Abbeyfield provides supported independent living and residential care for older people. All its houses are led by three core principles: volunteering, value for money and real integration with the community. Contact: 01727 857 536; website: www.abbeyfield.com.

Anchor provides flats and bungalows for older people located throughout England. Most of the developments have a communal area, laundry, alarm system and guest room. Contact: 0845 140 2020; website: www.anchor.org.uk.

Girlings offers private retirement property for rent on life-long tenancies on properties throughout the UK. Contact: 0800 52 51 84; website: www.girlings.co.uk.

Habinteg Housing Association provides homes that are accessible, adaptable and affordable. With over 40 years' experience in housing and disability, Habinteg creates neighbourhoods that allow everyone to live as independently as possible. Contact: 020 7822 8700; website: www.habinteg.org.uk.

Hanover offers one of the widest choices of housing options available in the UK to the over-55s, in towns, cities and rural locations. There are also more than 40 extra-care housing estates where care is available 24 hours a day. Contact: 0800 280 2575; website: www.hanover.org.uk.

Jewish Community Housing Association Ltd has some 600 sheltered flats primarily for Jewish people in housing need. Properties are located in London, Hemel Hempstead and Margate. Contact: 0208 381 4901; website: www.jcha.org.uk.

Southern Housing Group is one of Southern England's largest housing associations. Founded over 100 years ago, it owns and manages 24,000 homes with more than 66,000 residents. It provides a range of options for rent and home ownership, including sheltered accommodation, across the South of England and the Isle of Wight. Contact: 0300 303 1771; website: www.shgroup.org.uk.

Benevolent societies

These all cater for specific professional and other groups:

Housing 21 is a major national provider of housing, care and support services for older people. Established over 40 years ago, this not-for-profit organization with charitable status provides over 13,000 properties in 350 sheltered and extra-care housing schemes throughout England. Contact: 0345 606 6363; website: www.housing21.co.uk.

Royal Alfred Seafarers' Society, established as a charity in 1865 to help 'worn out and infirm seamen', provides quality long-term care for seafarers and their widows and dependants. Contact: 01737 353 763; website: www.royalalfredseafarers.com.

SSAFA Forces Help is restricted to those who have served in the armed forces (including reservists and those who have done National Service) and their families. Contact: 0845 1300 975; website: www.ssafa.org.uk.

Alternative ways of buying sheltered accommodation

For those who cannot afford to buy into sheltered housing either outright or through a mortgage, there are a variety of alternative payment methods.

Shared ownership and 'Sundowner' schemes

Part-ownership schemes are now offered by a number of developers. Would-be residents, who must be over 55 years, part-buy or part-rent, with the amount of rent varying according to the size of the initial lump sum. Residents can sell at any time, but they only recoup that percentage of the sale price that is proportionate to their original capital investment, with no allowance for any rental payments made over the intervening period.

'Investment' and gifted housing schemes

Some charities and housing associations operate these schemes, for which a capital sum is required, to obtain sheltered accommodation.

'Investment' schemes work as follows. The buyer puts in the larger share of the capital, usually 50 to 80 per cent, and the housing association puts in the remainder. The buyer pays rent on the housing association's share of the accommodation and also service charges for the communal facilities.

Gifted housing schemes differ in that an individual donates his or her property to a registered charity, in return for being housed and cared for in his or her own home. The attraction is that the owner can remain in his or her own property with none of the burden of its upkeep. However, it is advisable to consult a solicitor before signing anything, because such schemes have the big negative of reducing the value of the owner's estate, with consequent loss for any beneficiaries.

Age UK runs SeniorLine, a free advice and information service, available throughout the UK for older people and their carers. Trained advice workers can help with enquiries about community or residential care and housing options. Contact: 0800 169 6565; website: www.ageuk.org.uk.

Almshouses

Most almshouses are endowed by a charity for the benefit of older people of reduced means who live locally or have a connection with a particular trade. There are now over 2,000 groups of almshouses, providing about 35,000 dwellings. Although many are of considerable age, most of them have been modernized and new ones are being built. Rents are not charged, but there will be a maintenance contribution towards upkeep and heating.

A point you should be aware of is that almshouses do not provide the same security of tenure as some other tenancies. You would be well advised to have the proposed letter of appointment checked by a lawyer or other expert to ensure you understand exactly what the beneficiary's rights are. There is no standard way to apply for an almshouse, since each charity has its own qualifications for residence. Some housing departments and advice centres keep lists of local almshouses. An organization that could help is the **Almshouse Association**, which supplies information on almshouses and contact details in the county in which you are interested. Contact: 01344 452 922; website: www.almshouses.org.

Granny flats

A granny flat or annexe is a self-contained unit attached to a family house. A large house can be converted or extended for this purpose, but planning permission is needed. Enquire at your local authority planning department. Some councils, particularly new towns, have houses to rent with granny flats.

Housing for ethnic groups

LHA-ASRA is a not-for-profit organization with over 20 years' experience in providing affordable housing to meet the needs of single people and families of all ages, including Asian elders and single Asian women. There are also general family homes. Contact: 0116 257 6700; website: www.lha-asra.org.uk.

Salvation Army homes

The Salvation Army has 18 homes for elderly people in various parts of the UK, offering residential care for men and women unable to manage in their own homes. Christian caring is given within a family atmosphere, in pleasant surroundings, but the homes are not nursing homes. Contact: 0845 634 0101; website: www.salvationarmy.org.uk.

Extra-care schemes

A number of organizations that provide sheltered accommodation also have extra-care sheltered housing, designed for those who can no longer look after themselves without assistance. Cost ranges from about £100 to £450 a week. Although expensive, it is cheaper than most private care homes and often more appropriate than full-scale nursing care. A possible problem is that tenants of some of these schemes do not have security of tenure and, should they become frail, could be asked to leave if more intensive care were required. Among the housing associations that provide these facilities are Housing 21, Hanover Housing Association, Anchor, Abbeyfield (see the details listed earlier in this chapter).

Community Care

Since the start of Community Care in April 1993, anyone needing help in arranging suitable care for an elderly person should contact his or her social services department. Before making suggestions, the department will assess what type of provision would best meet the needs of the individual concerned. This could be services or special equipment to enable the person to stay in his or her own home, residential home accommodation or a nursing home. If residential or nursing home care is necessary, the department will arrange a place in either a local authority or other home, pay the charge and seek reimbursement from the individual according to his or her means.

It is anticipated that nearly 70 per cent of men and some 85 per cent of women over the age of 65 will need care at some time. One in five British adults has elderly parents who require some form of care or assistance. One in four of those aged over 65 will require some form of long-term care. According to the health think tank, the King's Fund, almost everyone in the UK will either need care or become a carer.

The Health Secretary set up the independent commission on the funding of care in July 2010, which is expected to report by mid-2011. The state has no responsibility to fund daily care, such as help with washing and dressing. Frailty in old age is quite different from actual illness, where elderly people are entitled to receive free treatment under the National Health Service. While some older people can afford to retire in comfort and others are confident and optimistic about how they will end their days, it is very sad when relatives have to sell their loved ones' property so that they can afford to pay for their growing care needs in their latter years.

Care homes

If your parents need to move into a care home, the state may help with the cost. The rules are complex and only a brief outline is given here. For more information, the local council is the point of contact.

If moving into a nursing home is a continuation of NHS treatment that your parents have been having for an illness – for example he or she is discharged from hospital direct to a home – this should be paid for by the NHS. However, this is a grey area and you may have to be persistent to get their costs met in this way.

If they do not qualify for NHS continuing care, they may still qualify for some state help with care-home fees, provided their needs assessment found this was the best option for them and their means are low.

If their capital (savings and other assets) are above a set threshold, they will have to pay for themselves. If their capital is less, their local council may pay part or, if their capital is below the lower threshold, the full amount. The capital limits (2010/11) are as follows:

Country	Lower limit	Upper limit	Personal expenses allowance per week
England	£14,000	£23,000	£21.90
Wales	£20,750	£22,000	£22.00
Scotland	£13,750	£22,500	£21.90
N Ireland	£14,000	£23,000	£21.90

Capital does not include the value of their home, if their spouse, civil partner or certain other dependants continue to live there. They will be expected to contribute most of their income towards the cost of the fees, but they can keep around £20 per week to meet their personal expenses. If they receive state help with their care home fees, they will no longer be eligible for attendance allowance.

Residential care homes (care homes registered to provide personal care)

There may come a time when it is no longer possible for an elderly person to manage without being in proper residential care. In a residential care home, sometimes known as a 'rest home', the accommodation usually consists of a bedroom plus communal dining rooms, lounges and gardens. All meals are provided, rooms are cleaned, and staff are at hand to give whatever help is needed. Most homes are fully furnished, though it is usually possible to take small items of furniture. Except in some of the more expensive private homes, bathrooms are normally shared. Intensive nursing care is not usually included.

Homes are run by private individuals (or companies), voluntary organizations and local authorities. All homes must be registered with the Commission for Social Care Inspection to ensure minimum standards. *An unregistered home should not be considered.* It is very important that the individual should have a proper chance to visit it and ask any questions. Before reaching a final decision, it is a good idea to arrange a short stay to see whether the facilities are suitable and pleasant.

It could also be sensible to enquire what long-term plans there are for the home. Moving to a new care home can be a highly distressing experience for an elderly person who has become attached to the staff and made friends among the other residents. Though a move can never be totally ruled out, awareness of whether the home is likely to remain a going concern could be a deciding factor when making a choice. Possible clues could include whether the place is short-staffed or in need of decoration. If it is run by a company or charity, you could request to see the latest accounts.

Private homes

Private care homes are often converted houses, taking up to about 30 people. As more companies move into the market, they can be purpose-built accommodation and may include a heated swimming pool and luxury facilities. The degree of care varies. If a resident becomes increasingly infirm, a care home will normally continue to look after him or her if possible. It may, however, become necessary at some point to arrange transfer to a nursing home or hospital. Fees vary enormously.

Voluntary care homes

These are run by charities, religious bodies or other voluntary organizations. Eligibility may be determined by age, background or occupation, depending on the criteria of the managing organization. Income may be a factor, as may general fitness, and individuals may be invited to a personal interview before acceptance on to the waiting list. Priority tends to be given to those in greatest need. Homes are often in large converted houses, with accommodation for under 10 people or up to 100. Fees vary depending on locality.

Local authority homes

These are sometimes referred to as 'Part III accommodation', and admission will invariably be arranged by the social services department. If someone does not like the particular accommodation suggested, he or she can turn it down and ask the department what other offers might be available. Weekly charges vary around the country. In practice, individuals are charged only according to their means.

Nursing homes (care homes registered to provide nursing care)

Nursing homes provide medical supervision and fully qualified nurses, 24 hours a day. Most are privately run, with the remainder being supported by voluntary organizations. All nursing homes in England must be registered with the Commission for Social Care Inspection, which keeps a list of what homes are available in the area. In Wales, the inspectorate is called the Care Standards Inspectorate for Wales, and in Scotland it is called the Scottish Commission for the Regulation of Care.

Private

These homes normally accommodate between 15 and 100 patients. Depending on the part of the country, charges vary. Some fees rise depending on how much nursing is required. For information about nursing homes in the UK, contact the following:

Elderly Accommodation Counsel maintains a nationwide database of all types of specialist accommodation for elderly people and gives advice and detailed information to help enquirers choose the support and care most suited to their needs. Contact: 020 7820 1343; website: www.eac.org.uk.

NHFA runs a free helpline that offers advice to individuals and their families on specialist accommodation and how to pay for care home fees, what state benefits are available to them and other related matters. Contact: 0800 99 88 33; website: www.nhfa.co.uk.

RNHA (Registered Nursing Home Association) is an organization that provides support for nursing home owners, requiring its members to meet high levels of standards and service. Patients in nursing homes that are members of the RNHA can expect to receive some of the best standards of service available. Contact: 0121 451 1088; website: www.rnha.co.uk.

Voluntary organizations

These normally have very long waiting lists, and beds are often reserved for those who have been in the charity's care home. Voluntary organizations that run care homes include:

Careways Trust	01903 276 030; website: www.carewaystrust.org.uk
Friends of the Elderly	020 7730 8263; website: www.fote.org.uk
IndependentAge	020 7605 4200; website: www.independentage.org.uk
Jewish Care	020 8922 2222; website: www.jewishcare.org

Free nursing care

Since October 2001, the nursing costs of being in a home have been made free to all patients. This does not include the personal care costs (eg help with bathing, dressing or eating), nor the accommodation costs; individuals will continue to be assessed for both of these under the rules described below. In Scotland, exceptionally, the personal care costs are also free. The provision of free nursing care may make only a fairly limited contribution to the cost of being in a home. Patients are assessed according to their needs and the amount of actual nursing care they require.

Financial assistance for residential and nursing home care

Under the Community Care arrangements, people needing to go into a residential or nursing home may receive help from their local authority social services department. As explained earlier, the department will make the arrangements direct with the home following its assessment procedure and will seek reimbursement from the person towards the cost, according to set means-testing rules.

People who were already in a residential or nursing home before April 1993 used to receive special levels of Income Support. This arrangement, known as 'preserved rights', ended in April 2002, and instead the full cost of residential care is now met by the individual's local authority.

People who had been or are currently paying for themselves but can no longer afford to do so may have the right to claim help, now or in the future, if they qualify on grounds of financial need. Help is provided on a sliding scale for those with assets. Even those on a very low income are required to make some contribution towards the cost of being in a home.

For further information, enquire at your local Citizens Advice Bureau: website: www.citizensadvice.org.uk or contact **Elderly Accommodation Counsel**, Contact: 020 7820 1343; website: www.eac.org.uk.

Additional help

A major worry for many people going into residential care is the requirement to sell their home to cover the costs. While this may still eventually be necessary, the rules have been made slightly more flexible to allow a short breathing space for making decisions. Under the rules introduced in April 2001, the value of a person's home is disregarded from the means-testing procedure in assessing their ability to pay for the first 12 weeks of their going into care. Also, instead of selling, they may be able to borrow the money (secured against their home) from the local council, which will eventually reclaim the loan at a later stage or from their estate.

But if you are thinking about funding care for your parents in future, you are ahead of the game. Most people leave it until it is needed and then have to sort things out in a hurry. Planning for care is a new sphere for most people and there are different types of care to consider: in the home, in residential care and then in nursing care. The funding aspect is always difficult. The starting point is to see what the local authority can provide. Beyond that, careful planning is required so that best use is made of your parents' income and assets.

Obtaining and paying for care is a complex area. An organization that can help is **EquityCare,** supported by First Stop Advice, an elderly care charity. It provides support and advice to seniors as well as an information service for carers. Contact: 0800 014 1640. Care funding advice is available on 0845 004 0301; Website: www.equitycare.co.uk.

Useful organizations

Care & Quality Commission   03000 616 161;
website: www.cqc.org.uk

Home Instead Senior Care   01925 730 271;
website: www.homeinstead.co.uk

Solicitors for the Elderly   0844 567 6173:
website: www.solicitorsfortheelderly.com

Further information

Key sources of information about voluntary and private homes are: the *Charities Digest* (available in libraries, housing aid centres and Citizens Advice Bureau) and the *Directory of Independent Hospitals and Health Services* (available in libraries). The *Charities Digest* also includes information about hospices.

Here are some sources of advice:

Action on Elder Abuse was founded to help prevent physical, psychological or financial exploitation and other types of abuse of elderly people. An estimated 340,000 older people are abused every year in this country in their own homes – and only 10 per cent of cases are acted upon. As well as providing guidance and training for professionals engaged in the care of vulnerable older people, it also runs a free confidential helpline offering advice and support to individuals who feel that they are the victims of abuse as well as to other members of the public who have grounds for concern about someone's welfare. Contact: 0808 808 8141; website: www.elderabuse.org.uk.

Age UK runs SeniorLine, a free advice and information service, available throughout the UK for older people and their carers. Trained advice workers can help with enquiries about community or residential care and housing options. Contact: 0800 169 6565; website: www.ageuk.org.uk.

The Cinnamon Trust maintains a register of care homes that allow pets to be kept. Contact: 01736 757 900; website: www.cinnamon.org.uk.

Elderly Accommodation Counsel maintains a nationwide database of all types of specialist accommodation for elderly people and gives advice and detailed information to help enquirers choose the support and care most suited to their needs. Contact: 020 7820 1343; website: www.eac.org.uk.

NHFA runs a free helpline that offers advice to individuals and their families on specialist accommodation and how to pay for care home fees, what state benefits are available to them and other related matters. Contact: 0800 99 88 33; website: www.nhfa.co.uk.

R&RA (Relatives & Residents Association) offers a support service to families and friends of older people in, or considering, long-term care. There are local groups around the country where relatives can meet and discuss any practical or emotional worries they may have about opting for residential care, and there is also a helpline that can give advice on most questions, from finding a home to concerns about the standard of care. Contact: 020 7359 8136; website: www.relres.org.

Useful reading

Finding Care Home Accommodation, a free fact sheet obtainable from **Age UK.** Contact: 0800 169 6565; website: www.ageuk.org.uk.

Some special problems

A minority of people, as they become older, suffer from special problems that can cause great distress. Because families do not like to talk about them, they may be unaware of what services are available and so may be missing out on practical help and sometimes also on financial assistance.

Hypothermia

Elderly people tend to be more vulnerable to the cold. If the body drops below a certain temperature, it can be dangerous, because one of the symptoms of hypothermia is that sufferers no longer actually feel cold. Instead, they may lose their appetite and vitality and may become mentally confused. Instead of doing all the sensible things like getting a hot drink and putting on an extra sweater, they are liable to neglect themselves further and can put themselves at real risk. Although heating costs are often blamed, quite wealthy people can also be victims by allowing their home to become too cold or not wearing sufficient clothing. For this reason, during a cold snap it is very important to check up regularly on an elderly person living alone.

British Gas, electricity companies and the Solid Fuel Association are all willing to give advice on how heating systems can be used more efficiently and economically. Insulation can also play a very large part in keeping a home warmer and cheaper to heat. It may be possible to obtain a grant from the local authority, although normally this would only be likely on grounds of real need.

Elderly and disabled people in receipt of Income Support may receive a cold weather payment to help with heating costs during a particularly cold spell – that is, when the temperature is forecast to drop to zero degrees Celsius (or below) for seven consecutive days. Those eligible should receive the money automatically. In the event of any problem, ask at your social security office. In the event of an emergency, such as a power cut, contact the Citizens Advice Bureau or Age UK.

Finally, every household with someone aged 60 or older will get an annual tax-free winter fuel payment of £250, while those with a resident aged 80 or older will receive £400. Contact **Winter Fuel Helpline: 0845 915 1515**; website: www.direct.gov.uk.

Incontinence

Bladder or bowel problems can cause deep embarrassment to sufferers as well as inconvenience to relatives. The problem can occur in an elderly person for all sorts of reasons, and a doctor should always be consulted, as it can often be cured or at least alleviated by proper treatment. To assist with the practical problems, some local authorities operate a laundry service that collects soiled linen, sometimes several times a week. Talk to the health visitor or district nurse (at their local health centre), who will be able to advise about this and other facilities.

B&BF (**Bladder and Bowel Foundation**) is the charity for people with bladder and bowel dysfunction. The charity operates a helpline that is staffed by nurses with specialist knowledge. Contact: 0845 345 0165; website: www.bladderandbowelfoundation.org.

Dementia

Sometimes an elderly person can become confused or forgetful, suffer severe loss of memory or have violent mood swings and at times be abnormally aggressive. It is important to consult a doctor as soon as possible, as the cause may be depression, stress or even vitamin deficiency. All of these can be treated and often completely cured. If dementia is diagnosed, there are ways of helping a sufferer to cope better with acute forgetfulness and other symptoms. Arguably the hardest aspect is the thought that there is no cure for a progressive disease that gradually erodes the personality of the person one loves. But there is ongoing research into finding a cure and there are some treatments that can delay the progression of some forms of dementia. Meanwhile there are many ways to make life for people with dementia more manageable and enjoyable.

The most common type of dementia is Alzheimer's disease, which is usually found in people aged over 65. Approximately 24 million people worldwide have dementia, of which the majority (over 60 per cent) is due to Alzheimer's. Clinical signs are characterized by progressive cognitive deterioration, together with a decline in the ability to carry out common daily tasks, and behavioural changes. The first readily identifiable symptoms of Alzheimer's disease are usually short-term memory loss and visual-spatial confusion. These initial symptoms progress from seemingly simple and fluctuating to a more pervasive loss of memory, including difficulty navigating familiar areas such as the local neighbourhood. This advances to loss of other familiar and well-known skills, as well as recognition of objects and persons.

Since family members are often the first to notice changes that might indicate the onset of Alzheimer's (or other forms of dementia) they should learn the early warning signs. They should serve as informants during initial clinical evaluation of patients. It is important to consult your doctor as soon as you have concerns. It is also a good idea to talk to the health visitor, as he or she will know about any helpful facilities that may be available locally. The health visitor is also able to arrange appointments with other professionals, such as the community psychiatric nurse and the occupational therapist.

It is important to remember that people with dementia are still people. The Alzheimer's Society recommends the following tips. Always treat the person with respect and dignity; be a good listener; be a good communicator; remember that little things mean a lot. Staying in touch shows that you care; offer practical help; organize a treat; and find out more about the condition so that you understand and feel comfortable spending time with the person with dementia.

Other sources of help and support for people with dementia and their carers are:

Alzheimer Scotland   0808 8083 000; website: www.alzscot.org

Alzheimer's Society   0845 300 0336; website: www.alzheimers.org.uk

Mind   0845 766 0163, website: www.mind.org.uk

Useful reading

Caring for the Person with Dementia, published by the Alzheimer's Society, website: www.alzheimers.org.uk, and *Understanding Dementia*, available from Mind, website: www.mind.org.uk.

Chapter Sixteen
No one is immortal

" A man should not leave this earth with unfinished business.
He should live each day as if it was a pre-flight check.
He should ask each morning, 'am I prepared for lift-off?'

DIANE FROLOV AND ANDREW SCHNEIDER (FROM NORTHERN EXPOSURE)

Life – as we all know – has no dress rehearsal. We get one shot at it and it passes all too quickly. In countries in the East, death is celebrated with glorious processions, merry-making and days of feasting. In Western society, we go to the other extreme. Some people rarely discuss death or how it will affect them. Even more worrying, they ignore the financial practicalities, in the subconscious belief perhaps that to do otherwise would be tempting fate. For the same reason, many people put off making a will or rationalize that it does not really matter. They believe perhaps that, whatever happens, their possessions will eventually go to their family. But this is not necessarily the case. A great deal of heartbreak and real financial worry could be avoided if people were more open about the subject of dying and discussed their wishes and choices with loved ones regarding their own mortality.

Wills

Anyone who is married, has children or is over the age of 35 should make a will. Despite a lot of publicity about it, thousands of people still do not do so. A will ensures that the deceased person's wishes are known and properly executed. But also very important, it will spare the family the legal complications that arise when someone dies intestate. A major problem, if someone dies without leaving a will, is that the surviving husband or wife will usually have to wait very much longer for badly needed cash. The legal

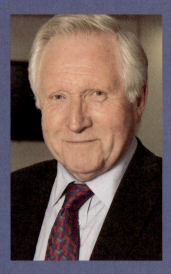

Many of you will remember my father, Richard Dimbleby, and his broadcasts up until his untimely death from cancer at 52. In the 1960s cancer was still a taboo subject and my father's decision to go public about his illness helped to lift that taboo. In his memory, a fund was set up that has been used both to support those who are affected by cancer, and to research more effective treatments. We need your help to expand our work, particularly to support the growing number of people who are living for longer with cancer.

Every year Dimbleby Cancer Care offers care and support to patients and their carers through its main centres at Guy's and St Thomas' Hospitals in London, providing psychological and practical help, support groups and complementary therapies. The charity's research arm funds national research projects which identify the support needs of people with cancer – and those of their families and carers – and provides strategies for how those needs can be met. Hitherto this field of research has been badly neglected. People who have been kind enough to make donations or remember us in their wills have allowed us to help thousands of people over the past 40 years. Please remember us when you are making your will and, if you can, make a donation to us now.

David Dimbleby

Making life better
for people living
with cancer

4th Floor Management Offices
Bermondsey Wing
Guy's Hospital
Great Maze Pond
London SE1 9RT

tel: 020 7188 7889
email: admin@dimblebycancercare.org
Registered charity number 247558

DIMBLEBY CANCER CARE

www.dimblebycancercare.or

Set up as a memorial to Richard Dimbleby, the broadcasting pioneer, who died of cancer at 52, Dimbleby Cancer Care's focus is on addressing the psychological and social impact on patients and their families which a cancer diagnosis inevitably brings.

The charity supports the DCC Cancer Support and Information Services at Guy's and St Thomas' Hospitals in London, offering psychological support and counselling; complementary therapies; benefits and financial advice; support groups which focus on specific cancers; and information about cancer.

The DCC Research Fund finances national research into the support needs of people with cancer, and those of their families and carers – for example, how can carers be of more help to patients undergoing chemotherapy? How can older care givers be helped to cope better? How helpful are telephone help-lines? How can children with cancer be involved in their own treatment decisions? The Research Fund is one of the UK's leading funders of this type of research.

Dimbleby Cancer Care is entirely dependent on legacies and donations to fund its work.

advertisement feature

formalities are infinitely more complex; there will be no executor. Also, the individual's assets will be distributed according to a rigid formula, which may be far from what he or she had intended. It may perversely result in the partner's security being quite unnecessarily jeopardized.

Laws of intestacy

The rules if you die without leaving a will are as follows:

- If there is *a surviving spouse but no surviving children, parents, brothers, sisters or direct nephews or nieces* of the deceased, the widow or widower inherits the whole of the estate.

- If there are *children but no surviving spouse,* the estate is divided equally among the children. If one child has died, his or her share goes to his or her own children.

- If there are *a spouse and children,* the partner receives all personal possessions, a maximum of £125,000 (if the estate is a large one) and a life interest in half of the remainder. The other half goes to the children.

- If there are *no children* but other close members of the family still living (parents, brothers, sisters or direct nephews or nieces), the surviving spouse receives all personal possessions, up to £200,000 where there is a large estate, and half of the remainder of the estate. The other half is divided between the rest of the family.

- *Non-married partners* do not inherit automatically; they have to make a court application.

- *Same-sex partners* who have entered into a civil partnership have the same inheritance rights as married spouses.

- If *a couple are separated* but not divorced, they are still legally married and, therefore, the separated partner could be a major beneficiary.

Making a will

You have three choices: you can do it yourself, you can ask your bank to help you, or you can use a solicitor or a specialist will-writing practitioner.

1. Doing it yourself

Home-made wills are not generally recommended. People often use ambiguous wording which, while perfectly clear to the individual who has written it, may be less obvious to others. This could result in the donor's wishes being misinterpreted and could also cause considerable delay in settling the estate. Wills forms are available from good stationers. They are not perfect and still leave considerable margin for error if the estate is complicated.

Two witnesses are needed, and an essential point to remember is that beneficiaries cannot witness a will, nor can the spouses of any beneficiaries. In certain circumstances, a will can be rendered invalid. A sensible precaution for those doing it themselves is to have it checked by a solicitor or by a legal expert from the Citizens Advice Bureau.

For individuals with sight problems, **RNIB** has produced a comprehensive guide to making or changing a will that is available in large print size, in Braille and on tape, as well as in standard print size. Contact: 0845 766 9999; website: www.rnib.org.uk.

2. Banks

Advice on wills and the administration of estates is given by the trustee companies of most of the major high street banks. In particular, the services they offer are to provide general guidance, to act as executor and to administer the estate. They will also introduce clients to a solicitor and keep a copy of the will – plus other important documents – in their safe, to avoid the risk of their being mislaid. Additionally, banks (as solicitors) can give tax planning and other financial guidance, including advice on Inheritance Tax. Some banks will draw up a will for you.

3. Solicitors and will-writing specialists

Solicitors may offer to draw up a will, act as executors and administer the estate. Like banks, they will also keep a copy of your will in safe keeping (most will not charge for storing a will). If you do not have a solicitor, your friends may be able to recommend one, or ask at the Citizens Advice Bureau. The **Law Society** can also provide you with names and addresses. Contact: 020 7242 1222; website: www.lawsociety.org.uk.

Alternatively, if you simply want help in writing a will, you could consult a specialist will-writing practitioner. The best approach is to contact one of the following organizations:

The Society of Will Writers	01522 687 888; website: www.willwriters.com
Trust Inheritance Limited	0800 097 8012; website: www.trustinheritance.com
The Will Bureau	020 8920 3360; website: www.twb.org.uk

A helpful organization is **Moneta Partnership,** which deals with inheritance tax and care costs planning using lifetime trusts. For further information contact: 0800 781 3487; website: www.monetapartnership.com.

Charges

These can vary enormously, depending on the size and complexity of the will. A basic will could cost around £120 or, if your affairs are more complicated, the cost could be considerably more. Always ask for an estimate before proceeding. Remember too that professional fees normally carry VAT. Some solicitors charge according to the time they spend on a job so, although the actual work may not take very long, if you spend hours discussing your will or changing it every few months the costs can escalate very considerably. However, many solicitors will give you a fixed-fee estimate for a will. The fees for will-writing practitioners are broadly in line with those of solicitors.

Community Legal Service funding (Legal Aid)

Financial assistance for legal help and advice is available to certain groups of people for making a will. These include people aged over 70, disabled people, and a parent of a disabled person whom the parent wishes to provide for in his or her will. Additionally, to qualify, the people will need to satisfy the financial eligibility criteria. For further information enquire at your Citizens Advice Bureau or other advice centre.

Executors

You will need to appoint at least one executor to administer your will. An executor can be a beneficiary under the estate and can be a member of your family or a friend whom you trust to act impartially, always provided of course that he or she is willing to accept the responsibility. Alternatively, and this is generally advisable for larger estates, you could appoint your solicitor or bank.

The fees will be additional. They are not paid at the time of making the will but instead come out of the estate. Pretty significant sums could be involved, so the advice on obtaining an estimate is, if anything, even more relevant. In certain instances, banks can be more expensive; in others, solicitors can be. The only way to establish the relative costs is to get an estimate from each.

Banks publish a tariff of their charges. Solicitors render bills according to the time involved so, although it is impossible for them to be precise, they should nevertheless be able to give a pretty accurate assessment – at least at the time of quoting. Both banks' and solicitors' fees may increase during the interval between their being appointed and their fulfilling their duties as executor.

Other points

- Wills should always be kept in a safe place – and their whereabouts known. The most sensible arrangement is for the solicitor to keep the original and for both you and the bank to have a copy.

- A helpful initiative devised by the Law Society is a mini-form, known as a *personal assets log*. This is for individuals drawing up a will to give to their executor or close relatives. It is, quite simply, a four-sided leaflet with space to record essential information: name and address of solicitor; where the will and other important documents, for example share certificates and insurance policies, are kept; the date of any codicils and so on. Logs should be obtainable from most solicitors.

- Wills may need updating in the event of an important change of circumstances, for example a divorce, a remarriage or the birth of a grandchild. An existing will normally becomes invalid in the event of marriage or remarriage and should be replaced. Any changes must be by codicil (for minor alterations) or by a new will, and must be properly witnessed.

- Another reason why you may need, or wish, to change your will is in consequence of changes in the Inheritance Tax rules. The Law Society had been advising all owners of homes and other assets worth more than the nil-rate band (£325,000 for the 2010/11 tax year) to review their wills.

- Partners who wish to leave all their possessions to each other should consider including a 'survivorship clause' in their wills, as an insurance against the intestacy rules being applied were they both, for example, involved in the same fatal accident. Legal advice is strongly recommended here.

- If you have views about your funeral, it is sensible to write a letter to your executors explaining your wishes and to lodge it with your will. If you have any pets, you may equally wish to leave a letter filed with

Every three minutes someone is diagnosed with diabetes. Every three minutes, someone's life changes forever.

With the number of people with diabetes growing year on year, there has never been a more urgent need for funding. Will you help them by remembering Diabetes UK in your will?

By leaving a gift to Diabetes UK in your will today, you can improve the lives of people with diabetes – today, tomorrow and in the years ahead. Call **0845 123 2399** or email **legacies@diabetes.org.uk** for more information.

 Diabetes UK

The charity for people with diabetes

Macleod House, 10 Parkway, London NW1 7AA

A charity registered in England and Wales (no.215199) and in Scotland (no. SCO39136)

FundRaising Standards Board

A Hope For The Future

For over 75 years Diabetes UK has provided help and support for people with diabetes, as well as to their family, friends and carers. Our mission remains to improve the lives of people with the condition and work towards a future without diabetes. Crucial to us achieving this is your support of:

- Our Careline which answered over 33,000 queries from people with diabetes in 2009
- Our Care Event Holidays which give more than 250 children each year the opportunity to learn how to manage their diabetes and meet other children with this condition
- Our vast range of publications which provide the latest news and advice for people of all ages and stages living with diabetes

One way in which you can support the vital work of Diabetes UK is by leaving a gift in your will. The idea that your hopes, beliefs and values

advertisement feature

can be encapsulated in this one document is inspiring. As the largest charity for people with diabetes, we are immeasurably grateful to those individuals who chose to remember us in this way. Much of our work is only possible because of people who care deeply about this debilitating condition and want to ensure their support continues through their will.

Naturally, family and loved ones must come first and there is great peace of mind from knowing those you care about most will be taken care of. But once those provisions are made, did you know that even a fraction of what's left can be immensely valuable to Diabetes UK?

Our greatest hope is that one day, we will find a cure for diabetes. It may not happen in this lifetime but there will be life-changing breakthroughs in treatments and prevention to be made along the way.

If you would like any more information on the work of Diabetes UK or how to go about leaving a gift in your will to charity, you can request a free copy of our will guide to help you. Simply contact our Legacy Manager on:

Telephone: 0845 123 2399
Email: legacies@diabetes.org.uk
Web: www.diabetes.org.uk/legacy

Become a legacy Pioneer by remembering a gift to Diabetes UK in your will. Thank you

your will explaining what arrangements you have made for their immediate and long-term welfare.

- Over the years there has been increased interest in advance decision making, otherwise known as *living wills*. For those who would like more information, the organization, **Dignity in Dying,** is very helpful and can supply you with forms and advice. Contact: 020 7479 7730; website: www.dignityindying.org.uk.

- If you would be willing to donate an organ that might help save someone else's life, you could indicate this in your will or alternatively obtain an organ donor card. These are available from most hospitals, doctors surgeries and chemists.

- **Age UK** can help with information on locally based wills and legacy advisers who provide confidential, impartial advice to older people in their own homes about all aspects of making or revising a will. The advice service is available free of charge to anyone of retirement age.

Useful reading

Will Information Pack, from Age UK; Tel: 0800 169 65 65; website: www.ageuk.org.uk.

How to Write Your Will (the complete guide to structuring your will, inheritance tax planning, probate and administering an estate) by Marlene Garsia published by Kogan Page, website: www.koganpage.com.

Provision for dependent adult children

A particular concern for parents with a physically or mentally dependent son or daughter is what plans they can make to ensure his or her care when they are no longer in a position to manage. There is no easy answer, as each case is individual, depending on the severity of the disability or illness, the range of helpful voluntary or statutory facilities locally, and the extent to which they, as parents, can provide for their child's financial security long term.

While social services may be able to advise, parents thinking ahead might do better to consult a specialist organization experienced in helping carers in this situation to explore the possible options available to them. Useful addresses are:

Carers UK   0808 808 7777;
                                            website: www.carersuk.org

The Princess Royal Trust for Carers   0844 800 4361;
                                            website: www.carers.org

Parents concerned about financial matters such as setting up a trust or making alternative provision in their will would also be advised to consult a solicitor or accountant.

Money and other worries – and how to minimize them

Many people say that the first time they really think about death, in terms of what would happen to their nearest and dearest, is after the birth of their first baby. As children grow up, requirements change, but key points that anyone with a family should consider – and review from time to time – include life insurance and mortgage protection. Both husbands and wives should have *life insurance cover*. If either were to die, not only would the partner lose the financial benefit of the other's earnings, but the partner would also lose immeasurably in other ways.

Most banks and building societies urge home-owners to take out *mortgage protection schemes*. If you die, the loan is paid off automatically and the family home will not be repossessed. Banks also offer *insurance to cover any personal or other loans*. This could be a vital safeguard to avoid leaving the family with debts.

Many people worry about *funeral costs*. Burial service costs can vary, according to different parts of the country, with the average price about £5,000 or even more depending on the choice of coffin and other arrangements. Although you may well hear of cheaper estimates, these are normally exclusive of disbursements, which include minister's fees, cremation fees, medical certificate fees and other items. While cremations are cheaper, prices have increased by at least 15 per cent over the past few years, with £2,500 being a rough average. But here again, costs can vary significantly according to area and how grand or simple the arrangements are.

As a way of helping, a number of insurance companies offer policies to cover funeral costs. While these could be sensible, a drawback is that you are budgeting today against an unknown cost in the future. Over the past four or five years, funeral costs have soared. There is no guarantee even with the best policies that the eventual payout would be sufficient to cover the expenses.

A rather different type of scheme, which overcomes the uncertainties and is growing in popularity, is the prepaid funeral plan, which is designed so you pay all the costs in advance, at present-day prices. In other words, if you join today, the funeral is paid at today's price, whenever the service is actually required and whatever the prices are at the time. Funeral plans are offered by the following:

Age UK Funeral Plan: 0800 028 3139; website: www.ageuk.org.uk.

Co-operative Funeralcare, a nationwide network of more than 600 funeral homes and founder member of the Funeral Planning Council, offers the choice of prepaid tailor-made arrangements or a selection of funeral plan packages, with the option to pay in monthly instalments or in a single payment. Contact: 0800 328 7083; website: www.co-operativefuneralcare.co.uk.

Dignity Caring Funeral Services offers a varied range of choices to suit different requirements, with in all cases the option of paying in a single payment or by monthly instalments. Contact: 0800 38 77 17; website: www.dignityfuneralplans.co.uk.

Golden Charter – the UK's largest independent funeral plan provider – allows provision to be made for increased disbursement costs, and the family would only be charged any extra in the event of these exceeding the amount provided for in the plan at the time of need. The company, which is recommended by the National Society of Allied and Independent Funeral Directors, offers a selection of four plans that can all be tailored to individual requirements. Contact: 0800 111 4514; website: www.golden-charter.co.uk.

Perfect Choice Funeral Plans, offered by the National Association of Funeral Directors (NAFD) has three standard plans and a 'bespoke' scheme, enabling you to choose all the details you want. Contact: 0845 230 1343; website: www.nafd.org.uk.

As with insurance policies, a point to check is whether there are any exclusions. Because of the large increases in fees being charged by some cemeteries and crematoria, as well as the rising cost of other disbursements, a number of funeral plan providers are now restricting their guarantee on price to those services within the control of the funeral director. This does not necessarily mean that there would be an excess to pay.

If you are considering this type of scheme, as with any other important purchase it is sensible to compare the different plans on the market to ensure that you are choosing the one that best suits your requirements. Contact: 0845 601 9619; website: www.funeralplanningauthority.com.

Helpful as these new measures are, before making any advance payment you would still be wise to investigate the following points:

- whether your money will be put into an insurance policy or trust fund or, if not, whether the plan provider is authorized by the Financial Services Authority;
- what fees are deducted from the investment;
- what exact expenses the plan covers;
- what freedom you have if you subsequently want to change any of the details of the plan; and
- if you cancel the plan, whether you can get all your money back – or only a part.

Before paying, you should receive a letter confirming the terms and conditions together with full details of the arrangements you have specified. It is important to check this carefully and inform your next of kin where the letter is filed.

Those in receipt of Income Support, Housing Benefit or Council Tax Benefit may qualify for a payment from the Social Fund to help with funeral costs. For details of eligibility and how you claim, see leaflet D49, *What to Do after a Death*, obtainable from any social security or Jobcentre Plus office. If the matter is urgent, make a point of asking for form SF200. See website: www.direct.gov.uk/moneytaxandbenefits/bereavement.

A very real crisis for some families is the need for immediate money while waiting for the estate to be settled. At least part of the problem can be overcome by couples having a *joint bank account,* with both partners having drawing rights without the signature of the other being required. Sole-name bank accounts and joint accounts requiring both signatures are frozen. For the same reason, it may also be a good idea for any savings or investments to be held in the joint name of the couple. However, couples who have recently made any changes – or were planning to do so – as a result of independent taxation could be advised to discuss this point with a solicitor or qualified financial adviser.

Additionally, an essential practical point for all couples is that any financial and other *important documents should be discussed together* and understood by both parties. Even today, an all-too-common situation is for widows to come across insurance policies and other papers that they have never seen before and do not understand, often causing quite unnecessary anxiety. A further common sense 'must' is for both partners to *know where important papers are kept.* The best idea is either to lock them, filed together, in a home safe, or to give them to the bank to look after.

When someone dies, *the bank manager should be notified as soon as possible* so he or she can assist with the problems of unpaid bills and help work out a solution until the estate is settled. The same goes for the *suppliers of essential services:* gas, electricity, telephone and so on. Unless they know the situation, there is a risk of services being cut off if there is a delay in paying the bill. Add, too, any credit card companies, where if bills lie neglected the additional interest could mount up alarmingly.

Another organization that may be able to help you after a loved one has died is the **Bereavement Register**. This organization has one aim: to reduce the amount of direct mail to those who are deceased. Originally launched in the UK in 2000, this service has since expanded into France and Canada. Coming to terms with the loss of a loved one takes time; receiving direct mail bearing the name of the deceased is often painful and unnecessary. The Bereavement Register puts an end to such occurrences. Contact: 0800 082 1230; website: www.the-bereavement-register.org.uk.

Useful reading

What to Do after a Death, a free booklet, from any social security office, and *Planning for a Funeral,* a free fact sheet from Age UK, Tel: 0800 169 65 65; website: www.ageuk.org.uk.

State benefits, tax and other money points

Several extra financial benefits are given to widowed people. Most take the form of a cash payment. However, there are one or two tax and other points that it may be useful to know.

Benefits paid in cash form

There are three important cash benefits to which widowed people may be entitled: Bereavement Benefit, Bereavement Allowance and Widowed Parent's Allowance. These have replaced the former widows' benefits, as all benefits are now payable on equal terms to men and women alike. To find out more information see website: www.direct.gov.uk/moneytaxandbenefits/

bereavement. You will be given a questionnaire (BD8) by the Registrar when you register the death. It is important that you complete this, as it acts as a trigger to speed up payment of your benefits.

1. Bereavement Benefit

This has replaced what used to be known as Widow's Payment. It is a tax-free lump sum of £2,000, paid as soon as people are widowed, provided that: 1) the widowed person's spouse had paid sufficient NI Contributions; 2) the widowed person personally is under state retirement age; or 3) if over state retirement age, the widowed person's husband or wife had not been entitled to retirement pension.

2. Bereavement Allowance

This has replaced the Widow's Pension. Women already in receipt of Widow's Pension before 6 April 2001 are not affected and will continue to receive it as normal.

Bereavement Allowance is for those aged between 45 and State pension age who do not receive Widowed Parent's Allowance. It is payable for 52 weeks and, as with Widow's Pension before, there are various levels of payment: the full rate and age-related allowance. Receipt in all cases is dependent on sufficient NI Contributions having been paid.

Full-rate Bereavement Allowance is paid to widowed people between the ages of 55 and 59 inclusive. The weekly amount is £97.65, which is the same as the current pension for a single person. *Age-related* Bereavement Allowance is for younger widows or widowers, who do not qualify for the full rate. It is payable to those who are aged between 45 and 54 inclusive when their partner dies. Rates depend on age and vary from £29.30 for 45-year-olds to £90.81 for those aged 54.

Bereavement Allowance is normally paid automatically once you have sent off your completed form BB1, so if for any reason you do not receive it you should enquire at your social security office. In the event of your being ineligible, owing to insufficient NIC having been paid, you may still be entitled to receive Income Support, Housing Benefit or a grant or loan from the Social Fund. Your social security or Jobcentre Plus office will advise you. See website: www.direct.gov.uk/moneytaxandbenefits/bereavement.

3. Widowed Parent's Allowance

This is paid to widowed parents with at least one child for whom they receive Child Benefit. The current value (2010/11) is £97.65 per week. The allowance is usually paid automatically. If for some reason, although eligible, you do not receive the money, you should inform your social security office.

Retirement pension

Once a widowed person reaches state retirement age, he or she should receive a State pension in the normal way. An important point to remember is that a widow or widower may be able to use the late spouse's NIC to boost the amount he or she receives. See leaflet RM1, *Retirement – A Guide to Benefits for People Who Are Retiring or Have Retired*.

Problems

Both pension payments and bereavement benefits are dependent on sufficient NIC having been paid. Your social security office will inform you if you are not eligible. If this should turn out to be the case, you may still be entitled to receive Income Support, Housing Benefit, Council Tax Benefit or a grant or loan from the Social Fund – so ask. If you are unsure of your position or have difficulties, ask at your Citizens Advice Bureau, which will at least be able to help you work out the sums and inform you of your rights.

Particular points to note

Most widowed people's benefits are taxable. However, the £2,000 Bereavement Benefit is tax-free, as are pensions paid to the widows or widowers of armed forces personnel.

Widowed people will normally be able to inherit their spouse's additional pension rights if they contributed to SERPS (see the note below) and/or the Second State Pension (S2P), or at least half their guaranteed minimum pension, if their spouse was in a contracted-out scheme. Additionally, where applicable, all widowed people are entitled on retirement to half the graduated pension earned by their husband or wife.

NB: SERPS benefits paid to surviving spouses are due to be halved over the coming years. The cuts were completed in October 2010. Anyone over State pension age before 6 October 2002 is exempt from any cuts and will keep the right to pass on his or her SERPS pension in full to a bereaved spouse. Equally, any younger widower or widow who inherited his or her late spouse's SERPS entitlement before 6 October 2002 will not be affected and will continue to receive the full amount.

Women in receipt of widow's pension who remarry, or live with a man as his wife, lose their entitlement to the payment, unless the cohabitation ends, in which case they can claim it again. If a woman is aged over 60, the fact that she is living with a man will not affect her entitlement to a retirement pension based on her late husband's contribution record.

Widows and widowers of armed forces personnel whose deaths were a direct result of their service are now entitled to keep their armed forces attributable pension for life, regardless of whether they remarry or cohabit.

Tax allowances

Widows and widowers receive the normal single person's tax allowance of £6,475 and, if in receipt of married couple's allowance, are also entitled to any unused portion of the allowance in the year of their partner's death. Those aged 65 and older may be entitled to a higher personal allowance.

Advice

Many people have difficulty in working out exactly what they are entitled to and how to claim it. The Citizens Advice Bureau is always very helpful. Additionally, Cruse and the National Association of Widows (see below) can assist you.

Organizations that can help

Problems vary. For some, the hardest thing to bear is the loneliness of returning to an empty house. For others, money problems seem to dominate everything else. For many older women, in particular, who have not got a job, widowhood creates a great gulf where for a while there is no real sense of purpose. Many widowed men and women go through a spell of feeling enraged against their partner for dying. Most are baffled and hurt by the seeming indifference of friends, who appear more embarrassed than sympathetic.

In time, problems diminish and individuals are able to recapture some of their joy for living with all its many pleasures. Talking to other people who know the difficulties from their own experience can be a tremendous help. The following organizations not only offer opportunities for companionship but also provide an advisory and support service:

Cruse Bereavement Care offers free help to anyone who has been bereaved by providing both one-to-one and group support through its 150 local branches throughout the UK. Contact: 0844 477 9400; website: www.crusebereavementcare.org.uk.

The National Association of Widows is a national voluntary organization. Its many branches provide a supportive social network for widows throughout the UK. Contact: 0845 838 2261; website: www.nawidows.org.uk.

Many professional and other groups offer a range of services for widows and widowers associated with them. These include:

The Civil Service Retirement Fellowship	020 8691 7411; website: www.csrf.org.uk
The War Widows Association of Great Britain	0845 2412 189; website: www.warwidows.org.uk

Many local Age UK groups offer a counselling service. Trade unions are often particularly supportive, as are Rotary Clubs, all the armed forces organizations and most benevolent societies.

Directory of useful organizations

Campaigning Organizations

Action for Sick Children, 32b Buxton Road, High Lane, Stockport, Cheshire, SK6 8BH. Tel: 01663 763 004; Website: www.actionforsickchildren.org

Action for Sick Children is the UK's leading children and young people's healthcare charity. For almost 50 years it has worked to improve the healthcare services for children, young people and their families.

National Pensioners Convention, Walkden House, 10 Melton Street, London NW1 2EJ. Tel: 020 7383 0388. www.npcuk.org.

The NPC is Britain's biggest older people's organization, with 1.5m members and 1,000 affiliated groups. The Convention is run by older people for older people and campaigns on issues such as pensions, health care, transport, housing, fuel poverty and age discrimination.

Disabilities

Calibre Audio Library, New Road, Weston Turville, Aylesbury, Bucks HP22 5XQ. Tel: 01296 432 339; E-mail: enquiries@calibre.org.uk; Web: www.calibre.org.uk.

A national charity providing a free postal library service of unabridged books on MP3 CDs, memory sticks and cassettes for people with sight problems, dyslexia or other disabilities which prevent them reading print. There are over 8,000 titles to choose from, 1,400 of which are in the Young Calibre library for under 16s. Catalogues are available online and in large print. No independent confirmation of eligibility required.

Funeral Planning

Funeral Planning Authority Ltd, Knellstone House, Udimre, Rye, East Sussex, TN31 6AR. Tel: 0845 601 9619. Web: www.funeralplanningauthority.co.uk.

The FPA is the self-regulatory authority for the funeral planning sector. It exists to help protect customers interests in this sector by, amongst other things, registering companies that comply with its Rules and Code of Practice (see website for details). The Financial Services Authority suggests customers considering buying a funeral plan should check whether the plan provider they are considering is registered with the FPA.

Healthcare

Alcoholics Anonymous, General Service Office, PO Box 1, 10 Tot Green, York YO1 7NJ. Tel: 01904 644026.

AA offers help through mutual support to those with a serious alcohol problem. There are no charges, we are independent and anonymity is carefully preserved. Members achieve and maintain sobriety using the 12 Step Recovery Programme. Over 4,000 groups nationwide – Helpline 0845 7697555.

Holidays

Explore Worldwide, Nelson House, 55 Victoria Road, Farnborough, Hampshire, GU14 7PA. Tel: 0844 499 0901; Web: www.explore.co.uk.

Explore Worldwide offers over 500 tours to more than 130 countries. Examples of recent tours include: Lakes and Mountains of Italy (from £905); cruising the Greek islands (from £745); China Highlights (from £1,980) and High Trails of the Incas (from £2,310). Prices quoted are per person and include return flights from the UK.

Fred. Olsen Cruise Lines, Fred. Olsen House, White House Road, Ipswich, Suffolk IP1 5LL. Tel: 021473 742424; Web: www.fredolsencruises.co.uk.

Fred. Olsen Cruise Lines operates a fleet of four, compact sized ships (the largest carries only 1,350 passengers) offering a selection of worldwide itineraries. For most of the year, cruises depart from a selection of ports around the UK. One ship operates a winter season of fly-cruises in the Caribbean with flights departing from Manchester and Gatwick. Cruise programmes vary in length from a two-night mini cruise, up to 108-nights Around the World. Many cruises also offer Fred. Olsen's Flagship Golf programme (at an additional cost), and *The ArtsClub* – Fred. Olsen's programme of special interest programmes that are offered at no extra charge, and which passengers are free to dip in and out of as they wish.

Insurance

The Private Health Partnership, Butterfield Park, Otley Road, Baildon, West Yorkshire, BD17 7HE. Tel: 01274 588862; Fax: 01274 530255. Web: www.php.co.uk.

The Private Health Partnership (PHP) is an independent healthcare intermediary providing advice on private medical insurance, health & wellbeing products and services to companies and individuals.

With over 8,000 clients, we've built an industry reputation for service excellence, placing emphasis on treating customers fairly and priding ourselves on our commitment to provide tailor-made solutions offering impartial and independent advice.

Leisure

Aldeburgh Music, Snape Maltings Concert Hall, Snape, Suffolk IP17 1SP. Tel: 01728 687100; Fax: 01728 687120; Web: www.aldeburgh.co.uk.

Founded by Benjamin Britten in 1948, Aldeburgh Music today has a year-round programme of events, many of them staged in Snape Maltings Concert Hall world-famous for its acoustics. It also has a growing reputation as a centre where everybody – from the local community to the world's finest musicians – can come to be inspired and reach their full potential.

The British Model Flying Association Tel: 0116 2440028; Web: www. bmfa.org.

Have you ever wanted to build and pilot your own aircraft? Our members build and fly aircraft of all types ranging from ultra-light indoor models to gas turbine powered fighters. We are the governing body for model aircraft flying in the UK with 36,000 members and 840 clubs providing a range of services and insurance.

NADFAS, NADFAS House, 8 Guilford Street, London WC1N 1DA. Tel: 020 7430 0730; Fax: 020 7242 0686; Web: www.nadfas.org.uk.

NADFAS is an Arts-based educational charity which promotes its aims through lectures on the decorative and fine arts through a network of over 350 societies. There is also range of volunteering activities such as Church Recording, Heritage Volunteering, and Young Arts projects. Visit our website for more details or phone our Volunteering Department on the number above.

National Philatelic Society, c/o The British Postal Museum & Archive, Freeling House, Phoenix Place, London WC1X 0DL. Tel: 020 7239 2571; Web: www. ukphilately.org.uk/nps.

If you are interested in philately – which these days embraces Postal History, Social Philately as well as the collecting of stamps – you might like to join the National Philatelic Society. As a member, you can buy and sell stamps through their auctions or postal packet scheme. Monthly Saturday meetings are held in London with occasional country meetings. Members get the magazine *Stamp Lover* six times a year and can borrow books from the Society's extensive library. Membership costs from £23 a year. For further information on the National and on philately generally, visit the website or contact the General Secretary at the above address.

Recruitment

Wrinklies Direct Limited, 6 Caronia Court, 71 Plough Way, London SE16 7AD. Tel: 08452 601116; Fax: 07091 013799. Web: www.wrinklies.org.

A recruitment service that focuses on placing experienced people into businesses that recognize the benefits of maturity in approach and outlook. Wrinklies people have a traditional work ethic, a high degree of integrity and loyalty and a level of experience that often limits training to that of induction. Much against the myth, most grasp new ideas and IT quickly.

SOS Help

Independent Age, 6 Avonmore Road, London W14 8RL.

Independent Age is a unique charity, providing lifelong support to older people on very low incomes. We provide information and advice, practical help and emergency financial aid through our network of staff and dedicated volunteers across the UK and Republic of Ireland.

Charity number 210729

Universal Aunts, PO Box 304, London SW4 0NN. Tel: 020 7738 8937; Web: www.universalaunts.co.uk.

Established 1921 and still supplying housekeeper/companions, carers, general household employment, caretaking property and pets, childcare, escorts for airports/stations and to your destination.

Volunteers

Riding for the Disabled Association (RDA), Norfolk House, 1a Tournament Court, Edghill Drive, Warwick, CV34 6LG. Tel: 0845 6581082; Fax: 0845 658 1082. Web: www.rda.org.uk.

RDA is dedicated to making a lasting difference to the lives of people with disabilities, enabling them to benefit from equestrian activities, improving their quality of life and achieving their potential. 18,000 volunteers support 25,000 people with physical or learning difficulties. RDA always needs volunteers, not only to work with horses, but also to support Groups in a variety of ways.

Index

NB: page numbers in *italic* indicate figures or tables

Index of Advertisers